Presented in Honor of

Mary Haldane Coleman

by the
Soroptimist Club
and Friends

Williamsburg
Regional Library

## Volume II:
## From the Scientific Revolution to the Present

# Western Civilization

# Volume II:
## From the Scientific Revolution to the Present

# Western Civilization

## Original and Secondary Source Readings

Benjamin C. Sax, professor of history,
University of Kansas, Book Editor

David L. Bender, Publisher
Bruno Leone, Executive Editor
Bonnie Szumski, Editorial Director
James Miller, Series Editor

Perspectives on History

GREENHAVEN PRESS, INC., SAN DIEGO, CA

**Every effort has been made to trace the owners of copyrighted material. The articles in this volume may have been edited for content, length, and/or reading level. Those interested in locating the original source will find the complete citation on the first page of each article.**

Library of Congress Cataloging-in-Publication Data

Western civilization / Benjamin Sax, book editor.
    p.    cm. — (Perspectives on history)
    Includes bibliographical references and index.
    Contents: v. 2. From the Scientific Revolution to the Present
    ISBN 1-56510-988-0 (v. 1 : pbk. : alk. paper). — ISBN 1-56510-989-9
(v. 1 : lib. : alk. paper) — ISBN 1-56510-990-2 (v. 2 : pbk. bdg. : alk. paper) —
ISBN 1-56510-991-0 (v. 2 : lib. : alk. paper)
    1. Civilization, Western—History, I. Sax, Benjamin C., 1950–    II. Series.

    CB245 .W475  2001
    909'.09821—dc21                                                    00-050339
                                                                              CIP

Cover photo: Planet Art

Every effort has been made to trace the owners of the copyrighted material.

Printed in the USA

# CONTENTS

INTRODUCTION     9

TIMELINE     14

# UNIT 1
# Science, Enlightenment, and Revolution

**CHAPTER 1:** Modern Europe: The Current Debate     18
*The Progress of History,* Marquis de Condorcet
*The Development of Feminist Consciousness,* Gerda Lerner
Science and the Modern World, Alfred North Whitehead
*An Alternative Viewpoint,* José Ortega y Gasset

**CHAPTER 2:** The Scientific Revolution: The Search for New Foundations     35
*Galileo Looks Through a Telescope,* Galileo Galilei
*Galileo's Significance in the History of Science,* Alexandre Koyré
*Scientific Method,* Isaac Newton
*Scientific Method and Technological Innovation,* Robert K. Merton

**CHAPTER 3:** Absolutism: Defended and Criticized     48
*The Concept of Sovereignty,* Jean Bodin
*Absolutism Defined,* Jacques-Bénigne Bossuet
*The Origins of Modern Bureaucracy,* Hans Rosenberg
*Absolutism in Action,* Robert Muchembled
*The English Bill of Rights*

**CHAPTER 4:** The Enlightenment: "To Change the Common Way     64
      of Thinking"
*The Method of "Right Reasoning,"* René Descartes
*The Philosophes Defined,* Peter Gay
*"To Change the Common Way of Thinking,"* Denis Diderot
*A New Science of the Economy,* Adam Smith
*Science vs. Morals,* Jean-Jacques Rousseau

**CHAPTER 5:** The French Revolution as a World Revolution    80
    *The Coming of the French Revolution,* Georges Lefebvre
    *"What Is the Third Estate?"* Emmanuel-Joseph Sieyès
    *The Declaration of the Rights of Man and Citizen*
    *The Declaration of the Rights of Woman and Female Citizen,*
        Olympe de Gouges
    *An Alternative Interpretation of the Revolution,* Alexis de
        Tocqueville

**CHAPTER 6:** The Age of Nationalism and Liberalism    98
    *The Continuity of the Enlightenment,* Jeremy Bentham
    *The Principles of Nineteenth-Century Liberalism,* John Stuart Mill
    *The Origins of Conservatism,* Edmund Burke
    *The Nation as Culture,* Johann Herder
    *The Garden of Humanity,* Giuseppe Mazzini

# UNIT 2
# The Nineteenth Century

**CHAPTER 7:** The Interrelated Processes of the Industrial Revolution    115
    *Factory Workers Observed,* Andrew Ure
    *Another Viewpoint,* James Phillips Kay
    *A Twentieth-Century View,* T.S. Ashton
    *The Rise of the Industrial City,* Paul M. Hohenberg and Lynn
        Hollen Lees
    *The Life of a Worker,* Otto Krille

**CHAPTER 8:** Family, Gender, and Class in the Early Industrial Era    134
    *Child Labor,* The British Parliamentary Report, 1816
    *Women and Industrial Labor,* Louise A. Tilly and Joan W. Scott
    *Women, Work, and Opportunity,* Marilyn J. Boxer and Jean H.
        Quataert
    *Working-Class Consciousness, Black Dwarf* (September 30, 1818)
    *Marx Explains Socialism,* Karl Marx

**CHAPTER 9:** Darwin, Nietzsche, and Freud    156
    *Positivism,* Auguste Comte
    The Origin of Species, Charles Darwin
    *Social Darwinism,* Herbert Spencer
    *An Attack on Western Morals,* Friedrich Nietzsche
    *The Origins of Depth Psychology,* Sigmund Freud

**CHAPTER 10:** Christianity in the Modern World     175
    *The Origins of Liberal Protestantism,* Friedrich Schleiermacher
    The Essence of Christianity, Ludwig Feuerbach
    *The Beginnings of Christian Existentialism,* Søren Kierkegaard
    *Catholicism in the Modern World,* Pope Leo XIII
    *Neo-Reformation Theology,* Karl Barth

# UNIT 3
# The Contemporary West

**CHAPTER 11:** Mass Democracy and World War I     195
    The Age of the Masses, Michael D. Biddiss
    *The New Nationalism,* E.J. Hobsbawm
    *Vienna and the New Politics,* Carl E. Schorske
    *The New Imperialism,* Hannah Arendt
    *War as a Shaper of Consciousness,* Paul Fussell

**CHAPTER 12:** Nazism and the Holocaust     220
    *The Party Program,* Anton Drexler, Gottfried Feder, and Adolf
       Hitler
    *The Nazi Seizure of Power,* Karl Dietrich Bracher
    *The* Volksgemeinschaft, Adolf Hitler
    The Racial State, Michael Burleigh and Wolfgang Wippermann
    *The "Final Solution" of the Jewish Question,* The Wannsee
       Conference

**CHAPTER 13:** From the Russian Revolution to the Fall of the     243
          Soviet Union
    *The Bolsheviks Take Control,* Leon Trotsky
    *The Bolshevik "Program,"* V.I. Lenin
    *How Did the Bolsheviks Take Over the Revolution?*
       Alexander Rabinowitch
    *The Cold War,* Charles S. Maier
    *The Fall of the Soviet Union,* Mikhail Gorbachev

**CHAPTER 14:** The Embattled Enlightenment Tradition     263
    *The Postmodern Condition,* Joyce Appleby et al.
    *Power and Discourse,* Michel Foucault
    *"The Question Concerning Technology,"* Martin Heidegger
    *Postmodern Feminism,* Hélène Cixous

**CHAPTER 15:** The West Within the World     276
    The Clash of Civilizations, Samuel P. Huntington

*The Non-Western World,* Frantz Fanon
Orientalism, Edward Said
*A Reply to Said,* Arif Dirlik
*A Defense of the West,* Jacques Ellul

INDEX                                                                    296

# INTRODUCTION

What is Western civilization? This is a difficult question to answer since it calls for a definition of what is a complex phenomenon consisting of disparate components. In the following two volumes of *Western Civilization: Perspectives on History*, no conclusive definition of the West will be offered. No simple identity will suffice to capture the variety of institutions, the multiplicity of political and social forms, and the diversity of values and beliefs we generally refer to as Western civilization. What will be offered are several ways of formulating possible answers to the question of the meaning of the West. There are, however, better and worse ways of doing so. In posing the question in this way, we seek an understanding of those features that make the West distinctive. To identify these distinctive features we need to proceed both internally and externally. Internally, we must strive to encompass the diversity and complexity of the West as we have come to know it in the present. Externally, we need to compare the West to other world civilizations. Only in the last two chapters of volume II will we be able to turn directly to this dual perspective. In the next-to-last chapter we will turn to the various challenges to the West, raised by a number of recent critics concerning the West's basic values and fundamental knowledge. In the final chapter, "The West Within the World," we will look at how Western civilization has come to be perceived by those outside the West. To define the term *Western Civilization* adequately, we also need to comprehend what constitutes a civilization and recognize what the West might share in common with other world civilizations.

The chapters of *Western Civilization* leading up to these final two will explore the long history of the civilization of the West. In them we will examine the various components that have formed the basis of and continue to shape the modern West. This history can be traced back to the origins of civilization itself, at least in the ways civilization arose in the first cities of the ancient Near East. There has not, however, been a simple unfolding of beliefs, values, and political and social forms from these origins. These early rituals, habits, customs, and institutions changed over time as they were interpreted and reinterpreted within changing situations. Equally important were the contributions from other civilizations. Ancient Greece and Rome contributed distinctive social and political forms and often alien values and beliefs. Christianity, especially as it evolved in late antiquity, combined and reinterpreted many strands inherited from these earlier civilizations. The Middle Ages continued to uphold several of these elements from the ancient world and added some of its own, creating a distinctive European phase to the civilization of the West. Finally, modern Europe developed new ways of understanding nature and refined the concepts of society, politics, and morals. These, in turn, would allow the West to develop forms of economic organization and instruments of technological control that were unknown to earlier phases of Western civilization as well as to the other civilizations of the world.

Even this brief sketch of the history of the West raises additional questions. How should we interpret the various components of this civilization and the complexities of its history? Is it sufficient for an understanding of a civilization merely to comprehend earlier and often alien political, social, or intellectual forms? Or should the historian reconstruct the various ways in which past individuals found meaning in their existence? Or should emphasis be placed only on what has come down today from the past, thereby downplaying what was historically specific to past societies and making only what interests us in the present the main criterion of historical significance and thus of historical study? Or does historical understanding involve not just a sense of the specific cultural forms of the past and the means through which they have been handed down by a tradition but also the various ways in which these forms and these traditions were formed, changed, and have continued—whether for good or bad, whether in acknowledged or unacknowledged ways—to define the present world?

As in every other great civilization, the West has no single line of continuity linking past and present. The history of the West lacks a single form of social organization, one type of political institution, one understanding of the nature of divinity, and a common set of shared values and attitudes about the world. In other words, none of these general areas of existence provides an uninterrupted line of continuity throughout history. Yet in studying this history we continually encounter a number of features that cut across the political, social, and ideational. Instead of simple continuity, we seem to have a continuum of multiple components, rearranged through the course of history into new, meaningful patterns. What has emerged as the modern form of Western civilization was actually a complex amalgam of differing institutions and values, social forms, and beliefs.

A distinctive historical dimension exists in the formation of this amalgam. Even if the theory of a progressive movement of history is entirely left aside, there is the sense that the West is the product of a long process of change and interchange, of formation and transformation. We should not conceive of the West as simply what has been handed down from earlier periods or built up through a steady series of increments from the past. Traditions are not constituted in such a fash-

ion, for much is lost and altered in the process of handing down. Those elements that can be inherited as a tradition, in other words, are not necessarily taken up in the forms and with the meanings established at their sites of origin. Traditions grow by repetition and constant use; they also progress by adding to and building on—that is, by transferring or transforming—what has been handed down within new situations. The original meanings given to various cultural forms can change as these forms are interpreted and incorporated in another epoch or by another people.

This process works in various ways. In accepting higher cultural forms, for example, less civilized peoples or epochs seem to degrade them. By adopting them to their needs, however, they also allow them to survive and thus provide possibilities of further development and even refinement in the future. Inheritance in this sense allows for the creation of new meanings, whether they are considered renaissances or entirely original forms. New patterns of civilization and new meanings are generated from these common components. The history of the West is not only long and complex, but also multilayered. Obvious changes on the political level and even on the level of social organization often reside on foundations of basic beliefs and interpretations about what constitutes reality. These foundations are not always clearly articulated or even recognized; yet they nevertheless continue to influence these other levels. And these foundations of the West themselves are neither simple nor uniform. They shift through time as weight is placed on the Hebraic rather than the Hellenic or the Christian rather than the classical side of the civilization.

What then is the meaning of Western civilization? If we need to understand the complex history of the West to answer this question, we also need to comprehend what is meant by the term *civilization*. Anthropologists would claim that *civilization* defines something distinctive of human existence. While civilization is obviously related to and interacts with biological processes and biological inheritances, it is perhaps best understood as all those aspects of human existence that escape biology. With this distinction established, we next confront the more vexing problem of the difference between *culture* and *civilization*. Although scholars do not agree on what distinguishes these two terms, or even that such a distinction exists, they concede that *culture* designates something generally human, in the sense that all humans have or are part of a culture, and that civilization seems to designate a "higher" or a "more complex" form of culture.

For historical reasons, the terms *civilization* and *culture* entered the Western vocabulary only as recently as the second half of the eighteenth century. *Civilization* clearly indicates the attitudes and intellectual qualities, or in Voltaire's usage, "good taste," that compose the "higher" forms of human existence and their intellectual and artistic expressions. *Culture*, on the other hand, was first employed by the German writer Johann Herder as a conscious reply to this notion of civilization. As Herder pointed out, no simple way exists to identify what are qualitatively higher or qualitatively lower forms of human life. A man or woman living within what we might consider a "primitive" culture could live a fuller and even a more humane existence—or as Herder would claim, even a more moral form of existence—than those who exist in supposedly "advanced" civilizations. This understanding led to a remarkable insight that only slowly emerged in the history of the West. Whereas Voltaire could only understand *civilization* in the singular, a single standard to measure the various human societies around the world and throughout history, Herder used the plural *cultures*, emphasizing that each culture contains its own values and its own "center" of existence. These values are incommensurate with those of any other.

Today, if we speak of "higher" cultures, it does not necessarily imply "better" but merely "more complex." The term *civilization*, in other words, does not express a value judgment; rather, it is used in a purely descriptive sense. Although we may agree that certain forms of human life are degrading and even less-than-human, we do not ascribe a hierarchy of human existence or forms of human society. However, a significant distinction exists between *culture* and *civilization*. Whereas the former term implies a generic quality of human existence, the latter indicates a higher, more com-

plex and perhaps a greater variety of the ways of being human. In this sense, we can still accept Voltaire's notion of civilization as expressing a higher form of life and combine it with Herder's emphasis on the great diversity of the forms of human existence.

Within the civilization of the West, questions immediately arise about the specific definitions and particular nature of these higher forms of life and how they should be understood. From the beginning, the term *human civilization* referred to many different civilizations. These civilizations arose independently in at least four major sites around the world: around the Tigris and Euphrates Rivers (ancient Mesopotamia—the land between the two rivers), in the Indus valley of India, along the Huang Ho (Yellow River) in China, and in Central America. Each developed distinctive forms of political and social organization, distinct notions of god and nature, and distinct sets of values and beliefs; yet, they all expressed definitive notions of what constituted the "civilized life."

Although the terms *culture* and *civilization* were coined during the eighteenth century as a result of the debates on the meaning and value of social existence, the notion of a civilized life, of course, did not first arise in this period. The ancient Romans, for instance, used the term *humanitas* to define a common human striving for the good life. The great Roman historian Tacitus drew an important distinction between a civilized and what only appeared to be a civilized form of life. He considered it barbaric and ignorant to think of civilization only in terms of fine buildings, material comforts, and technological power; civilization cannot be reduced to its material forms. And for Cicero, who developed this notion of *humanitas* to a high degree, civilization entailed a sense of dignity of one's own human existence, something that must be cared for and cultivated to the highest standards possible. Cicero does not, of course, mean this in a self-centered or egotistical way. Respect for oneself entails a recognition and respect for the worth of every other human being. In other words, *humanitas* implies self-restraint, compromise, consideration, and sympathy.

*Western Civilization: Perspectives on History* emphasizes those scholarly writings that have emphasized moral values, the relation of these values to the understanding of reality, and what earlier epochs have considered (for lack of a better term) "the good life." Again, in the history of the West, we find diversity and not uniformity. Is the good life a form of righteousness, following the commandments of the gods? This is how the early civilizations of the ancient Near East viewed the good life. Or is the good life a matter of individual striving for a type of human excellence that expresses itself in political leadership, the accumulation of material goods, in knowledge and control of the world? Such values were paramount among the ancient Greeks. Or is the good life understood as the type of spiritual equanimity and self-control favored by members of the ancient Roman elite? All these notions of the good life come into the modern West and indicate the richness and complexity of the Western heritage. Likewise. the modern West has developed its own ideas of the good life. The creation of a political and social community based on the freedom and equality of all—rich as well as poor, women as well as men—is part of our modern notion of the good life. With the technological and economic developments of the last two centuries, these ideals have been combined with the notion that a basic level of material security is also a necessary condition for the good life. These values provide a common background against which political actions, the establishment of institutions, and the reactions to social and economic forces are understood and evaluated.

Thus, what constitutes "the good life," varies with time and place, with various groups, and within various traditions. The notion of the good life is also connected to other ideas and beliefs. The fundamental ideals of a given people at a given time are intimately connected to what they consider the best way to be human. What is their understanding of truth, of nature, and of human beings' relation to nature? These questions have most often been related to conceptions of reality and the nature of divinity. Is the good life based on a belief in a transcendental god who created the world, directs its historical development, and provides an explicit notion of how human beings should lead their lives and organize their society? Or does the notion of divinity provide men and women with the freedom and responsibility to act on their own and to create their own political forms and social organizations, imploring the gods only for aid in achieving such ventures? Or, as has become characteristic of modern times, does an understanding of the workings of nature and of human nature provide a way of establishing universal notions of human rights and free association, which in turn legitimate governments and organize societies?

Questions of this nature also raise problems of how these truths are known and how they are interpreted. Is the knowledge of god revealed by him in sacred writings or through individuals called by him? Or are truths handed down by the ancestors, as with the ancient Romans, or discovered through the use of dialectical or logical reason, as with the ancient Greeks? The modern West is the heir of these competing and sometimes conflicting ways in which truth is known and the nature of reality defined. The ways in which nature has come to be defined, explained, and exploited in more recent times opened a new way of understanding truth and provided an insight into social organization and politics that have acted like catalysts for change.

Even within this limited range of the concerns, there is no consensus among modern scholars. In the following chapters, selections cover a wide range of interpretations by various historians, archaeologists, anthropologists, and mythologists who have attempted to address the questions of the meaning of the civilization of the West. Thus, this anthology brings together those scholars and philosophers who tend to think on the level of long-range trends and the meaning of civilizations, even when they are immediately addressing only limited questions dealing with specific events or historical periods.

In addition, the process of questioning the meaning of a civilization entails not only the verification of past facts—of historical dating or archaeological finds—but also the interpretation of these facts. And historical interpretation means not just interpreting within our own frame of references. Historical interpretation includes the various ways in which earlier ages interpreted themselves and gave meaning to their lives. These past interpretations must also be interpreted by the present-day historian. For this reason, a wide-ranging set of primary source materials, upon which these interpretations are based, have also been included. These historical documents are present because they illustrate the lives of past peoples and epochs (and in ways that secondary interpretations hardly ever can capture in their full richness) and because they provide the student with the opportunity of interpreting these sources themselves in relation to various scholarly interpretations.

# Timeline:
# From the Scientific Revolution to the Presen

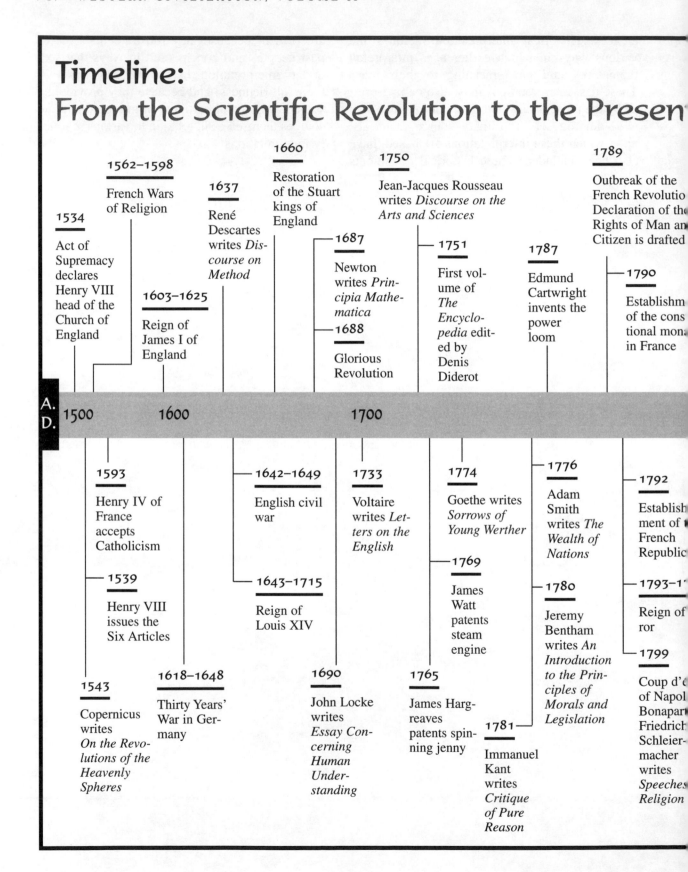

**A.D.** 1500 — 1600 — 1700

**1534**
Act of Supremacy declares Henry VIII head of the Church of England

**1562–1598**
French Wars of Religion

**1603–1625**
Reign of James I of England

**1637**
René Descartes writes *Discourse on Method*

**1660**
Restoration of the Stuart kings of England

**1687**
Newton writes *Principia Mathematica*

**1688**
Glorious Revolution

**1750**
Jean-Jacques Rousseau writes *Discourse on the Arts and Sciences*

**1751**
First volume of *The Encyclopedia* edited by Denis Diderot

**1787**
Edmund Cartwright invents the power loom

**1789**
Outbreak of the French Revolutio Declaration of the Rights of Man an Citizen is drafted

**1790**
Establishm of the cons tional mon in France

**1593**
Henry IV of France accepts Catholicism

**1539**
Henry VIII issues the Six Articles

**1543**
Copernicus writes *On the Revolutions of the Heavenly Spheres*

**1618–1648**
Thirty Years' War in Germany

**1642–1649**
English civil war

**1643–1715**
Reign of Louis XIV

**1690**
John Locke writes *Essay Concerning Human Understanding*

**1733**
Voltaire writes *Letters on the English*

**1774**
Goethe writes *Sorrows of Young Werther*

**1769**
James Watt patents steam engine

**1765**
James Hargreaves patents spinning jenny

**1776**
Adam Smith writes *The Wealth of Nations*

**1780**
Jeremy Bentham writes *An Introduction to the Principles of Morals and Legislation*

**1781**
Immanuel Kant writes *Critique of Pure Reason*

**1792**
Establish ment of French Republic

**1793–1**
Reign of ror

**1799**
Coup d'é of Napol Bonapar Friedrich Schleier-macher writes *Speeches Religion*

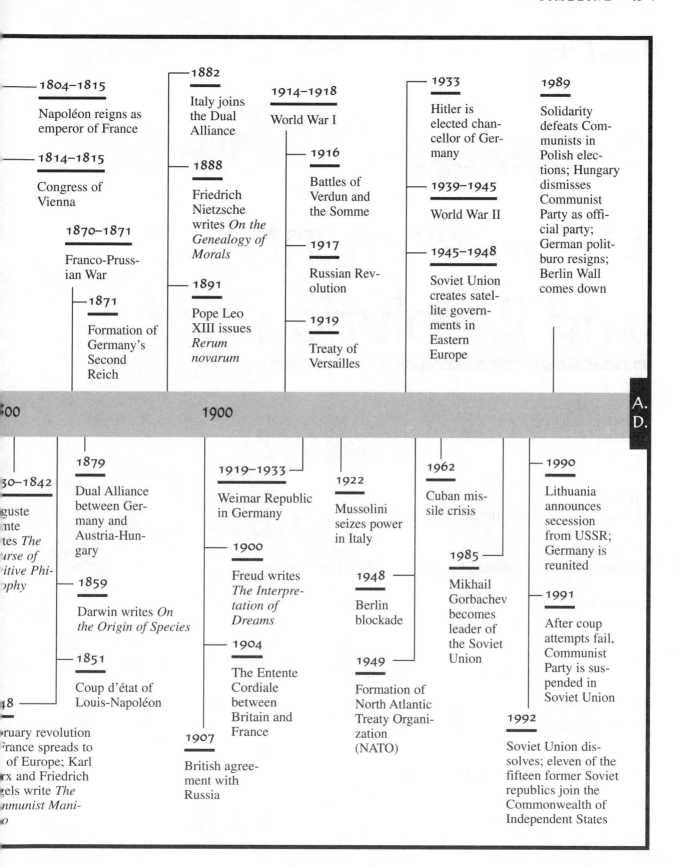

**1804–1815**

Napoléon reigns as emperor of France

**1814–1815**

Congress of Vienna

**1870–1871**

Franco-Prussian War

**1871**

Formation of Germany's Second Reich

**1882**

Italy joins the Dual Alliance

**1888**

Friedrich Nietzsche writes *On the Genealogy of Morals*

**1891**

Pope Leo XIII issues *Rerum novarum*

**1914–1918**

World War I

**1916**

Battles of Verdun and the Somme

**1917**

Russian Revolution

**1919**

Treaty of Versailles

**1933**

Hitler is elected chancellor of Germany

**1939–1945**

World War II

**1945–1948**

Soviet Union creates satellite governments in Eastern Europe

**1989**

Solidarity defeats Communists in Polish elections; Hungary dismisses Communist Party as official party; German politburo resigns; Berlin Wall comes down

**00**        **1900**        A.
D.

**30–1842**

guste
nte
tes *The
urse of
itive Phi-
ophy*

**1879**

Dual Alliance between Germany and Austria-Hungary

**1859**

Darwin writes *On the Origin of Species*

**1851**

Coup d'état of Louis-Napoléon

**1919–1933**

Weimar Republic in Germany

**1900**

Freud writes *The Interpretation of Dreams*

**1904**

The Entente Cordiale between Britain and France

**1907**

British agreement with Russia

**1922**

Mussolini seizes power in Italy

**1948**

Berlin blockade

**1949**

Formation of North Atlantic Treaty Organization (NATO)

**1962**

Cuban missile crisis

**1985**

Mikhail Gorbachev becomes leader of the Soviet Union

**1990**

Lithuania announces secession from USSR; Germany is reunited

**1991**

After coup attempts fail, Communist Party is suspended in Soviet Union

**1992**

Soviet Union dissolves; eleven of the fifteen former Soviet republics join the Commonwealth of Independent States

**48**

ruary revolution
France spreads to
of Europe; Karl
rx and Friedrich
gels write *The
nmunist Mani-
o*

# Unit 1

# Science, Enlightenment, and Revolution

## Contents

Maps                                                                            17

**Chapter 1:**
Modern Europe: The Current Debate                                               18

**Chapter 2:**
The Scientific Revolution: The Search for New Foundations                       35

**Chapter 3:**
Absolutism: Defended and Criticized                                             48

**Chapter 4:**
The Enlightenment: "To Change the Common Way of Thinking"                       64

**Chapter 5:**
The French Revolution as a World Revolution                                     80

**Chapter 6:**
The Age of Nationalism and Liberalism                                           98

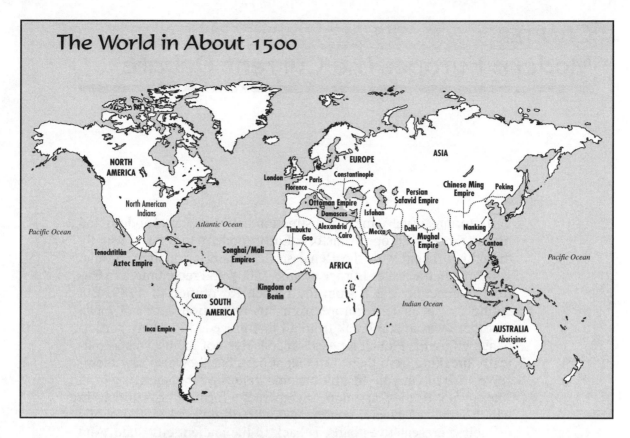

The World in About 1500

Europe at the Beginning of the Enlightenment

# CHAPTER 1
# Modern Europe: The Current Debate

Historians usually make a distinction between early modern and recent modern European history. Early modern Europe is usually thought to begin with the Renaissance (emerging in Italy around 1400 and in the rest of Europe around 1500), and recent modern Europe is generally dated from the French Revolution of 1789. But dating recent modern Europe from this revolution does not mean that there was a total break from all that preceded it. Many participants within the French Revolution conceived of themselves as radically breaking from their own recent past, but they also saw themselves as reviving the institutions and values of the ancient world. The revolutionaries' attempts to construct a form of government in which issues of general concern would be discussed by the public or their representatives harkens back to the ancient city-state. And the establishment of democratic and republican forms of government called for republican virtues and a public educated in democratic principles.

The French revolutionaries both succeeded and failed in these intentions. The revolution created a political sphere and a language of politics that we in the West (and indeed the whole contemporary world) continue to employ. We speak, for example, of the political right and the political left, of conservatives and radicals, of consensus politics and the will of the people. More importantly than the everyday language of politics, we legitimate the use of power in the political framework established by the French Revolution. This basic framework is constituted not only on the principles of majority rule and written constitutions but also in our concepts of human rights, civil liberties, and the right to vote. In addition, we define various liberation movements in the contemporary West—ranging from racial equality to feminism and gay liberation—in terms of the principles of a community comprising politically free and socially equal individuals. The French Revolution made real what had previously been only an ideal. Therefore, it also initiated unintended historical trends. In opposition to the revolution's definitions of politics and society, there arose a number of conservative and reactionary movements that threw up alternative models of legitimate rule and social justice. In a self-conscious appeal to prerevolutionary forms, they abandoned politics founded on autonomous individuals and societies based on equality and instead opted for ones defined by traditional values, inherited social hierarchy, and conventional notions of political power.

In the name of truth and justice, the French Revolution attempted to sweep away much of the inheritance from the past. Even during the revolution, conservative currents emerged, aimed at preserving various components of the prerevolutionary era. And beyond all intentions, there were bound to be links to the values and institutions of the recent past. For instance, the revolution attempted to change basic values and popular beliefs by promoting the scientific explanation of nature, man, and society. In this, the revolution only partly succeeded. It did not totally destroy Christian notions of a personal God and of an individual sense of sin, which would resurface not only during the revolution but again and again in the nineteenth and twentieth centuries.

The French Revolution did not emerge out of the blue. Whatever its intended or unintended consequences, the revolution itself depended on a number of earlier revolutions. The most important of these was the Scientific Revolution of the seventeenth century. In breaking from the foundations of truth in faith, the Bible, and the traditions that sustained them, the Scientific Revolution found a different source of truth in exact observation, in the ways in which individuals acquire knowledge, and ultimately in how to conceive of nature and of human beings' relation to it. In itself, the Scientific Revolution could not have caused the French Revolution. What would come to be called the scientific method, along with all of the assumptions that it entailed, had to be systematized and applied not just to nature but also to society and politics.

Beginning in the early seventeenth century and climaxing in the mid–eighteenth, what would eventually come to be called the Enlightenment extended the ideas and ideals of the Scientific Revolution to the understanding of social organization, political institutions, and individual morals. This extension not only encouraged a questioning of traditional values and inherited institutions (a questioning that would culminate in the French Revolution) but also provided the foundations for new types of knowledge—specifically, the scientific knowledge of the human domain we know as the social sciences. Our common understanding of legitimate state authority, of the just society, of the rights and freedoms of the individual, all derive from Enlightenment conceptions of state, society, law, and the individual.

# SELECTION 1:

# The Progress of History

Even before the outbreak of the French Revolution in 1789, both the Scientific Revolution and the application of the scientific method to the study of humankind led to the general belief in progress among the educated elite of Europe. The political philosopher Montesquieu (Charles Louis de Secondat, baron de LaBrède et de Montesquieu), the writer Voltaire, and the mathematician, scientist, and philosopher Jean Le Rond d'Alembert— to mention only the most prominent Enlightenment thinkers—all accepted the idea that the human race had materially, socially, and morally progressed over its long history. They also believed that this progress would inevitably continue into the infinite future. These authors wrote a new type of history that demonstrated this historical progress. More importantly, the idea of progress became a foundational assumption in their understanding of nature and society. Although they accepted that the scientific truths of nature were universal and thus ahistorical, human knowledge of these laws and their application to society were not. Over time more of nature's laws would be discovered and given practical applications to improve humanity's material and social condition. This progressive understanding of knowledge, and its application, would prove to be the foundation for the modern West's understanding of reality.

Although the notion of history as progress continued through the nineteenth and into the twentieth centuries, it found its original outlines in the eighteenth century. The marquis de Condorcet's "Sketch for the Historical Progress of the Human Mind" is perhaps its most exuberant expression. Condorcet (1743–1794) was a mathematician and a member of the French Academy of Sciences. Though born a noble, he—like many progressive aristocrats of his generation—wholeheartedly supported the French Revolution. Even before 1789, Condorcet was fascinated with questions of how governments could represent the people and how educational institutions could be created to produce an enlightened citizenry. With the onset of the more radical stage of revolution after 1792, Condorcet's attempts at liberal reform increasingly came under attack. Condorcet was labeled an enemy of the French Republic, and, in circumstances that have remained clouded, he was found strangled in his prison cell as he awaited execution. Though written in prison as he awaited execution, this "Sketch" still shows Condorcet's commitment to the principles of the Enlightenment and to the progressive view of history based on these principles.

No one has ever believed that the human mind could exhaust all the facts of nature, all the refinements of measuring and analyzing these facts, the interrelationship of objects, and all the possible combinations of ideas. . . .

But because, as the number of facts known increases, man learns to classify them, to reduce them to more general terms; because the instruments and the methods of observation and exact measurement are at the same time reaching a new precision; . . . the truths whose discovery has cost the most effort, which at first could be grasped only by men capable of profound thought, are soon carried further and proved by methods that are no longer beyond the reach of ordinary intelligence. If the methods that lead to new combinations are exhausted, if their application to problems not yet solved requires labors that exceed the time or the capacity of scholars, soon more general methods, simpler means, come to open a new avenue for genius. . . .

Applying these general reflections to the different sciences, we shall give, for each, examples of their successive improvement that will leave no doubt as to the certainty of the future improvements we can expect. . . . We shall point out how more universal education in each country, by giving more people the elementary knowledge that can inspire them with a taste for more advanced study and give them the capacity for making progress in it, can add to such hopes; how [these hopes] increase even more, if a more general prosperity permits a greater number of individuals to pursue studies, since at present, in the most enlightened countries, hardly a fiftieth part of those men to whom nature has given talent receive the education necessary to make use of their talents; and that, therefore, the number of men destined to push back the frontiers of the sciences by their discoveries will grow in the same proportion [as universal education increases].

We shall show how this equality of education, and the equality that will arise between nations,

will speed up the advances of those sciences whose progress depends on observations repeated in greater number over a larger area. . . .

If we now turn to the mechanical arts, we shall see that their progress can have no other limit than the reach of the scientific theories on which they depend; that the methods of these arts are capable of the same improvement, the same simplifications as methods in the sciences. Instruments, machines, looms will increasingly supplement the strength and skill of men; will augment at the same time the perfection and the precision of manufactures by lessening both the time and the labor needed to produce them. Then the obstacles that still impede this progress will disappear. . . .

Then a smaller and smaller area of land will be able to produce commodities of greater use or higher value; wider enjoyment will be obtained with less outlay; the same manufacturing output will call for less expenditure of raw materials or will be more durable. . . . Thus, without any sacrifice, the methods of conservation and of economy in consumption will follow the progress of the art of producing the various commodities, preparing them and turning them into manufactures.

Thus not only will the same amount of land be able to feed more people; but each of them, with less labor, will be employed more productively and will be able to satisfy his needs better. . . .

All these causes of the improvement of the human species, all these means that assure it, will by their nature act continuously and acquire a constantly growing momentum.

We have explained the proofs of this . . . ; we could therefore already conclude that the perfectibility of man is unlimited, even though, up to now, we have only supposed him endowed with the same natural faculties and organization. What then would be the certainty and extent of our hopes if we could believe that these natural faculties themselves and this organization are also susceptible of improvement? This is the last question remaining for us to examine.

The organic perfectibility or degeneration of races in plants and animals may be regarded as one of the general laws of nature.

This law extends to the human species; and certainly no one will doubt that progress in med-

From Marie Jean Antoine Nicolas Caritat, marquis de Condorcet, "Sketch for a Historical Picture of the Progress of the Human Spirit" (Paris: Masson, 1822).

ical conservation [of life], in the use of healthier food and housing, a way of living that would develop strength through exercise without impairing it by excess, and finally the destruction of the two most active causes of degradation—misery and too great wealth—will prolong the extent of life and assure people more constant health as well as a more robust constitution. We feel that the progress of preventive medicine as a preservative, made more effective by the progress of reason and social order, will eventually banish communicable or contagious illnesses and those diseases in general that originate in climate, food, and the nature of work. It would not be difficult to prove that this hope should extend to almost all other diseases, whose more remote causes will eventually be recognized. Would it be absurd now to suppose that the improvement of the human race should be regarded as capable of un-

limited progress? That a time will come when death would result only from extraordinary accidents or the more and more gradual wearing out of vitality, and that, finally, the duration of the average interval between birth and wearing out has itself no specific limit whatsoever? No doubt man will not become immortal, but cannot the span constantly increase between the moment he begins to live and the time when naturally, without illness or accident, he finds life a burden?

After reading this selection, consider these questions:

1. For Condorcet, what are the theoretical bases of human progress?
2. What role do the "mechanical arts" play in human progress?
3. How does Condorcet measure the impact of this progress?

# SELECTION 2:

# The Development of Feminist Consciousness

*The eighteenth-century Enlightenment was one of the clearest expressions of the principles of the Scientific Revolution. These principles, however, were not limited to the seventeenth and eighteenth centuries; their basic concerns for humanity and nature continue to be foundational for the modern West. In other words, our core definitions of the individual and our understanding of the individual's relation to nature and to society are still based on principles derived from the Enlightenment. Two popular ideas from that era state that society consists of individuals, and these individuals should all be equal in a basic sense. The belief that all forms of government derive their legitimacy from the will of the majority of these individuals is also an expression of these Enlightenment ideals. The attempts to reorganize society and found governments on these principles formed the basis of both the American and the French Revolutions. Even when these principles are contradicted by actual circumstances, the promise they hold out for the full emancipation of the individual continues to be the leading reason for present-day social and political reforms. Re-*

*form movements ranging from the enfranchisement of the entire population to the struggle for racial equality have taken the form of fulfilling these Enlightenment ideals.*

*The recognition of women as socially equal and politically active members of the nation is yet another example of how these basic Enlightenment principles continue to shape the modern West. In the following selection from* The Creation of Feminist Consciousness, *contemporary feminist historian Gerda Lerner sketches the history of women from ancient to modern times from the perspective of these Enlightenment principles.*

Feminist consciousness consists (1) of the awareness of women that they belong to a subordinate group and that, as members of such a group, they have suffered wrongs; (2) the recognition that their condition of subordination is not natural, but societally determined; (3) the development of a sense of sisterhood; (4) the autonomous definition by women of their goals and strategies for changing their condition; and (5) the development of an alternate vision of the future.

Because of the way women have been structured into patriarchal institutions, because of their long history of educational deprivation and of their economic dependence on males, women have had to overcome many obstacles before this process of coming-into-consciousness could be achieved. As we have seen, they first had to overcome their internalized feelings of mental and spiritual inferiority. In order to think and write at all, they had to prove to themselves and to each other that they were equal creatures before God, that they were able to communicate with God without male mediation and to conceptualize the Divine in their own way. This was the great contribution to women's thought made by the long line of women mystics whose work we have examined. Other groups of women authorized themselves to write because they were mothers. For centuries women conceptualized their group coherence on the basis of their actual experience of or their capacity for motherhood. Maternal thinking and responsibility gave them a special role in society and empowered them to resist certain aspects of patriarchal thought and practice. The experience of motherhood as empowering and as embodying specialized knowledge enabled women to subvert patriarchal religious ideas by insisting on a female aspect of the Divine. This could take the form of giving female characteristics to Jesus or of elevating the Virgin Mary to a position near to equality with the Trinity. It could lead to the various efforts we have traced by which women rewrote the story of the Redemption to make women's role essential in it. The patriarchal "glorification of motherhood," which began in the 18th century and culminated in the 19th-century glorification of women's role in the domestic sphere, led increasing numbers of women to the recognition that their collectivity needed to be defined not by their maternal role but by their personhood. This kind of reasoning contributed to the definition of "sisterhood" as the collective entity of women.

For over a thousand years women reinterpreted the biblical texts in a massive feminist critique, yet their marginalization in the formation of religious and philosophical thought prevented this critique from ever engaging the minds of the men who had appointed themselves as the definers of divine truth and revelation. Women's Bible criticism not only did not alter the patriarchal paradigm but also failed to spur the advancement of women's thought in a feminist direction, for women did not know that other women before them had already engaged in this enterprise of re-thinking and revision. It helped individual women to authorize themselves and in some cases to create important works of lasting impact. But what we need to note is the discontinuity in the story of women's intellectual effort. Endlessly, generation after generation of Penelopes [the faithful wife of the legendary Greek hero Odysseus] rewove the unraveled fabric only to unravel it again.

A different group of women authorized themselves to think and write by reliance on and an appeal to the gift of their special talent. Creativity became the instrument by which these women emancipated themselves intellectually to a level from which they could think their way out of patriarchy. There is a long history of these extraordinary women, which we have traced in this book. Their individual achievements are awesome and inspire respect, yet it must be noted that their individual effort could not lead to a collective advancement in consciousness. The women of talent existed, they struggled valiantly, they achieved—and they were forgotten. The women coming after them had to start all over again, repeating the process.

The awareness of a wrong is, as we have seen, something women developed over 1500 years from within patriarchal training and culture. Many women reasoned their way to an understanding that their condition was societally determined. This point was, in fact, the major insight provided by the generations of feminist Bible critics. The achievement of the next stage of awareness—namely, that they must join with other women to remedy the wrongs they suffered—was much harder to accomplish.

Crucial to the development of feminist consciousness are societal changes which allow substantial numbers of women to live in economic independence. We have earlier discussed these preconditions, most of them connected with industrialization, such as the decline in infant mortality and maternal death rates and the increase in life span. These are the developments that enable substantial numbers of women to choose not to be reproducers or, at the very least, to limit the number of years of their life span they devote to maternal work. Fully developed feminist consciousness rests on the precondition that women must have an economic alternative for survival other than marriage and that there exist large groups of single, self-supporting women. Only with such preconditions can women conceptualize alternatives to the patriarchal state; only with such preconditions can women elevate sisterhood to a uni-

fying ideal. In order for women to verify the adequacy, even the power, of their own thinking they needed cultural affirmation, exactly as men did. The mystics and religious women could find such affirmation in their actual or spiritual communities. Secular women attempted to and sometimes did find it in women's clusters or networks. Beginning with the 17th century, women were able to find it in the response of female readers of their books and audiences for their dramas.

But as long as the vast majority of women depended for their economic existence and that of their children on the support of a man, the formation of such female support networks was the privilege of a tiny minority of upper-class women. All positions of economic, legal and political power were in the hands of men, thus even the intellectually most emancipated women, those hoping to make changes in society, could not conceive of the process other than doing so with the help of powerful men. The learned women of the Reformation aimed no further than achieving a respectful dialogue with the men of their circles. The women in the left-wing sects of the Protestant Reformation saw themselves, at best, as equal partners with men in redefining religious belief and practice.

From the 17th century on, the main issue for religious and secular women on which they focused their strivings for equality was education. From [Mary] Astell [1666–1731; an English Quaker who proposed a woman's interpretation of the Bible] to [Mary] Wollstonecraft [1759–1797, author of *Vindication of the Rights of Woman* (1792)] to Catharine Beecher [1800–1878; an American promoter of higher education for women], women correctly defined the wrong they suffered as educational discrimination and defined their goal as equal access. But the arguments they used for a long time were focused on gaining male support and thus defined the issue in a way that still rested largely on patriarchal gender definitions. Because women were mothers and had responsibility for educating the young, they needed to be granted better education. Because they were the mothers of the Republic, their citizenship could best be expressed by their raising loyal [male] citizens and to do so, they needed to be better educated themselves.

Yet, again starting in the 17th century, the same advocacy for women's equal education took a different form, often originating with women who had also used the earlier arguments. Bathsua Makin, with the support of a network of women, founded women's schools. Mary Astell advocated a sex-segregated institution for the education of women, again with the support of other women. In the 19th-century United States, Emma Willard, Mary Lyon and Catharine Beecher, using the most traditional arguments for women's right to education, each set up sex-segregated educational institutions. To do so, they created female networks which quickly began to take on a life of their own. Female sponsors and alumnae of these institutions began to see their roles in society in a new light and many of them formed the core of activists who created the 19th-century woman's rights movement. The development of the British, French and German woman's rights movements was also connected with the growth and development of women's education.

Similar to the situation in the 1840s and 1850s in the United States, when voting rights for white men were being expanded, women in Great Britain petitioned to have voting rights for women included in the electoral reform legislation of 1832. Their petitions went unheeded, and the women put their energy into other channels. In the 1850s they formed organizations to press for educational reforms, the right of divorce, a Married Women's Property Bill (passed in 1855), and greater employment opportunities for women. Out of these clusters of women active in reforms *for women*, arose the first woman's rights organization, the National Society for Women's Suffrage in 1867.

In France, women had actively participated in the great revolutionary movements of 1792, 1848 and 1870, in each case forming sex-segregated organizations which made quite advanced feminist demands. These organizations were short-lived and ineffective; they were destroyed by repressive regimes and a conservative backlash. The *Code Napoléon*, backed by the Catholic Church and enacted in 1804, classified married women with children, the insane and criminals as politically incompetent; restricted women's legal and civil rights; made married women economically and legally subject to their husbands and declared that they belonged to the family, not to public life. The *Code* forbade women to attend political meetings or to wear trousers.

In the 1848 revolution against the monarchy, women played an active part. They established several feminist clubs and newspapers, took part in revolutionary battles and street actions, petitioned the provisional government for the vote, and even attempted to run female candidates. Working-class women raised economic demands specific to their own interests. But all of these efforts proved fruitless. Universal male suffrage, which was enacted in 1848, excluded women; a school reform bill setting up primary education for girls put these schools under the control of the Catholic Church. Several women who had participated in the Revolution were sent to prison or exile. The feminist organizations died in the wake of the general repression.

A similar sequence of events occurred during and after the Paris Commune in 1871. Its defeat devastated a tiny feminist movement and the few radical women who had participated in the Commune. It was not until 1883 that a feminist organization, *Société du Suffrage des Femmes* (Women's Suffrage Society), was formed. French women did not receive legal recognition of their personhood and voting rights until 1938.

In Germany, women's feminist consciousness was affected by the development of German nationalism. The journalist Louise Otto edited a feminist newspaper from 1849 to 1850 in Saxony as a result of her disappointment with the debates over a constitution for the future unified nation. "They think in their deliberations only about half the human race only about men," she commented. "When they speak of the people, they do not include the women." She and the other women who participated in the 1848 revolutions gained this basic insight over and over again. As fighters on the barricades they were subject to the same persecution and prison sentences as the male revolutionaries, but when they advanced a program for the full equality of women, they met male indifference and resistance. The reaction following the defeat of the revolution set back all organizational efforts. In most German states legislation enacted in 1850 forbade women and minors from attending any political meetings and joining political organizations. Yet in the 1850s autonomous women's organizations arose in many German cities out of welfare organizations for the victims of the defeated revolution. In Hamburg a woman's organization, set up to improve the discourse between Protestant and Jewish women, succeeded in developing plans for the establishment of a university for women, but their efforts, like those of other feminist groups, succumbed to the repression of all grassroots organizations after 1850. Adapting to this climate of repression, the *Allgemeiner Deutscher Frauenverein* (General German Women's Association), led by Louise Otto in the 1860s and '70s, limited itself to conservative demands and tactics. German national unification and statehood in 1870 under Prussia's leadership did not promote democracy. Nationalism, militarism and the most traditionalist emphasis on women's domestic role continued unchallenged. It was not until 1902 that it was possible for German women to form a major woman's suffrage association.

What emerges from this brief overview is that women's participation in general revolutionary movements did not bring them closer to advancing their own rights and interests. Time and time again, their sacrifices and contributions were appreciated, but their male colleagues and comrades considered their demands at best marginal and secondary and did not act on them. Interestingly, conservative political groups always considered the threat of feminism a central issue and made the repression of women's organizations an inevitable and essential feature of their political program. What also becomes clear is the necessary connection between women's work in sex-segregated groups under their own leadership and the advancement of feminist organizations.

Sex-segregated social space became the terrain in which women could confirm their own ideas and test them against the knowledge and experience of other women. Here, they could also, for the first time in history, test their theories in social practice. Unlike the social spaces in which women could have equal or nearly equal leadership roles, but in which the hegemony of men remained unchallenged—such as the salons, the utopian communities, the socialist and anarchist parties—these all-female spaces could help women to advance from a simple analysis of their condition to the level of theory formation. Or, in other words, to the level of providing not only their own autonomous definitions of their goals but an alternate vision of societal organization—a feminist world-view.

The sex-segregated institutions and organizations formed in the 19th century in the United States, England and on the European continent were usually driven by necessity. Women founded girls' academies because society did not adequately provide for the education of women. Women formed women's medical colleges, hospitals, nursing training institutions, because male-dominated schools and institutions excluded them. The earliest women's clubs in America, both those of white and of African-American women, were formed to counteract discriminatory practices by male clubs. The founders intended merely to right a wrong, to redress a grievance, to win limited equity and/or access. But the process of reaching that goal, the resistance they met, the struggles to overcome that resistance, all enhanced the process of consciousness-formation. It was this dynamic which enabled them to develop a sense of sisterhood and separate forms of women's culture, institutions and modes of living.

A similar development took place in social welfare and in religious organizations. In the United States throughout the 19th century we find women organizing first to help others, then to help themselves. In the social struggles they engaged in they experienced resistance to their efforts by men and by male-dominated institutions, ranging from universities to the state. It was only then, when they began not only to think of themselves as a coherent group, but when they began to act in society as such a group, that the concept of sisterhood could be more than a rhetorical term.

Throughout historical time, women have been discriminated against and disadvantaged economically, politically, legally and sexually. They have, depending on their class, race and ethnic affiliations with men, also participated in discriminating against, disadvantaging and exploiting men and women different from themselves by race and class and religion. In short, they have, while being victimized by patriarchy, continued to support the system and helped to perpetuate it. They have done so because their consciousness of their own situation could not develop in a manner commensurate with their advancement in other aspects of their lives. Thus, the systematic educational disadvantaging of women and their definition as being persons "out of history" have been truly the most oppressive aspect of women's condition under patriarchy.

I have argued in this book that women's marginalization in the process of History-making has set them back intellectually and has kept them for far longer than was necessary from developing a consciousness of their collectivity in sisterhood, not motherhood. The cruel repetitiousness by which individual women have struggled to a higher level of consciousness, repeating an effort made a number of times by other women in previous centuries, is not only a symbol of women's oppression but is its actual manifestation. Thus, even the most advanced feminist thinkers, up to and including those in the early 20th century, have been in dialogue with the "great men" before them and have been unable to verify, test and improve their ideas by being in dialogue with the women thinkers before them. Mary Wollstonecraft argued with [Edmund] Burke [1729–1797; British statesman] and [Jean-Jacque] Rousseau [1712–1798; French philosopher and writer], when arguing with Makin, Astell and Margaret Fell might have sharpened her thought and radicalized her. Emma Goldman argued for free love and a new sort of communal life against the models of [Karl] Marx and [anarchist Mikhail] Bakunin; a dialogue with the Owenite feminists Anna Wheeler and Emma Martin might have redirected her thinking and kept her from inventing "solutions" which had already proven unworkable fifty years earlier. Simone de Beauvoir, in a passionate dialogue with Marx, [Sigmund] Freud, [Jean-Paul] Sartre and [writer Albert] Camus, could go as far with a feminist critique of patriarchal values and institutions as it was possible to go when the thinker was male-centered. Had she truly engaged with Mary Wollstonecraft's thought, the works of Mary Astell, the Quaker feminists of the early 19th century, the mystical revisioners among the black spiritualists and the feminism of Anna Cooper, her analysis might have become woman-centered and therefore capable of projecting alternatives to the basic mental constructs of patriarchal thought. Her erroneous assertion that, "They [women] have no past, no history, no religion of their own," was not just an oversight and a flaw, but a manifestation of the basic limitations which have for millennia limited the power and effectiveness of women's thought.

Human beings have always used history in order to find their direction toward the future: to repeat the past or to depart from it. Lacking knowledge of their own history, women thinkers did not have the self-knowledge from which to project a desired future. Therefore, women have, up until very recently, not been able to create a social theory appropriate to their needs. Feminist consciousness is a prerequisite for the formulation of the kind of abstract thought needed to conceptualize a society in which differences do not connote dominance.

The hegemony of patriarchal thought in Western civilization is not due to its superiority in content, form and achievement over all other thought; it is built upon the systematic silencing of other voices. Women of all classes, men of different races or religious beliefs from those of the dominant, those defined as deviants by them—all these had to be discouraged, ridiculed, silenced. Above all they had to be kept from being part of the intellectual discourse. Patriarchal thinkers constructed their edifice the way patriarchal statesmen constructed their states: by defining who was to be kept out. The definition of those to be kept out was usually not even made explicit, for to have made it explicit would have meant to acknowledge that there was a process of exclusion going on. Those to be kept out were simply obliterated from sight, marginalized out of existence. When the great system of European universities secularized learning and made it more widely accessible, the very nature of the university was so defined as to exclude all women from it. In the 19th century, throughout Europe and in the United States, professions redefined their purposes, restructured their organizations, licensed and upgraded their services and enhanced their status in the societies in which they operated. All of this was based on the tacit assumption that women were to be excluded from these professions. It took nearly 150 years of organized struggle for women to make this assumption visible and, at least partially, reverse it.

An equally devastating pattern can be seen in the connection of advances in political democracy with contractions in the political/legal rights of women. I began this book by calling attention to this connection in the case of the democratic *polis* of ancient Greece and the democratic Constitution of the United States of America. The pattern becomes obvious when we contemplate the restrictions on the freedoms of noble women as a result of the Renaissance; the increase in witchhunts and persecution of heretics combined with the educational advancement of women after the Reformation; the backlash resulting in misogynist legislation after women's activism in the revolutions of the 18th and 19th centuries, such as the *Code Napoléon* after the French Revolution, the constraints on women's legal rights following the revolutions in Germany and in France in 1848; the inclusion of the word "male" as qualification for voting in the "liberalized" constitutions of the United States, the Netherlands and France in the 19th century. The pattern alters and begins to crack by the end of the 19th century, directly as the result of women's raised feminist consciousness and their militant organizing. It is worth recollecting, even as a historical artifact, because the achievements of women as thinkers and creators of ideas cannot be really appreciated unless we know the obstacles against which they had to struggle.

It appears then, that there were women as great as the greatest male thinkers and writers, but their significance and their work have been marginalized and obscured. It appears most likely also that there were many others of equal potential who have been totally silenced and remain forgotten in the long forward march of male dominance over Western civilization. Most important, the female questions, the woman's point of view, the paradigm which would include the female experience has, until very recently, never entered the common discourse.

But now, the period of patriarchal hegemony over culture has come to an end. Even though in most places in the world and even in the Western democracies male dominance in major cultural institutions persists, the intellectual emancipation of women has shattered the solid monopoly men have held so long over theory and definition. Women do not as yet have power over institutions, over the state, over the law. But the theoretical insights modern feminist scholarship has already achieved have the power to shatter the patriarchal paradigm. Marginalization, ridicule, name-calling, budgetcutting and other devices designed to halt the process of redefining the mental constructs of Western civilization will all, in the long run, have to fail. They can temporarily retard the ongoing process of intellectual transformation, but they cannot stop it. As Galileo on his death-bed, long after the power of the Inquisition had forced him to recant his heretical theories, said, "*E pure si muove*" (And still, it moves).

More than thirteen hundred years of individual struggles, disappointments and persistence have brought women to the historic moment when we can reclaim the freedom of our minds as we reclaim our past. The millennia of women's prehistory are at an end. We stand at the beginning of a new epoch in the history of humankind's thought, as we recognize that sex is irrelevant to thought, that gender is a social construct and that woman, like man, makes and defines history.

After reading this selection, consider these questions:

1. According to Lerner, what were the chief obstacles for the creation of women's consciousness?

2. What does Lerner mean by *patriarchy*?

3. How does Lerner describe the present state of women's consciousness?

# SELECTION 3:

# Science and the Modern World

*The principles of the Scientific Revolution proved to be historically creative. Their application to the human realm helped produce both the Enlightenment and the French Revolution in the eighteenth century. In addition, the Scientific Revolution has also had a more direct impact on the nineteenth and twentieth centuries. In fact, it would be difficult to conceive of the modern West without the specific ways in which science has shaped and reshaped the very definition of knowledge. In the various forms of technology, the Scientific Revolution has fundamentally altered the relation of human beings to nature, the economy, and society. It would be difficult to understand the West today without thinking of the role of science and technology.*

*Reflecting on both the extensiveness and the magnitude of this impact, a number of thinkers have even equated science in this broad sense with the modern West itself. In the following selection from his book* Science and the Modern World, *the eminent twentieth-century philosopher Alfred North Whitehead offers one interpretation of this relation between science and the modern West. After defining the modern scientific mentality and the principles on which it is based (which he traces back to the seventeenth century French philosopher René Descartes), Whitehead evaluates the various ways in which science has affected society.*

The general conceptions introduced by science into modern thought cannot be separated from the philosophical situation as expressed by Descartes. I mean the assumption of bodies and minds as independent individual substances, each existing in its own right apart from any necessary reference to each other. Such a conception was very concordant with the individualism which had issued from the moral discipline of the Middle Ages. But, though the easy reception of the idea is thus explained, the derivation in itself rests upon a confusion, very natural but none the less unfortunate. The moral discipline had emphasised the intrinsic value of the individual entity. This emphasis had put the notions of the individual and of its experiences into the foreground of thought. At this point the confusion commences. The emergent individual value of each entity is transformed into the independent substantial existence of each entity, which is a very different notion.

I do not mean to say that Descartes made this logical, or rather illogical transition, in the form of explicit reasoning. Far from it. What he did, was first to concentrate upon his own conscious experiences, as being facts within the independent world of his own mentality. He was led to speculate in this way by the current emphasis upon the individual value of his total self. He im-

From *Science and the Modern World,* by Alfred North Whitehead (New York: Macmillan, 1925).

plicitly transformed this emergent individual value, inherent in the very fact of his own reality, into a private world of passions, or modes, of independent substance.

Also the independence ascribed to bodily substances carried them away from the realm of values altogether. They degenerated into a mechanism entirely valueless, except as suggestive of an external ingenuity. The heavens had lost the glory of God. . . . This recoil was already in full strength antecedently to [before] Descartes. Accordingly, the Cartesian scientific doctrine of bits of matter, bare of intrinsic value, was merely a formulation . . . of a doctrine which was current before its entrance into scientific thought or Cartesian philosophy. . . . But science, as equipped by Descartes, gave stability and intellectual status to a point of view which has had very mixed effects upon the moral presuppositions of modern communities. Its good effects arose from its efficiency as a method for scientific researches within those limited regions which were then best suited for exploration. The result was a general clearing of the European mind away from the stains left upon it by the hysteria of remote barbaric ages. This was all to the good, and was most completely exemplified in the eighteenth century.

But in the nineteenth century, when society was undergoing transformation into the manufacturing system, the bad effects of these doctrines have been very fatal. The doctrine of minds, as independent substances, leads directly not merely to private worlds of experience, but also to private worlds of morals. The moral intuitions can be held to apply only to the strictly private world of psychological experience. Accordingly, self-respect, and the making the most of your own individual opportunities, together constituted the efficient morality of the leaders among the industrialists of that period. The western world is now [in 1925] suffering from the limited moral outlook of the three previous generations. . . .

The two evils are: one, the ignoration of the true relation of each organism to its environment; and the other, the habit of ignoring the intrinsic worth of the environment which must be allowed its weight in any consideration of final ends.

Another great fact confronting the modern world is the discovery of the method of training professionals, who specialise in particular regions of thought and thereby progressively add to the sum of knowledge within their respective limitations of subject. . . .

Professionals are not new to the world. But in the past, professionals have formed unprogressive castes. The point is that professionalism has now been mated with progress. The world is now faced with a self-evolving system, which it cannot stop. There are dangers and advantages in this situation. It is obvious that the gain in material power affords opportunity for social betterment. If mankind can rise to the occasion, there lies in front a golden age of beneficent creativeness. But material power in itself is ethically neutral. It can equally well work in the wrong direction. The problem is not how to produce great men, but how to produce great societies. The great society will put up the men for the occasions. The materialistic philosophy emphasised the given quantity of material, and thence derivatively the given nature of the environment. It thus operated most unfortunately upon the social conscience of mankind. For it directed almost exclusive attention to the aspect of struggle for existence in a fixed environment. To a large extent the environment is fixed, and to this extent there is a struggle for existence. It is folly to look at the universe through rose-tinted spectacles. We must admit the struggle. The question is, who is to be eliminated? In so far as we are educators, we have to have clear ideas upon that point; for it settles the type to be produced and the practical ethics to be inculcated.

But during the last three generations, the exclusive direction of attention to this aspect of things has been a disaster of the first magnitude. The watchwords of the nineteenth century have been, struggle for existence, competition, class warfare, commercial antagonism between nations, military warfare. The struggle for existence has been construed into the gospel of hate. The full conclusion to be drawn from a philosophy of evolution is fortunately of a more balanced character. Successful organisms modify their environment. Those organisms are successful which modify their environments so as to assist each other. This law is exemplified in nature on a vast scale. For example, the North American Indians accepted their environment, with the result that a scanty population barely succeeded in maintaining themselves over the whole continent. The European races when they arrived in the same continent pursued an opposite policy. They at once coöperated in modifying their environment. The result is that a population more than twenty times that of the Indian population now occupies the same territory, and the continent is not yet full. Again, there are associations of different species which mutually coöperate. This differentiation of species is exhibited in the simplest physical entities, such as the association between electrons and positive nuclei, and in the whole realm of animate nature. The trees in a Brazilian forest depend upon the association of various species of organisms, each of which is mutually dependent on the other species. A single tree by itself is dependent upon all the adverse chances of shifting circumstances. The wind stunts it: the variations in temperature check its foliage: the rains denude its soil: its leaves are blown away and are lost for the purpose of fertilisation. You may obtain individual specimens of fine trees either in exceptional circumstances, or where human cultivation has intervened. But in nature the normal way in which trees flourish is by their association in a forest. Each tree may lose something of its individual perfection of growth, but they mutually assist each other in preserving the conditions for survival. The soil is preserved and shaded; and the microbes necessary for its fertility are neither scorched, nor frozen, nor washed away. A forest is the triumph of the organisation of mutually dependent species. Further a species of microbes which kills the forest, also exterminates itself. Again the two sexes exhibit the same advantage of differentiation. In the history of the world, the prize has not gone to those species which specialised in methods of violence, or even in defensive armour. In fact, nature began with producing animals encased in hard shells for defence against the ills of life. It also experimented in size. But smaller animals, without external armour, warm-blooded, sensitive, and alert, have cleared these monsters off the face of the earth. Also, the lions and tigers are not the successful

species. There is something in the ready use of force which defeats its own object. Its main defect is that it bars coöperation. Every organism requires an environment of friends, partly to shield it from violent changes, and partly to supply it with its wants. The Gospel of Force is incompatible with a social life. By *force*, I mean *antagonism* in its most general sense.

Almost equally dangerous is the Gospel of Uniformity. The differences between the nations and races of mankind are required to preserve the conditions under which higher development is possible. One main factor in the upward trend of animal life has been the power of wandering. Perhaps this is why the armour-plated monsters fared badly. They could not wander. Animals wander into new conditions. They have to adapt themselves or die. Mankind has wandered from the trees to the plains, from the plains to the seacoast, from climate to climate, from continent to continent, and from habit of life to habit of life. When man ceases to wander, he will cease to ascend in the scale of being. Physical wandering is still important, but greater still is the power of man's spiritual adventures—adventures of thought, adventures of passionate feeling, adventures of aesthetic experience. A diversification among human communities is essential for the provision of the incentive and material for the Odyssey of the human spirit. Other nations of different habits are not enemies: they are godsends. Men require of their neighbours something sufficiently akin to be understood, something sufficiently different to provoke attention, and something great enough to command admiration. We must not expect, however, all the virtues. We should even be satisfied if there is something odd enough to be interesting.

Modern science has imposed on humanity the necessity for wandering. Its progressive thought and its progressive technology make the transition through time, from generation to generation, a true migration into uncharted seas of adventure. The very benefit of wandering is that it is dangerous and needs skill to avert evils. We must expect, therefore, that the future will disclose dangers. It is the business of the future to be dangerous; and it is among the merits of science that it equips the future for its duties. The prosperous middle classes, who ruled the nineteenth century, placed an excessive value upon placidity of existence. They refused to face the necessities for social reform imposed by the new industrial system, and they are now refusing to face the necessities for intellectual reform imposed by the new knowledge. The middle class pessimism over the future of the world comes from a confusion between civilisation and security. In the immediate future there will be less security than in the immediate past, less stability. It must be admitted that there is a degree of instability which is inconsistent with civilisation. But, on the whole, the great ages have been unstable ages.

After reading this selection, consider these questions:

1. How does Whitehead define modern science?
2. What were the major consequences of modern science on the nineteenth and twentieth centuries?
3. What does Whitehead mean by the terms *Gospel of Force* and *Gospel of Uniformity*?

# SELECTION 4:

# An Alternative Viewpoint

*Like science and technology, the principles of the Enlightenment have not always or unqualifiedly been accepted by all. While there are a great many opposing viewpoints to the Enlightenment, they cannot all be encompassed by our established categories of conservative thought or more traditional forms of religious belief. The twentieth-century Spanish philosopher José Ortega y Gasset challenged the interpretation that the modern West can be equated with the principles of the Enlightenment. Based on an alternative view of the individual and of the definition of knowledge, Ortega y Gasset understood the ideas of* human being *and* human society *as fundamentally historical. Both are shaped by traditions and evolve over time. Neither the individual nor society can be adequately comprehended by the Enlightenment's abstract and generalized concepts. Accordingly, the Enlightenment's idea of historical progress must also be questioned. In the following selection from his 1930 book* The Revolt of the Masses, *Ortega y Gasset draws attention to several unintended consequences of the spread of scientific and Enlightenment principles. While accepting the impact of Enlightenment thought on the history of the West, Ortega y Gasset draws attention to the problems of modern mass society.*

From *The Revolt of the Masses*, by José Ortega y Gasset (New York: Norton, 1932).

This essay is an attempt to discover the diagnosis of our time, of our actual existence. . . . Our life as a programme of possibilities is magnificent, exuberant, superior to all others known to history.

But by the very fact that its scope is greater, it has overflowed all the channels, principles, norms, ideals handed down by tradition. It is more life than all previous existence, and therefore all the more problematical. It can find no direction from the past. It has to discover its own destiny.

But now we must complete the diagnosis. Life, which means primarily what is possible for us to be, is likewise, and for that very reason, a choice, from among these possibilities, of what we actually are going to be. Our circumstances—these possibilities—form the portion of life given us, imposed on us. This constitutes what we call the world. Life does not choose its own world, it finds itself, to start with, in a world determined and unchangeable: the world of the present. Our world is that portion of destiny which goes to make up our life. But this vital destiny is not a kind of mechanism. We are not launched into existence like a shot from a gun, with its trajectory absolutely predetermined. The destiny under which we fall when we come into this world—it is always *this* world, the actual one—consists in the exact contrary. Instead of imposing on us one trajectory, it imposes several, and consequently forces us to choose. Surprising condition, this, of our existence! To live is to feel ourselves *fatally* obliged to exercise our *liberty*, to decide what we are going to be in this world. . . .

It is, then, false to say that in life "circumstances decide." On the contrary, circumstances are the dilemma, constantly renewed, in presence of which we have to make our decision; what actually decides is our character. All this is equally valid for collective life. In it also there is, first, a horizon of possibilities, and then, a determination which chooses and decides on the effective form of collective existence. This determination has its origin in the character of society, or what comes to the same thing, of the type of men dominant in it. In our time it is the mass-man who dominates. . . . It will not do to say that this is what happened in the period of democracy, of universal suffrage. Under universal suffrage, the masses do not decide, their role consists in supporting the decision of one minority or other. It was these who presented their "programmes"—excellent word. Such programmes were, in fact, programmes of collective life. In them the masses were invited to accept a line of decision.

To-day something very different is happening. If we observe the public life of the countries where the triumph of the masses has made most advance . . . we are surprised to find that politically they are living from day to day. The phenomenon is an extraordinarily strange one. Public authority is in the hands of a representative of the masses. These are so powerful that they have wiped out all opposition. . . . And yet public authority—the Government— . . . lives without any vital programme, any plan of existence. . . . Hence its activities are reduced to dodging the difficulties of the hour. . . . Such has public power always been when exercised directly by the masses: omnipotent and ephemeral. The mass-man is he whose life lacks any purpose, and simply goes drifting along. Consequently, though his possibilities and his powers be enormous, he constructs nothing. And it is this type of man who decides in our time. It will be well, then, that we analyse his character. . . .

The average type of European at present possesses a soul, healthier and stronger it is true than those of the [nineteenth] century, but much more simple. Hence, at times he leaves the impression of a primitive man suddenly risen in the midst of a very old civilisation. In the schools, which were such a source of pride to the [nineteenth] century, it has been impossible to do more than instruct the masses in the technique of modern life; it has been found impossible to educate them. They have been given tools for an intenser form of existence, but no feeling for their great historic duties; they have been hurriedly inoculated with the pride and power of modern instruments, but not with their spirit. Hence they will have nothing to do with their spirit, and the new generations are getting ready to take over command of the world as if the world were a paradise without trace of former footsteps, without traditional and highly complex problems. . . .

This type which at present is to be found everywhere, and everywhere imposes his own spiritual barbarism, is, in fact, the spoiled child of human history. The spoiled child is the heir who behaves exclusively as a mere heir. In this case the inheritance is civilisation—with its conveniences, its security; in a word, with all its advantages. As we have seen, it is only in circumstances of easy existence such as our civilisation has produced, that a type can arise, marked by such a collection of features, inspired by such a character. It is one of a number of deformities produced by luxury in human material. There might be a deceptive tendency to believe that a life born into a world of plenty should be better, more really a life than one which consists in a struggle against scarcity. Such is not the case, for reasons of the strictest and most fundamental nature, which this is not the place to enlarge upon. For the present, instead of those reasons, it is sufficient to recall the ever-recurrent fact which constitutes the tragedy of every hereditary aristocracy. The aristocrat inherits, that is to say, he finds attributed to his person, conditions of life which he has not created, and which, therefore, are not produced in organic union with his personal, individual existence. At birth he finds himself installed, suddenly and without knowing how, in the midst of his riches and his prerogatives. In his own self, he has nothing to do with them, because they do not come from him. They are the giant armour of some other person, some other human being, his ancestor. And he has to live as an heir, that is to say, he has to wear the trappings of another existence. What does this bring us to? What life is the "aristocrat" by inheritance going to lead, his own or that of his first noble ancestor? Neither one nor the other. He is condemned to *represent* the other man, consequently, to *be* neither that other nor himself. Inevitably his life loses all authenticity, and is transformed into pure representation or fiction of another life. The abundance of resources that he is obliged to make use of gives him no chance to live out his own personal destiny, his life is atrophied. *All life is the struggle, the effort to be itself.* The difficulties which I meet with in order to realise my existence are precisely what awaken and mobilise my activities, my capacities. If my body was not a weight to me, I should not be able to walk. If the atmosphere did not press on me, I should feel my body as something vague, flabby, unsubstantial. So in the "aristocratic" heir his whole individuality grows vague, for lack of use and vital effort. The result is that specific stupidity of "our old nobility" which is unlike anything else—a stupidity which, strictly speaking, has never yet been described in its intimate, tragic mechanism—that tragic mechanism which leads all hereditary aristocracy to irremediable degeneration.

So much merely to counteract our ingenuous tendency to believe that a superabundance of resources favours existence. Quite the contrary. A world superabundant in possibilities automatically produces deformities, vicious types of human life, which may be brought under the general class, the "heir-man," of which the "aristocrat" is only one particular case, the spoiled child another, and the mass-man of our time, more fully, more radically, a third. (It would, moreover, be possible to make more detailed use of this last allusion to the "aristocrat," by showing how many of his characteristic traits, in all times and among all peoples, germinate in the mass-man. For example: his propensity to make out of games and sports the central occupation of his life; the cult of the body—hygienic regime and attention to dress; lack of romance in his dealings with woman; his amusing himself with the "intellectual," while at bottom despising him and at times ordering his flunkeys or his bravoes to chastise him; his preference for living under an absolute authority rather than under a regime of free-discussion, etc.)

After reading this selection, consider these questions:
1. How does Ortega y Gasset define modern man as a type?
2. How is this type the "spoiled child of human history"?
3. What does Ortega y Gasset speak of power and the role of government?

# CHAPTER 2
# The Scientific Revolution:
# The Search for New Foundations

Emerging slowly and almost unobserved in the mid–sixteenth century, consolidated as a distinct method and view of nature in the seventeenth century, and expanded into a major "revolution" in the understanding of the world and truth in general in the eighteenth century, the Scientific Revolution was to have far-reaching consequences. In fact, the Scientific Revolution established a new foundation for the civilization of the West. Both the method for acquiring knowledge and the definition of what constituted reality were fundamentally and unalterably changed as a result of a new understanding of nature. This understanding challenged the notion of revealed truth and authority based on tradition that underlay the various forms of Christianity. With the consolidation of a distinct "scientific method" by Galileo Galilei and Isaac Newton, the eighteenth-century Enlightenment extended the scientific view of nature and the definition of truth to encompass human beings, political power, and social organization. In so doing, the Scientific Revolution challenged the more established and traditionally sanctioned foundations that had evolved from the Middle Ages. From this method and this challenge, the intellectual foundation for both the American and the French Revolutions were laid.

There were other consequences of the Scientific Revolution as well. Through the application of scientific method (and more widely a scientific mentality) to nature, technological innovations would eventuate in a series of industrial revolutions in the production of goods, the means of communication, and in the development of ever more powerful weapons. With these wide-ranging consequences, the Scientific Revolution dramatically marked off the West from all other civilizations of the world. In this sense, the Scientific Revolution would indirectly provide the means for the West's military, political, and economic domination of the rest of the world.

What was the origin of the Scientific Revolution? The answer is not easy to give or even to formulate appropriately. There were, of course, roots in the philosophical and scientific thought of the Hellenic (ancient Greek) and especially the Hellenistic (post–Alexander the Great) periods. Understanding the world as an organized cosmos, open to human comprehension and to critical reevaluation (and therefore not primarily known through myth or religious traditions) was one of the major inheritances from antiquity. More immediately, the Scientific Revolution emerged in the sixteenth and seventeenth centuries from rather esoteric problems concerning the calculation of planetary movements and the subsequent debates among scientists concerning the position of the earth relative to the sun. In 1543 the Polish clergyman Nicolaus Copernicus proposed that an easier method and mathematically more precise means of calculating the motions of the planets could be achieved theoretically by conceiving of the sun as the center of a series of concentric circles along which the seven known planets revolved. The resulting image of planetary motion resulted in a solar system.

By the first half of the seventeenth century, what Copernicus had suggested had become the centerpiece of a new view of the universe, a new method of ascertaining knowledge, and a new understanding of the relationship between human reason and this knowledge. Positioning our own planet among the other revolving planets undermined the traditional Christian meaning of earth as central to God's creation. In addition, the idea of a moving earth challenged the traditional understanding of motion in general. Instead of Aristotle's claim that rest, not motion, is the natural state of all entities, the new view posited motion as the norm not only for the planets but also for objects on earth. Such motion was mechanical and was open to human comprehension, and even to human experimentation, and could not be understood according to notions other than the traditional one of a divine (and ultimately mysterious) order created by God. Thus, the Scientific Revolution arose as a clash with traditional definitions of truth and authority, even when individual promoters of scientific knowledge such as Isaac Newton attempted through science to place belief in the Christian God and divine providence on firmer foundations.

To ask why this new understanding of truth came to challenge or reground Christian faith and to restructure knowledge and legitimate authority—to ask, in other words, why the Scientific Revolution evolved in the remarkable ways in which it did—is to inquire into a far wider set of problems than that of intellectual history. The new mentality behind the Scientific Revolution arose both as a response to, and a symptom of, the specific historical situation of Western civilization in the early modern period. This historical situation was characterized by the clashes among the divergent understandings of Christianity and the destruction of life and property during the religious wars that wracked Europe throughout the later sixteenth and the first half of the seventeenth centuries. Whatever the intentions of individual scientists and philosophers, the Scientific Revolution—once consolidated in the late seventeenth and early eighteenth century—allowed a new definition of truth and a new means of legitimating authority to emerge that, at least apparently, overcame religious dissension and ideological conflict.

SELECTION 1:

# Galileo Looks Through a Telescope

*Two names stand out in the early development of these new concepts of motion. Johannes Kepler (1571–1630) accepted Copernicus's idea that the movement of the planets could be calculated mathematically. Between 1609 and 1619 he formulated three laws of planetary motion, thus providing a clearer mathematical description of observed conditions. These laws appeared to be confirmed once Galileo Galilei (1564–1642) had perfected the telescope and observed the great diversity among heavenly phenomena—the pitted surface of the moon, the four satellites of Jupiter, the phases of Venus, and the eruption of sunspots. Galileo went on to study the motion of the stars and planets as well as moving spheres here on earth. Galileo proposed an alternative framework for comprehending motion that, theoretically, broke down the long-established division between celestial and terrestrial motion, between an assumed perfect translunar realm and the transitory nature of all things earthly. He proposed uniting the studies of motion within a single, universal system of absolute space and absolute time, which was a bold intellectual leap since it clearly went beyond direct observation. The following selection is taken from Galileo's* The Starry Messenger *(1610), in which he describes his most recent telescopic observations.*

Now let us review the observations made during the past two months, once more inviting the attention of all who are eager for true philosophy to the first steps of such important contemplations. Let us speak first of that surface of the moon which faces us. For greater clarity I distinguish two parts of this surface, a lighter and a darker; the lighter part seems to surround and to pervade the whole hemisphere, while the darker part discolors the moon's surface like a kind of cloud, and makes it appear covered with spots. Now those spots which are fairly dark and rather large are plain to everyone and have been seen throughout the ages; these I shall call the "large" or "ancient" spots, distinguishing them from others that are smaller in size but so numerous as to occur all over the lunar surface, and especially the lighter part. The latter spots had never been seen by anyone before me. From observations of these spots repeated many times I have been led to the opinion and conviction that the surface of the moon is not smooth, uniform, and precisely spherical as a great number of philosophers believe it (and the other heavenly bodies) to be, but is uneven, rough, and full of cavities and prominences, being not unlike the face of the earth, relieved by chains of mountains and deep valleys. The things I have seen by which I was enabled to draw this conclusion are as follows.

On the fourth or fifth day after new moon, when the moon is seen with brilliant horns, the

From "The Starry Messenger," by Galileo Galilei, in *Discoveries and Opinions of Galileo*, translated by Stillman Drake (Garden City, NY: Anchor/Doubleday, 1957).

boundary which divides the dark part from the light does not extend uniformly in an oval line as would happen on a perfectly spherical solid, but traces out an uneven, rough, and very wavy line as shown in the figure below. Indeed, many luminous excrescences extend beyond the boundary into the darker portion, while on the other hand some dark patches invade the illuminated part. Moreover a great quantity of small blackish spots, entirely separated from the dark region, are scattered almost all over the area illuminated by the sun with the exception only of that part which is occupied by the large and ancient spots. Let us note, however, that the said small spots always agree in having their blackened parts directed toward the sun, while on the side opposite the sun they are crowned with bright contours, like shining summits. There is a similar sight on earth about sunrise, when we behold the valleys not yet flooded with light though the mountains surrounding them are already ablaze with glowing splendor on the side opposite the sun. And just as the shadows in the hollows on earth diminish in size as the sun rises higher, so these spots on the moon lose their blackness as the illuminated region grows larger and larger.

Again, not only are the boundaries of shadow and light in the moon seen to be uneven and wavy, but still more astonishingly many bright points appear within the darkened portion of the moon, completely divided and separated from the illuminated part and at a considerable distance from it. After a time these gradually increase in size and brightness, and an hour or two later they become joined with the rest of the lighted part which has now increased in size. Meanwhile more and more peaks shoot up as if sprouting

now here, now there, lighting up within the shadowed portion; these become larger, and finally they too are united with that same luminous surface which extends ever further. An illustration of this is to be seen in the figure above. And on the earth, before the rising of the sun, are not the highest peaks of the mountains illuminated by the sun's rays while the plains remain in shadow? Does not the light go on spreading while the larger central parts of those mountains are becoming illuminated? And when the sun has finally risen, does not the illumination of plains and hills finally become one? But on the moon the variety of elevations and depressions appears to surpass in every way the roughness of the terrestrial surface, as we shall demonstrate further on.

At present I cannot pass over in silence something worthy of consideration which I observed when the moon was approaching first quarter, as shown in the previous figure. Into the luminous part there extended a great dark gulf in the neighborhood of the lower cusp. When I had observed it for a long time and had seen it completely dark, a bright peak began to emerge, a little below its center, after about two hours. Gradually growing, this presented itself in a triangular shape, remaining completely detached and separated from the lighted surface. Around it three other small points soon began to shine, and finally, when the moon was about to set, this triangular shape (which had meanwhile become more widely extended) joined with the rest of the illuminated region and suddenly burst into the gulf of shadow like a vast promontory of light, surrounded still by the three bright peaks already mentioned. Beyond the ends of the cusps, both above and below, certain bright points emerged which were quite detached from the remaining lighted part, as may be seen depicted in the same figure. There were also a great number of dark spots in both the horns, especially in the lower one; those nearest the boundary of light and shadow appeared larger and darker, while those more distant from the boundary were not so dark and distinct. But in all cases, as we have mentioned earlier, the blackish portion of each spot is turned toward the source of the sun's radiance, while a bright rim surrounds the spot on the side away from the sun in the direction of the shadowy region of the moon. This part of the moon's surface, where it is spotted as the tail of a peacock is sprinkled with azure eyes, resembles those glass vases which have been plunged while still hot into cold water and have thus acquired a crackled and wavy surface, from which they receive their common name of "ice-cups."

As to the large lunar spots, these are not seen to be broken in the above manner and full of cavities and prominences; rather, they are even and uniform, and brighter patches crop up only here and there. Hence if anyone wished to revive the old Pythagorean [based on the theory of the sixth-century B.C. mathematician and philosopher Pythagoras] opinion that the moon is like another earth, its brighter part might very fitly represent the surface of the land and its darker region that of the water. I have never doubted that if our globe were seen from afar when flooded with sunlight, the land regions would appear brighter and the watery regions darker. The large spots in the moon are also seen to be less elevated than the brighter tracts, for whether the moon is waxing or waning there are always seen, here and there along its boundary of light and shadow, certain ridges of brighter hue around the large

spots (and we have attended to this in preparing the diagrams); the edges of these spots are not only lower, but also more uniform, being uninterrupted by peaks or ruggedness.

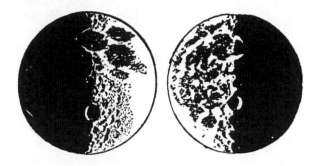

After reading this selection, consider these questions:

1. What did Galileo observe about the surface of the moon?
2. Why does Galileo conclude that his observations contradict earlier interpretations?
3. From this selection, what do you think were the main questions that guided Galileo's research?

# SELECTION 2:

# Galileo's Significance in the History of Science

*Galileo was quick to publish not only the results of his research but also the implications of such results for the understanding of celestial and terrestrial mechanics. And he published them in Italian, rather than the scholarly language Latin, in order to reach as wide an audience as possible. The Catholic Church immediately responded to these publications. In 1616 church authorities forbade Galileo to teach or publish that the earth revolved around the sun since this idea clearly contradicted the authority of both Scripture and the scholastic interpretation of Aristotle. In 1633 Galileo was brought before the Inquisition for having disobeyed the earli-*

*er injunction. This time he was forced to recant his views, was placed under house arrest, and was forbidden to publish any books on scientific matters.*

*A noted twentieth-century historian of science, Alexandre Koyré, emphasizes that it was Galileo's observations from experience as well as his development of a definite scientific method that led to his discoveries and to his conflict with church authorities.*

The name of Galileo Galilei is indissolubly linked with the scientific revolution of the sixteenth century, one of the profoundest, if not the most profound, revolution of human thought since the invention of the Cosmos by Greek thought. . . .

This revolution is sometimes characterized, and at the same time explained, as a kind of spiritual upheaval, an utter transformation of the whole fundamental attitude of the human mind. . . . Modern man seeks the domination of nature, whereas medieval or ancient man attempted above all its contemplation. The mechanistic trend of classical physics— . . . which was to render man "master and possessor of nature"—has, therefore, to be explained by this desire to dominate, to act; it has to be considered purely and simply an outflow of this attitude, an application to nature of the categories of thinking of *homo faber* ["man the maker"]. The science of [René] Descartes—and . . . that of Galileo—is nothing else than (as has been said) the science of the craftsman or of the engineer.

I must confess that I do not believe this explanation to be entirely correct. It is true, of course, that modern philosophy, as well as modern ethics and modern religion, lays much more stress on action . . . than ancient and medieval thought. And it is just as true of modern science: I am thinking of the Cartesian physics and its analogies of pulleys, strings and levers. Still the attitude we have just described is much more that of [English philosopher Francis] Bacon—whose rôle in the history of science is not of the same order—than that of Galileo or Descartes. Their science is made not by engineers or craftsmen, but by men who seldom built or made anything

more real than a theory. The new ballistics was made not by artificers and gunners, but against them. And Galileo did not learn *his* business from people who toiled in the arsenals and shipyards of Venice. Quite the contrary: he taught them *theirs*. Moreover, this theory explains too much and too little. It explains the tremendous scientific progress of the seventeenth century by that of technology. And yet the latter was infinitely less conspicuous than the former. Besides, it forgets the technological achievements of the Middle Ages. It neglects the lust for power and wealth which, throughout its history, inspired alchemy.

Other scholars have insisted on the Galilean fight against authority, against tradition, especially against that of Aristotle: against the scientific and philosophical tradition, upheld by the Church and taught in the universities. They have stressed the rôle of observation and experience in the new science of nature. It is perfectly true, of course, that observation and experimentation form one of the most characteristic features of modern science. It is certain that in the writings of Galileo we find innumerable appeals to observation and to experience, and bitter irony toward men who didn't believe their eyes because what they saw was contrary to the teaching of the authorities, or, even worse, who . . . did not want to look through Galileo's telescope for fear of seeing something which would contradict their traditional theories and beliefs. It is obvious that it was just by building a telescope and by looking through it, by careful observation of the moon and the planets, by his discovery of the satellites of Jupiter, that Galileo dealt a crushing blow to the astronomy and the cosmology of his times.

Still one must not forget that observation and experience, in the sense of brute, common-sense experience, did not play a major rôle—or, if it did, it was a negative one, the rôle of obstacle—in the foundation of modern science. The physics of Aris-

From Alexandre Koyré, "Galileo and Plato," *Journal of the History of Ideas*, vol. 4, no. 1 (1943), 400–19. Copyright © Journal of the History of Ideas, Inc. Reprinted by permission of the Johns Hopkins University Press.

totle . . . was . . . much nearer to common-sense experience than those of Galileo and Descartes.

It is not "experience," but "experiment," which played—but only later—a great positive rôle. Experimentation is the methodical interrogation of nature, an interrogation which presupposes and implies a *language* in which to formulate the questions, and a dictionary which enables us to read and to interpret the answers. For Galileo, as we know well, it was in curves and circles and triangles, in mathematical or even more precisely, in *geometrical language*—not in the language of common sense or in that of pure symbols— that we must speak to Nature and receive her answers. Yet obviously the choice of the language, the decision to employ it, could not be determined by the experience which its use was to make possible. It had to come from other sources.

Still other historians of science and philosophy have more modestly tried to characterize modern physics, as *physics,* by some of its salient traits: for instance, by the rôle which the principle of *inertia* plays in it. Perfectly right, once more: the principle of *inertia,* in contradistinction to that of the Ancients, holds an outstanding place in classical mechanics. It is its fundamental law of motion; it implicitly pervades Galilean physics and quite explicitly that of Descartes and of [Isaac] Newton. But this characteristic seems to me to be somewhat superficial. In my opinion it is not enough simply to state the fact. We have to understand and to explain it—to explain why *modern* physics was able to adopt this principle; to understand why, and how, the principle of inertial motion, which to us appears so simple, so clear, so plausible and even self-evident, acquired this status of self-evidence and *a priori* truth whereas for the Greeks as well as for the thinkers of the Middle Ages the idea that a body once put in motion will continue to move forever, appeared as obviously and evidently false, and even absurd.

I shall not try to explain here the reasons and causes that produced the spiritual revolution of the sixteenth century. It is for our purpose sufficient to describe it, to describe the mental or intellectual attitude of modern science by two (connected) characteristics. They are: 1) the destruction of the Cosmos, and therefore the disappearance in sci-

ence of all considerations based on that notion; 2) the geometrization of space—that is, the substitution of the homogeneous and abstract space of Euclidian geometry for the qualitatively differentiated and concrete world-space conception of the pre-Galilean physics. These two characteristics may be summed up and expressed as follows: the mathematization (geometrization) of nature and, therefore, the mathematization (geometrization) of science.

The dissolution of the Cosmos means the destruction of the idea of a hierarchically-ordered finite world-structure, of the idea of a qualitatively and ontologically differentiated world, and its replacement by that of an open, indefinite and even infinite universe, united and governed by the same universal laws; a universe in which, in contradiction to the traditional conception with its distinction and opposition of the two worlds of Heaven and of Earth, all things are on the same level of Being. The laws of Heaven and the laws of Earth are merged together. Astronomy and physics become interdependent, and even unified and united. And this implies the disappearance from the scientific outlook of all considerations based on value, on perfection, on harmony, on meaning and on purpose. They disappear in the infinite space of the new Universe. It is in this new Universe, in this new world of a geometry made real, that the laws of classical physics are valid and find their application.

The dissolution of the Cosmos—I repeat what I have already said: this seems to me to be the most profound revolution achieved or suffered by the human mind since the invention of the Cosmos by the Greeks. It is a revolution so profound and so far-reaching that mankind—with very few exceptions . . . —for centuries did not grasp its bearing and its meaning; which, even now, is often misvalued and misunderstood.

Therefore what the founders of modern science, among them Galileo, had to do, was not to criticize and to combat certain faulty theories, and to correct or to replace them by better ones. They had to do something quite different. They had to destroy one world and to replace it by another. They had to reshape the framework of our intellect itself, to restate and to reform its concepts, to evolve a new approach to Being, a new concept of knowledge, a new concept of science—and even to replace a pretty natural approach, that of common sense, by another which is not natural at all.

This explains why the discovery of things, of laws, which today appear so simple and so easy as to be taught to children—the laws of motion, the law of falling bodies—required such a long, strenuous, and often unsuccessful effort of some of the greatest geniuses of mankind, a Galileo, a Descartes. This fact in turn seems to me to disprove the modern attempt to minimize, or even to deny, the originality, or at least the revolutionary character, of Galileo's thinking; and to make clear that the apparent continuity in the development of medieval and modern physics . . . is an illusion. . . .

Aristotelian physics is false, of course; and utterly obsolete. Nevertheless, it is a "physics," that is, a highly though non-mathematically elaborated science. It is not a childish phantasy, nor a brute and verbal restatement of common sense, but a theory, that is, a doctrine which, starting of course with the data of common sense, subjects them to an extremely coherent and systematic treatment.

The facts or data which serve as a basis for this theoretical elaboration are very simple, and in practice we admit them just as did Aristotle. It still seems to all of us "natural" to see a heavy body fall "down." And just like Aristotle . . . we should be deeply astonished to see a ponderous body—a stone or a bull—rise freely in the air. This would seem to us pretty "unnatural"; and we would look for an explanation in the action of some hidden mechanism.

In the same way we still find it "natural" that the flame of a match points "up," and that we place our pots and pans "on" the fire. We should be astonished and should seek for an explanation if, for instance, we saw the flame turn about and point "down." Shall we call this conception, or rather this attitude, childish and simple? Perhaps. We can even point out that according to Aristotle himself science begins precisely by looking for an explanation for things that appear natural. Still, when thermodynamics asserts as a principle

that "heat" passes from a hot to a cold body, but not from the cold to a hot one, does it not simply translate an intuition of common sense that a "hot" body "naturally" becomes cold, but that a cold one does not "naturally" become hot? And even when we are stating that the center of gravity of a system tends to take the lowest position and does not rise by itself, are we not simply translating an intuition of common sense, the self-same intuition which Aristotelian physics expresses by its distinction of movement into "natural" and "violent"?

Moreover, Aristotelian physics no more rests content than thermodynamics with merely expressing in its language the "fact" of common sense just mentioned; it transposes it, and the distinction between "natural" and "violent" movements takes its place in a general conception of physical reality, a conception of which the principal features seem to be: (a) the belief in the existence of qualitatively determined "natures," and (b) the belief in the existence of a Cosmos—that is, the belief in the existence of principles of order in virtue of which the entirety of real beings form a hierarchically-ordered whole.

Whole, cosmic order, and harmony: these concepts imply that in the Universe things are (or should be) distributed and disposed in a certain determined order; that their location is not a matter of indifference (neither for them, nor for the Universe); that on the contrary each thing has, according to its nature, a determined "place" in the Universe, which is in some sense its own. A place for everything, and everything in its place: the concept of "natural place" expresses this theoretical demand of Aristotelian physics.

The conception of "natural place" is based on a purely static conception of order. Indeed, if everything were "in order," everything would be in its natural place, and, of course, would remain and stay there forever. Why should it depart from it? On the contrary, it would offer a resistance to any attempt to expel it therefrom. This expulsion could be effected only by exerting some kind of *violence*, and the body would seek to come back, if, and when, owing to such a *violence*, it found itself out of "its" place.

Thus every movement implies some kind of

cosmic disorder, a disturbance of the world-equilibrium, being either a direct effect of *violence*, or, on the contrary, the effect of the effort of Being to compensate for the *violence*, to recover its lost and troubled order and balance, to bring things back to their natural places, places where they can rest and remain. It is this returning to order latter's works, and even more clearly, more consistently and consciously, in those of the young Galileo, we find—under the obvious and unmistakable influence of the "suprahuman Archimedes" a determined attempt to apply to this physics the principles of "mathematical philosophy."

Nothing is more instructive than the study of this attempt—or, more exactly, of these attempts—and of their failure. They show us that it is impossible to mathematize, i.e., to transform into an exact, mathematical concept, the rude, vague and confused conception of *impetus*. In order to build up a mathematical physics following the lines of the statics of Archimedes, this conception had to be dropped altogether. A new and original concept of motion had to be formed and developed. It is this new concept that we owe to Galileo.

We are too well acquainted with, or rather too well accustomed to, the principles and concepts of modern mechanics, so well that it is almost impossible for us to see the difficulties which had to be overcome for their establishment. They seem to us so simple, so natural, that we do not notice the paradoxes they imply and contain. Yet the mere fact that the greatest and mightiest minds of mankind—Galileo, Descartes—had to struggle in order to make them theirs, is in itself sufficient to indicate that these clear and simple notions—the notion of movement or that of space—are not so clear and simple as they seem to be. Or they are clear and simple only from a certain point of view, only as part of a certain set of concepts and axioms, apart from which they are not simple at all. Or, perhaps, they are too clear and too simple: so clear and so simple that, like all prime notions, they are very difficult to grasp.

Movement, space—let us try to forget for a while all we have learnt at school; let us try to think out what they mean in mechanics. Let us try to place ourselves in the situation of a con-temporary of Galileo, a man accustomed to the concepts of Aristotelian physics which *he* learnt at *his* school, and who encounters for the first time the modern concept of motion. What is it? In fact something pretty strange. It is something which in no way affects the body which is endowed with it: to be in motion or to be at rest does not make any difference for, nor any change in, the body in motion or at rest. The body, as such, is utterly and absolutely indifferent to both. Therefore, we are not able to ascribe motion to a determined body considered in itself. A body is in motion only in relation to some other body which we assume to be at rest. All motion is relative. And therefore we may ascribe it to the one or to the other of the two bodies. . . .

Thus motion seems to be a relation. But at the same time it is a *state*, just as rest is another *state*, utterly and absolutely opposed to the former; besides which they are both *persistent states*. The famous first law of motion, the law of inertia, teaches us that a body left to itself persists eternally in its state of motion or of rest, and that we must apply a force in order to change a state of motion to a state of rest, and *vice versa*. Yet not every kind of motion is thus endowed with an eternal being, but only uniform movement in a straight line. Modern physics affirms, as well we know, that a body once set in motion conserves eternally its direction and speed, provided of course it is not subject to the action of any external force. Moreover, to the objection of the Aristotelian that though as a matter of fact he is acquainted with eternal motion, the eternal circular motion of the heavenly spheres, he has never yet encountered a persistent rectilinear one, modern physics replies: of course! rectilinear, uniform motion is utterly impossible, and can take place only in a vacuum.

Let us think it over, and perhaps we will not be too harsh on the Aristotelian who felt himself unable to grasp and to accept this unheard-of notion, the notion of a persistent, substantial relation-state, the concept of something which to him seemed just as abstruse, and just as impossible, as the ill-fated substantial forms of the scholastics appear to us. No wonder that the Aristotelian felt himself astonished and bewildered by this amazing attempt to explain the real by the impossible—or, which is the same thing, to explain real being by mathematical being, because, as I have mentioned already, these bodies moving in straight lines in infinite empty space are not *real* bodies moving in *real* space, but *mathematical* bodies moving in *mathematical* space.

After reading this selection, consider these questions:

1. According to Koyré, what were the main characteristics of Galileo's understanding of science?
2. How did it differ from earlier definitions of science?
3. How does Koyré describe Galileo's scientific method?

# SELECTION 3:

# Newton and Scientific Method

$A$s a distinct method and a new view of nature, the Scientific Revolution reached a climax and became solidified in the works of Isaac Newton (1642–1727). Building directly on the research of Johannes Kepler and Galileo, Newton formulated a coherent method of experimentation and a method for reaching conclusions from the results of these experiments. This is the scientific method as we have come to understand it. In the Principia Mathematica (1687), Newton clearly articulates the rules of this method.

By following these rules of reasoning, Newton developed a mechanical understanding of nature within the Galilean framework of absolute space and time. The key to Newton's system was the notion of universal gravitation, operating on earth and among heavenly bodies. Gravitation is a single force that explains all forms of motion that are not explainable in terms of direct contact. The law of gravitation holds that every body exerts over every other body an attractive force proportional to the product of their masses and inversely proportional to the square of the distance between them. From the notion of gravity, Newton could establish a universal science combining physics and astronomy, based on the concepts of mass, inertia, force, velocity, and acceleration. Having established the definitions of these basic terms, Newton was then able to formulate three universal laws of nature: (1) motion continues in a straight line if not interrupted by another force, (2) the rate of change in the motion of an object is a result of the forces acting on it, and (3) the action and reaction between two objects are equal and opposite.

From *The Mathematical Principles of Natural Philosophy*, by Isaac Newton, translated by A. Motte (London: 1729).

$R$ule I. We are to admit no more causes of natural things, than such as are both true and sufficient to explain their appearances.

To this purpose the philosophers say, that Nature does nothing in vain, and more is in vain, when less will serve; for Nature is pleased with simplicity, and affects not the pomp of superfluous causes.

*Rule II. Therefore to the same natural effects we must, as far as possible, assign the same causes.*

As to respiration in a man, and in a beast; the descent of stones in Europe and in America; the light of our culinary fire and of the sun; the reflection of light in the earth, and in the planets.

*Rule III. The qualities of bodies, which admit neither intension nor remission of degrees, and which are found to belong to all bodies within reach of our experiments, are to be esteemed the universal qualities of all bodies whatsoever.*

For since the qualities of bodies are only known to us by experiments, we are to hold for universal, all such as universally agree with experiments; and such as are not liable to diminution, can never be quite taken away. We are certainly not to relinquish the evidence of experiments for the sake of dreams and vain fictions of our own devising; nor are we to recede from the analogy of Nature, which is wont to be simple, and always consonant to itself. We no other way know the extension of bodies, than by our senses, nor do these reach it in all bodies; but because we perceive extension in all that are sensible, therefore we ascribe it universally to all others, also. That abundance of bodies are hard we learn by experience. And because the hardness of the whole arises from the hardness of the parts, we therefore justly infer the hardness of the undivided particles not only of the bodies we feel but of all others. That all bodies are impenetrable we gather not from reason, but from sensation. The bodies which we handle we find impenetrables and thence conclude impenetrability to be a universal property of all bodies whatsoever. That all bodies are moveable, and endowed with certain powers (which we call the forces of inertia) or persevering in their motion or in their rest, we only infer from the like properties observed in the bodies which we have seen. The extension, hardness, impenetrability, mobility, and force of inertia of the whole result from the extension, hardness, impenetrability, mobility, and forces of inertia of the parts: and thence we conclude that the least particles of all bodies to be also all extended, and hard, and impenetrable, and moveable, and endowed with their proper forces of inertia. And this is the foundation of all philosophy. Moreover, that the divided but contiguous particles of bodies may be separated from one another, is a matter of observation; and, in the particles that remain undivided, our minds are able to distinguish yet lesser parts, as is mathematically demonstrated. But whether the parts so distinguished, and not yet divided, may, by the powers of nature, be actually divided and separated from one another, we cannot certainly determine. Yet had we the proof of but one experiment, that any undivided particle, in breaking a hard and solid body, suffered a division, we might by virtue of this rule, conclude, that the undivided as well as the divided particles, may be divided and actually separated into infinity.

Lastly, if it universally appears, by experiments and astronomical observations, that all bodies about the earth, gravitate toward the earth; and that in proportion to the quantity of matter which they severally contain; that the moon likewise, according to the quantity of its matter, gravitates toward the earth; that on the other hand our sea gravitates toward the moon; and all the planets mutually one toward another; and the comets in like manner towards the sun; we must, in consequence of this rule, universally allow, that all bodies whatsoever are endowed with a principle of mutual gravitation. For the argument from the appearances concludes with more force for the universal gravitation of all bodies, than for their impenetrability, of which among those in the celestial regions, we have no experiments, nor any manner of observation. Not that I affirm gravity to be essential to all bodies. By their inherent force I mean nothing but their force of inertia. This is immutable. Their gravity is diminished as they recede from the earth.

*Rule IV. In experimental philosophy we are to look upon propositions collected by general induction from phenomena as accurately or very nearly true, notwithstanding any contrary hypotheses that may be imagined, till such time as other phenomena occur, by which they may either be made more accurate, or liable to exceptions.*

This rule we must follow that the argument of induction may not be evaded by hypotheses.

After reading this selection, consider these questions:

1. What are Newton's "four rules of philosophy"?
2. How does Newton define *gravity*?
3. What assumptions lie behind Newton's rules and theories?

# SELECTION 4:
# Scientific Method and Technological Innovation

*The modern sociologist Robert K. Merton has attempted to reinterpret the development of Isaac Newton's thought, as well as modern science in general, within the social and economic context of seventeenth-century England. In addition to Newton, Merton looks at the relationship between the group of scientists known as the Royal Society and the concerns and problems of the age.*

The interplay between socio-economic and scientific development is scarcely problematical. To speak of socio-economic influences upon science in general unanalyzed terms, however, barely poses the problem. The sociologist of science is specifically concerned with the *types* of influence involved (facilitative and obstructive), the *extent* to which these types prove effective in different social structures and the *processes* through which they operate. But these questions cannot be answered even tentatively without a clarification of the conceptual tools employed. All too often, the sociologist who repudiates the . . . heroic interpretation of the history of science lapses into a vulgar materialism which seeks to find simple parallels between social and scientific development. Such misguided efforts invariably result in a seriously biased and untenable discussion. . . .

The burgeoning of capitalistic enterprise in seventeenth century England intensified interest in more adequate means of transport and communication. . . . This and the relatively low cost of water-transport led to the marked growth of the merchant marine. More than forty per cent of the English production of coal was carried by water. Similarly, internal trade enhanced the need for improved facilities for land and river transport. Proposals for turnpikes and canals were common throughout the century.

Foreign trade was assuming world-wide proportions. The best available, though defective, statistics testify to these developments. Imports and exports increased by almost 300 per cent between 1613 and 1700. . . .

These developments were accompanied by increased emphasis upon a number of technical problems. Above all, the increase of commercial voyages to distant points—India, North America, Africa, Russia—stressed anew the need for accurate and expedient means of determining position at sea, of finding latitude and longitude. Scien-

From *Social Theory and Social Structure*, by Robert K. Merton (New York: Free Press, 1949).

tists were profoundly concerned with possible solutions to these problems. Both mathematics and astronomy were signally advanced through research oriented in this direction.

[Scottish mathematician John] Napier's invention of logarithms, expanded by [the mathematicians] Henry Briggs, Adrian Vlacq (in Holland), Edmund Gunter and Henry Gellibrand, was of aid to astronomer and mariner alike. Adam Anderson possibly reflects the general attitude toward this achievement when he remarks that "logarithms are of great special utility to mariners at sea in calculations relating to their course, distance, latitude, longitude, etc." Sprat, the genial historiographer of the Royal Society, asserted that the advancement of navigation was one of the chief aims of the group. . . .

[Isaac] Newton was likewise deeply interested in the same general problem. Early in his career, he wrote a now famous letter of advice to his friend, Francis Aston, who was planning a trip on the Continent, in which he suggested among other particulars that Aston "inform himself whether pendulum clocks be of any service in finding out the longitude." In a correspondence which we have reason to believe ultimately led Newton to the completion of the *Principia*, both [the English astronomer Edmond] Halley and [the English scientist Robert] Hooke urged Newton to continue certain phases of his research because of its utility for navigation. . . .

Newton's lunar theory was the climactic outcome of scientific concentration on this subject. . . . Halley, who had decided that the various methods of determining longitude were all defective and had declared that "it would be scarce possible ever to find the Longitude at sea sufficient for sea uses, till such time as the Lunar Theory be fully perfected," constantly prompted Newton to continue his work. [English astronomer John] Flamsteed, and (from 1691 to 1739) Halley, also endeavored to rectify the lunar tables sufficiently to attain "the great object, of finding the Longitude with the requisite degree of exactness." Observations of the eclipses of the moon were recommended by the Royal Society for the same purpose. . . .

Thus we are led to see that the scientific problems emphasized by the manifest value of a method for finding longitude were manifold. If the scientific study of various possible means of achieving this goal was not invariably dictated by the practical utility of the desired result, it is clear that at least part of the continued diligence exercised in these fields had this aim. In the last analysis it is impossible to determine with exactitude the extent to which practical concern focused scientific attention upon certain problems. What can be conscionably suggested is a certain correspondence between the subjects most intensively investigated by the contemporary men of science and the problems raised or emphasized by economic developments. It is an inference—usually supported by the explicit statements of the scientists themselves—that these economic requirements or, more properly, the technical needs deriving from these requirements, directed research into particular channels. The finding of the longitude was one problem which, engrossing the attention of many scientists, fostered profound developments in astronomy, geography, mathematics, mechanics, and the invention of clocks and watches.

After reading this selection, consider these questions:

1. What does Merton identify as the major reasons for scientific investigation in the seventeenth century?
2. What was the relationship between overseas exploration and scientific innovation, according to Merton?
3. Compare Merton's view of the Scientific Revolution with that of Alexandre Koyré in the previous selection.

# CHAPTER 3
# Absolutism: Defended and Criticized

The Reformation and Counter Reformation ushered in a series of religious wars in all the major European states between 1547 and 1660. These wars produced a number of intended and, perhaps more importantly, unintended consequences. The efforts of the Catholic monarchs of Europe, especially the Habsburg kings of Spain and the Habsburg Holy Roman Emperors, succeeded in returning large sections of Germany, Austria, Bohemia, and Hungary to the Catholic Church. They failed, however, in bringing all of Germany—let alone Scandinavia, the Netherlands, England, and Scotland—back into the Catholic fold. Europe was fated to remain divided between Catholics and Protestants. Even within a number of countries there were to be divisions along confessional lines. Perhaps the most significant unintended consequence was that the state's political power increased through these various conflicts over definitions of Christianity. Although all European states in the sixteenth, seventeenth, and eighteenth centuries still defined themselves and claimed their legitimacy in terms of power derived from God and often exercised their authority in terms of protecting the realm from heresy, this power increasingly became an end in itself. As a result, the wars of religion led to a more secular notion of political power and the spread of wordly values within society.

In the sixteenth century the kingdom of France became entangled in a religious and civil struggle known as the French Wars of Religion (1564–1598). These wars pitted not only Catholics against Calvinists but also fanatical Catholics against the more tolerant forms of Catholicism that the monarchy itself sought to support. Peace came only when Henry IV, a Protestant, inherited the kingdom upon the death of the last ruler of the Valois line and converted to Catholicism. A compromise was reached by the Edict of Nantes. French Protestants were allowed to practice their religion within certain restricted areas of the kingdom and even to protect themselves by maintaining an army.

Under Henry IV's successors—most notably Louis XII and Louis XIV—a form of monarchical government was consciously developed that emphasized the importance of the king as the sole expression of power on the earth. Although not above the law of God and the so-called fundamental laws of the kingdom (the royal succession and the Catholic definition of the kingdom, for instance), the monarch was above all forms of statutory and customary law since he was the source of all such laws. The king was also the only "public" authority in the realm. He alone unified the kingdom; and he alone could know and speak for the whole. The unity of France was both founded on and found expression in the person of the king. It would be incorrect, however, if we think of the origins of this form of absolute monarchy as arising from the mere desire of the king to amass power or even of the king's intention to exploit his subjects, noble as well as common. Absolutism arose for both internal reasons (the collapse of any security as a result of the Wars of Religion) and external ones (the highly competitive and expensive wars among states), and it demanded from the individuals in charge continuous and laborious involvement with state policies and the direction of large state bureaucracies.

By the seventeenth century the kingdom of France under Louis XII and especially Louis XIV emerged as the most powerful state in Europe. This was the result both of success on the battlefield and of the creation of a centralized authority. Military power in the seventeenth century demanded huge increases in the size of armies and keeping up with the revolutionary changes in military technology. Maintaining a large army in the field necessitated creating an effective bureaucracy able to raise sufficient taxes and keep them flowing to the king. In previous centuries France had evolved into one of the great feudal monarchies of the High and late Middle Ages; and various attempts had been made, as in England, to bring some type of centralized authority to bear on what previously had been diffused and shared forms of power. These early attempts at centralization basically failed as local interests, feudal notions of corporate rights of towns and orders of society, and the continued power of the great nobles limited all royal attempts to accrue power. The absolutist state of Louis XIV created France's first effective centralized bureaucracy. This centralized form of government successfully organized and exploited the potentials within the traditional military, political, and economic organization of the kingdom.

A system of royal commissioners, the intendants, formed the core of the new bureaucratic state of France. With this effective control from the center, we can begin to speak of the state as an entity with its own reasons and interests and of government as guided by policies. The state now could pursue goals of its own. Government became active and not just passive: It devised plans for better rule and no longer merely reacted to restore the just organization of things. One of the most important figures in the formation of these policies was Louis's chief economic minister, Jean-Baptiste Colbert (1619–1683). In addition to royal finances, Colbert was in charge of public works and the navy. He devised a wide range of policies to increase the wealth of the state by fostering the country's economic prosperity. He encouraged the development of industries through state monopolies, eliminated a number of internal tax barriers that frustrated commerce within the kingdom, and promoted overseas trade by establishing colonies in the Americas.

The second half of the seventeenth century and the first half of the eighteenth witnessed the decline of some states (such as Spain and Sweden) and the emergence of others. Blocked by constitutional reasons and the number of increasingly powerful local noble houses from centralizing powers within the Holy Roman Empire, the Austrian Habsburgs increasingly turned to their diverse holdings outside the frontiers of the empire. These lands included Hungary and all or parts of what are today the Czech Republic, Slovakia, Romania, and Croatia (and eventually also parts of Poland) as a basis of power. Within the empire itself, various principalities emerged as practically independent states, such as Bavaria and Saxony; but most remarkable of all, the electorate of Brandenburg (after 1701, the kingdom of Prussia) became a major power in central Europe. Russia, too, emerged from centuries of relative isolation to begin a Europeanization under Peter the Great and Catherine the Great.

What determined the success or failure of these states in many ways depended on the degree to which they could model themselves after French absolutism. In other words, the same conditions that called for the rise of absolutism in France—the need for greater legal, political, and economic unity at home and thus a centralized bureaucracy and a greater military force, as well as a greater diplomatic presence abroad—were always at work in these states as well. The exception was England. By the early eighteenth century, England (after 1707, the kingdoms of England and Scotland were combined to form the United Kingdom of Great Britain and Ireland) was clearly emerging as a major power in Europe and as a growing center of a worldwide empire. Aside from the American Revolutionary War, England won its wars in the eighteenth century, mostly at the expense of France. Why? This question intrigued the men and women of the eighteenth century as much as it does historians today. Great Britain had no large standing army and no centralized bureaucracy (at least to the extent that the continental powers did), and yet it was perhaps the leading power in Europe. The simple fact that Britain was an island and therefore did not need large standing armies to maintain its independence goes a long way in explaining this anomaly. The state found its strength in the Royal Navy, which necessitated both a different and a less expensive use of national resources and would also be employed to acquire and defend an overseas empire.

More surprisingly still, England seemed to have evolved political institutions directly out of the forms and practices of the medieval feudal monarchy. Unlike France and the other emerging continental states of the eighteenth century, England did not face the need either to suppress these older forms or to create new sets of institutions from scratch, as Prussia and Russia did. Although the political and constitutional history of England was one of continual evolution of these ancient institutions and ideas throughout the eighteenth and nineteenth centuries, it would be wrong to think of the preceding two centuries in these terms. England's political and religious history in the sixteenth and seventeenth centuries was as chaotic and violent as that of any continental state. The break from Rome and the establishment of an English church under Henry VIII (reigned 1509–1547) and his successors, especially Elizabeth I (reigned 1558–1603), resulted in a more powerful form of monarchical power. Under Elizabeth's successors, James I (reigned 1603–1625) and Charles I (reigned 1625–1649), various attempts were made to define the monarchy in ways similar to those of the absolutist state of the continent.

As a kingdomwide institution, the English Parliament evolved from the Middle Ages. It was an attempt to bring a limited type of order to the growing power and complexities of feudal power. Drawing on medieval notions that royal taxation depended on the consent of those taxed, Parliament maintained the right to vote for new taxes. In this sense, there was little difference between the English Parliament and the French Estates General. But Parliament in England developed into an institution with its own sense of its authority and privileges along lines differing from those of comparable continental institutions. Henry VIII and Elizabeth I looked to Parliament to confirm their power, especially the initial break from the Roman Catholic Church. Although not meeting on a regular basis, it still continued to maintain its identity even under the rule of James I and Charles I, claiming the right not just to discuss royal expenditures but also to intervene in religious reform and foreign affairs. Louis XIII learned to rule and thus raise money without calling the Estates General; Louis XIV and Louis XV never had to face such a body. The English Parliament claimed to share in sovereignty; and in the course of the eighteenth century, Great Britain evolved an alternative state system to that of continental absolutism.

# SELECTION 1:

# The Concept of Sovereignty

*As a result of the disastrous religious wars of the sixteenth century, the French became increasingly interested in providing their monarch with greater authority to ensure peace within the kingdom. The most important formulation of this new theory of kingship was offered by the lawyer and historian Jean Bodin (1530–1596). In* Six Books of the Commonwealth *(1576), Bodin argues that only the increased power of the king could avoid the ruin that France was experiencing in his time. More importantly, he gives a new justification for political power. Bodin uses the term* sovereignty, *the concept that there is something called a state beyond the concerns and desires of individual monarchs and with interests and ends beyond the diverse and often competing forces within the kingdom of France at any given time. These interests and ends Bodin called the "reason of state." Reason of state, argued Bodin, should be beyond religious divisions within the kingdom. (He therefore advocated religious toleration of French Protestants.) This notion of reason of state was also to play an important part in international relations. Under Louis XII, for instance, the great minister Cardinal Richelieu allied France with the Protestant powers of Europe. Beyond religious convictions and a religious approach to politics, the interests of the kingdom depended on defeating the Habsburg rulers and ending Spanish control of Europe. Richelieu's policies succeeded. France emerged from the Thirty Years' War (1618–1648) as the dominant military and diplomatic power on the continent. For these reasons alone, but also for the ways in which the notion of sovereignty and reason of state would come to define European concepts of the state and the relations among states, historians consider the* Six Books of the Commonwealth *as the most important work on political theory of the sixteenth century.*

Since there is nothing greater on earth, after God, than sovereign princes, and since they have been established by Him as His lieutenants for commanding other men, we need to be precise about their status so that we may respect and revere their majesty in complete obedience, and do them honor in our thoughts and in our speech. Contempt for one's sovereign prince is contempt toward God, of whom he is the earthly image. That is why God, speaking to Samuel, from whom the people had demanded a different prince, said, "It is me that they have wronged.". . .

In short, we have shown what intolerable absurdities would follow if vassals were sovereigns, especially when they have nothing that is not held of someone else. For this is to equate the lord and the subject, the master and the servant, him who gives the law and him who receives it, him who commands and him who owes obedience.

Since this is impossible, we have to conclude that dukes, counts, and all of those who hold of another or receive laws or commands from another, whether by force or legal obligation, are not sovereign. And we will say the same of the highest magistrates, lieutenant-generals of kings, governors, regents, dictators. No matter how much power they have, if they are bound to the laws, jurisdiction, and command of someone else, they are not sovereign. For the prerogatives of sovereignty have to be of such a sort that they apply only to a sovereign prince. If, on the contrary, they can be shared with subjects, one cannot say that they are marks of sovereignty. For just as a prince no longer has that name if it is breached, or if its rosettes are torn away, so sovereign majesty loses its greatness if someone makes a breach in it and encroaches on a part of its domain. . . .

By the same reasoning all [the jurists] agree that the rights of the prince cannot be relinquished or alienated, and cannot be prescribed by any period of time. And if it should happen that a sovereign prince does share them with a subject,

From *Six Books of the Commonwealth,* by Jean Bodin (1576), translated by Benjamin C. Sax.

he would make a companion of his servant and, in so doing, would cease to be sovereign. For the notion of a sovereign (that is to say, of someone who is above all subjects) cannot apply to someone who has made a subject his companion. Just as God, the great sovereign, cannot make a God equal to Himself because He is infinite and by logical necessity two infinites cannot exist, so we can say that the prince, whom we have taken as the image of God, cannot make a subject equal to himself without annihilation of his power.

This being so, it follows that the mark of sovereignty is not to do justice, because that is shared by prince and subject, nor is it to establish or remove all officers, because both the prince and subject have that power too. This applies not only to officers serving in the administration of justice, police, war, or finance, but also to those who have command in peace or war. . . . To clarify this point, we must assume that the term "law," used without qualification, signifies the just command of the person or persons who have full power over everyone else without excepting anybody, and no matter whether the command affects subjects collectively or as individuals, and exception only the person or persons who made the law. . . .

We may thus conclude that the first prerogative of a sovereign prince is to give law to all in general and each in particular. But this is not sufficient. We have to add "without the consent of any other, whether greater, equal, or below him." For if the prince is obligated to make no law without the consent of a superior, he is clearly a subject; if of an equal, he has an associate; if of subjects, such as the senate or the people, he is not sovereign. . . .

When I say that the first prerogative of sovereignty is to give law to all in general and to each in particular, the latter part refers to privileges, which are in the jurisdiction of sovereign princes to the exclusion of all others. I call it a privilege when a law is made for one or a few private individuals, no matter whether it is for the profit or the loss of the person with respect to whom it is decreed. . . .

This same power of making and repealing law includes all the other rights and prerogatives of sovereignty, so that strictly speaking we can say that there is only this one prerogative of sovereignty, inasmuch as all the other rights are comprehended in it—such as declaring war or making peace; hearing appeals in last instance from the judgements of any magistrate; instituting and removing the highest officers; imposing taxes and aids on subjects or exempting them; granting pardons and dispensations against the rigor of the law; determining the name, value, and measure of the coinage; requiring subjects and liege vassals to swear that they will be loyal without exception to the person to whom their oath is owed. These are the true prerogatives of sovereignty, which are included in the power to give law to all in general and to each in particular, and not to receive law from anyone but God. For the prince or duke, who has power to give law to all his subjects in general and to each in particular, is not sovereign if he also takes law from a superior or an equal—I include equal because to have a companion is to have a master—and he is even less a sovereign if he has this power only in the capacity of a vicar, a lieutenant, or regent.

But since the word law is too general, it is best to specify the rights of sovereignty which are included, as I have said, in the lawmaking power of the sovereign. Thus declaring war or making peace is one of the most important points of majesty, since it often entails the ruin or the preservation of a state.

After reading this selection, consider these questions:
1. What, according to Bodin, are the attributes of sovereignty?
2. Why did Bodin see a need to define this term in the sixteenth century?
3. How does sovereignty differ from feudal notions of power?

# SELECTION 2:

# Absolutism Defined

*At least in the seventeenth century, absolutism was a popular form of government. Large sections of French society saw in the concentration of powers in the hands of one man the living symbol of order and justice— indeed, the living image of God. To this conception was added the humanist dream of the king as a lover of glory in war, promoter of the arts and sciences, and protector of the church. At the time, royal absolutism was seen as the highest expression of just authority. Bishop Jacques-Bénigne Bossuet, a leading clergyman within France and the man selected by Louis XIV as the tutor for the heir apparent, defined and legitimized the monarchy according to Scriptures.*

*Third Book, Article I. There are four characteristics or qualities essential to royal authority.*

First, royal authority is sacred;
Secondly, it is paternal;
Thirdly, it is absolute;
Fourthly, it is subject to reason.

All of this must be established, in order, in the following articles.

*Article II, Royal authority is sacred. 1st Proposition, God establishes kings as his ministers, and reigns through them over the peoples.* We have already seen that all power comes from God.

"The prince, St. Paul adds, is God's minister to thee for good. But if thou do that which is evil, fear: for he beareth not the sword in vain. For he is God's minister: an avenger to execute wrath upon him that doth evil."

Thus princes act as ministers of God, and his lieutenants on earth. It is through them that he exercises his Empire. "And now say you that you are able to withstand the kingdom of the Lord, which he possesseth by the sons of David?"

It is in this way that we have seen that the royal throne is not the throne of a man, but the throne of God himself. "God hath chosen Solomon my son, to sit upon the throne of the kingdom of the Lord over Israel." And again: "Solomon sat on the throne of the Lord.". . .

*2nd Proposition, The person of kings is sacred.* It appears from all this that the person of kings is sacred, and that to attempt anything against them is a sacrilege.

God anoints them through his prophets, with a sacred unction, as he anoints the pontiffs and their altars. . . .

*3rd Proposition, One must obey the prince by reason of religion and conscience.* St. Paul, after having said that the prince is the minister of God, concludes thus: "wherefore be subject of necessity, not only for wrath, but also for conscience' sake."

This is why "one must serve, not to the eye, as it were pleasing men, but, as the servants of Christ doing the will of God, from the heart."

And again: "Servants, obey in all things your temporal masters, not serving to the eye, as pleasing men, but in simplicity of heart, fearing God. Whatsoever you do, do it from the heart, as to the Lord, and not to men; knowing that you shall receive of the Lord the reward of inheritance. Serve ye the Lord Christ.". . .

*4th Proposition, Kings should respect their own power, and use it only for the public good.* Their power coming from on high, as has been

From *Politics Derived from the Words of Holy Scripture*, by Jacques-Bénigne Bossuet (1709), translated by Benjamin C. Sax.

said, they must not believe that they are the owners of it, to use it as they please; rather must they use it with fear and restraint, as something which comes to them from God, and for which God will ask an accounting of them. "Hear, therefore, ye kings, and understand: learn ye that are judges of the ends of the earth. Give ye ear, you that rule the people, and that please yourselves in multitudes of nations: For power is given you by the Lord, and strength by the most High, who will examine your works, and search out your thoughts.". . .

*Article III, Royal authority is paternal. 2nd Proposition, The prince is not born for himself, but for the public.* This is a consequence of the preceding proposition; and God confirms this truth by the example of Moses.

He gave him his people to lead, and at the same time he made him forget himself. . . .

*3rd Proposition, The prince must provide for the needs of the people.* "The Lord said to David: thou shalt feed my people Israel, and thou shalt be prince over Israel."

"God has chosen David, and took him from the flocks of sheep . . . to feed Jacob his servant, and Israel his inheritance." He merely changed the flock: instead of grazing sheep, he grazed men. "To graze" in the language of Scripture is "to govern," and the name "pastor" signifies the prince—so much are these things united. . . .

*7th Proposition, The bounty of the prince must not be altered by the ingratitude of the people.* No one was ever so ungrateful to Moses as the Jewish people. No one was ever so good to the Jewish people as Moses. Throughout Exodus and Numbers one hears only the insolent murmurings of this people against him: all their complaints are seditious, and never does he hear from their mouths any quiet remonstrances. From threats they passed on to actions. "All the multitude cried out, and would have stoned him" [Numbers 14:10]. But during this fury he pleaded their cause before God, who wanted to abandon them. "I will strike them therefore with pestilence, and will consume them: but thee I will make a ruler over a great nation, and mightier than this is. Yes, Lord, Moses answered, so that the Egyptians can blaspheme against you. Rather let the strength of the Lord be magnified, O God patient and full of

mercy . . . and forgive, I beseech thee the sins of his people, according to the greatness of his mercy" [Numbers 14:12-19].

*Fourth Book, On the characteristics of royalty. First Article, Royal authority is absolute.* In order to make this term [absolute] odious and insupportable, many [writers] pretend to confuse absolute government and arbitrary government. But nothing is more distinct, as we shall make clear when we speak of justice.

*1st Proposition, The prince need account to no one for what he ordains.* "Observe the mouth of the king, and the commandments of the oath of God. Be not hasty to depart from his face, and do not continue in an evil work: for he will do all that pleaseth him. And his word is full of power: neither can any man say to him: Why dost thou so? He that keepeth the commandment, shall find no evil."

Without this absolute authority, he can neither do good nor suppress evil: his power must be such that no one can hope to escape him; and, in fine, the sole defense of individuals against the public power, must be their innocence.

This doctrine is in conformity with the saying of St. Paul: "Wilt thou then not be afraid of the power? Do that which is good."

*2nd Proposition, When the prince has decided, there can be no other decision.* The judgments of sovereigns are attributed to God himself. When Josaphat established judges to judge the people, he said: "It is not in the name of man that you judge, but in the name of God."

This is what Ecclesiasticus is made to say: "Judge not against a judge," for still stronger reasons [one must not judge] against the sovereign judge who is the king. And the reason which is given [by Ecclesiasticus] is that, "he judgeth according to that which is just." It is not that he is always so judging, but that he is assumed to be so judging; and that no one has the right to judge or to review after him.

One must, then, obey princes as if they were justice itself, without which there is neither order nor justice in affairs.

*3rd Proposition, There is no coercive force against the prince.* One calls coercive force a power to constrain and to execute what is legitimately ordained. To the prince alone belongs legitimate command; to him alone belongs coactive force as well.

It is for that reason also that St. Paul gives the sword to him alone. "If thou do that which is evil, fear; for he beareth not the sword in vain."

In the state only the prince should be armed: otherwise everything is in confusion, and the state falls back into anarchy.

He who creates a sovereign prince puts everything together into his hands, both the sovereign authority to judge and all the power of the state. "Our king shall judge us, and go out before us, and fight our battles for us." This is what the Jewish people said when they asked for a king. Samuel declares to them upon this basis that the power of their prince will be absolute, incapable of being restrained by any other power. "This will be the right of the king, that shall reign over you, saith the Lord: He will take your children, and put them in his service: he will seize your lands and the best of that which you have in order to give it to his servants," and so forth. . . .

*4th Proposition, Nonetheless kings are not freed from the laws.* "When he is made king, he shall not multiply horses to himself. . . . He shall not have many wives, that may allure his mind, nor immense sums of silver and gold. But after he is raised to the throne of his kingdom, he shall copy out to himself the Deuteronomy of this law in a volume, taking the copy of the priests of the Levitical tribe. And he shall have it with him, and shall read it all the days of his life, that he may learn to fear the Lord his God, and keep his words and ceremonies. Let his heart not be lifted up with pride over his brethren, nor decline to the right or to the left, that he and his sons may reign a long time. . . ."

It must be remarked that this law comprehends not only religion, but also the law of the kingdom, to which the prince is subject as much as anyone else—or rather more than the others, through the rightness of his will.

*5th Proposition, The people must keep itself in a condition of repose under the authority of the prince.* So it appears in the tale in which the trees choose a king. They speak to the olive-tree, to the fig-tree, and to the vine. These delightful trees, content with their natural abundance, did not want to weigh themselves down with the cares of government. "And all the trees said to the bramble-bush: Come thou and reign over us." The bramble-bush is accustomed to thorns and to cares. It is the only one that is born armed; it has its natural protection in its thorns. Thereby it could seem worthy of reigning. Thus it is made to speak in a way befitting a king. "It answered the trees which had chosen it: If you truly make me your king, come ye and rest under my shadow; but if you mean it not, let fire come out from the bramble-bush and devour the cedars of Lebanon."

As soon as there is a king, the people has only to remain at rest under his authority. If an impatient people stirs, and does not want to keep itself tranquil under royal authority, the fire of division will flare up in the state, and consume the bramble-bush together with all the other trees, that is to say the King and the nations. The cedars of Lebanon will be burned: in addition to the great power, which is the royal one, the other powers will be overturned, and the whole state will no longer be anything but a single cinder. . . .

*6th Proposition, The people must fear the prince; but the prince must only fear doing evil.* "He that will be proud, and refuse to obey the commandment of the priest . . . and the decree of the judge, that man shall die, and thou shalt take away the evil from Israel: and all the people hearing it shall fear, that no one afterwards swell with pride."

Fear is a bridle necessary to men because of their pride and their natural indocility.

The people must thus fear the prince; but if the prince fears the people, all is lost.

After reading this selection, consider these questions:

1. How does Bossuet define royal authority?
2. What, according to Bossuet, are the sources of legitimate authority?
3. What does Bossuet mean by the term *absolute power*?

SELECTION 3:

# The Origins of Modern Bureaucracy

*Absolutism was not just a theory of government or a way of legitimating the increase in royal authority. The absolutism of the rule of Louis XIII and especially of Louis XIV realized these claims to power in practice. Again, the monarch did not move toward accruing more power simply for personal reasons. The demand for maintaining order within the kingdom, and especially for achieving an independent and even dominant role among the states of Europe called for greater centralization. Effective and unquestioned rule by the king required that his commands be carried out throughout the kingdom. The king and his representatives had to discipline, but not abolish, the various feudal relationships upon which the kingdom was founded and from which it derived its legitimacy. This, in turn, required an organization directed from the center and carried out by the king's agents (the* intendants*) throughout the kingdom. It demanded, in other words, the creation of a centralized bureaucracy, which was unknown to European monarchies in the previous centuries. Modern historian Hans Rosenberg gives an overview of how this centralized state structure evolved, originating in France and then being copied by many of the other states of the continent.*

All the states of the contemporary world, despite enormous differences in the moral, legal, and material basis of their authority and in the function, efficiency, control, and responsibility of governmental action, form part of a single political order. Everywhere government has developed into a big business because of the growing complexity of social life and the multiplying effect of the extension of the state's regulative functions. Everywhere government engages in service-extracting and service-rendering activities on a large scale. Everywhere the supreme power to restrain or to aid individuals and groups has become concentrated in huge and vulnerable organiza-

tions. For good or for evil, an essential part of the present structure of governance consists of its far-flung system of professionalized administration and its hierarchy of appointed officials upon whom society is thoroughly dependent. . . .

Bureaucratic public administration in the modern sense is based on general rules and prescribed routines of organized behavior: on a methodical division of the integrated activities of continuously operating offices, on clearly defined spheres of competence, and a precise enumeration of official responsibilities and prerogatives. Thus, in principle, nothing is left to chance and personal caprice. . . . In the [eighteenth and nineteenth] centuries, this impersonal method of minutely calculated government management by a standing army of accountable salaried employees has acquired world-wide significance.

In the free societies of our time, nonbureaucratic forms of administration remain important. Even the totalitarian dictatorships make substantial use of nonprofessional agents for policy enforcement, although here bureaucracy is the intolerant and vindictive master of the government. . . .

The New Monarchy [of early modern Europe], as it is sometimes called, modified but did not destroy the confused mass of jurisdictions which had been transmitted from the past. It merely made a start in disengaging public prerogatives from the law of private property, from vested family interests, and from the grip of the possessors of legal, social, and political privilege. The new bureaucrats epitomized this trend which in medieval times had been noticeable only in the cities.

France, the most populous political unit of Europe in the sixteenth and seventeenth centuries, was then the chief model of the absolute monarchy. Here law and political theory drew a sharp distinction between the numerous patrimonial officials, the strongly entrenched *officiers*, and the rising small body of absolutist bureaucrats, the *commissaires*. All the modernized states of Europe, in their own peculiar and fleeting ways, developed striking analogies to this dual personnel pattern which reflected two antagonistic principles of officeholding and the coëxistence of two distinct managerial hierarchies.

The *officiers*, as defined and protected by French law, gave concrete expression to the close association of public authority with rights of private ownership, which the feudal state had passed on to its successors. The *officiers* were holders of administrative and judicial jobs whose appointment had legally to be approved by the crown. Actually, in the course of the fourteenth and fifteenth centuries . . . the purchase of offices was common enough to reduce royal confirmation to a formality. Through this practice the buyer gained a personal proprietary title to a particular *charge* or *fonction*. . . .

The *commissaire* appeared in the sixteenth century as an irregular and more carefully selected representative of the king. He differed fundamentally from the *officier*, with regard to both legal status and political function. The *commissaire* was the new bureaucrat, the official champion of monarchical centralization, and a salaried subordinate, although his emoluments were seldom confined to a fixed stipend. He was a "permanent probationer," subservient to the wishes of his ruler. Entrusted with a revocable *commission*, he was subject to specific instructions regulating his functions and duties, to disciplinary controls, to sudden transfer or dismissal. He was the creature but also the maker and chief direct beneficiary of the absolute form of government. . . .

From the outset, the power elite of "commissars" was built up, like their age-old competitors, on gradations of rank and permeated with hierarchical conceptions. Their initial political status was that of a mere transmission belt. They were commissioned by the monarch to ensure his sovereignty by curbing or destroying the powers of the traditional leadership groups in general and by working out a *modus vivendi* with the corporate organizations of the *officiers* in particular. They had to make a place for themselves in a neatly stratified and predominantly noncompetitive society, founded on status, unequal rights, class privileges, and the persistent aristocratic conviction "that the inequalities which distinguish one body of men from another are of essential and permanent importance. In such a social order, the commissars, loosely scraped together from heterogeneous strata, could not relax until they, too, had arrived.

The long and bitter struggle of these interlopers for dominance in the management of public administration, for political leadership, and for recognition as a superior status group was concentrated on two fronts. They could not attain their ends without putting into their place the old political and executive elites and without effecting their own emancipation from monarchical autocracy.

Nowhere in Europe under the absolutist Old Regime were the new administrative bureaucracy and the time-honored bodies of aristocratic rulership implacable enemies. The upper brackets of the commissar class found their social identity in close interaction with those very forces who as independent *seigneurs* or as semi-independent *officiers* had heretofore owned the means of government and administration. The commissars gained an assured social position and extended their power by infiltration and limited amalgamation, chiefly through holding interlocking positions. Thus they developed into a social elite which was not merely a self-perpetuating official aristocracy but also a highly prominent segment of the nobility and of the plutocracy. Thus they fortified themselves as a political hierarchy. . . .

This whole process was accompanied by the regrouping of all the competing governing elites. The principal political result was the subtle conversion of bureaucratized monarchical autocracy into government by an oligarchical bureaucracy, self-willed, yet representative of the refashioned privileged classes. Everywhere, earlier or later, dynastic absolutism was superseded by bureaucratic absolutism before the absolute state itself was seriously challenged by modern liberalism.

The transition to the more advanced stage in the evolution of the Old Regime began to be quite conspicuous in France in the late days of Louis XIV, in Russia under the successors of Peter I, and in the monarchy of the Austrian Habsburgs during the reign of Maria Theresa. In Prussia this development did not become clearly discernable before the latter part of the eighteenth century.

After reading this selection, consider these questions:
1. How does Rosenberg characterize the absolutist state?
2. According to Rosenberg, how did they differ from earlier forms of monarchical rule?
3. What were the main agencies of the absolute monarchies?

# SELECTION 4:

# Absolutism in Action

The French absolutist state reached down to levels of society that earlier forms of state power were neither willing nor able to touch. The new bureaucratic machinery of government not only involved itself with the rule of the cities and towns but also with village life and practices. One significant measure of this phenomenon is the way in which local customs and traditional beliefs throughout the diverse provinces of the kingdom became a concern of religious as well as state authorities.

Historian Robert Muchembled studied the suppression of witchcraft in seventeenth-century France. He shows how the united power of the Tridentine church—that is, the reformed Catholic Church, as defined by the Council of Trent (1545–1564) that emerged during the Counter Reformation—and the absolutist state collaborated to suppress and exterminate witchcraft. In this way, the church and the state sought to restructure and control the lives of individuals throughout the kingdom of France, down to the parish and village levels.

From *Popular Culture and Elite Culture in France*, by Robert Muchembled, translated by Lydia Cochrane. Copyright © 1985 by Louisiana State University Press.

Witch-hunting . . . was tied to the widespread movement for the acculturation of rural areas that took place in France from the middle of the sixteenth century on. Representatives of the Church, the king, and the governing orders of society directed all their efforts to the constraint of bodies and the submission of souls and to the imposition of total obedience to the absolute king and to God. This overall movement, which persisted up to the great changes that preceded the Revolution, in the middle of the eighteenth century, was not uniform, however. It had peaks and troughs that become evident when we study the fluctuations of witch-hunting. The beginning of these persecutions, around 1580, corresponded to the discovery on the part of the various elites—and first of all, by the missionaries—of an ocean of superstitions and of practices they considered abominable. The violence of the clash between traditional popular rural culture and regenerate Christianity, with its global conception of the City of God, explains the proliferation of witchcraft trials from 1580 to 1610.

The principal method for the acculturation of rural areas was frontal and violent clash, for the implantation of schools and seminaries was only at its beginnings, and ecclesiastics and agents of the king were only starting to infiltrate the land. The only way to modify the traditional intellectual framework of the peasant world was through the new generations, and even then the task was so immense that the results were imperfect. Around 1610, when the first wave of the persecution of witches was drawing to a close, only one generation could have been affected by this cultural conquest, and this to a varying degree from one region and one social category to another. In Wissous (Essonne) around 1600, twenty-five out of one hundred villagers knew how to sign their names. All the rural notables, a fourth of the wine growers, and nine independent farmers out of fifteen could do so, which indicates that the embryonic elementary instruction organized during the Wars of Religion concerned the upper levels of the rural world alone. In Languedoc at the same epoch "nine agricultural proletarians out of ten remained spiritually estranged from civilizations of writing," but 10 percent of the independent farmers could sign their names, one fourth of them could sign their initials, and two thirds used just a mark.

For one generation the persecution of witches

slowed somewhat, however, after which it underwent a new general upsurge, only slightly less intense than the first, around 1640–1660. Christianization, literacy, and political control all showed progress in rural areas during this half century. But spiritual conquest, strictly speaking, was not yet widespread. Around 1640, when the stakes and the pyres multiplied once more, there remained old peasants and old village women still attached to their traditional mindsets. Their sons and their grandsons had not all been enrolled by the missionaries, by more learned priests, or by schools, which were still sparse. The many popular revolts of the first half of the seventeenth century contributed to the insecurity of the times, and they worked against the efforts of the Church and the servants of the king. Was the exasperation felt by the cultural elites and the clergy, now increasingly well prepared, when they considered the mental inertia of the peasant world at least in part responsible for setting off the second wave of persecution? The agents of God and the State must surely have sensed more distinctly the gap between the new ideas and the reality of life among the people. The missionary enthusiasm born in the middle of the sixteenth century continued, but the passive resistance of the superstitions was becoming apparent. Saint Vincent de Paul, among many others, lucidly observed that the villagers fell back into error after the missionaries had left, and that to avoid this danger the missions should return regularly to each community. . . .

The stereotype of the witch proves that popular culture was the target of persecution, for this stereotype was a total fabrication of the judges and the demonologists. It tells us more about the mentality of the prosecutors than about the reality of witchcraft. It presents an ethical inversion of the values that were then dominant in society. In this sense, the theme of the "world upside down" or the "topsy-turvy world," which was used in the seventeenth century just as well as in the twentieth to describe witchcraft, does not refer to any sort of phenomenon of subversion, but it does define the anxieties and the fears, and thus by antithesis, the ideals of representatives of the governing orders of society.

This definition can be found as early as the end of the Middle Ages. The *Hammer of Witchcraft*, for example, which was published in 1486/1487 in Strasbourg, presents woman as "an evil of nature, painted with fair colours." This is because the daughters of Eve were on an average judged guilty of the crime of witchcraft four times more often than men, as we have seen. In general they were old women (more rarely, young girls), and more or less destitute, but a strong sexual dimension always surfaced in the course of the trials.

These considerations relate directly to the sociocultural values that the Church and state were trying to implant into the minds of rural folk. A more general repression of sexuality was expressed through a persecution of women. The missionaries of the Catholic Reformation combatted the relative liberty of mores that existed in rural areas before 1550. They imposed effective "sexual brakes" on the peasant world. The "confessions" extorted from the supposed witches can be interpreted in relation to this very real puritanical struggle. Copulation with Satan or with demons recalls the survival within the rural world of the "trial engagements" and concubinages that the authorities were attempting to uproot. The sabbath, that "sacrilegious feast," was just a diabolical transposition of the many popular festivities that we have studied, which often ended up, with the aid of drunkenness, in sexual excesses,

as in the . . . harvest festivals.

In reality, the many sins imputed to the witches were the result of the missionaries' profound dissatisfaction when peasant sexual conduct continued to conform insufficiently well to the theoretical mold urged by the Counter Reformation. Evil seemed to be everywhere. The witchcraft trials, in this context, created a sense of guilt among the people by linking extramarital sex with the Devil. Could the fall in the number of illegitimate children and in prenuptial conceptions in the seventeenth century be the result, at least in part, of the existence of this mechanism? The witch, in any event, stood as an example of an extreme form of censurable behaviors, but also of the victory of the new sexual norms. . . .

In short, witch-hunting was to find a more favorable terrain in communities in which the pastor kept a careful check on his own mores and those of his parishioners and in which sexual repression had affected at least part of the population.

After reading this selection, consider these questions:

1. How does Muchembled define the process of acculturation?
2. In what decades of what century did the suppression of witchcraft reach a height in France?
3. Why did the church and the state suppress the practice of witchcraft?

# SELECTION 5:

# The English Bill of Rights

*U*nder the early Stuart monarchs of England (1603–1649), questions of absolutist rule came to a head. James I and Charles I considered parliamentary interference with their governance of church and state presumptive and intolerable, challenging their own claims to rule by divine right. A collision course seemed to be set from the start between the Stuart kings of England and Parliament. The first five decades of the seventeenth century, in fact, saw Parliament in uninterrupted squabbles with the monar-

*chy. When Charles attempted to rule without calling Parliament from 1629 to 1640 and to raise funds through arbitrary nonparliamentary levies, the country faced a crisis. Led by the House of Commons, Parliament directly challenged the king when he finally was forced to call them together to issue new taxes. The subsequent English civil war (1642–1649) was fought between these royal forces and those raised in the name of Parliament. Although fought out in terms of distinct and highly different notions of royal authority, this civil war was also a religious war. Like similar civil wars earlier in France (the Wars of Religion) and simultaneously in the empire (the Thirty Years' War), constitutional issues were inextricably intertwined with religious differences. While Charles supported a form of high church Anglicanism (and his opponents even accused him of desiring Catholic doctrines and institutions), his Parliamentary opponents for the most part wanted more Calvinist forms of Protestantism established in England. Parliamentary forces eventually won the war, executed Charles I for high treason, and established more reformed types of worship throughout the kingdom. Although England was a republic after 1649, it did not remain so for long. In 1660 the monarchy was restored under the son of the executed monarch, who reigned as Charles II from 1660 until his death in 1685. Through this reign a compromise between royal prerogatives and parliamentary rule was worked out. After further difficulties resulted in the bloodless Glorious Revolution of 1688, which expelled James II and placed William and Mary on the throne, the relations between king and Parliament were eventually resolved.*

*One of the foundations of this new constitutional monarchy is contained in the* English Bill of Rights, *drafted in 1689.*

---

**W**hereas the said late King James II having abdicated the government, and the throne being thereby vacant, his Highness the prince of Orange (whom it hath pleased Almighty God to make the glorious instrument of delivering this kingdom from popery and arbitrary power) did (by the advice of the lords spiritual and temporal, and diverse principal persons of the Commons) cause letters to be written to the lords spiritual and temporal, being Protestants, and other letters to the several counties, cities, universities, boroughs, and Cinque Ports, for the choosing of such persons to represent them, as were of right to be sent to parliament, to meet and sit at Westminster upon the two and twentieth day of January, in this year 1689, in order to such an establishment as that their religion, laws, and liberties might not again be in danger of being subverted; upon which letters elections have been accordingly made.

And thereupon the said lords spiritual and temporal and Commons, pursuant to their respective letters and elections, being new assembled in a full and free representation of this nation, taking into their most serious consideration the best means for attaining the ends aforesaid, do in the first place (as their ancestors in like case have usually done), for the vindication and assertion of their ancient rights and liberties, declare:

1. That the pretended power of suspending laws, or the execution of laws, by regal authority, without consent of parliament is illegal.

2. That the pretended power of dispensing with the laws, or the execution of law by regal authority, as it hath been assumed and exercised of late, is illegal.

3. That the commission for erecting the late

From *The Statutes*, rev. ed. (London: Eyre & Spottiswode, 1871).

court of commissioners for ecclesiastical causes, and all other commissions and courts of like nature, are illegal and pernicious.

4. That levying money for or to the use of the crown by pretense of prerogative, without grant of parliament, for longer time or in other manner than the same is or shall be granted, is illegal.

5. That it is the right of the subjects to petition the king, and all commitments and prosecutions for such petitioning are illegal.

6. That the raising or keeping a standing army within the kingdom in time of peace, unless it be with consent of parliament, is against law.

7. That the subjects which are Protestants may have arms for their defense suitable to their conditions, and as allowed by law.

8. That election of members of parliament ought to be free.

9. That the freedom of speech, and debates or proceedings in parliament, ought not to be impeached or questioned in any court or place out of parliament.

10. That excessive bail ought not to be required, nor excessive fines imposed, nor cruel and unusual punishments inflicted.

11. That jurors ought to be duly impaneled and returned, and jurors which pass upon men in trials for high treason ought to be freeholders.

12. That all grants and promises of fines and forfeitures of particular persons before conviction are illegal and void.

13. And that for redress of all grievances, and for the amending, strengthening, and preserving of the laws, parliament ought to be held frequently.

And they do claim, demand, and insist upon all and singular the premises, as their undoubted rights and liberties. . . .

Having therefore an entire confidence that his said Highness the prince of Orange will perfect the deliverance so far advanced by him, and will still preserve them from the violation of their rights, which they have here asserted, and from all other attempt upon their religion, rights, and liberties:

The said lords spiritual and temporal, and Commons, assembled at Westminster, do resolve that William and Mary, prince and princess of Orange, be, and be declared, king and queen of England, France, and Ireland. . . .

Upon which their said Majesties did accept the crown and royal dignity of the kingdoms of England, France, and Ireland, and the dominions thereunto belonging, according to the resolution and desire of the said lords and commons contained in the said declaration.

After reading this selection, consider these questions:

1. What role did Parliament play in sixteenth- and seventeenth-century England?
2. What prevented the development of full-scale absolutism in England?
3. What was the English Bill of Rights of 1689?

# CHAPTER 4
# The Enlightenment: "To Change the Common Way of Thinking"

Although not named until the middle of the eighteenth century, the historical phenomenon we now call the Enlightenment is not merely one more event or stage within the history of the West. The Enlightenment has continued to provide the basic assumptions, values, and attitudes we have come to consider modern and Western. We owe our common understanding of legitimate state authority, of the just society, and of individual freedom to Enlightenment concepts. If we compare our own world with those of non-Western civilizations, we become immediately aware to what degree we define the individual person in terms of basic human rights within an ideal of a common humanity.

What was the Enlightenment? Or, better yet, What were the origins of the principles that became identified as "enlightened"? The simplest and most direct answer is that the Enlightenment was an intellectual movement of the eighteenth century that applied the methods of the modern natural sciences and their redefinition of knowledge to the understanding of human beings, society, and politics. By the mid-eighteenth century, the adherents of the Enlightenment provided a historical definition of themselves. Beginning with the Renaissance, there developed a greater interest in understanding and experimenting with natural phenomena, with explaining the operations of nature entirely in physical and mechanical terms. Francis Bacon and Nicolaus Copernicus, Johannes Kepler and Galileo Galilei all contributed to a worldview that Isaac Newton fully articulated and synthesized. The evolving notions of a universe determined by natural (as opposed to supernatural) powers provided both a method and a model of knowledge that, although anticipated by the Greeks and Romans, were only fully realized in modern science.

Beginning in the late seventeenth century, this new definition of knowledge was extended to the understanding of phenomena outside the realm of the natural sciences. Within the grand structure of the laws of nature, scientific method could now be applied to the new sciences of chemistry and biology. From biology, a new understanding of the human being and individual psychology could be developed; and from these sciences, in turn, new sciences of society and politics would also evolve. As the English poet Alexander Pope stated in his *Essay on Man* (1733), "The science of human nature [may be] like all other sciences reduced to a few clear points." Thus, advocates of the Enlightenment claimed a few simple governing laws similar to those discovered by Newton in the physical sciences. These laws would focus on human nature, society, and the rise and fall of nations.

The English philosopher John Locke (1632–1704) made the all-important move from the methods of the natural sciences to a general understanding of human reason; he then applied this understanding to the study of individuals and political organizations. To the Enlightenment, Locke was the philosopher who taught people to abandon traditional notions of metaphysics and to instead carefully build up series of empirical observations into larger bodies of knowledge. Empiricism was thus to be the foundation of Enlightenment thinking. Yet commonsensical as this method appears today, the belief that empirical knowledge would result in comprehensive bodies of knowledge could not be proved empirically. As David Hume and other philosophers later in the eighteenth century pointed out, empiricism had its limitations. Most philosophers did not share Hume's radical skepticism, and instead continued to believe in an order of the natural and human worlds—that there was indeed a rational order to the universe and that this order could be known through human intelligence. At the base of Locke's social and political theory lay the conception of the autonomous individual. The individual was no longer to be thought of as a dependent, subject to the guidance and protection of king and church. Each person was now considered a citizen, free to decide not only matters of personal concern but also the direction of the state itself.

Also fundamental to this understanding of nature was the principle, most fully articulated by Locke, that the human race as a whole could be educated in this new knowledge and that through this knowledge the human condition would infinitely be improved. Although the principles of sciences could thus be extended into areas that few of the greatest thinkers of the sixteenth and seventeenth centuries had imagined, the primary goal of the Enlightenment was to systematize these findings in all fields and to popularize them. The goal of the Enlightenment, in the words of one of its leading advocates, Denis Diderot, was to change society by changing "the common way of thinking" of humankind. Proponents of the Enlightenment were often referred to as *philosophes,* the French word for philosopher. The term, however, is a little misleading since no one besides David Hume, Adam Smith, and Immanuel Kant were original thinkers and only a few, including Smith and Kant, were academic teachers of philosophy. In general, the philosophes remained throughout the eighteenth century a rather loosely united group of men and women who shared a basic attitude toward the world and its reform.

Basing all knowledge on scientific method and mechanical causation, the philosophes saw themselves as critics and reformers. To explain the working of the universe in natural terms led them to oppose both the revealed truth of religion and the traditions of the various forms of Christianity. This is not to say that the philosophes were all atheists (though several clearly were); rather, the Enlightenment offered a new and wider range of beliefs in God. In the eighteenth century, this range generally followed geographical patterns. In France, the philosophes were the most critical of Christianity and its institutions, especially of the ways in which Christianity had been employed to justify both an absolutist and a hierarchical definition of society. While opposed to Christianity, these philosophes remained for the most part believers in the divine governance of the world. They were deists, believing in a God who transcended not only all forms of Christianity but also who lay behind all the world's religions. In Protestant England and its North American colonies, the evolution of more tolerant attitudes toward a variety of religious beliefs made the philosophes in these places less concerned with attacking the religious establishment. In Spain, Italy, and Austria, where the Catholic Church was powerfully entrenched, the philosophes attempted to work within the system. In Protestant Germany, the Enlightenment inspired less a total rejection than a critical rethinking of the meaning and moral principles of the Christian faith.

Across Europe and North America, the philosophes also adopted a wide range of attitudes to existing forms of government and society. They shared a common concern with spreading the ideas of the Enlightenment, with the reform of the educational systems, and with changing the penal codes and forms of punishment. Although the philosophes in France were generally considered to be the model, both in the originality of their ideas and in the means of effecting reform, they were also the most radical and the most organized. The French philosophes were organized around a major publishing venture, *The Encyclopedia*, and both individually and collectively became directly involved with criticizing the policy of the monarchy and shaping public opinion.

Although *The Encyclopedia* brought together all of the major writers and intellectuals of France in the middle of the eighteenth century, divisions among the philosophes arose in the third quarter of the century. These divisions had several sources. Beyond personal antagonisms, there were debates over the political and religious opposition to the publication of *The Encyclopedia*, over the role of the philosophes in the increasingly crisis-ridden politics of the French monarchy, and over the further development of Enlightenment thought itself. On this last point, a number of philosophes, including Diderot, increasingly moved to a more radical, atheistic, and materialist position. In no small measure, their criticism of existing conditions as well as their image of a better world played a definite role in bringing about and in shaping the course of the French Revolution of 1789.

## SELECTION 1:

# The Method of "Right Reasoning"

*The belief in an ordered and knowable universe had been established by a seventeenth-century group of philosophers. These rationalists posited that, beyond empirical evidence and as a foundation for all empirical knowledge, there was a nonempirical principle within human reason itself. René Descartes (1596–1650) provided the best-known and most debated argument for rationalism in the seventeenth and eighteenth centuries. The Cartesian foundation for Enlightenment thought allowed the philosophes to investigate the world empirically within a meaningful but empirically unprovable rational structure.*

*Descartes was a powerful thinker. From the clutter of traditional philosophy and inherited ways of thinking, he retrieved the primary grounds of human rationality: the capacity of the human mind to go beyond all immediate objects of thought. In this way, Descartes—without knowing it himself—reinaugurated the fundamental step of early Greek philosophy. But Descartes interpreted this intuition in ways that the ancient Greeks never did. From a radical skepticism of all knowledge and even the knowledge of his own existence, he found that the one idea that he could not doubt was that he was thinking and that this thinking implied existence: "I think therefore I am." The thinking subject then stood before an "objective" world, the truth of which could now be determined in terms of the accurate "representation" before the mind.*

*Descartes was a superb mathematician and natural scientist, and he applied his knowledge in these fields to his understanding of philosophy. In his* Discourse on Method *(1637), he proposed a general method of reasoning developed through his own thinking. From a skeptical starting point and with mathematical precision, Descartes analyzes representations down to their "clear and distinct" foundations and then synthesizes them into ever larger bodies of knowledge. In this manner, a clear and deducible metaphysics can be established and a process can be started to reform knowledge of nature and medicine. In the following selection from the* Discourse on Method, *Descartes lays out the simple steps of this way of reasoning.*

---

From *Discourse on Method*, by René Descartes (1637), translated by Benjamin C. Sax.

To make it possible to judge whether the foundations I have chosen are firm enough, I am in a way obliged to speak of them. For a long time I had observed . . . that in practical life it is sometimes necessary to act upon opinions which one knows to be quite uncertain just as if they were indubitable. But since I now wished to devote myself solely to the search for truth, I thought it necessary to do the very opposite and reject as if absolutely false everything in which I could imagine the least doubt, in order to see if I was left believing anything that was entirely indubitable. Thus, because our senses sometimes deceive us, I decided to suppose that nothing was such as they led us to imagine. And since there are men who make mistakes in reasoning, committing logical fallacies concerning the simplest questions in geometry, and because I judged that I was as prone to error as anyone else, I rejected as unsound all the arguments I had previously taken as demonstrative proofs. Lastly, considering that the very thoughts we have while awake may also occur while we sleep without any of them being at that time true, I resolved to pretend that all the things that had ever entered my mind were no more true than the illusions of my dreams. But immediately I noticed that while I was trying thus to think everything false, it was necessary that I, who was thinking this, was something. And observing that this truth *"I am thinking, therefore I exist"* [cogito ergo sum] was so firm and sure that all the most extravagant suppositions of the sceptics were incapable of shaking it, I decided that I could accept it without scruple as the first principle of the philosophy I was seeking.

Next I examined attentively what I was. I saw that while I could pretend that I had no body and that there was no world and no place for me to be in, I could not for all that pretend that I did not exist. I saw on the contrary that from the mere fact that I thought of doubting the truth of other things, I followed quite evidently and certainly that I existed; whereas if I had merely ceased thinking, even if everything else I had ever imagined had been true, I should have had no reason to believe that I existed. From this I knew I was a substance whose whole essence of nature is simply to think, and which does not require any place, nor is, the soul by which I am what I am— is entirely distinct from the body, and indeed is easier to know than the body, and would not fail to be whatever it is, even if the body did not exist.

After this I considered in general what is required of a proposition in order for it to be true and certain; for since I had just found one that I knew to be such, I thought that I ought also to know what this certainty consists in. I observed that there is nothing at all in the proposition *"I am thinking, therefore I exist"* to assure me that I am speaking the truth, except that I see very clearly that in order to think it is necessary to exist. So I decided that I could take it as a general rule that the things we conceive very clearly and very distinctly are all true; only there is some difficulty in recognizing which are the things that we distinctly conceive.

After reading this selection, consider these questions:
1. How does Descartes define *truth*?
2. How does he differentiate truth from opinion?
3. What is the foundation of all truths for Descartes?

# SELECTION 2:
# The Philosophes Defined

Yale *University historian Peter Gay presents in his book* The Enlightenment: An Interpretation *a synthesis of the international movement of the*

*Enlightenment. In the following selection, Gay gives a collective biography of the philosophes in the second half of the eighteenth century.*

The men of the Enlightenment united on a vastly ambitious program, a program of secularism, humanity, cosmopolitanism, and freedom, above all, freedom in its many forms—freedom from arbitrary power, freedom of speech, freedom of trade, freedom to realize one's talents, freedom of aesthetic response, freedom, in a word, of moral man to make his own way in the world. In 1784, when the Enlightenment had done most of its work, [Immanuel] Kant defined it as man's emergence from his self-imposed tutelage, and offered as its motto *Sapere aude*—"Dare to know": take the risk of discovery, exercise the right of unfettered criticism, accept the loneliness of autonomy. Like the other philosophes . . . Kant saw the Enlightenment as man's claim to be recognized as an adult, responsible being. It is the concord of the philosophes in staking this claim, as much as the claim itself, that makes the Enlightenment such a momentous event in the history of the Western mind.

Unity did not mean unanimity. The philosophic coalition was marked, and sometimes endangered, by disparities of philosophical and political convictions. A few—a very few—of the philosophes held tenaciously to vestiges of their Christian schooling, while others ventured into atheism and materialism; a handful remained loyal to dynastic authority, while radicals developed democratic ideas. The French took perverse pleasure in the opposition of church and state to their campaigns for free speech and a humane penal code, and to their polemics against "superstition." British men of letters, on the other hand, were relatively content with their political and social institutions. The German *Aufklärer* ["Enlighteners"] were isolated, impotent, and almost wholly unpolitical. . . . Thus the variety of political experience produced an Enlightenment with distinct branches; the philosophes were neither a disciplined phalanx nor a rigid school of thought. If they composed anything at all, it was something rather looser than that: a family.

But while the philosophes were a family, they were a stormy one. They were allies and often friends, but second only to their pleasure in promoting the common cause was the pleasure in criticizing a comrade-in-arms. They carried on an unending debate with one another, and some of their exchanges were anything but polite. . . .

To the delight of their enemies, the philosophes generated a highly charged atmosphere in which friendships were emotional, quarrels noisy, reconciliations tearful, and private affairs public. [Denis] Diderot, generous to everyone's faults except [Jean-Jacques] Rousseau's, found it hard to forgive [Jean Le Rond] d'Alembert's prudent desertion of the *Encyclopédie*. Voltaire, fondest of those who did not threaten him with their talent, gave Diderot uneasy and uncomprehending respect, and collaborated on an *Encyclopédie* in which he never really believed; in return, Diderot paid awkward tributes to the literary dictator of the age. He honored Voltaire . . . despite his bizarre behavior: "Someone gives him a shocking page which Rousseau, citizen of Geneva, has just scribbled against him. He gets furious, he loses his temper, he calls him villain, he foams with rage; he wants to have the miserable fellow beaten to death. 'Look,' says someone there, 'I have it on good authority that he's going to ask you for asylum, today, tomorrow, perhaps the day after tomorrow. What would you do?' 'What would I do?' replies Voltaire, gnashing his teeth, 'What would I do? I'd take him by the hand, lead him to my room, and say to him, 'Look, here's my bed, the best in the house, sleep there, sleep there for the rest of your life, and be happy.'". . .

The metaphor of a philosophic family is not my invention. The philosophes used it themselves. . . . Some of the harshest recriminations remained in the family, and when they did become public, they were usually sweetened by large doses of polite appreciation. Moreover, harassment or the fear of harassment drove the philosophes to remember

From *The Enlightenment*, vol. 2, by Peter Gay. Copyright © 1969 by Peter Gay. Reprinted by permission of Alfred A. Knopf, a division of Random House, Inc.

what they had in common and forget what divided them. The report of a book burned, a radical writer imprisoned, a heterodox passage censured, was enough. Then, quarrelsome officers faced with sudden battle, they closed ranks. . . .

In fact, the philosophes tolerated a wider range of opinions than fanatical preachers could have: Voltaire was happy to admit that while atheism is misguided and potentially dangerous, a world filled with Holbachs [Baron d'Holbach, a German-born philosopher who lived in France, was an outspoken atheist] would be palatable, far more palatable than a world filled with Christians, and Holbach, who thought little of deism, returned the compliment. . . .

The Enlightenment, then, was a single army with a single banner, with a large central corps, a right and left wing, daring scouts, and lame stragglers. And it enlisted soldiers who did not call themselves philosophes but who were their teachers, intimates, or disciples. The philosophic family was drawn together by the demands of political strategy, by the hostility of church and state, and by the struggle to enhance the prestige and increase the income of literary men. But the cohesion among the philosophes went deeper than this: behind their tactical alliances and personal fellowship there stood a common experience from which they constructed a coherent philosophy. This experience—which marked each of the philosophes with greater or lesser intensity, but which marked them all—was the dialectical interplay of their appeal to antiquity, their tension with Christianity, and their pursuit of modernity. This dialectic defines the philosophes and sets them apart from other enlightened men of their age: they, unlike the others, used their classical learning to free themselves from their Christian heritage, and then, having done with the ancients, turned their face toward a modern world view. The Enlightenment was a volatile mixture of classicism, impiety, and science; the philosophes, in a phrase, were modern pagans.

To call the Enlightenment pagan is to conjure up the most delightfully irresponsible sexual license: a lazy, sun-drenched summer afternoon, fauns and nymphs cavorting to sensual music, and lascivious paintings. . . . There is some reality in this fantasy: the philosophes argued for a positive appreciation of sensuality and despised asceticism. But these preachers of libertinism were far less self-indulgent, far more restrained in their habits, than their pronouncements would lead us to believe. . . . Generally, the philosophes worked hard—made, in fact, a cult of work—ate moderately, and knew the joys of faithful affection, although rarely with their wives. . . . As a group, the philosophes were a solid, respectable clan of revolutionaries, with their mission continually before them.

In speaking of the Enlightenment as pagan, therefore, I am referring not to sensuality but to the affinity of the Enlightenment to classical thought.

After reading this selection, consider these questions:

1. How does Peter Gay define the group known as the philosophes?
2. What joins the philosophes together? What divides them?
3. In what sense does Gay mean that the Enlightenment was "pagan"?

# SELECTION 3:

# "To Change the Common Way of Thinking"

*It is understandable that, with this popular interest in the new sciences and in the recent increases in knowledge in general, that a major encyclopedic work would find a ready audience in the eighteenth century. What is less understandable to us is that the undertaking of such a work as* The Encyclopedia or Reasoned Dictionary of the Sciences, Arts, and Trades *(1751–1772) would draw together the major writers and intellectual figures of France or that it would also serve as a source of criticism of the church and the monarchy. Under the general editorship of the popular writer Denis Diderot (1713–1784) and the mathematician Jean Le Rond d'Alembert (1717–1783), this massive publishing venture—seventeen thick volumes of text and eleven more volumes of plates—became a major engine of the Enlightenment vision and its reformist projects. In the following selection, excerpted from* The Encyclopedia, *Diderot explains the purpose of this project.*

Encyclopedia, noun, feminine gender (*Philosophy*). This word signifies *unity of knowledge*; it is made up of the Greek prefix EN, *in*, and the nouns KYKLOS, *circle*, and PAIDEIA, *instruction, science, knowledge*. In truth, the aim of an *encyclopedia* is to collect all the knowledge that now lies scattered over the face of the earth, to make known its general structure to the men among whom we live, and to transmit it to those who will come after us, in order that the labors of past ages may be useful to the ages to come, that our grandsons, as they become better educated, may at the same time become more virtuous and more happy, and that we may not die without having deserved well of the human race. . . .

Without doubt it would be very useful to have all that one could obtain from each particular learned society; and the sum of what they could

all provide would advance a universal dictionary a long way toward completion. There is, indeed, a task which, if undertaken, would render the academicians' labors even more directly subservient to the purpose of such a dictionary, and which the academies ought to be asked to do. I can conceive of two ways of cultivating the sciences: one is to increase the general fund of knowledge by making discoveries, and it is by this method that one comes to deserve the name of *inventor*; the other is to bring past discoveries together and reduce them to an ordered scheme so that more men may be enlightened and that each may contribute within the limits of his capacity to the intellectual progress of his age; we use the term *writers of texts* to apply to those who succeed in this second kind of enterprise, which is by no means an easy one. . . .

An encyclopedia ought to make good the failure to execute such a project hitherto, and should encompass not only the fields already covered by the academies, but each and every branch of human knowledge. This is a work that cannot be completed except by a society of men of letters and skilled workmen, each working separately on his own part, but all bound together solely by their zeal for the best interests of the human race and a feeling of mutual good will.

I say, *a society of men of letters and of skilled workmen*, for it is necessary to assemble all sorts of abilities. I wish the members of this society to work separately because there is no existing society from which one could obtain all the knowledge one needs, and because if one wanted the work to be perpetually in the making, but never finished, the best way to secure that result would be to form a permanent society. For every society has its meetings; there are intervals between meetings; each meeting lasts for only a few hours; part of this time is wasted in disputes; and so the simplest problems consume entire months. . . .

I add: *men bound together by zeal for the best interests of the human race and by a feeling of mutual good will*, because these motives are the most worthy that can animate the souls of upright people and they are also the most lasting. One has an inward sense of self-approval for all that one does; one becomes enthusiastic, and one undertakes, out of regard for one's friends and colleagues, many a task that one would not attempt for any other consideration. I can certainly testify from my own experience that the success of such attempts is all the more assured. The *Encyclopedia* has brought together its materials in a very short time. It is no sordid self-interest that has assembled and spurred on the authors; rather they have seen their efforts seconded by the majority of the men of letters from whom they expected assistance, and the only annoyance they have suffered in the course of their work has been caused by persons who had not the talent necessary to contribute one single good page.

If the government were to meddle with a work of this sort it would never be finished. All that the authorities ought to do is encourage its completion. A monarch may, by a single word, cause a palace to rise up out of the grass; but a society of men of letters is not the same thing as a gang of laborers. An encyclopedia cannot be produced on order. It is a task that needs rather to be pursued with perseverance than to be begun with ardor.

An enterprise of this sort may on occasion be proposed in the course of a conversation at Court; but the interest which it arouses in such circles is never great enough to prevent its being forgotten amidst the tumult and confusion of an infinite number of more or less pressing affairs. Literary projects which great noblemen conceive are like the leaves that appear in the spring, grow dry in the autumn and fall in a heap in the depths of the forest, where the sustenance they give to a few sterile plants is all the effect they can be seen to produce. . . . Private individuals are eager to harvest the fruits of what they have sown; the government has none of this economic zeal. I do not know what reprehensible motive it is that leads people to deal less honestly with a prince than with his subjects. One assumes the lightest of obligations and then expects the most handsome rewards. Uncertainty as to whether the project will ever have any useful results fills the workmen with inconceivable indolence. To lend to all these disadvantages the greatest possible force, projects ordered by sovereigns are never conceived in terms of pure utility, but always in terms of the dignity of the sponsor; that is to say, the scale is as large as possible; obstacles are continually arising; men, special abilities, and time are needed in proportion to surmount them; and before the end is in sight, there is sure to intervene a change of ministers. . . . If the average life expectancy of an ordinary man is less than twenty years, that of a minister is less than ten. And not only are interruptions more frequent when it is a question of some literary project; they are also more damaging when the government is the sponsor than when the publishing enterprise is conducted by private individuals. In the event of shipwreck, the individual at least gathers up the debris of his undertaking and carefully preserves the materials that may be of service to him in a happier time; he hastens to salvage something from his investment. But the spirit of monarchy scorns this sort of prudence; men die, and the fruit of their toil disappears so completely that no one can discover what became of it. . . .

But the circumstance that will give a superannuated appearance to the work and bring it the public's scorn will be above all the revolution that will occur in the minds of men and in the national character. Today, when philosophy is advancing with gigantic strides, when it is bringing under its sway all the matters that are its proper concern, when its tone is the dominant one, and when we are beginning to shake off the yoke of authority and tradition in order to hold fast to the laws of reason, there is scarcely a single elementary or dogmatic book which satisfies us entirely. We find that these works are put together out of the productions of a few men and are not founded upon the truths of nature. We dare to raise doubts about the infallibility of Aristotle and Plato, and the time has come when the works that still enjoy the highest reputation will begin to lose some of their great prestige or even fall into complete oblivion. Certain literary forms—for want of the vital realities and actual custom that once served them as models—will no longer possess an unchanging or even a reasonable poetic meaning and will be abandoned; while others that remain, and whose intrinsic value sustains them will take on an entirely new meaning. Such are the consequences of the progress of reason, an advance that will overthrow so many old idols and perhaps restore to their pedestals some statues that have been cast down. The latter will be those of the rare geniuses who were ahead of their own times. We have had, if one may thus express it, our contemporaries in the age of Louis XIV. . . .

In a systematic, universal dictionary, as in any work intended for the general education of mankind, you must begin by contemplating your subject in its most general aspects; you must know the state of mind of your nation, foresee the direction of its future development, hasten to anticipate its progress so that the march of events will not leave your book behind but will rather overtake it along the road; you must be prepared to work solely for the good of future generations because the moment of your own existence quickly passes away, and a great enterprise is not likely to be finished before the present generation ceases to exist. But if you would have your work remain fresh and useful for a long time to come—by virtue of its being far in advance of the national spirit, which marches steadily forward—you must shorten your labors by multiplying the

number of your helpers, an expedient that is not, indeed, without its disadvantages, as I shall try to make plain hereafter.

Nevertheless, knowledge is not infinite, and cannot be universally diffused beyond a certain point. To be sure, no one knows just where this limit may be. Still less does anyone know to what heights the human race might have attained nor of what it might be capable, if it were in no way hampered in its progress. Revolutions are necessary; there have always been revolutions, and there always will be; the maximum interval between one revolution and another is a fixed quantity, and this is the only limit to what we can attain by our labors. For there is in every science a point beyond which it is virtually impossible to go. Whenever this point is reached, there will be created landmarks which will remain almost forever to astonish all mankind.

But if humanity is subject to certain limitations which set bounds to its strivings, how much narrower are the limits that circumscribe the efforts of individuals! The individual has but a certain quantity of energy both physical and intellectual. He enjoys but a short span of existence, he is constrained to alternate labor with repose; he has both instincts and bodily needs to satisfy, and he is prey to an infinite number of distractions. Whenever the negative elements in this equation add up to the smallest possible sum, or the positive elements add up to the largest possible sum, a man working alone in some branch of human knowledge will be able to carry it forward as far as it is capable of being carried by the efforts of one man. Add to the labors of this extraordinary individual those of another like him, and of still others, until you have filled up the whole interval of time between one scientific revolution and the revolution most remote from it in time, and you will be able to form some notion of the greatest perfection attainable by the whole human race—especially if you take for granted a certain number of accidental circumstances favorable to its labors, or which might have diminished its success had they been adverse.

But the general mass of men are not so made that they can either promote or understand this forward march of the human spirit. The highest level of enlightenment that this mass can achieve is strictly limited; hence it follows that there will always be literary achievements which will be above the capacities of the generality of men; there will be others which by degrees will fall short of that level; and there will be still others which will share both these fates.

No matter to what state of perfection an encyclopedia may be brought, it is clear from the very nature of such a work that it will necessarily be found among this third class of books. There are many things that are in daily use among the common people, things from which they draw their livelihood, and they are incessantly busy gaining a practical knowledge of these things. As many treatises as you like may be written about these matters and still there will always come a time when the practical man will know more about them than the writer of the book. There are other subjects about which the ordinary man will remain almost totally ignorant because the daily accretions to his fund of knowledge are too feeble and too slow ever to form any considerable sum of enlightenment, even if you suppose them to be uninterrupted.

Hence both the man of the people and the learned man will always have equally good reasons for desiring an encyclopedia and for seeking to learn from it.

After reading this selection, consider these questions:

1. How does Diderot define the term *encyclopedia*?
2. How does this encyclopedia differ from encyclopedias of today?
3. What is the relationship of Diderot's *Encyclopedia* to power?

# SELECTION 4:

# A New Science of the Economy

*One area in which the spread of Enlightenment principles would prove most fruitful was that of economics. Economics emerged as a science in its own right through the pioneering works of Adam Smith (1723–1790). A professor of logic and moral philosophy at Glasgow University in Scotland, Smith developed the new science of political economy. In 1776 he published* An Inquiry into the Nature and Causes of the Wealth of Nations, *which was widely read at the time and made its author internationally famous. Rejecting the state regulation of economic policy that was advocated not just by absolutism but by most forms of government in the eighteenth century, Smith proposed a notion of laissez faire—the restriction of governmental interference in economic matters. Also opposed to the protectionist policies of his time, which proposed increasing a nation's exports and minimizing its imports, Smith argued that free trade would increase the wealth of all nations. Before moving on to these larger theses, Smith opens* The Wealth of Nations *with a discussion of the division of labor.*

This great increase of the quantity of work, which, in consequence of the division of labour, the same number of people are capable of performing, is owing to three different circumstances: first, to the increase of dexterity in every particular workman; secondly, to the saving of the time which is commonly lost in passing from one species of work to another; and lastly, to the invention of a great number of machines which facilitate and abridge labour, and enable one man to do the work of many.

First, the improvement of the dexterity of the workman necessarily increases the quantity of the work he can perform; and the division of labour, by reducing every man's business to some one simple operation, and by making this operation the sole employment of his life, necessarily increases very much the dexterity of the workman. A common smith, who, though accustomed to handle the hammer, has never been used to make nails, if upon some particular occasion he is obliged to attempt it, will scarce, I am assured, be able to make above two or three hundred nails in a day, and those too very bad ones. A smith who has been accustomed to make nails, but whose sole or principal business has not been that of a nailer, can seldom with his utmost diligence make more than eight hundred or a thousand nails in a day. I have seen several boys under twenty years of age who had never exercised any other trade but that of making nails, and who, when they exerted themselves, could make, each of them, upwards of two thousand three hundred nails in a day. The making of a nail, however, is by no means one of the simplest operations. The same person blows the bellows, stirs or mends the fire as there is occasion, heats the iron, and forges every part of the nail: in forging the head too he is obliged to change his tools. The different operations into which the making of a pin, or of a metal button, is subdivided, are all of them much more simple, and the dexterity of the person, of whose life it has been the sole business to

From *An Inquiry into the Nature and Causes of the Wealth of Nations*, by Adam Smith, edited by James E. Thorold Rogers, vol. 1, 2nd ed. (Oxford: Clarendon Press, 1880).

perform them, is usually much greater. The rapidity with which some of the operations of those manufactures are performed, exceeds what the human hand could, by those who had never seen them, be supposed capable of acquiring.

Secondly, the advantage which is gained by saving the time commonly lost in passing from one sort of work to another, is much greater than we should at first view be apt to imagine it. It is impossible to pass very quickly from one kind of work to another, that is carried on in a different place, and with quite different tools. A country weaver, who cultivates a small farm, must lose a good deal of time in passing from his loom to the field, and from the field to his loom. When the two trades can be carried on in the same workhouse, the loss of time is no doubt much less. It is even in this case, however, very considerable. A man commonly saunters a little in turning his hand from one sort of employment to another. When he first begins the new work he is seldom very keen and hearty; his mind, as they say, does not go to it, and for some time he rather trifles than applies to good purpose. The habit of sauntering and of indolent careless application, which is naturally, or rather necessarily, acquired by every country workman who is obliged to change his work and his tools every half hour, and to apply his hand in twenty different ways almost every day of his life, renders him almost always slothful and lazy, and incapable of any vigorous application even on the most pressing occasions. Independent, therefore, of his deficiency in point of dexterity, this cause alone must always reduce considerably the quantity of work which he is capable of performing.

Thirdly, and lastly, everybody must be sensible how much labour is facilitated and abridged by the application of proper machinery. It is unnecessary to give any example. I shall only observe, therefore, that the invention of all those machines by which labour is so much facilitated and abridged, seems to have been originally owing to the division of labour. Men are much more likely to discover easier and readier methods of attaining any object, when the whole attention of their minds is directed towards that single object, than when it is dissipated among a great variety of things. But in consequence of the division of labour, the whole of every man's attention comes naturally to be directed towards some one very simple object. It is naturally to be expected, therefore, that some one or other of those who are employed in each particular branch of labour should soon find out easier and readier methods of performing their own particular work, wherever the nature of it admits of such improvement. A great part of the machines made use of in those manufactures in which labour is most subdivided, were originally the inventions of common workmen, who, being each of them employed in some very simple operation, naturally turned their thoughts towards finding out easier and readier methods of performing it. Whoever has been much accustomed to visit such manufactures, must frequently have been shown very pretty machines, which were the inventions of such workmen, in order to facilitate and quicken their own particular part of the work. In the first fire-engines, a boy was constantly employed to open and shut alternately the communication between the boiler and the cylinder, according as the piston either ascended or descended. One of those boys, who loved to play with his companions, observed that, by tying a string from the handle of the valve which opened this communication to another part of the machine, the valve would open and shut without his assistance, and leave him at liberty to divert himself with his play-fellows. One of the greatest improvements that has been made upon this machine, since it was first invented, was in this manner the discovery of a boy who wanted to save his own labour.

All the improvements in machinery, however, have by no means been the inventions of those who had occasion to use the machines. Many improvements have been made by the ingenuity of the makers of the machines, when to make them became the business of a peculiar trade; and some by that of those who are called philosophers or men of speculation, whose trade is not to do anything, but to observe everything; and who, upon that account, are often capable of combining together the powers of the most distant and dissimilar objects. In the progress of society, philosophy or speculation becomes, like every other employment, the principal or sole trade and occupation of a particular class of citizens. Like every other employment too, it is subdivided into a great number of different branches, each of which affords occupation to a peculiar tribe or class of philosophers; and this subdivision of employment in philosophy, as well as in every other business, improves dexterity, and saves time. Each individual becomes more expert in his own peculiar branch, more work is done upon the whole, and the quantity of science is considerably increased by it.

It is the great multiplication of the productions of all the different arts, in consequence of the division of labour, which occasions, in a well-governed society, that universal opulence which extends itself to the lowest ranks of the people. Every workman has a great quantity of his own work to dispose of beyond what he himself has occasion for; and every other workman being exactly in the same situation, he is enabled to exchange a great quantity of his own goods for a great quantity, or, what comes to the same thing, for the price of a great quantity of theirs. He supplies them abundantly with what they have occasion for, and they accommodate him as amply with what he has occasion for, and a general plenty diffuses itself through all the different ranks of the society.

After reading this selection, consider these questions:
1. What does Smith mean by the phrase *division of labor*?
2. What are the benefits of the division of labor, according to Smith?
3. How does Smith understand the relationship of capitalism to society?

## SELECTION 5:

# Science vs. Morals

*The notion that the scientific method and the spirit of inquiry developed by the sciences could be extended into every area of human knowledge and would improve the human condition did not go unchallenged in the eighteenth century, even by the philosophes themselves. As a professor of moral philosophy in Glasgow, Adam Smith argued that morals themselves had to be understood independently of economics. Jean-Jacques Rousseau (1712– 1778) drove home the point that the advancement of knowledge and even control over nature proposed by the Enlightenment did not necessarily result in the improvement of individuals' or society's morals; just the opposite, he thought. Rousseau reasoned that the advancement of knowledge and exploitation of nature, especially with the increase of luxury, led to moral decline. Initially responding to a question proposed by the Academy of Sciences of Dijon on whether the recent advances of the arts and sciences improved morals, Rousseau wrote an essay disputing this idea. He won first prize and saw his essay published the next year (1750) as the* Discourse on the Moral Effects of the Arts and Sciences. *This "first discourse" made Rousseau instantly famous. In the next decade he published a second essay on the origins of inequality and a series of works—*Émile *(on education),* The Social Contract *(on political organization), and* La Nouvelle Héloïse *(a sentimental novel)—all of which emphasized the need for both individual and social reform based on a more independent and natural understanding of the self. The following selection is from Rousseau's first discourse.*

The question before me is: "Whether the Restoration of the arts and sciences has had the effect of purifying or corrupting morals." Which side am I to take? That, gentlemen, which becomes an honest man, who is sensible of his own ignorance, and thinks himself none the worse for it.

I feel the difficulty of treating this subject fittingly, before the tribunal which is to judge of what I advance. How can I presume to belittle the sciences before one of the most learned assemblies in Europe, to commend ignorance in a famous Academy, and reconcile my contempt for study with the respect due to the truly learned?

I was aware of these inconsistencies, but not discouraged by them. It is not science, I said to myself, that I am attacking; it is virtue that I am defending, and that before virtuous men—and goodness is ever dearer to the good than learning to the learned.

What then have I to fear? The sagacity of the assembly before which I am pleading? That, I acknowledge, is to be feared; but rather on account of faults of construction than of the views I hold. Just sovereigns have never hesitated to decide against themselves in doubtful cases; and indeed the most advantageous situation in which a just claim can be, is that of being laid before a just and enlightened arbitrator, who is judge in his own case.

From *"The Social Contract" and "Discourses,"* by Jean-Jacques Rousseau, translated by G.D.H. Cole (London: J.M. Dent, 1913).

To this motive, which encouraged me, I may add another which finally decided me. And this is, that as I have upheld the cause of truth to the best of my natural abilities, whatever my apparent success, there is one reward which cannot fail me. That reward I shall find in the bottom of my heart.

It is a noble and beautiful spectacle to see man raising himself, so to speak, from nothing by his own cxcrtions; dissipating, by the light of reason, all the thick clouds in which he was by nature enveloped; mounting above himself; soaring in thought even to the celestial regions; like the sun, encompassing with giant strides the vast extent of the universe; and, what is still grander and more wonderful, going back into himself, there to study man and get to know his own nature, his duties and his end. All these miracles we have seen renewed within the last few generations.

Europe had relapsed into the barbarism of the earliest ages; the inhabitants of this part of the world, which is at present so highly enlightened, were plunged, some centuries ago, in a state still worse than ignorance. A scientific jargon, more despicable than mere ignorance, had usurped the name of knowledge, and opposed an almost invincible obstacle to its restoration.

Things had come to such a pass, that it required a complete revolution to bring men back to common sense. This came at last from the quarter from which it was least to be expected. It was the stupid Mussulman [Muslim], the eternal scourge of letters, who was the immediate cause of their revival among us. The fall of the throne of Constantine brought to Italy the relics of ancient Greece; and with these precious spoils France in turn was enriched. The sciences soon followed literature, and the art of thinking joined that of writing: an order which may seem strange, but is perhaps only too natural. The world now began to perceive the principal advantage of an intercourse with the Muses, that of rendering mankind more sociable by inspiring them with the desire to please one another with performances worthy of their mutual approbation.

The mind, as well as the body, has its needs: those of the body are the basis of society, those of the mind its ornaments.

So long as government and law provide for the security and well-being of men in their common life, the arts, literature, and the sciences, less despotic though perhaps more powerful, fling garlands of flowers over the chains which weigh them down. They stifle in men's breasts that sense of original liberty, for which they seem to have been born; cause them to love their own slavery, and so make of them what is called a civilized people.

Necessity raised up thrones; the arts and sciences have made them strong. Powers of the earth, cherish all talents and protect those who cultivate them. Civilized peoples, cultivate such pursuits: to them, happy slaves, you owe that delicacy and exquisiteness of taste, which is so much your boast, that sweetness of disposition and urbanity of manners which make intercourse so easy and agreeable among you—in a word, the appearance of all the virtues, without being in possession of one of them.

It was for this sort of accomplishment, which is by so much the more captivating, as it seems less affected, that Athens and Rome were so much distinguished in the boasted times of their splendour and magnificence: and it is doubtless in the same respect that our own age and nation will excel all periods and peoples. An air of philosophy without pedantry; an address at once natural and engaging, distant equally from Teutonic clumsiness and Italian pantomime; these are the effects of a taste acquired by liberal studies and improved by conversation with the world. What happiness would it be for those who live among us, if our external appearance were always a true mirror of our hearts; if decorum were but virtue; if the maxims we professed were the rules of our conduct; and if real philosophy were inseparable from the title of a philosopher! But so many good qualities too seldom go together; virtue rarely appears in so much pomp and state.

Richness of apparel may proclaim the man of fortune, and elegance the man of taste; but true health and manliness are known by different signs. It is under the homespun of the labourer, and not beneath the gilt and tinsel of the courtier, that we should look for strength and vigour of body.

External ornaments are no less foreign to virtue, which is the strength and activity of the mind. The honest man is an athlete, who loves to wrestle stark naked; he scorns all those vile trappings, which prevent the exertion of his strength, and were, for the most part, invented only to conceal some deformity.

Before art had moulded our behaviour, and taught our passions to speak an artificial language, our morals were rude but natural; and the different ways in which we behaved proclaimed at the first glance the difference of our dispositions. Human nature was not at bottom better then than now; but men found their security in the ease with which they could see through one another, and this advantage, of which we no longer feel the value, prevented their having many vices.

In our day, now that more subtle study and a more refined taste have reduced the art of pleasing to a system, there prevails in modern manners a servile and deceptive conformity; so that one would think every mind had been cast in the same mould. Politeness requires this thing; decorum that; ceremony has its forms, and fashion its laws, and these we must always follow, never the promptings of our own nature.

We no longer dare seem what we really are, but lie under a perpetual restraint; in the meantime the herd of men, which we call society, all act under the same circumstances exactly alike, unless very particular and powerful motives prevent them. Thus we never know with whom we have to deal; and even to know our friends we must wait for some critical and pressing occasion; that is, till it is too late; for it is on those very occasions that such knowledge is of use to us.

What a train of vices must attend this uncertainty! Sincere friendship, real esteem, and perfect confidence are banished from among men. Jealousy, suspicion, fear, coldness, reserve, hate, and fraud lie constantly concealed under that uniform and deceitful veil of politeness; that boasted candour and urbanity, for which we are indebted to the light and leading of this age. We shall no longer take in vain by our oaths the name of our Creator; but we shall insult Him with our blasphemies, and our scrupulous ears will take no offence. We have grown too modest to brag of our own desserts; but we do not scruple to decry those of others. We do not grossly outrage even our enemies, but artfully calumniate them. Our hatred of other nations diminishes, but patriotism dies with it. Ignorance is held in contempt; but a dangerous scepticism has succeeded it. Some vices indeed are condemned and others grown dishonourable; but we have still many that are honoured with the names of virtues, and it is become necessary that we should either have, or at least pretend to have them. Let who will extol the moderation of our modern sages, I see nothing in it but a refinement of intemperance as unworthy of my commendation as their artificial simplicity.

Such is the purity to which our morals have attained; this is the virtue we have made our own. Let the arts and sciences claim the share they have had in this salutary work. I shall add but one reflection more; suppose an inhabitant of some distant country should endeavour to form an idea of European morals from the state of the sciences, the perfection of the arts, the propriety of our public entertainments, the politeness of our behaviour, the affability of our conversation, our constant professions of benevolence, and from those tumultuous assemblies of people of all ranks, who seem, from morning till night, to have no other care than to oblige one another. Such a stranger, I maintain, would arrive at a totally false view of our morality.

After reading this selection, consider these questions:

1. How does Rousseau define the arts and sciences?
2. What threat do the arts and sciences pose to morals?
3. How does Rousseau define virtue?

# CHAPTER 5
# The French Revolution as a World Revolution

Two events, both beginning in the last quarter of the eighteenth century, were to have profound effects on the course of Western and even world history. And both were related to, but not necessarily caused by, the development of the new sciences and the spread of the Enlightenment. The first of these transforming events was the beginning of the Industrial Revolution in England of the 1770s. Comparable in its consequences to the Neolithic Revolution of the fifth and fourth millennia B.C., the Industrial Revolution also marked a gradual but totally transforming "event" in world history. Like the earlier shift to agriculture, the eighteenth-century change to mechanical production not only fundamentally changed economic relations but also altered the basic organization of society.

The other transforming event was the French Revolution of 1789. Although not as obviously influential as the global impact of industrialization, the French Revolution should not be thought of as limited either to France or to the eighteenth century. As a direct result of the Revolution, the various states of Europe came to redefine political legitimacy in terms of the will of the nation. But what is a nation? As both the French Revolution and subsequent history have shown, the answer to this question is not easy. The idea of the nation as the only legitimate source of power entailed a theoretical acceptance of both some notion of democracy and the ideal of legal and social equality. In this sense, the impact of the French Revolution was European-wide and, by the twentieth century, worldwide.

The French Revolution broke out in the spring of 1789. Over the course of the next decade, it went through a number of distinct phases: an initial constitutional monarchy (1789–1792), a republic and the radical Reign of Terror (1792–1794), and a moderate "caretaker" government from 1794 until Napoléon Bonaparte consolidated his personal rule in 1799. If the course of the Revolution was complex, its causes were even more so. The immediate cause was the calling in May 1789 of the Estates General. The king and his ministers were forced to call this representative body into session because the government had reached a state of financial crisis. After various schemes were attempted to meet the crisis, it was finally realized that the only solution was to levy new taxes. When the king's minister as well as the nobles and clergy of France refused to establish on their own authority new forms of taxation, Louis XVI was forced to convene the Estates General, which had not met since 1614. Louis's consent to the calling of the Estates General was a tacit admission that absolutism had failed: The king could not rule alone. What precisely was to replace absolutism was not directly considered by Louis or his ministers. Although certain ministers early in Louis's reign had distinct ideas on how to reform royal administration, in 1789 most of them envisioned only a return to a pre-absolutist form of government in which the king shared power with various high law courts (the *parlements*) and representative bodies throughout France. Others, especially those outside the royal administration, had more radical ideas.

The origins of the Revolution cannot be totally comprehended in terms of a response to the financial crisis alone. The French Revolution was a radical, world-historical event not only because the absolutist government was overthrown but also because a new model of the state and a new image of society were brought into existence as a result of this overthrow. In large measure, this model and this image had been created by the advanced critical thinking of the preceding half century. In other words, the Revolution became a highly significant event as a result of an attempt to change radically the established definitions of state and society. The Enlightenment's questioning of traditions and the clear and reasonable way of suggesting alternatives must have come like a breath of fresh air. Against mere customary ways of doing things, the philosophes proposed a practical way of evaluating forms of government and the organization of society. Utility was the measure. In this way, the Enlightenment by midcentury began a discussion on the purposes and ends of government, which was soon to widen out across France, the rest of Europe, and the European colonies in the Americas.

There were other reasons why the French Revolution took a radical direction. Nobles and the clergy did not pay taxes. In lieu of taxes, the nobles (members of the Second Estate) served the state as defenders of the kingdom and by advising the king. The clergy (the First Estate) was by definition also exempt. Their service consisted in praying for all those in the kingdom. In practice, by the eighteenth century certain forms of taxes were in fact paid by both the nobles and the clergy. Nonetheless, the members of the Third Estate (all those not members of the First and Second Estates) contributed the vast share of the direct taxes in France. They served the kingdom through their labor. Additional divisions also existed within the Third Estate. Most citizens of the incorporated towns of the kingdom did not pay taxes directly to the crown, having over the centuries negotiated more favorable conditions. This left the great burden of taxation on citizens of unincorporated (and generally smaller) towns and on the peasantry. In eighteenth-century France, the vast bulk of the population and the major source of the economy were agricultural. Although the older manorial system had mostly broken down and feudal dues in most instances had been transformed into money relationships, still the peasants remained tied in a number of ways to the land of their seigneurial lords. Adding royal taxes on top of these seigneurial rents and dues placed a great financial burden on the peasantry. This burden, heavy in the best of times, became unbearable in times of poor harvests and famine. Members of the peasantry saw in the promise of a new system of taxation and later in the French Revolution itself a means of changing their situation.

## SELECTION 1:

# The Coming of the French Revolution

*With a number of bad harvests in the 1780s, the French peasantry suffered from economic hardships and sometimes starvation. Peasants looked to the king for assistance and generally blamed his ministers for the failure of the government to help them. Significantly, they increasingly came to couch their grievances in the new language of rights and citizenship rather than in the traditional terms of the king as father and protector of his people. In the spring and summer of 1789 numerous uprisings erupted in the countryside. The peasants attacked the local château in the hope of destroying all the documents listing their feudal ties and dues.*

*The peasant uprisings alone did not lead to the outbreak of the revolution; they were only one factor in a very complex set of causes. The more pressing concerns for the royal government in 1789 was not unrest in the countryside but the continuing problem of taxation and the unintended consequences of the actions taken by the royal ministers to deal with the financial crisis. The twentieth-century French historian Georges Lefebvre, in his monumental history of the Revolution, divides up the events of 1789 into a number of separate revolutions. In addition to the peasant uprisings, Lefebvre identifies an aristocratic and a bourgeois revolution. Lefebvre's aristocratic revolution involved the relation between the royal administration and the high law courts of France, the parlements.*

Louis [XVI] opened the meeting [of the Estates-General] on May 5. His brief address was applauded. . . . Then [Minister of Finance Jacques] Necker, with the aid of an acting official who relieved him from time to time, harangued the anxious deputies. His listeners were soon disappointed and seriously annoyed. For three hours the minister of finance explained the detailed situation of the Treasury and the proposed improvements, made no allusion to constitutional reform, expressed confidence in the generosity of the privileged classes, then repeated the method of voting which had been announced in December. On the following day the nobility and clergy began to verify their powers separately. The Third Estate refused to follow suit. The Estates-General was paralysed.

Deputies from Brittany and the Dauphiné favoured outright refusal to vote by order, but that would have been an infringement of legality, and the politicians did not want to take chances so early in the game. The representatives were not yet familiar with one another, and no one knew how far each would agree to advance. Some found the ardour of the Bretons alarming. A delaying tactic was necessary, and Necker's refusal to grant the Council of State power of verification provided an escape. The Third Estate alleged that each order had to establish whether the two other orders were legally constituted, and that powers should therefore be inspected in common session. During this stalemate the Third refused to constitute itself as a separate order: no minutes were taken, no rules established; not even a steering committee was set up. They consented only to choose a "dean," who after June 3 was [astronomer and politician Jean-Sylvain] Bailly. At the beginning the Third had taken the name Commons (*communes*) for itself. Although no one other than a few of the more erudite knew exactly what the medieval communes were, the word evoked a vague memory of popular resistance to feudal lords, an idea strengthened by

what knowledge they had of English history. To the Third Estate the name meant refusal to recognize a social hierarchy that had relegated it to third rank.

This attitude had its drawbacks. The people were told that the Third Estate was responsible for delaying the abolition of fiscal privileges. . . . Everyone, however, sensed the need for some new tactical issue, and it was the clergy which furnished them with just that. The nobility, in no way perturbed, on May 11 announced itself constituted as a separate order. Because a large proportion of the parish priests supported the Commons, the clergy instead proposed that designated members of the three orders meet in conference. To humour the other order, the Third Estate agreed. But the discussions of May 23 and 25 came to nothing: the nobles retreated behind precedents which the Third Estate either challenged or fought with arguments of reason and natural right. They next tried to get the clergy to agree that the three orders should be fused. The bishops sensed imminent defection from the parish priests and asked the king to intervene. On May 28 Louis asked that the conferences be resumed in the presence of his ministers, and on June 4 Necker drafted a conciliatory proposal: each order should first verify the powers of its own members, then announce the results to the others and consider any objections that were raised. If no agreement could be reached, the king was to deliver a final decision. Once more the Third found itself in a difficult position. This time it was the nobility that came to its rescue by rejecting royal arbitration except for the "complete" delegations—those which . . . had been chosen in common by the three orders. This was the signal for revolutionary action.

On June 10 the Third Estate followed a proposal from [Emmanuel-Joseph] Sieyès and invited the privileged members to join it. Those who did not appear to answer a roll call would be considered to have defaulted. The roll was begun on June 12 and finished on the 14th: several parish priests had responded, but not one noble. After two days' debate the Third Estate on June 17 conferred the title "National Assembly" upon the combined and enrolled orders. It immediately arrogated to itself the power to consent to taxation,

From *The French Revolution: From Its Origins to 1793*, by Georges Lefebvre, translated by Elizabeth Moss Evanson. (London: Routledge & Kegan Paul, 1962). Reprinted by permission of the publisher.

confirming existing taxes provisionally. Had sovereignty passed to the nation? Not exactly. On June 20 Bailly acknowledged that these revolutionary resolutions required the king's approval.

Louis had no intention of approving them. The Dauphin had died on June 4, and the king had withdrawn to Marly, where the queen and royal princes instructed him. The nobility finally abdicated in favour of the throne and begged the king to make the Third Estate return to the path of duty. On June 19 the majority of the clergy declared itself in favour of fusing the three orders. The bishops hastily called for assistance. Royal ministers and even Necker agreed that intervention was necessary. The Council of State announced that a royal session would be held on June 22. But what would the king declare then? . . . Necker hoped to manage the Commons by simply ignoring their decrees rather than by overriding them. At last he came out into the open, proposing to establish equality of taxation, to admit all Frenchmen to public office, and to authorize the vote by head in constituting future Estates-General, stipulating that the king would agree to this only if the Estates met as two houses and if he were granted full executive power with a legislative veto. Necker protected aristocratic prerogatives and property with the vote by order, but [Keeper of the Seals François de] Barentin objected: did this mean they were to adopt the British system of government? Louis hesitated, postponing the decision. The royal session was put off until June 23.

On June 20 the Third Estate discovered its hall closed without notice or warning. It finally found asylum in a neighbouring tennis court, where, because there was talk of retiring to Paris and seeking the protection of the people, [lawyer Jean-Joseph] Mounier stepped in and proposed the famous oath, that they remain united until a constitution was established. A threatened *lit de justice*[1] had provoked enough indignation to incite the deputies, with few exceptions, to sign the oath. The Third Estate, like the Parlement of Paris, rebelled in advance against the royal will.

On June 21 Louis admitted his brothers to the Council and, finally, withdrew his support from Necker, whose programme was defeated the next day. On the 23rd an impressive show of armed force surrounded the Hôtel des Menus-Plaisirs [in Versailles], from which the public was excluded. Received in silence, Louis had Barentin read two declarations of capital interest in that they revealed quite clearly what was at stake in the struggle. They granted the Estates-General power to consent to taxes and loans and to various budget allocations, including the funds set aside for upkeep of the court. Personal liberty and freedom of the press would be guaranteed; decentralization would be carried out through the provincial estates; an extensive programme of reforms would be studied by the Estates-General. In sum, the proposals meant that a constitutional system, civil liberty, and achievement of national unity were to be the common inheritance of monarch and nation. Louis made an exception only for the clergy: its special consent was required for everything touching upon ecclesiastic organization and religious matters. Furthermore, he appeared as arbiter among the orders—if the Third Estate's decrees were overridden, so were the binding mandates that the privileged orders had invoked to compel voting by order and to postpone equality of taxation. Verification of powers would follow the system proposed on June 4. The orders were authorized to meet together to deliberate matters of general interest. The king strongly hoped that the clergy and nobility would agree to assume their share of public burdens.

But Louis failed to impose equal taxation and remained silent upon the question of admittance to public office; he expressly retained the orders and excluded vote by head from such matters as organization of future Estates-General, the manorial system, and honorific privileges. The throne thereby committed itself to preservation of the traditional social hierarchy and aristocratic preeminence. As a result of this decision, the Revolution was to mean conquest of equality of rights.

The king concluded by ordering the Estates to separate into orders and by giving them to understand that he would dissolve the assembly if its members did not obey. He then departed, followed

---

1. A constitutional procedure under the royal government by which the king could overrule decisions made by the various high law courts.

by the nobility and most of the clergy. The Third Estate did not stir. Brezé, grand master of ceremonies, repeated his sovereign's command, to which Bailly replied: "The assembled nation cannot receive orders." Sieyès declared: "You are today what you were yesterday." Ignoring, as the Parlement of Paris had done previously, the existence of a royal session, the Third Estate confirmed its own decrees and declared its members inviolable. The expressive and significant statements made by Bailly and by Sieyès deserve to be those remembered by posterity, but [Honoré-Gabriel Riqueti, comte de] Mirabeau's epigraph has proved more popular: "We will not stir from our seats unless forced by bayonets." The Commons could not have carried out this challenge, but the court thought itself in no position to find out, as agitation had already reached menacing proportions. After this point, resistance to the Third Estate disintegrated: a majority of the clergy and forty-seven nobles joined the Commons; on June 27 the king asked the others to follow suit.

The legal, peaceful revolution of the bourgeoisie, achieved by lawyers who borrowed their methods from the Parlement of Paris, was to all appearances victorious. On July 7 the Assembly appointed a committee on the constitution and two days later Mounier delivered its first report. From that day, and for history, the Assembly was the Constituent Assembly. On July 11 Lafayette[2] submitted his draft for a declaration of human rights.

The Third Estate did not lose its composure. Dictatorship of the constituent power, advocated by Sieyès, was not instituted. Royal approval was still considered necessary. The modern idea that a constitution creates its own powers before it regulates them had not yet been formulated; instead, Louis XVI, invested with his own power rooted in history, would contract with the nation. On the other hand, although the Third Estate fused the three orders, it did not proclaim their disappearance within the nation, nor did it call for election of a new assembly: the bourgeoisie therefore did not aspire to class dictatorship. On the contrary, it seemed possible that a moderate majority would be formed: the clergy, the liberal nobility, and a segment of the Commons favoured a party of the middle. Most of the nobles, however, made it known that they by no means considered the matter settled, and when troops were seen thronging around Paris and Versailles the king was suspected of preparing a show of force. He had excuses: agitation was growing; hunger multiplied disturbances; at the end of June disorderly conduct of the French guards caused a riot in Paris.

The court had not yet fixed a plan of action. To draw one up, it had to get rid of Necker and his friends. . . . Wisdom commanded that a cabinet be formed secretly, ready to appear when sufficient forces were on hand. This was a game with fearful consequences. We can understand that the king regarded deputies of the Third Estate as rebels and that the nobility considered surrender a humiliation. But if a show of arms failed, the blood spilled would stain both king and aristocracy. Nevertheless, on July 11 Necker was hastily dismissed and banished from the kingdom. . . . No further steps were taken. But the Assembly expected the worst, and the bourgeois revolution seemed lost. They were saved by popular force.

After reading this selection, consider these questions:

1. What were the issues confronting the Estates General in 1789?
2. Why did relations between the king and the Estates General break down?
3. What was the significance of the Tennis Court Oath?

---

2. Marie Joseph Yves Gilbert du Motier, Marquis de Lafayette, served on the colonists' side during the American Revolution but supported a constitutional monarchy in France.

# SELECTION 2:

# "What Is the Third Estate?"

*In preparation for the meeting of the Estates General in 1789, the monarchy called both for popular elections for representatives to the upcoming assembly and for the drawing up of lists of all popular grievances. In a remarkable democratic moment, throughout all of the cities, towns, and parishes of France, individuals from all social groups stated what they considered abuses at all levels of royal and local government. The writing of these* Cahiers de Doléance *intensified the increasingly politicized atmosphere of the winter and spring of 1789. Coupled with these elections and lists of grievances, there circulated a large number of political pamphlets directed not only at the issues to be discussed by the Estates General but also at the very organization and voting procedures of this body. The most important of these pamphlets was entitled "What Is the Third Estate?" Written by a middle-class cleric, Emmanuel-Joseph Sieyès, this pamphlet was not solely his own handiwork. As Sieyès makes clear, the Patriot Party and its vision of reforming the royal government lay behind the pamphlet's publication and wide circulation. "What Is the Third Estate?" called for the redefinition of the kingdom as a nation, an association of free individuals living under a single law of their own devising.*

*This definition of the nation as the sole source of political legitimacy was highly controversial. Under this idea of the nation, the members of the First Estate (the clergy) and the Second Estate (the nobility) were excluded by definition. According to medieval tradition and practices of the time, these groups lived under separate laws: canon law for the clergy and the so-called private law, or privilege, for the nobles. Sieyès thus defined the nation as consisting only of the Third Estate. He also further defined members of the Third Estate as citizens—those who worked and produced or otherwise were "useful" to the nation could actively participate in the government of the nation.*

**W**hat is necessary that a nation should subsist and prosper?

Individual effort and public functions.

*Individual Efforts.* All individual efforts may be included in four classes:

1. Since the earth and the waters furnish crude products for the needs of man, the first class, in logical sequence, will be that of all families which devote themselves to agricultural labor.

2. Between the first sale of products and their consumption or use, a new manipulation, more or less repeated, adds to these products a second value more or less composite. In this manner human industry succeeds in perfecting the gifts of nature, and the crude product increases two-fold, ten-fold, one

From "What Is the Third Estate?" by Emmanuel-Joseph Sieyès (1789), translated by Benjamin C. Sax.

hundred-fold in value. Such are the efforts of the second class.

3. Between production and consumption, as well as between the various stages of production, a group of intermediary agents establish themselves, useful both to producers and consumers; these are the merchants and brokers: the brokers who, comparing incessantly the demands of time and place, speculate upon the profit of retention and transportation; merchants who are charged with distribution, in the last analysis, either at wholesale or at retail. This species of utility characterizes the third class.

4. Outside of these three classes of productive and useful citizens, who are occupied with real objects of consumption and use, there is also need in a society of a series of efforts and pains, whose objects are directly useful or agreeable to the individual. This fourth class embraces all those who stand between the most distinguished and liberal professions and the less esteemed services of domestics.

Such are the efforts which sustain society. Who puts them forth? The Third Estate.

*Public Functions.* Public functions may be classified equally well, in the present state of affairs, under four recognized heads; the sword, the robe, the church and the administration. It would be superfluous to take them up one by one, for the purpose of showing that everywhere the Third Estate attends to nineteen-twentieths of them, with this distinction; that it is laden with all that which is really painful, with all the burdens which the privileged classes refuse to carry. Do we give the Third Estate credit for this? That this might come about, it would be necessary that the Third Estate should refuse to fill these places, or that it should be less ready to exercise their functions. The facts are well known. Meanwhile they have dared to impose a prohibition upon the order of the Third Estate. They have said to it: "Whatever may be your services, whatever may be your abilities, you shall go thus far; you may not pass beyond!" Certain rare exceptions, properly regarded, are but a mockery, and the terms which are indulged in on such occasions, one insult the more.

If this exclusion is a social crime against the Third Estate; if it is a veritable act of hostility, could it perhaps be said that it is useful to the public weal? Alas! who is ignorant of the effects of monopoly? If it discourages those whom it rejects, is it not well known that it tends to render less able those whom it favors? Is it not understood that every employment from which free competition is removed, becomes dear and less effective?

In setting aside any function whatsoever to serve as an appanage for a distinct class among citizens, is it not to be observed that it is no longer the man alone who does the work that it is necessary to reward, but all the unemployed members of that same caste, and also the entire families of those who are employed as well as those who are not? Is it not to be remarked that since the government has become the patrimony of a particular class, it has been distended beyond all measure; places have been created not on account of the necessities of the governed, but in the interests of the governing, etc., etc.? Has not attention been called to the fact that this order of things, which is basely and—I even presume to say—beastly respectable with us, when we find it in reading the History of Ancient Egypt or the accounts of Voyages to the Indies, is despicable, monstrous, destructive of all industry, the enemy of social progress; above all degrading to the human race in general, and particularly intolerable to Europeans, etc., etc.? But I must leave these considerations, which, if they increase the importance of the subject and throw light upon it, perhaps, along with the new light, slacken our progress.

It suffices here to have made it clear that the pretended utility of a privileged order for the public service is nothing more than a chimera; that with it all that which is burdensome in this service is performed by the Third Estate; that without it the superior places would be infinitely better filled; that they naturally ought to be the lot and the recompense of ability and recognized services, and that if privileged persons have come to usurp all the lucrative and honorable posts, it is a hateful injustice to the rank and file of citizens and at the same a treason to the public.

Who then shall dare to say that the Third Estate has not within itself all that is necessary for the formation of a complete nation? It is the strong and robust man who has one arm still shackled. If the privileged order should be abolished, the nation would be nothing less, but something more. Therefore, what is the Third Estate? Everything; but an everything shackled and oppressed. What would it be without the privileged order? Everything, but an everything free and flourishing. Nothing can succeed without it, everything would be infinitely better without the others.

It is not sufficient to show that privileged persons, far from being useful to the nation, cannot but enfeeble and injure it; it is necessary to prove further that the noble order does not enter at all into the social organization; that it may indeed be a burden upon the nation, but that it cannot of itself constitute a nation.

In the first place, it is not possible in the number of all the elementary parts of a nation to find a place for the caste of nobles. I know that there are individuals in great number whom infirmities, incapacity, incurable laziness, or the weight of bad habits render strangers to the labors of society. The exception and the abuse are everywhere found beside the rule. But it will be admitted that the less there are of these abuses, the better it will be for the State. The worst possible arrangement of all would be where not alone isolated individuals, but a whole class of citizens should take pride in remaining motionless in the midst of the general movement, and should consume the best part of the product without bearing any part in its production. Such a class is surely estranged to the nation by its indolence.

The noble order is not less estranged from the generality of us by its civil and political prerogatives.

What is a nation? A body of associates, living under a common law, and represented by the same legislature, etc.

Is it not evident that the noble order has privileges and expenditures which it dares to call its rights, but which are apart from the rights of the great body of citizens? It departs there from the common law. So its civil rights make of it an isolated people in the midst of the great nation. This is truly *imperium in imperia* [a kingdom within a kingdom].

In regard to its political rights, these also it exercises apart. It has its special representatives, which are not charged with securing the interests of the people. The body of its deputies sit apart; and when it is assembled in the same hall with the deputies of simple citizens, it is none the less true that its representation is essentially distinct and separate: it is a stranger to the nation, in the first place, by its origin, since its commission is not derived from the people; then by its object, which consists of defending not the general, but the particular interest.

The Third Estate embraces then all that which belongs to the nation; and all that which is not the Third Estate, cannot be regarded as being of the nation.

What is the Third Estate?

It is the whole.

After reading this selection, consider these questions:

1. How does Sieyès define the Third Estate?
2. What are the requirements for participation within the nation?
3. Why, according to Sieyès, should the clergy and nobility be excluded from the nation?

## SELECTION 3:

# The Declaration of the Rights of Man and Citizen

In the pamphlet "What Is the Third Estate?" Emmanuel-Joseph Sieyès provided a new way to perceive and evaluate government. The legitimate use of power did not derive from the authority of kings or the traditions of the kingdom; rather, it derived from the will of the people. This was the only legitimate form of authority, and the relation to means of production was the only just form of society. Although similar definitions had been evolving in Great Britain and had just received an original formulation in the U.S. Constitution, Sieyès and the ways in which his ideas worked themselves out in the course of the French Revolution were to have world-wide significance in the definitions of nation and citizenship.

In retrospect, "What Is the Third Estate?" functioned as a blueprint for the coming Revolution. The early debates in the Estates General and the transformation of that body into the National Assembly used the language and followed the plans laid out by this pamphlet. But it was not only the early stages of the revolution that followed Sieyès's vision. He also defined the nation as a "common will." In the political language of Jean-Jacques Rousseau, Sieyès spoke of the "general will" and the actions of sovereignty as acts of this collective political will. In this sense, the deliberations of all citizens through their legitimate representative bodies paled in importance to the direct will of the nation, which lay beyond all questions of representation. In practice, this meant that above and beyond all debates, the expression of this national will and the protection of the nation could be defined by any individual or group who claimed to speak on behalf of the nation and who were willing to fight in its defense. As the French Revolution faced increasing threats from both external and internal enemies, radicals and militants adopted this language of the national will.

By the summer of 1789 the first phase of the Revolution was well under way. The absolutist state had been transformed into a constitutional monarchy, and the Estates General became the National Assembly. On August 26, 1789, the National Assembly approved a set of basic principles upon which the revolution and the new government were to be based. These principles were entitled the Declaration of the Rights of Man and Citizen. Similar in many ways to the principles of the U.S. Declaration of Independence, these principles were expressed in the Enlightenment's universal terms of individual rights and citizenship.

The representatives of the French people, organized as a National Assembly, believing that the ignorance, neglect, or contempt of the rights of man are the sole cause of public calamities and of the corruption of governments, have determined to set forth in a solemn declaration the natural, unalienable, and sacred rights of man, in order that this declaration, being constantly before all the members of the Social body, shall remind them continually of their rights and duties; in order that the acts of the legislative power, as well as those of the executive power, may be compared at any moment with the objects and purposes of all political institutions and may thus be more respected, and, lastly, in order that the grievances of the citizens, based hereafter upon simple and incontestable principles, shall tend to the maintenance of the constitution and redound to the happiness of all. Therefore the National Assembly recognizes and proclaims, in the presence and under the auspices of the Supreme Being, the following rights of man and of the citizen:

## Articles:

1. Men are born and remain free and equal in rights. Social distinctions may be founded only upon the general good.
2. The aim of all political association is the preservation of the natural and imprescriptible rights of man. These rights are liberty, property, security, and resistance to oppression.
3. The principle of all sovereignty resides essentially in the nation. No body nor individual may exercise any authority which does not proceed directly from the nation.
4. Liberty consists in the freedom to do everything which injures no one else; hence the exercise of the natural rights of each man has no limits except those which assure to the other members of the society the enjoyment of the same rights. These limits can only be determined by law.

5. Law can only prohibit such actions as are hurtful to society. Nothing may be prevented which is not forbidden by law, and no one may be forced to do anything not provided for by law.
6. Law is the expression of the general will. Every citizen has a right to participate personally, or through his representative, in its foundation. It must be the same for all, whether it protects or punishes. All citizens, being equal in the eyes of the law, are equally eligible to all dignities and to all public positions and occupations, according to their abilities, and without distinction except that of their virtues and talents.
7. No person shall be accused, arrested, or imprisoned except in the cases and according to the forms prescribed by law. Any one soliciting, transmitting, executing, or causing to be executed, any arbitrary order, shall be punished. But any citizen summoned or arrested in virtue of the law shall submit without delay, as resistance constitutes an offense.
8. The law shall provide for such punishments only as are strictly and obviously necessary, and no one shall suffer punishment except it be legally inflicted in virtue of a law passed and promulgated before the commission of the offense.
9. As all persons are held innocent until they shall have been declared guilty, if arrest shall be deemed indispensable, all harshness not essential to the securing of the prisoner's person shall be severely repressed by law.
10. No one shall be disquieted on account of his opinions, including his religious views, provided their manifestation does not disturb the public order established by law.
11. The free communication of ideas and opinions is one of the most precious of the rights of man. Every citizen may, accordingly, speak, write, and print with freedom, but shall be responsible for such abuses of this freedom as shall be defined by law.
12. The security of the rights of man and of

---

*The Declaration of the Rights of Man* (1789). Reprinted from the website of the Avalon Project, Yale University School of Law, at http://www.yale.edu/lawweb/avalon/rightsof.htm.

the citizen requires public military forces. These forces are, therefore, established for the good of all and not for the personal advantage of those to whom they shall be intrusted.

13. A common contribution is essential for the maintenance of the public forces and for the cost of administration. This should be equitably distributed among all the citizens in proportion to their means.

14. All the citizens have a right to decide, either personally or by their representatives, as to the necessity of the public contribution; to grant this freely; to know to what uses it is put; and to fix the proportion, the mode of assessment and of collection and the duration of the taxes.

15. Society has the right to require of every public agent an account of his administration.

16. A society in which the observance of the law is not assured, nor the separation of powers defined, has no constitution at all.

17. Since property is an inviolable and sacred right, no one shall be deprived thereof except where public necessity, legally determined, shall clearly demand it, and then only on condition that the owner shall have been previously and equitably indemnified.

After reading this selection, consider these questions:

1. How does the declaration define citizenship?
2. What are the basic rights of the individual?
3. How does the Declaration of the Rights of Man and Citizen compare to the Declaration of Independence?

# SELECTION 4:

# The Declaration of the Rights of Woman and Female Citizen

*The fact that the Declaration of the Rights of Man and Citizen was couched in the ambiguous language of "man" and not of "men and women" or of "all human beings" did not go unnoticed. Whether women were to be included under its universal language was debated in the National Assembly; but it was generally agreed that the term* man *referred to males only. When a constitution for the new monarchy was finally drawn up in 1790, further distinctions were drawn between types of citizenship. The constitution defined "active" and "inactive" citizens. Active citizens had full civil and political rights in the new nation; inactive ones had only civil rights. For males, active citizenship was based on age and income level. All women, regardless of age and income, were excluded. The women of France did not unanimously accept these decisions. One of the most outspoken and most articulate opponents of these new definitions of citizenship was Olympe de Gouges. The daughter of a Parisian butcher, she challenged the dominant interpretation of the Declaration of the Rights of Man and Citizen by issuing in 1791 the Declaration of the Rights of Woman and Female Citizen. During the Reign of Terror (1793–1794), Gouges was executed for continuing to crusade for the recognition of women as full, active citizens.*

For the National Assembly to decree in its last session or in those of the next legislature:

*Preamble.* Mothers, daughters, sisters [and] representatives of the Nation demand to be constituted into a National Assembly. Believing that ignorance, forgetfulness, or contempt for the rights of woman are the only causes of public misfortunes and of the corruption of governments, [the women] have resolved to set forth in a solemn declaration the natural, inalienable, and sacred rights of women in order that this declaration, constantly exposed before all the members of the body of society, will ceaselessly remind them of their rights and duties; in order that the authoritative acts of women and the authoritative acts of men may be at any moment compared with and respectful of the purpose of all political institutions; and in order that female citizens' demands, henceforth based on the simple and incontestable principles, will always support the constitution, good morals, and the happiness of all.

Consequently, the sex that is superior in beauty as it is in courage during the sufferings of maternity recognizes and declares in the presence and under the auspices of the Supreme Being, the following Rights of Woman and of the Female Citizen.

*Article 1.* Woman is born free and lives equal to man in her rights. Social distinctions can be based only on common utility.

*Article 2.* The end of any political association is the conservation of the natural and undeniable rights of Woman and Man; these rights are liberty, property, security, and especially resistance to oppression.

*Article 3.* The principle of all sovereignty rests essentially with the Nation, which is nothing but the reunion of woman and man; no body and no individual can exercise any authority which does not come expressly from it [the nation].

*Article 4.* Liberty and justice consist of restoring all that belongs to others; thus, the exercise of the natural rights of woman are not to be limited except by the perpetual tyranny that mankind itself opposes; these limits are to be reformed by the laws of nature and reason.

*Article 5.* Laws of nature and reason proscribe all acts harmful to society; everything which is not prohibited by these wise and divine laws cannot be prevented, and no one can be constrained to do what they do not command.

*Article 6.* The law must be the expression of the general will; all female and male citizens must contribute either personally or through their representatives to its formation; it must be the same for all; male and female citizens, being equal in the eyes of the law, must be equally admitted to all dignities, positions, and public employment according to their capacity and without other distinctions besides those of their virtue and talents.

*Article 7.* No woman is an exception; she is accused, arrested, and detained in cases determined by law. Women obey like men this rigorous law.

*Article 8.* The law must establish only those penalties that are strictly and obviously necessary, and no one can be punished except by virtue of a law established and promulgated prior to the crime and legally applicable to woman.

*Article 9.* Once any woman is declared guilty, complete rigor is [to be] exercised by the law.

*Article 10.* No one is to be disquieted for his very basic opinions; woman has the right to mount the scaffold; she must equally have the right to mount the rostrum, provided that her demonstrations do not disturb the legally established public order.

*Article 11.* The free communication of thoughts and opinions is one of the most precious rights of woman, since that liberty assures that recognition

From Olympe de Gouges, *Ecrits Politiques: 1788–1791* (Paris: Ct-femmes Editions, 1993). Translation by Benjamin C. Sax.

of children by their fathers. Each female citizen thus must say freely, I am the mother of a child which belongs to you, without being forced by a barbarous prejudice to hide the truth; [an exception may be made] to respond to the abuse of this liberty in cases determined by the law.

Article 12. The guarantee of the rights of woman and the female citizen implies a major utility; this guarantee must be instituted for the advantage of all, and not for the particular benefit of those to whom it is entrusted.

Article 13. For the support of the public force and the expenses of administration, the contributions of woman and man are equal; she shared all the duties and all the painful tasks; therefore, she must have the same share in the distribution of positions, employment, offices, dignities, and work.

Article 14. Female and male citizens have the right to verify, either by themselves or through their representatives, the necessity of the public contribution. This can only apply to women if they are granted an equal share, not only of wealth, but also of public administration, and in the determination of the proportion, the base, the collection, and the duration of the tax.

Article 15. All women, joined for the tax purposes to the aggregate of men, have the right to demand an accounting of his administration from any public agent.

Article 16. No society has a constitution without the guarantee of rights and the separation of powers; the constitution is null if the majority of individuals comprising the Nation have not cooperated in drafting it.

Article 17. Property belongs to both sexes whether united or separate; for each it is an inviolable and sacred right; no one can be deprived of it, since it is the true patrimony of nature, unless the legally determined public need obviously dictates it, and then only with a just and prior indemnity.

*Postscript.* Woman, wake up; the tocsin [warning signal] of reason is being heard throughout the whole universe; discover your rights. The powerful empire of nature is no longer surrounded by prejudice, fanaticism, superstition, and lies. The flame of truth has dispersed all the clouds of folly and usurpation. Enslaved man has multiplied his strength and needs recourse to yours to break his chains. Having become free, he has become unjust to his companion. Oh, women, women! When will you cease to be blind? What advantage have you received from the Revolution? A more pronounced contempt, a more marked disdain. In the centuries of corruption you ruled only over the weakness of men. Your empire is destroyed. What will you rest on then— the conviction in the injustices of man? The reclamation of your patrimony, based on the wise decrees of nature—what have you to dread from such a fine undertaking? The *bon mot* of the legislator of the marriage of Cana [the occasion of Christ's first miracle of turning water into wine]? Do you fear that our French legislators, improvers of that morality, long ensnared by political practices now out of date, will only say again to you: Women, what is there in common between you and us? Everything, you will have to answer. If they persist in their weakness in putting this non sequitur in contradiction to their principles, courageously oppose the force of reason to the empty pretensions of superiority; unite yourselves beneath the standards of philosophy, deploy all the energy of your character, and you will soon see these haughty men, not as servile admirers at your feet, but as proud to share with you the treasures of the Supreme Being. Regardless of what barriers confront you, it is in your power to free yourselves; you have only to want to. Let us pass now to the shocking tableau of what you have been in society; and since national education is in question at this moment, let us see whether our wise legislators will think judiciously about the education of women.

Women have done more harm than good. Constraint and dissimulation have been their lot. What force had robbed them of, ruse returned to them; they had recourse to all the resources of their charms, and the most irreproachable person did not resist them. Poison and the sword were both subject to them; they commanded in crime as in fortune. The French government, especially, depended through the centuries on the nocturnal administration of women; the cabinet kept no secret from their indiscretion; ambassadorial post, command, ministry, presidency, pontificate, college of cardinal; finally, anything which characterizes the folly of men, profane and sacred, all have been subject to the cupidity and ambition of their sex, formerly contemptible and respected, and since the Revolution, respectable and scorned.

In this sort of contradictory situation, what remarks could I not make! I have but a moment to make them, but this moment will fix the attention of the remotest posterity. Under the Old Regime, all was vicious, all was guilty; but could not the amelioration of conditions be perceived even in the substance of vices? A woman only had to be beautiful or amiable; when she possessed these two advantages, she saw a hundred fortunes at her feet. If she did not profit from them, she had a bizarre character or a rare philosophy which made her scorn wealth; then she was deemed to be like a crazy woman; the most indecent made herself respected with gold; commerce in women was a kind of industry in the first class [of society], which, henceforth, will have no more credit. If it still had it, the Revolution would be lost, and under the new relationships we would always be corrupted; however, reason can always be deceived [into believing] that any other road to fortune is closed to the woman whom a man buys, like the slave on the African coasts. The difference is great; that is known. The slave is commanded by the master; but if the master gives her liberty without recompense, and at an age when the slave has lost all her charms, what will become of this unfortunate woman? The victim of contempt, even the doors of charity are closed to her; she is poor and old, they say; why did she not know how to make her fortune. Reason finds other examples that are even more touching. A young, inexperienced woman, seduced by a man whom she loves, will abandon her parents to follow him; the ingrate will leave her after a few years, and the older she has become with him, the more inhuman is his inconstancy; if she has children, he will likewise abandon them. If he is rich, he will consider himself excused from sharing his fortune with his noble victims. If some involvement binds him to his duties, he will deny them,

trusting that the laws will support him. If he is married, any other obligation loses its rights. Then what laws remain to extirpate vice all the way to its roots? The law of dividing wealth and public administration between men and women. It can easily be seen that one who is born into a rich family gains very much from such equal sharing. But the one born into a poor family with merit and virtue, what is her lot? Poverty and opprobrium. If she does not precisely excel in music or painting, she cannot be admitted to any public function when she has all the capacity for it. I do not want to give only a sketch of things; I will go more deeply into this in the new edition of all my political writings, with notes, which I propose to give to the public in a few days.

I take up my text again on the subject of morals. Marriage is the tomb of trust and love. The married woman can with impunity give bastards to her husband, and also give them the wealth which does not belong to them. The woman who is unmarried has only one feeble right; ancient and inhuman laws refuse to her for her children the right to the name and the wealth of their father; no new laws have been made in this matter. If it is considered a paradox and an impossibility on my part to try to give my sex an honorable and just consistency, I leave it to men to attain glory for dealing with this matter; but while we wait, the way can be prepared through national education, the restoration of morals, and conjugal conventions.

(14 September 1791)

After reading this selection, consider these questions:
1. What is the purpose of Gouges's declaration?
2. What does Gouges mean by the "social contract" between man and woman?
3. How does Gouges define equality for women?

## SELECTION 5:

# An Alternative Interpretation of the Revolution

*From one perspective, the French Revolution marked a radical break from what preceded it. It clearly overthrew absolutism and established a new concept of legitimate political power in the idea of the nation. From another perspective, however, this break was less radical than it appeared. Although the exercise of political power was now legitimated in the name of the will of the people, its actual institutional practices remained the same as those of the centralizing bureaucratic state of absolutism. The new government created by the Revolution, especially as it was consolidated under Napoléon, relied on a vast and highly organized bureaucratic setup, directly run by the government in Paris. In the face of this bureaucracy, the right to vote and elect various representatives, as well as the power to change administrations and even forms of government (as France often did in the course of the nineteenth century), mattered less than the preservation of a basic structure of the centralized, bureaucratic state. This alternate interpretation of the Revolution—increasingly accepted by historians today—was originally proposed by Alexis de Tocqueville (1805–1859). Best known for his study of democratic principles as they were realized in the United States (*Democracy in America, *1835*), Tocqueville first put forth his thesis of the continuity of institutional forms from absolutism to the nineteenth-century state in his unfinished history of the revolution. In *The Old Regime and the French Revolution, *he argues that the French Revolution of 1789 actually fulfilled the plans for centralized political authority that lay behind the administrative innovations of the absolutist state. The following selection opens with Tocqueville's discussion of Louis XVI's administrative reforms of 1787.*

A year before the Revolution the King issued an edict overhauling the entire judicial system. Several new jurisdictions were introduced, a number of others abolished, and all the rules defining the powers of the various courts were altered. Now, as I have already pointed out, the number of persons engaged in trying cases or executing orders passed by the courts was at this time immense; one might almost say that the whole middle class was concerned in one way or another with the administration of justice. Thus the changes made in the judicial system of the country had a disturbing effect on both the social status and the pecuniary situation of thousands of families; they felt as if the ground had been cut from under their feet. . . .

But it was above all the drastic reform of the administration (in the widest sense of the term) which took place in 1787 that not only threw

From *The Old Regime and the French Revolution,* by Alexis de Tocqueville, translated by Stuart Gilbert. Copyright © 1955 by Doubleday and Company. Used by permission of Doubleday, a division of Random House, Inc.

public affairs into confusion but had repercussions on the private life of every Frenchman. . . .

Totally unlike the old system of administration and changing out of recognition both the manner in which public business was transacted and, more, the social status of private citizens, the new system (so the King decreed) was to come into force everywhere simultaneously and under practically the same form; that is to say without the least respect for ancient customs, local usages, or the particular conditions of each province. So deeply had this notion of standardized administration, destined to be a characteristic of the Revolution, already permeated the monarchical government which it was soon to sweep away.

It was easy then to see how large a part is played by habit in the functioning of political institutions and how much more easily a nation can cope with complicated, well-nigh unintelligible laws to which it is accustomed than with a simpler legal system that is new.

There had previously existed in France a host of authorities, widely varying from province to province and none of them with recognized, well-defined limits, the result being that their fields of action often overlapped. Nonetheless, the administration of the country under the old order had come to run relatively smoothly. The new authorities, however, who were fewer in number, with similar but carefully restricted powers, tended in practice to become entangled with each other, the result being a state of confusion often ending in a deadlock. Moreover, the new system had a grave defect which alone would have been enough (anyhow in its early days) to prevent its working efficiently. This was that all the powers it instituted were *collective*. . . .

These being the only known forms of administration, when one was given up the other was adopted. It is a singular fact that in a nation so enlightened and one in which a central administration had so long played a vital part, nobody should have thought of trying to combine the two systems and distinguishing, without divorcing, the executive from the legislative, directive power. It was left to the nineteenth century to hit on this idea, self-evident though it seems to us today. Indeed, it is the only great discovery in the field of

public administration for which we can claim credit. But the nation opted for the other alternative: the administrative methods of the past were transposed into the political sphere, and following the tradition of the old régime, detested though it was, the system practiced in the provincial Estates and small urban municipalities was adopted by the National Convention [the legislative body of France during the radical phase of the revolution]. Thus what had formerly been no more than an impediment to the proper handling of public affairs gave rise directly to the Reign of Terror.

Meanwhile, in 1787, the provincial assemblies were invested with most of the powers that had hitherto been the Intendants'. It was now their duty, subject to the orders of the central government, to assess the *taille* [tax] and supervise its collection; to decide what public works were to be undertaken and to have them duly carried out. All employees of the Highways Department, from the Inspector down to the foremen of the labor gangs, were under their direct control. The assembly was responsible for seeing that these men carried out its orders, and was instructed to report on their work to the Minister and advise him as to suitable rates of pay. The administration of the villages was now transferred almost entirely to the assembly, which was to try as a court of first instance most of the suits which up to now had been heard by the Intendant. Some of these functions were obviously quite unsuitable for such a large and irresponsible body of men, complete novices, moreover, in such matters. . . .

Sometimes, however, the new governing bodies . . . [displayed] an excess of zeal and misdirected energy. In their eagerness for reform they sought to sweep away the old system altogether or to amend long-standing defects in the administration at a moment's notice. Alleging that the management of the towns now devolved on them, they took charge of all municipal affairs and, full of excellent intentions, created total chaos.

When we reflect on the immense power that had been exercised for so long a time by the central government, the host of private interests in which it had a hand, how many enterprises linked up with it or needed its support; when we remember that it was on the administration more than on his personal efforts that the Frenchman relied for the success of his business undertakings, for the regular supply of his daily needs, for the upkeep of the roads he used, and in fact for everything that could ensure his peace of mind and material well-being—when we remember all this, we can easily realize the vast number of people whose personal interests were injuriously affected by the malady that had attacked the body politic. . . .

Thus, though there had been as yet no changes in the constitutional law of the country and the structure of the State had not been tampered with, the innovations introduced in secondary laws had given rise to much confusion and ill-feeling. Even such as had remained intact were threatened, for the central power itself had announced the abolition of practically every existing law. Though this is hardly mentioned by present-day historians, the abrupt, wholesale remodeling of the entire administration which preceded the political revolution had already caused one of the greatest upheavals that have ever taken place in the life of a great nation. This first revolution had an incommensurable influence on the second, and, indeed, caused it to differ entirely from all the revolutions the world had known before or has witnessed during the last half century. . . .

We have had several other revolutions in France since '89, revolutions which changed the whole structure of the government of the country from top to bottom. Most of them broke out suddenly and were carried through by force in flagrant violation of existing laws. All the same, the disturbances they caused never were widespread or lasted long; usually, in fact, the majority of the population was almost unaffected by them; sometimes it hardly knew a revolution was taking place.

The reason is that since '89 the administrative system has always stood firm amid the debacles of political systems. There might be dynastic changes and alterations in the structure of the State machine, but the course of day-to-day affairs was neither interrupted nor deflected. Everyone kept to the rules and customs with which he was familiar in coping with the situations, trivial in themselves but of much personal import, which so frequently recur in the life of the ordinary citizen. He had to deal with and take orders from the same subaltern [subordinate] authorities as in the past and, oftener than not, the same officials. For though in each successive revolution the administration was, so to speak, decapitated, its body survived intact and active. The same duties were performed by the same civil servants, whose practical experience kept the nation on an even keel through the worst political storms. These men administered the country or rendered justice in the name of the King, then in that of the Republic, thereafter in the Emperor's. And when, with the changing tides of fortune, the cycle repeated itself in the present century, the same men continued administering and judging, first for the King, then for the Republic, then for the Emperor on exactly the same lines. Their business was less to be good citizens than good judges or administrators, and whenever the initial shock had spent its force, one might well have imagined that the nation had never swerved from the old groove.

After reading this selection, consider these questions:
1. What is Tocqueville's thesis on the relation of absolutism to post-revolutionary forms of government?
2. What changes did the royal government make in administration in the years before the French Revolution?
3. In what ways did post-revolutionary France continue the administrative forms of the absolutist state?

# CHAPTER 6
# The Age of Nationalism and Liberalism

The French Revolution lasted from 1789 through 1799. If we add the years of Napoléon Bonaparte's rule of France and domination of continental Europe, which ended to his defeat at Waterloo in 1815, we see that Europe and especially France experienced more than a quarter century of revolution, threats of revolution, and wars. It is therefore understandable that when the Congress of Vienna met between 1814 and 1815 to restore order and redraw the boundaries of continental Europe, not only heads of state but also most individuals welcomed peace and stability. The congress established this peace by creating a system of international treaties. By these treaties, the great powers—Great Britain, Prussia, Austria, and Russia (and beginning in the 1820s, France)—also agreed to restore, as far as possible, the older, "legitimate" rulers to their prerevolutionary or pre-Napoleonic positions of power.

Generally referred to as the Age of Restoration, the next thirty years witnessed the dominance of more conservative and definitely antirevolutionary forces throughout Europe. The French Revolution itself had gone through several distinct and very different stages. From the liberal phase of the constitutional monarchy to the republic and its radical Reign of Terror, the Revolution meant various things to various groups. Conservatives tended to emphasize the wars, violence, and destruction, blaming them on the principles of the Enlightenment. To some degree in Great Britain and France, but especially in Prussia, Austria, and Russia, attempts were undertaken to control the spread of revolutionary thought and strengthen the ties between the crown and the church. Clemens von Metternich, the foreign minister of the Austrian Empire, emerged as Europe's most influential statesman. He dominated international relations on the continent and controlled much of the internal affairs within the thirty-nine states of the German Confederation.

At the other end of the political spectrum, more liberal and definitely more revolutionary individuals saw in the French Revolution not just the confirmation of the basic ideas of sovereignty based on popular consent and the political and legal equality of all citizens. After the Revolution, liberals wanted to strengthen democratic institutions where they already existed (in France, for instance, or in embryonic forms as in Great Britain) or to create them where they did not (Prussia, Austria, and Russia). One way to understand the history of recent modern Europe is to trace the growth of liberalism not only in Great Britain and France but also in Prussia, Austria, and (at the end of the nineteenth century) in Russia. Within this framework, the twentieth century was to witness the challenges to liberalism in various types of fascism and Marxism.

Complicating this interpretation, however, is the idea of nationalism. *Nationalism* does not simply mean that an individual belongs to a particular people or tradition. Such recognition must be as old as the human race itself. As it came to be defined during the nineteenth century, *nationalism* emphasized that the nation represented one of the forms—if not the most important form—of group identification for the individual. The nation gave to the individual a language, a set of values, and a culture. Politically, it should be the basis of citizenship of all individuals who shared this language, values, and culture. The nation should be the foundation of all legitimate political authority within the state and for the independent actions among other nation-states.

Nationalism in this sense had to do with birth, culture, and the united will of a particular people. Such notions were bound at some point to run counter to the ideas of rational citizenship based on universal human rights, rational politics founded on a universal notion of human happiness, and an overall commitment to improving the lot of humanity as a whole. In other words, liberalism and nationalism, although not diametrically opposed to each other, definitely pointed in different directions in their basic definitions of the individual, political institutions, and social organization. These tensions can be seen in the "founding document" of the French Revolution—the pamphlet "What Is the Third Estate?". Emmanuel-Joseph Sieyès was unaware of this tension, but his definition of the nation as based on those living under a common law and thus having the right to change the law—a nation as a particular division of a universally human condition—conflicted with his second definition of the nation as a group of individuals united by a common will that transcended reason and representative politics.

During the first half of the nineteenth century, however, liberal principles and national will seemed to be united. The call for the creation of a nation went hand in hand with the call for liberal institutions. Liberals sought to create states based on the distinctive national cultural groupings of Europe and within these states to establish representative forms of government. These forces gained ground in the Europe of the 1840s. In 1848 a series of revolutions broke out throughout continental Europe, from Hungary through Italy and Spain to Austria, Prussia, and the smaller German states. This remarkable series of revolutions was sparked by the outbreak in February of a revolution in France. The time seemed to have come to complete the unfinished business of liberal reform begun by the great French Revolution of 1789. Each of these revolutions mixed to varying degrees liberal principles with national aspirations. Throughout Europe these revolutions were for the most part unsuccessful. France witnessed a change of regimes, becoming a republic once more. Austria saw a change in monarch but no new institutions or even a change of dynasty; and Prussia did not even have a change in its monarch.

Although these revolutions were all repressed by 1849, order was often restored by the government's promise to bring about more liberal reforms in the near future. These promises kept the principles of liberal government alive, but they remained for the most part merely plans until the 1860s and 1870s; even then, they were only partially instituted. The more direct and longer lasting consequences of 1848 were the strengthening of state power and the further attempts to unite their people in support of the state. In other words, after 1848 nationalism was no longer exclusively a liberal principle. The more conservative forces of Europe were to find in nationalism a way to sustain their control and increase their power. Such a combination was to last for the most part until World War I. Although the most prominent political leaders of the second half of the nineteenth century, such as Napoléon III in France and Otto von Bismarck in a newly united Germany, played with both liberal and conservative elements in different stages of their political careers, they always called on the strengthening of the ties between the government, the ruling classes, and the nationalism of the great mass of the population. Even in Great Britain, politics in the second half of the century saw the Conservative Party and not the Liberals seeking the support of the majority of the citizens through various land reforms and social welfare policies.

# SELECTION 1:

# The Continuity of the Enlightenment

*Even in the face of these conservative currents, the basic principles of the Enlightenment that had become actualized during the French Revolution were neither totally repudiated nor entirely forgotten. England, of course, did not experience a political revolution or foreign domination in the eighteenth century; but the principles of the Enlightenment were given a dis-*

*tinctive English form in the philosophy of utilitarianism. Jeremy Bentham (1748–1832), the father of utilitarianism, came out of the English empiricist tradition of John Locke and David Hume. He devised a general principle of "utility" as the central axiom of a systematic philosophy, comparable in the fields of morals and politics to the concept of gravity in Isaac Newton's* Principia Mathematica. *As the following selection from* An Introduction to the Principles of Morals and Legislation *(1780) indicates, Bentham argues from a universal definition of human nature to the notion of utilitarian ethics in terms of "the greatest good for the greatest number."*

Nature has placed mankind under the governance of two sovereign masters, *pain* and *pleasure*. It is for them alone to point out what we ought to do, as well as to determine what we shall do. On the one hand the standard of right and wrong, on the other the chain of causes and effects, are fastened to their throne. They govern us in all we do, in all we say, in all we think: every effort we can make to throw off our subjection, will serve but to demonstrate and confirm it. In words a man may pretend to abjure their empire: but in reality he will remain subject to it all the while. The *principle of utility* recognises this subjection, and assumes it for the foundation of that system, the object of which is to rear the fabric of felicity by the hands of reason and of law. Systems which attempt to question it, deal in sounds instead of sense, in caprice instead of reason, in darkness instead of light.

But enough of metaphor and declamation: it is not by such means that moral science is to be improved.

The principle of utility is the foundation of the present work: it will be proper therefore at the outset to give an explicit and determinate account of what is meant by it. By the principle of utility is meant that principle which approves or disapproves of every action whatsoever, according to the tendency which it appears to have to augment or diminish the happiness of the party whose interest is in question: or, what is the same thing in other words, to promote or to oppose that happiness. I say of every action whatsoever; and there-

fore not only of every action of a private individual, but of every measure of government.

By utility is meant that property in any object, whereby it tends to produce benefit, advantage, pleasure, good, or happiness, (all this in the present case comes to the same thing) or (what comes again to the same thing) to prevent the happening of mischief, pain, evil, or unhappiness to the party whose interest is considered: if that party be the community in general, then the happiness of the community: if a particular individual, then the happiness of that individual.

The interest of the community is one of the most general expressions that can occur in the phraseology of morals: no wonder that the meaning of it is often lost. When it has a meaning, it is this. The community is a fictitious *body*, composed of the individual persons who are considered as constituting as it were its *members*. The interest of the community then is, what?—the sum of the interests of the several members who compose it.

It is in vain to talk of the interest of the community, without understanding what is the interest of the individual. A thing is said to promote the interest, or to be *for* the interest, of an individual, when it tends to add to the sum total of his pleasures: or, what comes to the same thing, to diminish the sum total of his pains.

An action then may be said to be conformable to the principle of utility, or, for shortness sake, to utility, (meaning with respect to the community at large) when the tendency it has to augment the happiness of the community is greater than any it has to diminish it.

A measure of government (which is but a particular kind of action, performed by a particular person or persons) may be said to be conformable

---

From *An Introduction to the Principles of Morals and Legislation*, by Jeremy Bentham (Oxford: Clarendon Press, 1879).

to or dictated by the principle of utility, when in like manner the tendency which it has to augment the happiness of the community is greater than any which it has to diminish it.

When an action, or in particular a measure of government, is supposed by a man to be conformable to the principle of utility, it may be convenient, for the purposes of discourse, to imagine a kind of law or dictate, called a law or dictate of utility: and to speak of the action in question, as being conformable to such law or dictate.

A man may be said to be a partizan of the principle of utility, when the approbation or disapprobation he annexes to any action, or to any measure, is determined by and proportioned to the tendency which he conceives it to have to augment or to diminish the happiness of the community: or in other words, to its conformity or unconformity to the laws or dictates of utility.

Of an action that is conformable to the principle of utility one may always say either that it is one that ought to be done, or at least that it is not one that ought not to be done. One may say also, that it is right it should be done: at least that it is not wrong it should be done; that it is a right action; at least that it is not a wrong action. When thus interpreted, the words *ought*, and *right* and *wrong*, and others of that stamp, have a meaning: when otherwise, they have none.

After reading this selection, consider these questions:
1. How does Bentham define *utility*?
2. How is utility related to the principles of government?
3. What does Bentham mean by the phrase *principle of utility*?

## SELECTION 2:

# The Principles of Nineteenth-Century Liberalism

*Utilitarianism reached its highest expression in the philosophy of John Stuart Mill (1806–1873). He was also the nineteenth century's foremost spokesman for the principles of liberalism. In* On Liberty *(1859), Mill concedes that the history of liberty up to the nineteenth century consisted of the contests between monarchical centralization and the good of the people at large. Throughout the ages the problem, then, was of limiting the powers of government. In the nineteenth century, however, Mill contends, political power had passed through liberal institutions into the hands of greater numbers of individuals. Now, the threats to liberty were different. The majority was inclined to limit or even deny the freedom of individuals, whether explicitly through legislation (what Mill calls "acts of public authority") or more subtly through moral and social pressure (what Mill refers to as "collective opinion" or "the tyranny of the majority").*

The aim, therefore, of patriots was to set limits to the power which the ruler should be suffered [permitted] to exercise over the community; and this limitation was what they meant by liberty. It was attempted in two ways. First, by obtaining a recognition of certain immunities, called political liberties or rights, which it was to be regarded as a breach of duty in the ruler to infringe; and which if he did infringe, specific resistance, or general rebellion, was held to be justifiable. A second, and generally a later expedient, was the establishment of constitutional checks, by which the consent of the community, or of a body of some sort, supposed to represent its interests, was made a necessary condition to some of the more important acts of the governing power. To the first of these modes of limitation, the ruling power, in most European countries, was compelled, more or less, to submit. It was not so with the second; and, to attain this, or when already in some degree possessed, to attain it more completely, became everywhere the principal object of the lovers of liberty. And so long as mankind were content to combat one enemy by another, and to be ruled by a master, on condition of being guaranteed more or less efficaciously against his tyranny, they did not carry their aspirations beyond this point.

A time, however, came, in the progress of human affairs, when men ceased to think it a necessity of nature that their governors should be an independent power, opposed in interest to themselves. It appeared to them much better that the various magistrates of the State should be their tenants or delegates, revocable at their pleasure. In that way alone, it seemed, could they have complete security that the powers of government would never be abused to their disadvantage. By degrees this new demand for elective and temporary rulers became the prominent object of the exertions of the popular party, wherever any such party existed; and superseded, to a considerable extent, the previous efforts to limit the power of

rulers. As the struggle proceeded for making the ruling power emanate from the periodical choice of the ruled, some persons began to think that too much importance had been attached to the limitation of the power itself. That (it might seem) was a resource against rulers whose interests were habitually opposed to those of the people. What was now wanted was, that the rulers should be identified with the people; that their interest and will should be the interest and will of the nation. The nation did not need to be protected against its own will. There was no fear of its tyrannizing over itself. Let the rulers be effectually responsible to it, promptly removable by it, and it could afford to trust them with power of which it could itself dictate the use to be made. Their power was but the nation's own power, concentrated, and in a form convenient for exercise. This mode of thought, or rather perhaps of feeling, was common among the last generation of European liberalism, in the Continental section of which it still apparently predominates. . . .

In time, however, a democratic republic [the United States] came to occupy a large portion of the earth's surface, and made itself felt as one of the most powerful members of the community of nations; and elective and responsible government became subject to the observations and criticisms which wait upon a great existing fact. It was now perceived that such phrases as "self-government," and "the power of the people over themselves," do not express the true state of the case. The "people" who exercise the power are not always the same people with those over whom it is exercised; and the "self-government" spoken of is not the government of each by himself, but of each by all the rest. The will of the people, moreover, practically means the will of the most numerous or the most active part of the people; the majority, or those who succeed in making themselves accepted as the majority; the people, consequently may desire to oppress a part of their number; and precautions are as much needed against this as against any other abuse of power. The limitation, therefore, of the power of government over individuals loses none of its importance when the holders of power are regularly accountable to the community, that is, to the strongest party therein. This view of

From "On Liberty," by John Stuart Mill (New York: Longman, 1892).

things, recommending itself equally to the intelligence of thinkers and to the inclination of those important classes in European society to whose real or supposed interests democracy is adverse, has had no difficulty in establishing itself; and in political speculations "the tyranny of the majority" is now generally included among the evils against which society requires to be on its guard.

Like other tyrannies, the tyranny of the majority was at first, and is still vulgarly, held in dread, chiefly as operating through the acts of the public authorities. But reflecting [thinking] persons perceived that when society is itself the tyrant— society collectively over the separate individuals who compose it—its means of tyrannizing are not restricted to the acts which it may do by the hands of its political functionaries. Society can and does execute its own mandates: and if it issues wrong mandates instead of right, or any mandates at all in things with which it ought not to meddle, it practices a social tyranny more formidable than many kinds of political oppression, since, though not usually upheld by such extreme penalties, it leaves fewer means of escape, penetrating much more deeply into the details of life,

and enslaving the soul itself. Protection, therefore, against the tyranny of the magistrate is not enough; there needs protection also against the tyranny of the prevailing opinion and feeling; against the tendency of society to impose, by other means than civil penalties, its own ideas and practices as rules of conduct on those who dissent from them; to fetter the development, and, if possible, prevent the formation, of any individuality not in harmony with its ways, and compel all characters to fashion themselves upon the model of its own. There is a limit to the legitimate interference of collective opinion with individual independence: and to find that limit, and maintain it against encroachment, is as indispensable to a good condition of human affairs, as protection against political despotism.

After reading this selection, consider these questions:

1. How does Mill describe the recent political history of Europe?
2. What is "the tyranny of the majority"?
3. What are the solutions to this problem of tyranny, according to Mill?

# SELECTION 3:
# The Origins of Conservatism

*Conservatism, as a political doctrine, had its origins in a reaction to the French Revolution of 1789. Even when the Revolution was in its initial phases, the British politician and political theorist Edmund Burke laid out its principles. In his book* Reflections on the Revolution in France *(1790), Burke criticized the French for thinking they could construct an entirely new form of government and reorganize society along the rational lines proposed by the philosophes. Burke predicted, correctly as it turned out, that implementation of rational principles would eventually lead to acts of violence and the use of force as reality was made to conform to the demands of reason. For Burke, all change in government and society must be gradual and in accordance with the specific national characteristics of the people.*

A state without the means of some change is without the means of its conservation. Without such means it might even risk the loss of that part of the constitution which it wished the most religiously to preserve. The two principles of conservation and correction operated strongly at the two critical periods of the Restoration and Revolution, when England found itself without a king. At both those periods the nation had lost the bond of union in their [ancient] edifice; they did not, however, dissolve the whole fabric. On the contrary, in both cases they regenerated the deficient part of the old constitution through the parts which were not impaired. They kept these old parts exactly as they were, that the part recovered might be suited to them. They acted by the ancient organized states in the shape of their old organization, and not by the organic *moleculae* of a disbanded people. At no time, perhaps, did the sovereign legislature manifest a more tender regard to that fundamental principle of British constitutional policy, than at the time of the Revolution, when it deviated from the direct line of hereditary succession. The crown was carried somewhat out of the line in which it had before moved; but the new line was derived from the same stock. It was still a line of hereditary descent; still an hereditary descent in the same blood, though an hereditary descent qualified with protestantism. When the legislature altered the direction, but kept the principle, they shewed that they held it inviolable.

On this principle, the law of inheritance had admitted some amendment in the old time, and long before the [era] of the Revolution. Some time after the conquest great questions arose upon the legal principles of hereditary descent. It became a matter of doubt, whether the heir *per capita*[1] or the heir *per stirpes*[2] was to succeed; but

1. by head. An inheritance equally distributed among all beneficiaries.   2. by the roots. A preference given to certain beneficiaries of an inheritance.

From *Reflections on the Revolution in France*, by Edmund Burke (Oxford: Clarendon Press, 1898).

whether the heir *per capita* gave way when the heirdom *per stirpes* took place, or the Catholic heir when the Protestant was preferred, the inheritable principle survived with a sort of immortality through all transmigrations—["through the years the fortune of the house stands, and grandfathers' grandfathers augment the roll"]. This is the spirit of our constitution, not only in its settled course, but in all its revolutions. Whoever came in, or however he came in, whether he obtained the crown by law, or by force, the hereditary succession was either continued or adopted.

The gentlemen of the Society for Revolutions see nothing in that of 1688 but the deviation from the constitution; and they take the deviation from the principle for the principle. They have little regard to the obvious consequences of their doctrine, though they must see, that it leaves positive authority in very few of the positive institutions of this country. When such an unwarrantable maxim is once established, that no throne is lawful but the elective, no one act of the princes who preceded their [era] of fictitious election can be valid. Do these theorists mean to imitate some of their predecessors, who dragged the bodies of our [ancient] sovereigns out of the quiet of their tombs? Do they mean to attaint and disable backwards [retroactively condemn] all the kings that have reigned before the Revolution, and consequently to stain the throne of England with the blot of a continual usurpation? Do they mean to invalidate, annul, or to call into question, together with the titles of the whole line of our kings, that great body of our statute law which passed under those whom they treat as usurpers? To annul laws of inestimable value to our liberties—of as great value at least as any which have passed at or since the period of the Revolution? If kings, who did not owe their crown to the choice of their people, had no title to make laws, what will become of . . . the *petition of right?*—of the act of *habeas corpus?* Do these new doctors of the rights of men presume to assert, that King James the Second, who came to the crown as next of blood, according to the rules of a then unqualified succession, was not to all intents and purposes a lawful king of England, before he had done any of those acts which were justly construed into an abdication of his crown? If he was not, much trouble in parliament might have been saved at the period these gentlemen commemorate. But King James was a bad king with a good title, and not an usurper. The princes who succeeded according to the act of parliament which settled the crown on the electress Sophia and on her descendants, being Protestants, came in as much by a title of inheritance as King James did. He came in according to the law, as it stood at his accession to the crown; and the princes of the House of Brunswick [now known as the House of Windsor, the present British royal family] came to the inheritance of the crown, not by election, but by the law, as it stood at their several accessions of Protestant descent and inheritance, as I hope I have shewn sufficiently.

The law by which this royal family is specifically destined to the succession, is the act of the 12th and 13th of King William [III]. The terms of this act bind "us and our *heirs,* and our *posterity,* to them, their *heirs,* and their *posterity,*" being Protestants, to the end of time, in the same words as the declaration of right had bound us to the heirs of King William and Queen Mary. It therefore secures both an hereditary crown and an hereditary allegiance. On what ground, except the constitutional policy of forming an establishment to secure that kind of succession which is to preclude a choice of the people for ever, could the legislature have fastidiously rejected the fair and abundant choice which our own country presented to them, and searched in strange lands for a foreign princess, from whose womb the line of our future rulers were to derive their title to govern millions of men through a series of ages? . . .

You might, if you pleased, have profited of our example, and have given to your recovered freedom a correspondent dignity. Your privileges, though discontinued, were not lost to memory. Your constitution, it is true, whilst you were out of possession, suffered waste and dilapidation; but you possessed in some parts the walls, and in all the foundations of a noble and venerable castle. You might have repaired those walls; you might have built on those old foundations. Your constitution was suspended before it was perfected; but you had the elements of a constitution

very nearly as good as could be wished. In your old states [the Estates General] you possessed that variety of parts corresponding with the various descriptions of which your community was happily composed; you had all that combination, and all that opposition of interests, you had that action and counteraction which, in the natural and in the political world, from the reciprocal struggle of discordant powers, draws out the harmony of the universe. These opposed and conflicting interests, which you considered as so great a blemish in your old and in our present constitution, interpose a salutary check to all precipitate resolutions; they render deliberation a matter not of choice, but of necessity; they make all change a subject of *compromise,* which naturally begets moderation; they produce *temperaments,* preventing the sore evil of harsh, crude, unqualified reformations; and rendering all the headlong exertions of arbitrary power, in the few or in the many, for ever impracticable. Through that diversity of members and interests, general liberty had as many securities as there were separate views in the several orders; whilst by pressing down the whole by the weight of a real monarchy, the separate parts would have been prevented from warping and starting from their allotted places.

You had all these advantages in your [ancient] states; but you chose to act as if you had never been moulded into civil society, and had every thing to begin anew. You began ill, because you began by despising every thing that belonged to you. You set up your trade without a capital. If the last generations of your country appeared without much lustre in your eyes, you might have passed them by, and derived your claims from a more early race of ancestors. Under a pious predilection for those ancestors, your imaginations would have realized in them a standard of virtue and wisdom, beyond the vulgar practice of the hour: and you would have risen with the example to whose imitation you aspired. Respecting your forefathers, you would have been taught to respect yourselves. You would not have chosen to consider the French as a people of yesterday, as a nation of low-born servile wretches until the emancipating year of 1789. In order to furnish, at the expence of your honour, an excuse to your apologists here for several enormities of yours, you would not have been content to be represented as a gang of Maroon [fugitive] slaves, suddenly broke loose from the house of bondage, and therefore to be pardoned for your abuse of the liberty to which you were not accustomed and ill fitted. Would it not, my worthy friend, have been wiser to have you thought, what I, for one, always thought you, a generous and gallant nation, long misled to your disadvantage by your high and romantic sentiments of fidelity, honour, and loyalty; that events had been unfavourable to you, but that you were not enslaved through any illiberal or servile disposition; that in your most devoted submission, you were actuated by a principle of public spirit, and that it was your country you worshipped, in the person of your king? Had you made it to be understood, that in the delusion of this amiable error you had gone further than your wise ancestors; that you were resolved to resume your ancient privileges, whilst you preserved the spirit of your ancient and your recent loyalty and honour; or, if diffident of yourselves, and not clearly discerning the almost obliterated constitution of your ancestors, you had looked to your neighbours in this land, who had kept alive the ancient principles and models of the old common law of Europe meliorated and adapted to its present state—by following wise examples you would have given new examples of wisdom to the world. You would have rendered the cause of liberty venerable in the eyes of every worthy mind in every nation. You would have shamed despotism from the earth, by shewing that freedom was not only reconcileable, but as, when well disci-

plined it is, auxiliary to law. You would have had an unoppressive but a productive revenue. You would have had a flourishing commerce to feed it. You would have had a free constitution; a potent monarchy; a disciplined army; a reformed and venerated clergy; a mitigated but spirited nobility, to lead your virtue, not to overlay it; you would have had a liberal order of commons, to emulate and to recruit that nobility; you would have had a protected, satisfied, laborious, and obedient people, taught to seek and to recognize the happiness that is to be found by virtue in all conditions; in which consists the true moral equality of mankind, and not in that monstrous fiction, which, by inspiring false ideas and vain expectations into men destined to travel in the obscure walk of laborious life, serves only to aggravate and imbitter that real inequality, which it never can remove; and which the order of civil life establishes as much for the benefit of those whom it must leave in an humble state, as those whom it is able to exalt to a condition more splendid, but not more happy. You had a smooth and easy career of felicity and glory laid open to you, beyond any thing recorded in the history of the world; but you have shewn that difficulty is good for man.

After reading this selection, consider these questions:
1. How does Burke define *liberty*?
2. What, according to Burke, are the problems with plans based on reason?
3. How should governments function and, if necessary, change?

# SELECTION 4:

# The Nation as Culture

*In the previous selection, Edmund Burke provided one way of defining the nation and understanding it within a notion of conservative politics. He did so in the throes of the French Revolution and the immediate reactions to the Revolution. Burke, however, was not the first to speak of the nation and history in these terms. The German thinker, literary scholar, and Protestant minister Johann Herder (1744–1803) had defined the nation and the ways in which the nation was essential to the lives of the individuals within it. No single thinker was more significant in providing the new idea of a nationalism with a theoretical and indeed philosophical basis than Herder. He coined the word* culture *(*kultur *in German) precisely to convey the idea that there is a set of customs and values, beliefs and ideals, that are particular to specific peoples at specific times. As a culture, the nation is opposed on the one hand to the Enlightenment's abstract definition of* society. *On the other, Herder understood the nation and its culture historically. A nation moved through time, and if left free to develop, it intensified its basic characteristics over the course of history. Understanding history, especially as the history of the nation, became the way to understand the reality of the nation and its culture. Herder did not see the need to evaluate one culture in relation to others. They all had their own virtues and vices—their own "centre of gravity," as he termed it. Herder proposed that independent cultures allowed human beings greater diversity. Particularity was a greater value for Herder than universality.*

*In enunciating such principles, Herder was to bring out a basic conflict in modern Western values. Between particularity and universality, between the free expression of a specific people and the universal claims of human rights, there is an unresolvable conflict and a split allegiance. Whatever the tension, we in the West want both—and want them at the same time. Herder himself did not see such tensions; he understood cultural diversity only within the universal structure of humankind. He first articulated these new concepts of the nation, culture, and history in a highly polemical and highly satirical booklet he published in 1775. In* And Yet Another Philosophy of History, *Herder satirizes the Enlightenment with its universalist notion of society, its single definition of human virtue, and its rational notion of governmental administration. Herder poured particular scorn on the Enlightenment claim that there is a single measure of human happiness, that this history is one of the progress of reason and science, and that there is one goal for the history of humankind. The title of his booklet—*And Yet Another Philosophy of History*— jibes against the histories of Hume, Montesquieu, and Voltaire with their generalized notions of "culture" and history.*

**I** should . . . not be surprised to come across more or less trivial contradictions within the wealth of detail of peoples and times. That no people long remained, or could remain, what it was, that each, like the arts and sciences and everything else in the world, had its period of growth, flowering and decay; that each of these modifications has lasted only the minimum of time which could be given to it on the wheel of human destiny; that, finally, no two moments in the world were ever identical and that therefore the Egyptians, the Romans and the Greeks have not stayed the same through all time—I tremble to think what clever objections could be raised on this subject by clever people, especially historians! . . .

From *J.G. Herder on Social and Political Culture*, translated and edited by F.M. Barnard. Copyright © Cambridge University Press 1969. Reprinted by permission of Cambridge University Press.

How tiresome to address the public when one always has to guard against objections of this kind and worse, and delivered in such a tone, from the vociferous section of the public (the nobler-thinking section keeps quiet!) And yet at the same time one has to bear in mind that the great mass of sheep who cannot tell their right paw from their left will bleat in concert. Can there be a general picture without grouping and arrangement? Can you have a wide view without height? If you hold your face up against the picture, if you cut off this splinter of it, pick out that little lump of paint, you will never see the picture whole—indeed you will not see a picture at all. And if your head is full of one particular group with which you are infatuated, how can you possibly view the flux of ever-changing events as a totality? How can you order them, follow their course, distinguish the essential effect in each scene, quietly trace the influences and finally give a name to it all? But if you cannot do all this, history just flickers and wavers before your eyes like a confusion of scenes, peoples and times. First you must read and learn to see. I concede, however, that to give a general description, to provide a general concept, is inevitably an abstraction. For only the Creator can conceive the immense variety within one nation or all nations without losing sight of their essential unity. . . .

A learned society of our time proposed, doubtless with the best of intentions, the following question: "Which was the happiest people in history?" If I understand the question aright, and if it does not lie beyond the horizon of a human response, I can only say that at a certain time and in certain circumstances, *each* people met with such a moment or else there never was one. Indeed, human nature is not the vessel of an absolute, unchanging and independent happiness, as defined by the philosopher; everywhere it attracts that measure of happiness of which it is capable: it is a pliant clay which assumes a different shape under different needs and circumstances. Even the image of happiness changes with each condition and climate. (What is it then, if not the sum of "satisfaction of desires, realization of ends and a quiet surmounting of needs," which everyone interprets according to the land, the time and the

place?) Basically, therefore, all comparison is unprofitable. When the inner sense of happiness has altered, this or that attitude has changed; when the external circumstances and needs fashion and fortify this new sentiment: who can then compare the different forms of satisfaction perceived by different senses in different worlds? Who can compare the shepherd and the Oriental patriarch, the ploughman and the artist, the sailor, the runner, the conqueror of the world? Happiness lies not in the laurel wreath or in the sight of the blessed herd, in the cargo ship or in the captured field-trophy, but in the soul which needs this, aspires to that, has attained this and claims no more—each nation has its centre of happiness within itself, just as every sphere has its centre of gravity.

Mother Nature has taken good care of this. She placed in men's hearts inclinations towards diversity, but made each of them so little pressing in itself that if only some of them are satisfied the soul soon makes a concert out of the awakened notes and only senses the unawakened ones as if they mutely and obscurely supported the sounding melody. She has put tendencies towards diversity in our hearts; she has placed part of the diversity in a close circle around us; she has restricted man's view so that by force of habit the circle became a horizon, beyond which he could not see nor scarcely speculate. All that is akin to my nature, all that can be assimilated by it, I hanker and strive after, and adopt; beyond that, kind nature has armed me with insensibility, coldness and blindness, which can even turn into contempt and disgust. Her aim is only to force me back on myself so that I find satisfaction in my own centre. The Greek adopts as much of the Roman, the Roman of the Greek, as he needs for himself; he is satisfied, the rest falls to the earth and he no longer strives for it. If, in this development of particular national tendencies towards particular forms of national happiness, the distance between the nations grows too great, we find prejudices arising. The Egyptian detests the shepherd and the nomad and despises the frivolous Greek. Similar prejudices, mob judgment and narrow nationalism arise when the dispositions and spheres of happiness of two nations collide. But prejudice is good, in its time and place, for happiness may spring from it. It urges nations to converge upon their centre, attaches them more firmly to their roots, causes them to flourish after their kind, and makes them more ardent and therefore happier in their inclinations and purposes. The most ignorant, most prejudiced nations is often superior in this respect. The moment men start dwelling in wishful dreams of foreign lands from whence they seek hope and salvation they reveal the first symptoms of disease, of flatulence of unhealthy opulence, of approaching death!

The general, philosophical, philanthropical tone of our century wishes to extend "our own ideal" of virtue and happiness to each distant nation, to even the remotest age in history. But can one such single ideal act as an arbiter praising or condemning other nations or periods, their customs and laws; can it remake them after its own image? Is good not dispersed over the earth? Since one form of mankind and one region could not encompass it, it has been distributed in a thousand forms, changing shape like an eternal Proteus [the morphing Greek sea god] throughout continents and centuries. And even if it does not strive, as it keeps on changing, towards the greater virtue and happiness of the individual— for man remains forever man—nonetheless a plan of progressive endeavour becomes evident. This is my great theme.

Those who have so far undertaken to explain the progress of the centuries have mostly cherished the idea that such progress must lead towards greater virtue and individual happiness. In support of this idea they have embellished or invented facts, minimized or suppressed contrary facts; covered whole pages; taken words for works, enlightenment for happiness, greater sophistication for virtue, and in this way invented the fiction of the "general, progressive amelioration of the world" which few believed, least of all the true student of history and the human heart.

Others, who saw the harmfulness of this dream without knowing a better one, saw vices and virtues alternating like climates, perfections sprouting and dying like spring leaves, human customs and preferences strewn about like leaves of fate. No plan! No progress, but an endless revolution! Weaving and unravelling like Penelope! They fell into a whirlpool of scepticism about all virtue, about all happiness and the destiny of man, and introduced into history, religion and ethics the latest fad of recent philosophy.

After reading this selection, consider these questions:
1. What does Herder mean by *individuality*?
2. How does he define *culture*?
3. How does Herder understand the processes of history?

# SELECTION 5:

# The Garden of Humanity

*Johann Herder's ideas were quick to spread throughout Europe. The Italian writer and champion of the cause of Italian unification, Giuseppe Mazzini (1805–1872), developed Herder's idea in terms of more direct and practical programs for the creation of new national states. For Mazzini, the idea of the nation was still combined with the principles of liberalism. His writings were to become highly influential not only among his fellow Italians but also for many other Europeans, especially the peoples of central and eastern Europe. Like Herder, Mazzini did not argue for the superiority of one national culture, not even his native Italian culture. Also like Herder, he believed in a humanity consisting of all the nations of the world. Both in principle and in his political activities, Mazzini promoted the development of all national cultures and their achievement of political independence. The following selection is taken from Mazzini's very influential "Duties of Man," written in 1858. It was originally addressed to the Italian Workingmen's Association.*

To you, Sons and Daughters of the People, I dedicate this book. In it I have traced for you the Principles, in the name and by the aid of which you may, if you will, fulfil your mission in Italy; a mission of Republican Progress for all your countrymen and of emancipation for yourselves.

Let those among you whom favourable circumstances or superior ability have rendered more capable of penetrating the deep meaning of these Principles, explain them to the others in the same loving spirit in which I thought, while writing, of your sufferings, your aspirations, and that new life which it will be yours to diffuse over our Italian country, so soon as the unjust inequalities now so fatal to the free development of your faculties shall be overcome.

I have loved you from my earliest years. I was taught by the Republican instincts of my mother to seek out among my fellows neither the rich man nor the great, but the true *Man;* while the simple and unconscious virtues of my father accustomed me to value the silent unmarked spirit of self-sacrifice so frequently found in your class, far above the external and assumed superiority of semi-education.

In later years the pages of our history revealed to me the fact that the true life of Italy is the life of her People; and I saw how, during the slow progress of the ages, the shock of different races, and the superficial ephemeral changes wrought by usurpation and conquest, had been ordained to elaborate and prepare our great democratic National Unity.

And I devoted myself to you thirty years ago.

I saw that our Country, our One Country of free men and equals, could never be founded by an Aristocracy such as ours, possessed neither of initiative power nor collective life; nor by a Monarchy destitute of special mission, and devoid of all idea of Unity or Emancipation—a Monarchy which had merely crept in amongst us in the sixteenth century, and in the track of the foreigner.

I saw that our United Italian Country could only be founded by the Italian people, and I declared this to the world.

I saw the necessity that your class should free themselves from the yoke of *hire*, and gradually elevate Labour, through the medium of Association, to be master alike of the soil and capital of the State; and, long before any French sects of Socialists had distorted the question amongst us, I proclaimed it.

I saw that an Italy such as the aspirations of our hearts foretell, can never exist until the Papacy shall be overthrown in the name of the Moral Law, acknowledged as high above all pretended Intermediates between God and the People; and I avowed it.

Nor, amid the wild accusations, calumnies, and derision by which I have been assailed, have I ever betrayed your cause, nor deserted the banner of the Future, even when you—led astray by the teachings of men, not *believers*, but *idolaters*—forsook me for those who but trafficked in your blood, to withdraw their thoughts from you in the sequel.

The hearty and sincere grasp of the hand of some of the best among you, sons and daughters of the People, has consoled me for the faithlessness of others, and for the many bitter delusions heaped upon me by men whom I loved, and who professed to love me. I have but few years of life left to me, but the bond sealed between me and those few among yourselves will remain inviolate to my last day, and will live beyond it.

From *Life and Writings of Joseph Mazzini*, anonymous editor, vol. 4: *Critical and Literary* (London: Smith, Elder, 1891).

Think, then, of me as I think of you. Let us commune together in affection for our country. The special element of her future is in you.

But our country's future, and your own, can only be realised by ridding yourselves of two great sores, which still (though I hope for no long while) contaminate our upper classes, and threaten to misdirect the advance of Italy.

These two sores are *Macchiavellism* and *Materialism*.

The first, an ignoble travesty of the doctrine of a great but unhappy man [the political philosopher Niccolò Machiavelli], would lead you away from the frank, brave, and loyal adoration of Truth; the second, through the worship of *Interest*, would inevitably drag you down to egotism and anarchy.

If you would emancipate yourselves from the arbitrary rule and tyranny of man, you must begin by rightly adoring God. And in the world's great battle between the two principles of Good and Evil you must openly enrol yourselves beneath the banner of the first and ceaselessly combat the second; rejecting every dubious symbol, and every cowardly compromise or hypocrisy of all leaders who seek to strike a middle course.

Beneath the banner of the first you will ever find me by your side while life lasts.

It was because I saw these two lies of Macchiavellism and Materialism too often clothe themselves before your eyes with the seductive fascinations of hopes which only the worship of God and Truth can realise, that I thought to warn you by this book. I love you too well either to flatter your passions or caress the golden dreams by which others seek to win your favour. My voice may sound too harsh, and I may too severely insist on proclaiming the necessity of virtue and sacrifice; but I know, and you too—untainted by false doctrine and unspoiled by wealth—will soon know also, that the sole origin of every Right is in a Duty fulfilled.

After reading this selection, consider these questions:

1. What do men and women owe to their nation, according to Mazzini?
2. What do men and women owe to humanity?
3. How does Mazzini draw on the idea of Emmanuel-Joseph Sieyès?

# Unit 2

# The Nineteenth Century

## Contents

Map     114

**Chapter 7:**
The Interrelated Processes of the Industrial Revolution     115

**Chapter 8:**
Family, Gender, and Class in the Early Industrial Era     134

**Chapter 9:**
Darwin, Nietzsche, and Freud     156

**Chapter 10:**
Christianity in the Modern World     175

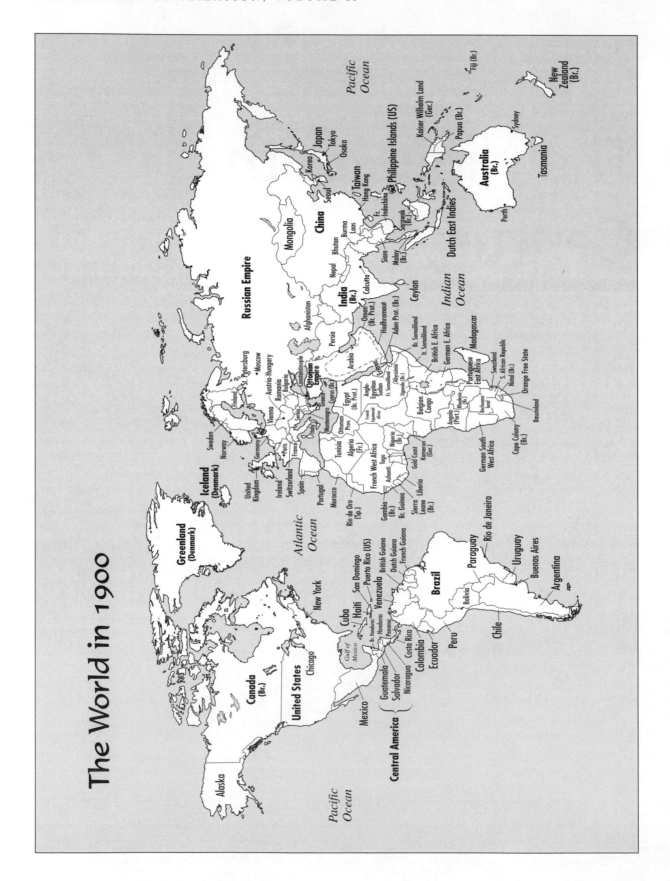

The World in 1900

# CHAPTER 7
# The Interrelated Processes of the Industrial Revolution

The term *Industrial Revolution* encompasses a complex set of interrelated phenomena. At its center lies the application of machine power to the transformation of raw materials into commodities. In place of the age-old forms of work, which were largely agricultural, home-based, and human- and animal-driven, the Industrial Revolution substituted manufacturing, the factory system, and machine power. Although various types of machines had always been employed in agriculture and production, the application of new sources of power and a whole new type of machinery radically increased productivity in ways and in magnitudes undreamt of in previous ages. The production of cotton cloth was the first form of manufacture to be industrialized. In Great Britain, inventions such as the "flying shuttle" in 1733 and the "spinning jenny" in 1764 raised productivity dramatically. James Watt's invention of the modern steam engine in 1769 and its adaptation to weaving and then spinning caused productivity to increase by 20, 30, and then 100 percent. By 1830 the cotton industry in Great Britain employed more than 1 million individuals and accounted for more than 50 percent of the nation's exports.

In addition, the introduction of industrial processes in one area of an industry put pressure upon related areas of the same industry to industrialize as well. Whether intended or not, this pressure resulted in the industrialization of all aspects of an industry. Other effects rippled out from this initial stage of industrialization. With the industrialization of cotton cloth production, for example, there soon developed various support industries. To produce the machines themselves, more coal and steel were needed, thus calling for unprecedented demands for increased production in these areas. To bring in raw materials and to send out finished products increased the need for more powerful modes of transportation. The vast increase in railway construction and the building of larger steam-driven ships were part of this wide-ranging set of changes associated with the process of industrialization. As both sources and potential sources of raw materials and as widening markets and potential markets, a large part of the rest of the world would be drawn into the British economic orbit in the second half of the nineteenth century.

Industrialization would also redistribute political power both within countries and among them. The origins and earliest developments of the Industrial Revolution, however, were limited to the English region known as the Midlands. Industrialization spread outside Great Britain unevenly. On the continent, industrialization was introduced first in Belgium in the 1820s and then gradually in France from the 1820s until it climaxed in the 1860s and 1870s. Much like the United States, Germany began industrialization relatively late; but once begun, industrialization was quick, extensive, and efficient. Beginning with the unification of the German states in 1871, the German Reich overtook Britain in steel production by the 1890s. Countries that lacked the coal and iron ore necessary for industrialization in the eighteenth and nineteenth centuries, like Italy, would have to wait until the development of lighter metals, plastics, and electrical power in the twentieth century.

The consequences of the application of machine power were not limited to the production and transportation of more and cheaper goods and to the growth of markets and the creation of new markets for these goods. The production process itself demanded a new type of social organization, the factory, in which large numbers of men, women, and children were trained to work with, and align themselves to, the stages of a machine's operations. Factory conditions were dismal, even for the relatively skilled workers. Monotonous activities demanded by working with the tempo of machinery and under the sometimes harsh discipline of overseers made work extremely burdensome. Hours were long: before 1850, usually twelve to fourteen hours per day. Cloth production often involved working with steam and sometimes toxic chemicals, which produced unhealthy environments. Surrounded by large, unprotected machinery, often inhaling harmful dust in unventilated conditions, and laboring in generally unsanitary conditions, the workers of the early Industrial Revolution experienced constant health hazards and sometimes physical harm.

The Industrial Revolution had a wide range of unintended consequences. The most obvious of these involved changes in population growth and population distributions. By the end of the nineteenth century, the populations of European nations had increased dramatically. In 1800 Europe had a population of approximately 190 million. By 1900 this figure had grown to over 500 million, despite the emigration of more than 40 million Europeans, largely to North America. There was also a major shift of this growing population to the cities. Over the course of the century, the number of individuals living in large cities (over 100,000 people) increased tenfold, from 3 to 11 percent of the aggregate population.

Factories themselves tended to become large complexes, employing huge labor forces. And the need for a large workforce in turn necessitated a great concentration of relatively poor individuals living near the factory site. Machines and the factories that housed them would eventually destroy more traditional forms of work and patterns of habitation as well as redefine social relations both between individuals and among classes.

## SELECTION 1:

# Factory Workers Observed

*Andrew Ure (1778–1857), a physician and professor of chemistry at Glasgow University, observed the conditions of workers in the early stages of the Industrial Revolution in Manchester. To Ure, the conditions of child workers and of workers in general were definitely improving. The following selection is taken from his 1835 book* The Philosophy of Manufactures, or, an Exposition of the Scientific, Moral, and Commercial Economy of the Factory System of Great Britain.

Of all the common prejudices that exist with regard to factory labour, there is none more unfounded than that which ascribes to it excessive tedium and irksomeness above other occupations, owing to its being carried on in conjunction with the "unceasing motion of the steam-engine." In an establishment for spinning or weaving cotton, all the hard work is performed by the steam-engine, which leaves for the attendant no hard labour at all, and literally nothing to do in general; but at intervals to perform some delicate operation, such as joining the threads that break, taking the cops off the spindles, &c. And it is so far from being true that the work in a factory is incessant, because the motion of the steam-engine is incessant, that the fact is, that the labour is not incessant on that very account, because it is performed in conjunction with the steam-engine. Of all manufacturing employments, those are by far the most irksome and incessant in which steam-engines are not employed, as in lace-running and

stocking-weaving; and the way to prevent an employment from being incessant, is to introduce a steam-engine into it. These remarks certainly apply more especially to the labour of children in factories. Three-fourths of the children so employed are engaged in piecing at the mules. "When the carriages of these have receded a foot and a half or two feet from the rollers," says Mr. Tufnell, "nothing is to be done, not even attention is required from either spinner or piecer." Both of them stand idle for a time, and in fine spinning particularly, for three-quarters of a minute, or more. Consequently, if a child remains at this business twelve hours daily, he has nine hours of inaction. And though he attends two mules, he has still six hours of non-exertion. Spinners sometimes dedicate these intervals to the perusal of books. The scavengers, who, in Mr. Sadler's report, have been described as being "constantly in a state of grief, always in terror, and every moment they have to spare stretched all their length upon the floor in a state of perspiration," may be observed in cotton factories idle for *four* minutes at a time, or moving about in a sportive mood, utterly unconscious of the tragical scenes in which they were dramatized.

From *The Philosophy of Manufactures*, by Andrew Ure, 3rd ed. (London: Bohn, 1861).

Occupations which are assisted by steam-engines require for the most part a higher, or at least a steadier, species of labour than those which are not; the exercise of the mind being then partially substituted for that of the muscles, constituting skilled labour, which is always paid more highly than unskilled. On this principle we can readily account for the comparatively high wages which the inmates of a factory, whether children or adults, obtain. Batting cotton by hand for fine spinning seems by far the hardest work in a factory; it is performed wholly by women, without any assistance from the steam-engine, and is somewhat similar in effort to threshing corn; yet it does not bring those who are engaged in it more than 6s.6d.[1] weekly, while close by is the stretching-frame, which remunerates its tenters or superintendents, women, and even children fourteen years old, with double wages for far lighter labour. In power-loom weaving also, the wages are good, and the muscular effort is trifling, as those who tend it frequently exercise themselves by following the movement of the lay, and leaning on it with their arms. It is reckoned a very healthy mill occupation, as is shown by the appearance of the females engaged in it, in every well-regulated establishment in England and Scotland.

The more refined the labour in factories is, it becomes generally the lighter and the pleasanter. Thus the fine spinning is the least laborious in Manchester, owing to the slowness with which the machinery moves in forming fine threads. The mule for No. 30 or No. 40 makes in general three stretches in a minute; but the mule for higher numbers makes only one stretch in the same time. During at least three-fourths of this minute, the four, five, or more piecers, who attend the pair of mules of 460 spindles each, have absolutely nothing to do but are seen in an easy attitude, till the carriage begins to start for a new stretch, when they proceed immediately to mend the threads, which break, or are purposely broken on account of some unsightly knot. The pieceing is soon over, as the carriage does not stop an instant in the frame, but forthwith resumes its spinning routine, and when it has again come out somewhat less than two feet, it places the rollers and roving beyond the reach of the hands of the piecers, and gives them another interval of repose. There is so little scavenger work required in fine spinning, on account of the small quantity of waste from the long-stapled cotton, that it is usually performed by one of the piecers. From the same cause there is hardly any dust to be seen in the air of the rooms. . . .

Under what pretext, or with what face of pretension, operatives, whose labour is assisted by steam or water power, can lay claim to a peculiar privilege of exemption from more than ten hours' daily labour it is hard to conjecture. They compare their toil with that of the small class, comparatively speaking, of artisans, such as carpenters, bricklayers, stone-masons, &c., who, they say, work only from six to six, with two one-hour intervals for meals: a class, however, in this material respect distinguished from most factory operatives, that their work is done entirely by muscular effort, and after serving a long apprenticeship with no little outlay. But what do the factory people think of the numerous class of domestic operatives, the stocking or frame-work knitters, the hand-loom weavers, the wool-combers, the lace-manufacturers, and a variety of others, who work, and very hardly too, from twelve to sixteen hours a-day, to earn a bare subsistence; and this frequently from a very early age, and in a state of confinement irksome to the mind and injurious to the body? The consideration is also overlooked by these interested reasoners, that by reducing the hours of labour, and thereby the amount of subsistence derivable from the less objectionable occupations, they would cause a corresponding increase of competition for employment in the more objectionable ones, and thus inflict an injury on the whole labouring community, by wantonly renouncing the fair advantages of their own.

On the principles expounded above, the woollen manufacturers in the large mills pay much better wages to their workmen than the domestic manufacturers do to theirs.

The factory system, then, instead of being

---

1. Shilling is abbreviated s. Until 1971 there were 20 shillings in an English pound. Pence or penny is abbreviated d. Until 1971 there were 12 pence in a shilling.

detrimental to the comfort of the labouring population, is its grand Palladium; for the more complicated and extensive the machinery required for any manufacture, the less risk is there of its agents being injured by the competition of foreign manufactures, and the greater inducement and ability has the mill-owner to keep up the wages of his work-people. The main reason why they are so high is, that they form a small part of the value of the manufactured article, so that if reduced too low by a sordid master, they would render his operatives less careful, and thereby injure the quality of their work more than could be compensated by his saving in wages. The less proportion wages bear to the value of the goods, the higher, generally speaking, is the recompense of labour. The prudent master of a fine spinning-mill is most reluctant to tamper with the earnings of his spinners, and never consents to reduce them till absolutely forced to it by a want of remuneration for the capital and skill embarked in his business. . . .

It deserves to be remarked, moreover, that hand-working is more or less discontinuous from the caprice of the operative, and never gives an average weekly or annual product at all comparable to that of a like machine equably driven by power. For this reason hand-weavers very seldom turn off in a week much more than one-half of what their loom could produce if kept continuously in action for twelve or fourteen hours a day, at the rate which the weaver in his working paroxysms impels it.

A gentleman in Manchester, one of the greatest warehousemen in the world, told me that 1,800 weavers, whom he employed in the surrounding districts, seldom brought him in more than 2,000 pieces per week, but he knew that they could fabricate 9,000, if they bestowed steady labour on their looms. One young woman in his employment, not long ago, produced by her own industry upon a hand-loom six pieces a week; for each of which she received 6s.3d. This fact strongly confirms what Mr. Strutt told me concerning the discontinuous industry of handicraft people. Learning that the inhabitants of a village a few miles from Belper, occupied chiefly by stocking weavers, was in a distressed state from the depreciation of their

wages, he invited a number of the most necessitous families to participate in the better wages and steadier employment of their great spinning-mills. Accordingly they came with troops of children, and were delighted to get installed into such comfortable quarters. After a few weeks, however, their irregular habits of work began to break out, proving both to their own conviction, and that of their patrons, their unfitness for power-going punctuality. They then renounced all further endeavours at learning the new business, and returned to their listless independence. . . .

In hand-weaving . . . the depreciation of wages has been extraordinary. Annexed are the prices paid at different periods in Manchester for weaving a sixty reed ¾ cambric, as taken in the month of March each year; the weaver paying threepence out of each shilling, for winding his warp, for brushes, past, &c.

In 1795, 39s.9d.   In 1810, 15s.   In 1830, 5s.
    1800, 25s.          1820, 8s.

The following painful statements made to the Factory Commissioners will show in how abject a condition are our so-called independent handicraft labourers, compared with that of those much-lamented labourers who tend the power-driven machines of a factory. The former class needs all the sympathy which Mr. Sadler's faction so perniciously expended upon the latter. . . .

The most recent, and perhaps most convincing, evidence regarding the healthiness of factory children is that given in the official report of Mr. Harrison, the Inspecting Surgeon appointed for the mills of Preston and its vicinity. There are 1,656 under 18 years of age, of whom 952 are employed in spinning-rooms, 468 in carding-rooms, 128 at power-looms, and 108 in winding, skewering cops, &c. "I have made very particular inquiries respecting the health of every child whom I have examined, and I find that the average annual sickness of each child is not more than four days; at least, that not more than four days on an average are lost by each child in a year, in consequence of sickness. This includes disorders of every kind, for the most part induced by causes wholly unconnected with factory labour. I have been not a little surprised to find so little sickness which can fairly be attributable to mill work. I have met with very few children who have suffered from injuries occasioned by machinery: and the protection, especially in new factories, is now so complete, that accidents will, I doubt not, speedily become rare. I have not met with a single instance out of the 1,656 children whom I have examined, of deformity, that is referable to factory labour. It must be admitted, that factory children do not present the same blooming robust appearance, as is witnessed among children who labour in the open air, but I question if they are not more exempt from acute diseases, and do not, on an average, suffer less sickness than those who are regarded as having more healthy employments. The average age at which the children of this district enter the factories is ten years and two months; and the average age of all the young persons together is fourteen years.". . . .

I examined samples of bacon as sold in several respectable shops in Manchester, and found it to be much more rank than the average in the London shops. In this *piquant* state, it suits vitiated palates accustomed to the fiery impressions of tobacco and gin. These three stimulants are too much used by that order of work-people in Manchester who receive the highest wages, and they are quite adequate to account for many chronic maladies of the stomach, liver, or spleen, without tracing them to mere factory labour or confinement. Were a judicious plan of cookery and diet, combining abundance of vegetable matter with light animal food, introduced among them, as it is among the families of the work-people at Belper, Hyde, New Lanark, Catrine, &c., joined to abstinence from tobacco and alcohol, I am confident that the health of the Manchester spinners would surpass that of any class of operatives in the kingdom. . . . Hypochondriasis from indulging too much the corrupt desires of the flesh and the spirit, is in fact the prevalent disease of the highest-paid operatives, a disease which may be aggravated by drugs, but must seek its permanent cure in moral regimen. Nothing strikes the eye of a stranger more in Manchester than the

swarms of empirical practitioners of medicine. Nearly a dozen of them may be found clustered together in one of the main streets; all prepared with drastic pills and alterative potions to prey upon the credulous spinners. . . .

Since they can purchase their favourite bacon at four-pence or five-pence a pound, they need not nor do they actually, content themselves with a *sprinkling*, for they swallow a substantial rasher. This consequently creates thirst, which must be quenched with tea at bagging-time, qualified with some ardent spirit to aid as they think the digestion of their dinner. . . .What is carried about for distribution in dwelling-houses by the milkmen is inferior even to the average London milk. The mill-owners of Manchester could, in my humble opinion, do nothing more conducive to the welfare of their operatives than to establish an extensive dairy, under the superintendence of one of their benevolent societies. . . .Were the workpeople of the factories to adopt also the *pot au feu* cookery of the French, they might live in the most comfortable manner upon their wages. I know two talented young men. . .who. . .practised the said system of diet for several years, by which small pieces of animal food are made to impart a relish to a large quantity of esculent and farinaceous vegetables of various kinds. . . .On this plan they ascertained that they could board themselves comfortably for 2*s*.6*d*. each per week. The most savoury and salubrious cookery requires the slowest fire. A sumptuous French dinner could be dressed with one-tenth of the fuel consumed by an English cook in broiling a few beef-steaks or mutton-chops.

After reading this selection, consider these questions:
1. How does Ure describe working conditions in Manchester?
2. How many children were employed in Manchester?
3. What were the health conditions of these children, according to Ure?

# SELECTION 2:

# Another Viewpoint

*The first large factory complexes arose in Manchester and Birmingham in the second half of the eighteenth century. One of the most interesting evaluations of the impact of early industrialization on the working-class families of Manchester was that of the physician James Phillips Kay (1804–1877). To his career as a doctor, Kay added service on various administrative agencies in Manchester that sought to alleviate harsh working conditions, end the squalor in which most laborers and their families lived, and improve their overall educational opportunities. He went from being an assistant Poor Law commissioner to secretary of the education committee of the city's Privy Council. During the cholera epidemic of 1832, Kay served as secretary of the Manchester Board of Health. He also published widely on the conditions of the working class. The following selection is taken from Kay's* The Moral and Physical Condition of the Working Classes employed in the Cotton Manufacture in Manchester *(1832), in which he describes the wretched conditions of most of the city's population.*

The township of Manchester chiefly consists of dense masses of houses, inhabited by the population engaged in the great manufactories of the cotton trade. Some of the central divisions are occupied by warehouses and shops, and a few streets by the dwellings of some of the more wealthy inhabitants; but the opulent merchants chiefly reside in the country, and even the superior servants of their establishments inhabit the suburbal [*sic*] townships. Manchester, properly so called, is chiefly inhabited by shopkeepers and the labouring classes. Those districts where the poor dwell are of very recent origin. The rapid growth of the cotton manufacture has attracted hither operatives from every part of the kingdom, and Ireland has poured forth the most destitute of her hordes to supply the constantly increasing demand for labour. This immigration has been, in one important respect, a serious evil. The Irish have taught the labouring classes of this country a pernicious lesson. The system of cottier farming, the demoralisation and barbarism of the people, and the general use of the potato as the chief article of food, have encouraged the population in Ireland more rapidly than the available means of subsistence have increased. Debased alike by ignorance and pauperism, they have discovered, with the savage, what is the minimum of the means of life, upon which existence may be prolonged. They have taught this fatal secret to the population of this country. . . . Instructed in the fatal secret of subsisting on what is barely necessary to life, the labouring classes have ceased to entertain a laudable pride in furnishing their houses, and in multiplying the decent comforts which minister to happiness. What is superfluous to the mere exigencies of nature, is too often expended at the tavern; and for the provision of old age and infirmity, they too frequently trust either to charity, to the support of their children, or to the protection of the poor laws.

When the example is considered in connexion with the unremitting labour of the whole popula-

From *The Moral and Physical Condition of the Working Classes Employed in the Cotton Manufacture in Manchester*, by James Phillips Kay (London: 1832).

tion engaged in the various branches of the cotton manufacture, our wonder will be less excited by their fatal demoralisation. Prolonged and exhausting labour, continued from day to day, and from year to year, is not calculated to develop the intellectual or moral faculties of man. The dull routine of a ceaseless drudgery, in which the same mechanical process is incessantly repeated, resembles the torment of [Greek mythology's] Sisyphus—the toil, like the rock, recoils perpetually on the wearied operative. The mind gathers neither stores nor strength from the constant extension and retraction of the same muscles. The intellect slumbers in supine inertness; but the grosser parts of our nature attain a rank development. To condemn man to such severity of toil is, in some measure, to cultivate in him the habits of an animal. He becomes reckless. He disregards the distinguishing appetites and habits of his species. He neglects the comforts and delicacies of life. He lives in squalid wretchedness, on meagre food, and expends his superfluous gains on debauchery.

The population employed in the cotton factories rises at five o'clock in the morning, works in the mills from six till eight o'clock, and returns home for half an hour to forty minutes to breakfast. This meal generally consists of tea or coffee with a little bread. Oatmeal porridge is sometimes, but of late rarely used, and chiefly by the men; but the stimulus of tea is preferred, and especially by the women. The tea is almost always of a bad, and sometimes of a deleterious quality, the infusion is weak, and little or no milk is added. The operatives return to the mills and workshops until twelve o'clock, when an hour is allowed for dinner. Amongst those who obtain the lowest rates of wages this meal generally consists of boiled potatoes. The mess of potatoes is put into one large dish; melted lard and butter are poured upon them, and a few pieces of fried fat bacon are sometimes mingled with them, and but seldom a little meat. Those who obtain better wages, or families whose aggregate income is larger, add a greater proportion of animal food to this meal, at least three times a week; but the quantity consumed by the labouring population is not great. The family sits round the table, and each rapidly appropriates his portion on a plate, or, they all plunge their spoons into the dish, and with an animal eagerness satisfy the cravings of their appetite. At the expiration of the hour, they are all again employed in the workshops or mills, where they continue until seven o'clock or a later hour, when they generally again indulge in the use of tea, often mingled with spirits accompanied by a little bread. Oatmeal or potatoes are however taken by some a second time in the evening.

The comparatively innutritious qualities of these articles of diet are most evident. We are, however, by no means prepared to say that an individual living in a healthy atmosphere, and engaged in active employment in the open air, would not be able to continue protracted and severe labour, without any suffering, whilst nourished by this food. . . . But the population nourished on this aliment is crowded into one dense mass, in cottages separated by narrow, unpaved, and almost pestilential streets, in an atmosphere loaded with the smoke and exhalations of a large manufacturing city. The operatives are congregated in rooms and workshops during twelve hours in the day, in an enervating, heated atmosphere, which is frequently loaded with dust or filaments of cotton, and impure from constant respiration, or from other causes. They are engaged in an employment which absorbs their attention, and unremittingly employs their physical energies. They are drudges who watch the movements, and assist the operations, of a mighty material force, which toils with an energy ever unconscious of fatigue. The persevering labour of the operative must rival the mathematical precision, the incessant motion, and the exhaustless power of the machine.

Hence, besides the negative results—the total abstraction of every moral and intellectual stimulus—the absence of variety—banishment from the grateful air and the cheering influences of light, the physical energies are exhausted by incessant toil, and imperfect nutrition. Having been subjected to the prolonged labour of an animal—his physical energy wasted—his mind in supreme inaction—the artisan has neither moral dignity nor intellectual nor organic strength to resist the seductions of appetite. His wife and children, too frequently subjected to the same process, are unable to cheer his remaining moments of leisure. Domestic economy is neglected, domestic comforts are unknown. A meal of the coarsest food is prepared with heedless haste, and devoured with equal precipitation. Home has no other relation to him than that of shelter—few pleasures are there—it chiefly presents to him a scene of physical exhaustion, from which he is glad to escape. Himself impotent to all the distinguishing aims of his species, he sinks into sensual sloth, or revels in more degrading licentiousness. His house is ill-furnished, uncleanly, often ill ventilated, perhaps damp; his food, through want of forethought and domestic economy, is meagre and innutritious; he is debilitated and hypochondriacal, and falls the victim of dissipation.

These artisans are frequently subject to a disease, in which the sensibility of the stomach and bowels is morbidly excited; the alvine secretions are deranged, and the appetite impaired. Whilst this state continues, the patient loses flesh, his features are sharpened, the skin becomes pale, leaden coloured, or of the yellow hue which is observed in those who have suffered from the influence of tropical climates. The strength fails, all the capacities of physical enjoyment are destroyed, and the paroxysms of corporal suffering are aggravated by the horrors of a disordered imagination, till they lead to gloomy apprehension, to the deepest depression, and almost to despair. We cannot wonder that the wretched victim of this disease, invited by those haunts of misery and crime the gin shop and the tavern, as he passes to his daily labour, should endeavour to cheat his sufferings of a few moments, by the false excitement procured by ardent spirits; or that the exhausted artisan, driven by ennui and discomfort from his squalid home, should strive, in the delirious dreams of a continued debauch, to forget the remembrance of his reckless improvidence, of the destitution, hunger, and uninterrupted toil, which threaten to destroy the remaining energies of his enfeebled constitution. . . .

Some idea of the want of cleanliness prevalent in their habitations, may be obtained from the report of the number of houses requiring whitewashing; but this column fails to indicate their gross neglect of order, and absolute filth. Much

less can we obtain satisfactory statistical results concerning the want of furniture, especially of bedding, and of food, clothing, and fuel. In these respects, the habitations of the Irish are the most destitute. They can scarcely be said to be furnished. They contain one or two chairs, a mean table, the most scanty culinary apparatus, and one or two beds, loathsome with filth. A whole family is sometimes accommodated in a single bed, and sometimes a heap of filthy straw and a covering of old sacking hide them in one undistinguished heap, debased alike by penury, want of economy, and dissolute habits. Frequently, the inspectors found two or more families crowded into one small house, containing only two apartments, in one of which they slept, and another in which they ate; and often more than one family lived in a damp cellar, containing only one room, in whose pestilential atmosphere from twelve to sixteen persons were crowded. To these fertile sources of disease were sometimes added the keeping of pigs and other animals in the house, with other nuisances of the most revolting character. . . .

The houses of the poor . . . are too generally built back to back, having therefore only one outlet, no yard, no privy, and no receptacle for refuse. Consequently the narrow, unpaved streets, in which mud and water stagnate, become the common receptacle of offal and ordure. Often low, damp, ill ventilated cellars exist beneath the houses; an improvement on which system, consists in the erection of a stage over the first storey, by which access is obtained to the second, and the house is inhabited by two separate families. More than one disgraceful example of this might be enumerated. The streets . . . are generally unsewered, and the drainage is consequently superficial. The houses are often built with a total neglect of order, on a summit of natural irregularities of the surface, or on mounds left at the side of artificial excavations on the brick grounds, with which these parts of the town abound.

These districts are inhabited by a turbulent population, which, rendered reckless by dissipation and want—misled by the secret intrigues, and excited by the inflammatory harangues of demagogues, has frequently committed daring assaults on the liberty of the more peaceful portions of the working classes, and the most frightful devastations on the property of their masters. Machines have been broken, and factories gutted and burned at mid-day, and the riotous crowd has dispersed ere the insufficient body of police arrived at the scene of disturbance. . . . The police form, in fact, so weak a screen against the power of the mob, that popular violence is now, in almost every instance, controlled by the presence of a military force.

The wages obtained by operatives in the various branches of the cotton manufacture are, in general, such, as with the exercise of that economy without which wealth itself is wasted, would be sufficient to provide them with all the decent comforts of life—the average wage of all persons employed (young and old) being from nine to twelve shillings per week. Their means are consumed by vice and improvidence. But the wages of certain classes are exceedingly meagre. The introduction of the power-loom, though ultimately destined to be productive of the greatest general benefits, has, in the present restricted state of commerce, occasioned some temporary embarrassment, by diminishing the demand for certain kinds of labour, and, consequently, their price. The hand-loom weavers, existing in the state of transition, still continue a very extensive class, and though they labour fourteen hours and upwards daily, earn only from five to seven shillings per week. They consist chiefly of Irish, and are affected by all the causes of moral and physical depression which we have enumerated. Ill-fed, ill-clothed, half-sheltered and ignorant; working in close, damp cellars, or crowded, ill-ventilated workshops, it only remains that they should become, as is too frequently the case, demoralised and reckless, to render perfect the portraiture of savage life. . . .

With unfeigned regret, we are . . . constrained to add, that the standard of morality is exceedingly debased, and that religious observances are neglected amongst the operative population of Manchester. . . .

The children . . . are often neglected by their parents. The early age at which girls are admitted into the factories, prevents their acquiring much knowledge of domestic economy; and even supposing them to have had accidental opportunities of making this acquisition, the extent to which women are employed in the mills, does not, even after marriage, permit the general application of its principles. The infant is the victim of the system; it has not lived long, ere it is abandoned to the care of a hireling or neighbour, whilst its mother pursues her accustomed toil. Sometimes a little girl has care of the child, or even of two or three collected from neighbouring houses. Thus abandoned to one whose sympathies are not interested in its welfare, or whose time is too often also occupied in household drudgery, the child is ill-fed, dirty, ill-clothed, exposed to cold and neglect, and, in consequence, more than one-half of the offspring of the poor (as may be proved by the bills of mortality of the town) die before they have completed their fifth year. The strongest survive; but the same causes which destroy the weakest, impair the vigour of the more robust; and hence the children of our manufacturing population are proverbially pale and sallow, though not generally emaciated, nor the subjects of disease. We cannot subscribe to those exaggerated and unscientific accounts of the physical ailments to which they are liable, which have been lately revived with an eagerness and haste equally unfriendly to taste and truth; but we are convinced that the operation of these causes, continuing unchecked through successive generations, would tend to depress the health of the people; and that subsequent physical ills would accumulate in an unhappy progression.

After reading this selection, consider these questions:

1. According to Kay, what was the typical workday for laborers in Manchester?
2. What impact did working and living conditions have on the moral and spiritual lives of the workers and their families?
3. What were the conditions of children in early industrial Manchester?

# SELECTION 3:

# A Twentieth-Century View

*The twentieth-century historian T.S. Ashton reexamines the impact of the first stage of industrialization on the workers of the British Isles.*

Most of the economists who lived through the period of rapid economic changes took a somewhat gloomy view of the effect of these changes on the workers. "The increasing wealth of the nation," wrote Thomas Malthus in 1798, "has had little or no tendency to better the conditions of the labouring poor. They have not, I believe, a greater command of the necessaries and conveniences of life; and a much greater proportion of them, than at the period of the Revolution, is employed in manufactories and crowded together in close and unwholesome rooms." A couple of generations later J.R. McCulloch declared that "there seems, on the whole, little room for doubting that the factory system operates unfavourably on the bulk of those engaged in it." And, in 1848, John Stuart Mill wrote words that, if they gave some glimmer of hope, were nevertheless highly critical of the society from which the technological changes had sprung. "Hitherto," he said, "it is questionable if all the mechanical inventions yet made have lightened the day's toil of any human being. They have enabled a greater proportion to live the same life of drudgery and imprisonment and an increased number of manufacturers and others to make fortunes. They have increased the comforts of the middle classes. But they have not yet begun to effect those great changes in human destiny, which it is in their nature and in their futurity to accomplish." Alongside the economists was a miscellany of poets, philosophers, and demagogues; parsons, deists, and infidels; con-

servatives, radicals, and revolutionaries—men differing widely one from another in fundamentals but united in their hatred of factories and in their belief that economic change had led to the degradation of labor.

In the opposing camp there were publicists whose opinions are no less worthy of respect and whose disinterestedness and zeal for reform can hardly be called in question. . . . To offset the passage from Mill, let me quote two sentences from [reformer Edwin] Chadwick, who surely knew as much as anyone else of the squalor and poverty of large numbers of town dwellers in the forties: "The fact is, that hitherto, in England, wages, or the means of obtaining the necessaries of life for the whole mass of the labouring community, have advanced, and the comforts within the reach of the labouring classes have increased with the late increase of population. . . . We have evidence of this advance even in many of the manufacturing districts now in a state of severe depression." (He wrote in 1842.)

If a public opinion poll could have been taken, it is probable that the adherents of the first group would have been found to outnumber those of the second. But this is not a matter to be settled by a show of hands. . . . Writing to [English poet Robert] Southey in 1816, [reformer John] Rickman observed, "If one listens to common assertion, everything in grumbling England grows worse and worse"; and in a later letter, to a Frenchman, in which he pointed to the way in which the poor had benefited from public relief and cheap food, Rickman was careful to add, "But these arguments would encounter contradiction in England." The romantic revival in literature, which coincided in time with the Industrial Revo-

From "Standard of Life of the Workers in England," by T.S. Ashton, in *Capitalism and the Historians*, edited by F.A. Hayek. Copyright © 1954 by The University of Chicago. Reprinted by permission of the University of Chicago Press.

lution, tended to strengthen the despondency. Popular writers, like William Cobbett, pictured an earlier England peopled with merry peasants or sturdy beef-eating, beer-drinking yeomen, just as their predecessors of the age of [poet John] Dryden had conjured up the vision of a Patagonia peopled with noble savages. But neither native pessimism nor unhistorical romanticism is sufficient in itself to explain the prevalence of the view that the condition of the workers had deteriorated. It is part of my thesis that those who held this view had their eyes on one section of the working classes only.

After reading this selection, consider these questions:

1. What evidence does Ashton provide to counter the image of the total material and moral degradation of the working class in early industrialization?
2. For Ashton, what are the significant periods of early industrialization?
3. According to Ashton, what comparisons can be drawn between living conditions in early industrial England and in other parts of the world?

# SELECTION 4:

# The Rise of the Industrial City

A *new type of city emerged from the factory organization and the resulting population shifts. Whereas preindustrial cities often included a diversity of manufacturing and commercial activities and mixed large numbers of people across the social spectrum, the industrial cities of the nineteenth and twentieth centuries were different. Often dedicated to a single industry or to a number of related industries and divided into socially defined districts, these new cities had more clearly demarcated living and manufacturing sites as well as rich and poor neighborhoods. In its economic foundations, its class structure, its geographic layout, and especially its unprecedented growth in both population and size, the new industrial city formed the churning center of all the economic, social, political, and cultural forces that we understand by the term* Industrial Revolution. *From this center radiated changes that were to affect not only the towns and villages of Great Britain but also the economies and societies of other European countries in the decades to come.*

*The rise of industrial cities such as Manchester, Birmingham, and Lancaster was something new to history. In* The Making of Urban Europe, *the social historians Paul M. Hohenberg and Lynn Hollen Lees trace the gradual emergence of industrialization in the late eighteenth and early nineteenth century, before turning to a comparison between development of the industrial city of Manchester and the Ruhr Valley in Germany.*

Reprinted by permission of the publisher from *The Making of Urban Europe, 1000–1950,* by Paul M. Hohenberg and Lynn Hollen Lees (Cambridge, MA: Harvard University Press). Copyright © 1985, 1995 by the President and Fellows of Harvard College.

When William Cobbett wrote in the 1820s of his tours of England, he called his journey "rural rides." Most of the settlements he passed through were sleepy market centers or older county and cathedral towns, where farm houses and pasture-land were an easy walk from the central square. Even though he was quite ready, and indeed eager, to denounce the results of the new technology, only in a few places, like "black Sheffield," did he encounter the results of industrial urbanization. And Sheffield, of course, had a long protoindustrial manufacturing tradition. Travelers from town to town in continental Europe at about that time would have had even fewer glimpses of the impact of economic transformation. The new industrial order began in the countryside and only slowly worked its way into the established urban networks that spanned the Continent.

An analysis of industrial urbanization must therefore begin in the countryside. For it was there, notably in regions of rural protoindustry, that the force of economic growth together with demography—migration and heightened fertility—brought new industrial towns into being. Only in a second phase of industrial development did scores of factories appear along the streets and on the fringes of older cities. But even then, many towns were bypassed by the new army of smoke-belching, coal-consuming mills. Despite the rapid growth of urban industry in England, Belgium, France, Germany, and northern Italy after 1840 or so, economic development was a spatially selective process. Some regions deindustrialized while others were transformed by the new technology. Here a new urban network was quickly built around production sites; there adaptation meant taking on the newer modes of production at a measured pace. Within regions some towns could mushroom while others stagnated. While industrialization and urbanization are certainly intertwined in the history of modern Europe, the links between them cannot be reduced to the dual phenomena of factories springing up in towns and towns growing up around factories. . . .

What prompted the concentration of rural protoindustry? One partial explanation hinges on local social factors. Certain institutional systems of inheritance and certain agrarian structures were more favorable to protoindustry than others; equal inheritance, fixed land rents, and tenancy seem to have encouraged rural industry more than did primogeniture [inheritance by the eldest son only], sharecropping, or direct working of farms by landowners. It can also be argued that success in a given region was cumulative because human capital was amassed there. Entrepreneurial, commercial, and technical skills were "learned by doing." Natural resources also had a part to play, notably the presence of streams that could be harnessed or good access to food and markets. Finally, the choice of staple proved important. Cotton and light wool draperies (worsteds) had a bright future, linen a somber one. Primary metallurgy based on charcoal smelting would not only become obsolete, but it also tended to migrate ever deeper into the forests after fresh timber. Metalworking, on the other hand, nurtured skills that withstood shifts in process and product.

The rise and eventual transformation of protoindustrial regions was highly dependent upon one important factor: the availability of entrepreneurs. They could come from two different sources, each of which is compatible with one of our models of urban systems. First, the energy for change could arise in the countryside or in a village from a local producer. Industrial enterprises often originated with a craftsman who devised machinery to improve productivity and eventually expanded his operations to become an industrialist. His efforts would require the markets of nearby towns to supply raw materials, customers, and possibly capital for expansion. The business would expand to larger centers and through them to other regions along the links of the Central Place System.[1] Development proceeded from the base up with supply leading the way.

As we have seen in our expositions of the Network System,[2] urban elites in trading centers could also take the initiative to expand production. Similarly, landlords and territorial authorities often took leading roles in developing natural resources, such as mineral deposits and waterways. Merchant or gentry capitalists, whether traders, financiers, clothiers, or ironmasters, were

---

1. A city is a central location supplying its surrounding areas with various economic, administrative, and cultural services.   2. A network of trade, information, and influence links a city to the outside world.

driven to innovate. They also could muster the resources to overcome the technical, organizational, and spatial limits of protoindustry. One common strategy was, of course, to concentrate the work force in a single indoor location. This familiar scenario of factory development paved the way for new divisions of labor and for the introduction of expensive or large-scale equipment. Development from the top in this manner depended, however, on access to markets, ideas, and finance via an urban center or gateway to the region. Towns, then, performed several economic roles in the protoindustrial era. Even where rural industry was much more dynamic than urban, city elites helped to direct and to finance manufacturing in the countryside. Cities provided markets, transportation facilities, and skilled workmen to finish goods. Town dwellers and country workers both contributed to the complex divisions of labor that underlay production and distribution.

Over time, protoindustry reshaped urban networks in two ways. Under the spur of economic growth, hamlets swelled into villages and villages became towns. By 1800 in the West Riding of Yorkshire, Dewsbury and Barnsley, which would not become incorporated towns until after 1860, had turned into sizable settlements. The populations of Halifax, Wakefield, and Bradford had passed the 10,000 mark. A wide scattering of settlements along the valleys of Yorkshire had become by 1800 a partly urban manufacturing network of woolens and worsteds centered on Leeds, which served as a gateway city to the region. Protoindustry had provided the impetus for substantial urbanization. The outposts of the network expanded and revised to fit the changing geography of production. In general, protoindustrial urbanization bypassed the regularly spaced market towns in favor of more concentrated growth, where the combination of entrepreneurs, work force, and raw materials permitted expansion.

A second sort of protoindustrial urbanization affected the upper ranks of urban hierarchies. Regional capitals such as Leeds, Leipzig, and Lille, which already had substantial marketing and service functions, gained new importance with the growth of manufacturing in both town and hinterland. Cities that combined major central place functions with an expanding role in manufacturing and trading networks grew particularly rapidly. In fact, national capitals and major ports, where economic influence kept pace with political dominance, consolidated their position as primate cities. Manufacturing supported their growth and profited from it. Note that protoindustry did not produce major new cities but worked through the upper ranks of existing urban systems. The urban legacy of protoindustry, therefore, combined new growth in some areas with substantial amounts of continuity. . . .

Let us look at the process of economic change in two sorts of areas in order to clarify the relationship of towns to the exploding numbers of factories. Two regions of intensive, coal-based industrialization and one with more diffuse, adaptive development will serve as examples. Our first case is the Ruhr.

Around 1800 what was to become the center of German heavy industry was an impoverished region of backward agriculture bordering on the protoindustrial areas of the Siegerland, Sauerland, and the Wupper valley. Its few small towns, by origin medieval commercial centers, were evenly spaced along the line of an east-west trade route. The largest, Soest, had only 5,000 inhabitants. Around 1850 came the exploitation of the Ruhr coal deposits. As deep mineshafts bored into the hillsides and fields, cottages sprang up along the roadsides. Nearby nucleated villages housed the local population of farmers and small-holding miners. Entrepreneurs in the iron industry rushed into the local towns. Friedrich Krupp began his works in Essen, and Jacob Mayer moved into Bochum. Exponential rates of growth soon lifted those towns, along with Duisburg and Dortmund, into the ranks of the urban giants and turned groups of villages into sprawling cities like Gelsenkirchen, Wattenscheid, and Castrop. By 1900 almost half the Ruhr's two million people lived in its five largest towns. Two sorts of settlements grew in profusion: mining villages scattered over the coalfields and cities based on iron and steel production, often dominated by a single firm. The need to bring in iron ore and to market the flood of metal products pouring from the furnaces of Thyssen, Hoesch, and Krupp produced a spiderweb of railroads and canals that linked these cities via the Rhine to Rotterdam and other major European towns. The products of mine and forge were whisked out of the region to the markets of the world. These new networks brought the Ruhr into an international city system. Meanwhile, local central place hierarchies were hesitantly readjusted. Soest remained a sleepy market center dwarfed by its neighbors to the west, and a host of new cities rearranged local marketing patterns. Political hierarchies, moving to their own dynamics, remained separate from economic ones. Split among several rulers in 1800, the region fell under the authority of the Prussian state in 1815, becoming part of the province of Westphalia. But it was divided among several county units (*Regierungsbezirke*) whose administrative centers were Münster, Arnsberg, and Düsseldorf. Even after they rose to dominate the region, the newer industrial superstars were not given administrative functions by the state. Growth brought no automatic gift of local political influence.

Relatively similar economic functions characterized the towns of the Ruhr, which formed a complex but not highly differentiated urban system. In other areas, coal resources combined with a richer protoindustrial heritage to produce a much more specialized urban network. In Lancashire, coal-fired steam power drew cotton mills away from the fast streams of the Yorkshire border and into the ring of towns around Manchester. They stayed even after fuel costs ceased to be critical because by then there were no compelling reasons for change. Over time, Lancashire developed into a finely articulated industrial system, more sophisticated than the popular image of endless cotton mills and workers' slums suggests. Liverpool and Manchester divided the functions of a regional capital, and the composition of their employment reflected the shared leadership roles. By 1851 only 24 percent of Manchester's work force was actually in textiles, and much of

that outside the basic spinning and weaving branches. Machine building and other auxiliary industries were important, but Manchester's principal role was that of commercial and service center to the circle of cotton towns around it: Bolton, Bury, and Stockport nearby, Preston, Blackburn, and Burnley further north. Liverpool was even less industrial in the narrow sense, and then mainly in support of trade and shipping. In brief, Manchester was the summit of the array of central places, whereas Liverpool served as the gateway city linking the region to European and trans-Atlantic urban networks.

A zone devoted to processing industries—glassworks, metal smelters, and chemical plants—stretched from Saint Helens south to the Cheshire coalfields, between the two regional centers. Even in those undemanding times, it was deemed prudent to segregate the worse nuisances; good transportation and deposits of salt and coal added positive locational attractions. It was transportation, in fact, that sealed the unity of the whole region. In 1835 one George Head entertained himself by exploring the various ways of going from Manchester to Liverpool. He found three quite distinct routes without subjecting himself to the inconvenience of a road journey. The date is noteworthy because it marks the precise changeover point between canals and railroads for passenger traffic in England. By mid-century the regional system was finely tuned and of unequaled efficiency and technical as well as economic sophistication.

After reading this selection, consider these questions:

1. How do Hohenberg and Lees characterize the first phase of industrialization?
2. What is meant by the term *protoindustrialization*?
3. Compare early industrialization in England and Germany.

# SELECTION 5:
# The Life of a Worker

*The growth of urban centers created social needs, but governments were slow to respond. At first, laissez-faire advocates and interventionists argued about the government's role in disputes between workers and factory owners and whether it should intervene to improve housing conditions and social services for the growing populations. Ultimately, however, municipal, regional, and national authorities created and extended their police forces, mail and rail services, census bureaus, public health agencies, and similar state functions. Politicians gradually recognized their responsibilities for public education and the general improvement of the lot of the urban workers and their families.*

*Although conditions were never to be as bad in later phases of industrialization or in the first stages of industrialization on the continent of Europe, the lives of the individual workers were still extremely difficult. What is perhaps worse, their lives offered little hope of improvement. The following selection is drawn from the autobiography of the editor, poet, and playwright Otto Krille (1878–1954). The son of a mason who died before he was born, Krille had to find his way through a number of jobs as an unskilled worker in the German city of Dresden. Although he wrote his autobiography from the perspective of a worker who had eventually made his way out of early poverty, Krille never lost the sense of hopelessness or the search for dignity that he had experienced as a young and often unemployed worker.*

It was humiliating to have to run from factory to factory and from business to business to offer myself as a scribe, a packer, an errand boy, and a work boy. But what else could I do since my knowledge of practical workaday life was very small, and my mother was unable to pay for me to learn a profitable trade. The first times were the worst for me. The false sense of shame that I had from the military school made me hesitate at the doors or even turn around. When I had gotten up the courage and shyly and blushingly stammered out my request and softly answered all questions, the end result would kill all my hopes for the rest of the day. Except for my discharge certificate from the noncommissioned officers' school, I had neither testimony of work performed nor anything else that could speak for me. All I had was my honest seventeen-year-old face. But on my discharge certificate was written in fine neat letters: Discharged as unsuitable to be a noncommissioned officer. You could make everything or nothing out of that, and my dear fellow citizens (in all their humanity) probably thought the very worst. The searching looks that they gave my face revealed their thoughts. I secretly clenched my fist during this silent inquisition; and my shame was even more oppressive when I still didn't get the position or was sent away with the remark that they would write if I got it.

From *The German Worker: Working-Class Autobiographies from the Age of Industrialization*, translated and edited by Alfred Kelly. Copyright © 1987 by the Regents of the University of California. Reprinted by permission of the University of California Press.

I'd had such a colorful, glowing vision of life and had yearned so greatly for my freedom, but after these secret tortures there wasn't a glimmer of all my dreams left. Any thoughts of a career as an actor were obliterated, and I even missed out on the sense of regret that often gives consolation to weak-willed people. What did I know about life anyway? It looked so different than in books. . . . I was suddenly confronted with the mystery of life, whose stony indifferent face could only preach: Work so that you don't go under. I was a slender, pale, and shy boy, and must have offered to the world a conflicting picture. Although my mother didn't reproach me, I could tell from her anxious looks how much my fate and my continued unemployment worried her. But not for a minute did I have any remorse or secret yearning to go back to the military school. Even as a simple worker I had the freedom to think and do as I pleased outside the factory, and I had control over my own fate. Or so it seemed to me. . . .

For the first time I had a feeling of powerlessness toward life. My mother worked for the big Dresden Lace and Curtain Factory. She worked at home, removing the superfluous threads that the machine production left in the pieces of cloth. She succeeded in getting me work at the factory. So I started work—for the first few days fetching spools, shuttles, and other things that were needed for the power looms. Then I got my own winding machine. It transferred the thread from big wooden spools onto the little spools, made out of two connected metal plates, which could be used at the looms. You had to pay some attention while threading the spools, and then while the machine was going you had to see that any breaks in the thread were immediately retied. As soon as I had the necessary dexterity, I occupied my mind by examining the completely unfamiliar surroundings. Only a few of the men and women workers were organized. My desire to learn something of socialism and Social Democracy wasn't satisfied here. With respect to all social life there was a general stupor of the sort that we associate with a virtually extinct generation of workers. During the breaks the talk was of personal experiences and pleasures, or else there was erotic banter or dirty jokes, directed especially at the younger women. I was completely isolated.

The fate of an entire class of people was soon frighteningly clear to me. Day after day, week after week, year after year, always this monotonous life with no variety. For centuries, thousands of lives had just been unwinding, like the threads on my machine. The thought oppressed me and demanded some kind of release. This was the origin of my poems "The Winder" and others. The heavier that all this lay on me, the more urgent was my desire to get to know the new doctrine that promised an ascent from the misery.

My religious views had fallen away piece by piece. What was left, the machine unwound from my soul. No matter how much I racked my brains, I could find no sense in the order of the world, least of all in a divine order. That millions have to do without and sacrifice their humanity to a wretched existence, while, on the other hand, fantastic wealth arises and brings with it new cultural wonders every day—the very thought was torture. But I could no longer believe that it was all necessary, in principle necessary, and that there was divine purpose in this principle. That was not a life-affirming but rather a murderous belief, and doubting it was a blessing. It seemed to me even more horrible that millions embraced this faith and that philosophers wrote about life without choking on this question.

The little time that remained to me between work and rest was taken up by reading the Social Democratic *Saxon Workers' Paper* [*Sächsischer Arbeiterzeitung*] and some current political pamphlets. That wasn't enough for me; I yearned for support. My eldest brother brought me a ticket to the founders' day festival of the Social Democratic club and I decided to go.

On the evening of the festival I sat alone at a table in the hall of the "Golden Meadow" and watched with curiosity the gestures and faces of the workers streaming in. My romantic fears made me feel ill at ease. But there was absolutely nothing conspiratorial in anyone's behavior. I was still affected by the ideas from the military school. All the people around me were conspirators against law and order, and yet I couldn't see anything that made them different from anyone else. I didn't dare to speak. A man of about thirty had sat down at my table, and I looked him over mistrustfully with a few stolen glances. My brother had warned me about police spies since I wasn't a member of the club. I took it for granted that the man across from me was one of those whom the government hired to snoop around everywhere and bring misfortune to honest people.

All around the hall, in the gallery and down below, there were shields and placards with sayings on them: "Through the night to the light"; "Undeterred by our enemies"; "Light our minds and fire our hearts"; and a lot more things like that. These heightened my tension to an almost unbearable level. I could feel my heart beating in my throat. Up in front next to the podium there were several large potted plants and behind them you could see two plaster heads. As I learned later these were busts of Marx and Lassalle.

Then the music started up. For a while it was just like any other harmless festival. The strangeness, the rebelliousness that would stir me up so much was a long time in coming. Then a man of average height with black hair and a thin mustache and beard stepped up to the podium. His voice had something weak about it, with nothing of the power of a field marshall's or a leader's voice. He almost whispered the word "comrade." You could tell it was hard for him to talk. He stood there, bent forward as though he wanted to say his words specially to each individual. He had consumption [tuberculosis]. But I only learned that later.

At first his words made no sense to me. But then something came into his voice that made me listen. Something in his voice flickered, grew, and came nearer and nearer, and finally became a huge flame that lit me up totally. And then I began to understand.

He condemned the social conditions that I'd gotten to know myself. Then he spoke of the growth of Social Democracy, and he said that the founding of the smallest workers' club was more significant to culture than a battle victory. That was all new and strange to me. In the history lessons in military school they placed the greatest significance on the wars and battles that had been fought between individual rulers. Sometimes we even had to learn the uniforms and the colors of

the collars and the facings of the fighting regiments. But now here was a worker (at least judging by his simple clothes) standing up there turning this view of the world upside down. How was it possible? Either he was lying or my teachers had lied.

And yet everything that the man said gave the impression of truth and moved you by its simplicity. The speech ended with a salute to Social Democracy. Everyone stood up and joined in. I did too and then sat there with peculiar feelings and thoughts for the whole evening, so that everything that followed went right by me.

The speaker, whose name was Eichhorn, was the president of the club. He was an old and revered Social Democrat, as was his wife who had accomplished fine and brave things for the party and the socialist women's movement. Both had been severely persecuted by the police. Both of them died, tragically, of consumption, which they had gotten as a result of the deprivations and persecutions under the Socialist Law.

The feelings that I took home with me from the festival were almost religious. Here was a way out of the despair. But this was soon followed by sober reflection, and I asked myself if it wasn't all deception and consolation in a never-never land. In the end, the future state seemed to be like the heaven of the religious. There was so much in the newspapers about the lies and troublemaking of Social Democracy that it was possible to be very wrong about it. But in spite of myself I felt deep down that the victory belonged to socialism. The heart is a funny thing; it allows the head to reason but still rules almost unrestrictedly. Often we take pride in our reasonable actions and don't even notice that it is actually the heart that has decided for us. I grabbed at the new gospel as a thirsty man grabs for a drink. I had to have faith in order to bear life. And of the millions who adhere to socialism today only a tiny fraction are socialists from scientific conviction; most come to socialism from a vast internal and external wasteland like the people of Israel out of the wilderness. They have to believe in order not to despair. They are socialists because socialism is their cause, material and spiritual. The worker needs it as he needs air and bread. I soon observed also that the more intellectually alive workers were generally Social Democrats.

After this I often attended mass meetings, and I slowly became familiar with Social Democratic ideas. In the past the idea of the state had seemed to me to have a kind of medieval crudity that was embodied in barracks and prisons. This attitude changed imperceptibly, because I learned to see myself as a citizen of this state who, though oppressed, still had an interest in it because I hoped to take it over for my own class. And the strangest thing was—and this revealed itself only later—that I, the despiser of unconditional military discipline, willingly submitted to party discipline. As contradictory as it may seem, socialist ideology reconciled me to a certain extent with my proletarian existence, and taught me to respect common manual labor. I no longer shied away from the name "worker.". . .

In the long run I didn't like it at the curtain factory, even though the work suited me OK. It was more the surroundings that caused me to quit. I missed a spirit of brotherhood among the workers.

After reading this selection, consider these questions:

1. How would you describe Krille's early life?

2. What were his feelings about life and work?

3. What were his attitudes toward politics?

# CHAPTER 8
# Family, Gender, and Class in the Early Industrial Era

As we have seen, the term *Industrial Revolution* means more than the application of machine power to the production of commodities. It involved new forms of economic activities and new types of social organization. The new factories were only the most obvious examples of these innovations; the development of large industrial cities was another. Industrialization also impacted the family and the organization of society as a whole. Industrialization would also alter the relations between men and women. Young women especially would in increasing numbers have to find work outside the home, thus providing them with new problems and new opportunities. Working-class children, too, were to be employed in ways unknown to previous generations.

Society began to be thought of differently. As the Industrial Revolution progressed, social relations assumed the structure of class relations. Society was now seen in terms of the classes—in the relation of groups to the means of production—and less in terms of the quasi-caste distinctions of earlier ages. A larger middle class emerged, wealthier and more politically secure than earlier members of this bourgeoisie. Before the Industrial Revolution and the French Revolution, the word *bourgeoisie* referred to people who lived in cities and enjoyed the privileges associated with urban residence, regardless of their economic status. From this group there arose a new class of wealthy and often extremely wealthy industrialists, who would assume positions of political, social, and cultural dominance. Industrial workers, coming from the countryside and farm labor, tended to experience harsh living conditions and low wages. Like the middle class, the working class was divided into various subgroups, determined by skill, wages, and workplace. This class included the skilled workers from preindustrial modes of production as well as the equally skilled workers who made and maintained the new machinery of the industrial age. It also included workers who tended these machines and those who worked the mines that produced the coal and iron ore for the machines. Women and children also labored in small shops and at home under what we would today call sweatshop conditions. Wages in such places were extremely low, based not on hours worked but on the amount of product produced. Beneath these workers were the men, women, and children who performed the least skilled occupations—dock workers, porters, domestic servants, cooks, cleaning women, prostitutes, messengers, and newsboys.

The massive and radical changes brought on by the Industrial Revolution produced a wide range of responses. The class organization of society eventually gave rise to new types of collective consciousness—class consciousness. New economic forces, new social organizations, and the rise of new forms of consciousness would before long have their effects upon politics. From the second half of the nineteenth century and into the twentieth century, the question of the relation between the nation-state (the legacy of the French Revolution) and the class organization of society brought on by the Industrial Revolution would arise again and again.

What is "class consciousness"? Does the formation of social classes generate specific forms of consciousness? In the second half of the eighteenth century, the social and moral problems posed by industrialization as well as the question of class consciousness—which would become so prominent in the nineteenth century—were hardly recognized. Adam Smith, for instance, envisioned little of the ill effects of industrialization. His classic work *The Wealth of Nations* (1776) argues for the openness of world markets, the disinvolvement of governments in the economic sphere, and the free contractual relation between workers and factory owners. Smith's notion of laissez-faire—of leaving economic relations of all types free to regulate themselves—has come to be interpreted as the basis of a new ethic. Individuals, groups, and nations should seek the greatest profits, and somehow through the operations of what Smith called the "invisible hand," these selfish motives would lead to the greater benefit of all. Smith's own opinions on ethical issues are more complex than this. In *The Theory of Moral Sentiments* (1759), Smith developed a theory of morals that was not contradicted by his later *Wealth of Nations*. For Smith, individual moral commitment and the growth of a free economy seemed to go hand in hand.

In the early nineteenth century, however, economists and social reformers increasingly saw that industrial society brought about a wide range of problems, most of which were unknown to earlier generations. The solution to these problems appeared to lie in the reorganization of government and society. One of the earliest and most influential thinkers to propose such solutions was the French social reformer Claude-Henri de Rouvroy, comte de Saint-Simon (1760–1825). Saint-Simon was reacting less directly to early industrialization than to the economic and social convulsions associated with the French Revolution. Having personally witnessed the ways in which government and social interests often collided to the detriment of individuals, Saint-Simon preached a new doctrine of socialism. In a forward-looking program of thoroughgoing reforms, he sought to reorganize social relations in order that they fit in better with the new economic relations of what he called "industrialism." Industrialism was to be spearheaded by the new class of "industrialists." His followers in France were proponents of entrepreneurship and the standardization and centralization of the financial system. Saint-Simon's utopian vision for social planning would later be derided by Karl Marx (1818–1886) as impractical and nonscientific "utopian socialism." Nonetheless, Saint-Simonianism would champion a number of practical concerns, which would have immediate impact on economic and social organization.

Working-class movements, socialist or otherwise, have forever been influenced by the writing of Marx. What would gradually become known as Marxism would exceed the appeal of earlier forms of socialism, such as utopian socialism, and provide a basis for the several types of socialist parties that would emerge in the various European states. Marx himself was born into a middle-class family in Germany and received a doctorate in philosophy at the University of Berlin. In 1842 he became editor of the *Rhineland Gazette*, but his attempts to make the newspaper an engine of economic and social reform soon put him at odds with his publisher. Marx then left Germany, moving first to Paris and then to Brussels. While in Paris in 1844, Marx began to think through the causes and the consequences of industrialization. He read the works of the French socialists Saint-Simon, Charles Fourier, and René-François-Armand Prudhomme, and he then turned to an analysis of English political economy.

While in Belgium, Marx became politically active. He helped found the Communist League, dedicated to overthrowing the existing political and social order. At the request of the Communist League, Marx and his friend and fellow socialist Friedrich Engels published a declaration of the league's principles. *The Communist Manifesto* appeared in 1848, intended to give direction to the growing revolutionary tide arising throughout the nations of Europe. In the *Manifesto,* Marx and Engels not only itemize their criticisms of existing political and social conditions but also outline a theory of revolution and project a future form of social organization.

# SELECTION 1:

# Child Labor

*Industrialization brought increasing numbers of working-class children into the mines and factories of Great Britain. In the early 1840s, more than fifty thousand children and young adults worked in mining, hauling and sorting coal. In the factories, children were hired because it was thought that, with their smaller hands and arms and greater agility, they would be able to maneuver around and repair broken threads and clean and maintain the moving parts of machines.*

*The physical and moral debilitation that resulted from such work did not go entirely unnoticed. The often harsh conditions of child and woman labor induced national governments rather than municipal or local governments to intervene to protect them. Although doctrinaire liberals opposed all state intervention in the "free" contractual relations between workers and factory owners, the increasing numbers of women and children in factories and mines led to further parliamentary investigations and actual legislation protecting children in the 1830s. The Factory Acts of 1842 and 1844 also prescribed a maximum workday for women. Similar legislation was passed in France and Germany in the 1880s and 1890s and the United States in the early twentieth century.*

*The first government investigation into child labor occurred in 1816, when a committee of the British Parliament was commissioned to investigate working conditions. Its chairman was the industrialist Sir Robert Peel, the father of the future prime minister.*

[Interview of Sir Gilbert Blane, M.D., examined by Sir Robert Peel:] You are by profession a physician?—[Blane:] I am.

[Peel:] It is well known you have had much experience in your profession?—[Blane:] I have.

[Peel:] Supposing that children are employed in close rooms, regularly day by day, for thirteen hours and a half, one hour and a half being occupied in meals, is it your opinion that the children, so employed, at the early age of from six to twelve, would receive no injury in their health?—[Blane:] It is necessary I should premise: I have no experience as to manufactories, and therefore my answer must depend on general analogy. From what I have observed in the course of my experience, for the last three-and-thirty years, in all ranks; and from being twelve years physician to one of the largest hospitals in London, I certainly should say it was greatly too much for the health of the children. My grounds of inference, with regard to the health of children, is founded on the natural appetency of all young creatures to loco-motive exercise, and the open air; from what

I have witnessed in the lower orders, and particularly from the bills of mortality in this town, in which I have observed, in the course of the last century, the mortality diminished from one in twenty to one in thirty-eight; and upon casting my eyes upon the different periods of life, I find that the great difference has arisen from the diminished mortality of children; and this diminished mortality, I apprehend, has arisen from children being brought up in purer air, with more cleanliness and greater warmth: that cleanliness, warmth, and ventilation, are the great cause of the health of young persons, and to which the great diminution of mortality, in this metropolis, has been chiefly owing. The diminution of mortality in grown persons has been owing chiefly to the same causes, preventing the generation and propagation of infectious fevers.

[Peel:] If children, at a very early age, were to be confined from fourteen to sixteen hours each day, though an immediate indisposition might not take place, do not you conceive that they would be prevented acquiring their full growth and strength when arrived at maturity?—[Blane:] I am assuredly of that opinion; for the consequence of confinement is to produce two or three diseases, which are particularly produced by confinement and want of exercise, I mean rickets and

From the Minutes of Evidence of the Select Committee on the State of Children Employed in Manufactories, Parliament, London, 1816.

mesenteric obstructions, weakness of body, and imbecility of mind.

[Peel:] Those disorders are particularly to be apprehended in children from seven to ten years of age?—[Blane:] Certainly, that is the period of life; I would say from birth to ten.

[Peel:] Have you had any opportunity of seeing the condition of children in any of the manufacturing towns, either lately or at an earlier period of life?—[Blane:] I was about twenty years ago in Buckinghamshire, and saw the lace manufactories, which evidently have an injurious effect on the health of children.

[Peel:] You conceive the employment of children, under ten years of age, from twelve to fourteen hours a day, is particularly likely to produce those complaints, and generally to be disadvantageous to their condition?—[Blane:] Most assuredly; that great length of time in the day, I should conceive to be highly injurious.

[Peel:] To what number of hours do you mean to refer, when you speak of that great length of confinement?—[Blane:] I think any thing above ten hours, at that early age.

[Peel:] Do you happen to know what number of children, in the lace manufactories, were employed?—[Blane:] I did not enter into the detail; I was merely on a visit.

[Peel:] Did you observe from their appearance that they had sallow countenances and other indications of ill health?—[Blane:] I certainly did.

[Peel:] What was the apparent age of them?—[Blane:] From seven or eight to fifteen.

[Peel:] Did it occur to you, to make any remark upon what you conceived to be the cause of that sickly appearance of the children?—[Blane:] I should say it was confinement in bad air.

[Peel:] Are you acquainted with the general state of the stature of the people in that country?—[Blane:] They are not the most robust, according to my observation. . . .

[Interview of G.L. Turkill, M.D. Peel:] Do you think that a room in a factory, one hundred feet long, five-and-thirty feet wide, and eight feet high, containing eight-and-twenty persons, the temperature of the air being from sixty to sixty-six degrees of the thermometer, would be a degree of closeness injurious to health?—[Turkill:] I should think the height of the room insufficient.

[Peel:] The room ventilated?—[Turkill:] I think it would not be injurious to health.

[Peel:] Have you had any practical experience of the effects on the health of children employed in manufactories?—[Turkill:] I have not.

[Peel:] From your general and extensive observation amongst the lower classes of people, the labouring classes, have you ever had reason to observe a want of affection and tenderness on the part of parents towards their children?—[Turkill:] I have occasionally had much reason to observe it. I have known a case, in which the parents refused to inoculate their children, or to have them vaccinated, because they hoped they might take the disease, and die of it.

[Peel:] Do not you know, that there prevails in a great part of the kingdom an opinion, that it is contrary to the principles of religion to convey to any child the smallpox by artificial means?—[Turkill:] There are individuals who have that opinion.

[Peel:] Does it not extend over a great part of the kingdom?—[Turkill:] Not to my knowledge.

[Peel:] Do you mean to extend the want of feeling and affection, on the part of parents to their child, beyond the single case you have mentioned of inoculation or vaccination?—[Turkill:] I do not mean to say, that there prevails a general disinclination in parents, by any means, towards their children.

[Peel:] From the general tenor of your experience, which has been so extensive, what has been the general impression on your mind, of the feelings of the lower orders towards their children?—[Turkill:] I think they are generally affectionate. . . .

[Interview of Robert Owen. Peel:] You have stated, that children of four years old are employed; will you please to specify where such children are employed?—[Owen:] Such children have been employed in Stockport; on Sunday fortnight I went to the Sunday school in Stockport, for the purpose of obtaining information upon a variety of points; I was introduced to the treasurer, to the secretary, and to another respectable gentleman, whose name I have not now in my memory; I asked them what was the earliest age at which they knew children to be employed in the manufactories at Stockport; the treasurer informed me that he knew a child (a boy) whose name he has given me, was employed at the age of four; the secretary immediately replied, "I know one child, a girl, who was employed at the age of three," and that it was a very common practice to employ children at the ages of five or six; the treasurer's name is Turner, and the secretary's, George Oughton.

[Peel:] In what did you understand this infant of three years old to be employed?—[Owen:] In a cotton mill.

[Peel:] You never heard of one of two years?—[Owen:] I was only one hour in Stockport; if I had made particular enquiries for a day or two days, I do not know what I might have discovered.

[Peel:] In what possible way do you believe a child of that age could be employed?—[Owen:] Not in any way to advantage.

[Peel:] Do you really believe such a child could be employed?—[Owen:] I confess, although I have known for so many years the miseries the children have suffered in many manufactories, I was astonished at this last fact.

[Peel:] You are requested to state, whether you really think any such child could be employed?—[Owen:] I believe what was told me by Mr. Turner, whose word I have every reason to believe may be relied upon.

[Peel:] Do you really conceive that a child of three years could be employed in any branch of the spinning business?—[Owen:] It is possible, and very probable, and the way in which many of these infants are first employed is to pick up the waste cotton from the floor; to go under the machines, where bigger people cannot creep, and the smaller they are the more conveniently they can go under the machines.

[Peel:] What other children do you know employed under the age of five years old?—[Owen:] I enquired of several individuals, and they informed me that children were very commonly employed at five and six years of age.

[Peel:] Do you not know that there is a fashion of listening very often to what they call hoax people?—[Owen:] If you went into a mill, knowing you were unacquainted with the matter, individuals might wish to hoax you; but those individuals knew that I was acquainted with all the details, and I think they would not attempt to hoax me upon such a subject.

[Peel:] Did you ever in any instance see or hear of any other case of a child of that age being employed?—[Owen:] I have seen very young children employed frequently; I cannot say what their ages were, but they appeared very young, and very unfit for the situation.

[Peel:] Did you ever hear of any children being actually engaged to pick up cotton in cotton mills, and being paid for such employment?—[Owen:] Yes, frequently; I have employed them myself, and do so now.

[Peel:] At what age?—[Owen:] At the ages of six, seven and eight formerly, now at ten to twelve.

[Peel:] What wages do you suppose a child of three years old got?—[Owen:] The case stated is a very extraordinary case, but the gentleman who related it to me can, I doubt not, state all the particulars.

# SELECTION 2:

# Women and Industrial Labor

W*omen, too, were increasingly employed in factory work. There are a number of good reasons why this labor force tended to be dominated by young women. Spinning and cloth production were traditionally considered*

*to be "women's work." By the 1830s tens of thousands of women were em-
ployed in the production of cotton, woolen, and silk cloth in Manchester,
England; Lyon, France; and Lowell, Massachusetts. In addition, women,
like children, could usually be hired for about half of a man's wage.*

*In* Women, Work, and Family *(1978), Louise A. Tilly and Joan W. Scott
trace the gradual move of women into the factories and other related occupations of the early Industrial Revolution. Drawing on representative
occupational and demographic samples from urban households in Great
Britain and France, they demonstrate that throughout the nineteenth century traditional forms of women's employment continued to dominate the
lives of women. In 1851 the largest group of wage-earners in Britain (40
percent) were employed as domestic servants. In 1866 in France, 40 percent of the female labor force was still involved in agriculture. Only one-
fifth of the total female labor force in Britain and one-tenth in France
worked in the textile industry. Providing examples from a wide range of
first-person accounts, Tilly and Scott offer vivid pictures of the impact of
the changing economic and social forces on the lives of individual women.*

Early industrialization did not create dramatic changes in the types of jobs women did. Yet the changes associated with economic and urban growth did alter the location of work and increased the numbers of women working for wages. Most significant, in fact, was the spread of wage labor which accompanied industrialization. The decline of the household mode of production meant that women more often worked away from their homes. The concentration of certain jobs in specific regions or cities, moreover, drew young rural women farther from home than their predecessors had gone to find employment. For increasing numbers of women, as well, the essence of work was earning a wage. Since they were members of family wage economies, their work was defined not by household labor needs, but by the household's need for money to pay for food and to meet other expenses, such as rent. In the family wage economy the interdependence of family members and their sense of obligation to the family unit remained strong. The importance of family membership and family ties continued. As in the past, daughters and wives worked in the family interest. The old rules of the family econ-

omy continued to operate in new contexts. But changing conditions, and particularly the spread of wage labor, began to change the relationships of daughters to their families as well as the allocation of married women's time among their productive and household activities.

We do not mean to suggest that all lower-class families were family wage economies. The household mode of production continued among French peasants and among some English and French craftsmen. In 1860, the French reporter Audiganne described weavers' cottages in the countryside outside Rouen:

> Here, the life of the family is rooted in custom: father, mother, sons and daughters spend all day around looms, producing together, each according to his strength. . . . The fruits of their labor and daily expenditures are shared by all.

Agricole Perdiguier, recalling his early-nineteenth-century childhood on a farm in France, wrote that his father made everyone work, even the girls and "especially the two oldest. . . . Madeleine and Babet worked with us, like men." The French sociologist Frédéric Le Play collected numerous case histories from the 1850s through the 1870s which document the continuation of the family economy among English and French workers' families. Nonetheless this mode of production and family organization was on the decline in both countries.

Reprinted by permission of the authors from *Women, Work, and Family,* by Louise A. Tilly and Joan W. Scott (New York: Holt, Rinehart & Winston, 1978).

The family wage economy was an increasingly prevalent form of family organization. The wages of family members formed a common fund which paid for expenses and supported the group. A twentieth-century observer described the family wage economy among the poor of London in 1908. She called it a "joint family."

> Joint households are perhaps the most distinguishing feature of domestic life among the poor; there are few homes in which no trace of the system is to be found. . . .The joint household is only tolerable so long as it maintains an accepted head, and each member pays the mother a sum to cover all expenses and shares in the common meals.

The composition of the household no longer was dictated by a need for household laborers, as in the family economy, but by a need for cash. The balance among wage earners and consumers in the household determined family fortunes. Reybaud, the French commentator on the work and family life of the popular classes, first described what Seebohm Rowntree was later to call the "poverty cycle." Family prosperity or poverty, wrote Reybaud, was closely tied to family composition. When a couple first married, they prospered, for both worked for wages. But after the babies came,

> the household was full of young children who needed supervision, cost money, and brought none in. Pregnancy and lactation diminished the resources the wife could contribute. The man carried the common burden practically alone. As the children grew, this situation improved; between 8 and 15 years of age, they stopped being a burden and became a resource; now all hands were occupied, and as small as their wages might be, they added a supplement to the budget that could not be disdained.

When the children moved out to set up their own households, the parents were again on their own. The parents' wage-earning ability declined, sickness and other crises overtook them, and misery often ensued again. The need to balance wage-earners and consumers in the household underlay many of the decisions about women's work and domestic responsibilities in the family wage economy. . . .

Once a girl embarked on her work, family ties changed. Daughters could become more independent of family controls than in the past. The location of work away from home, and the fact that they earned individual wages and lived in cities instead of small village communities, increased the autonomy of working-class daughters. Even if a working girl lived at home, her relationship to her family might change. As a wage earner she learned about money and what it could buy. She could contribute her wages and her knowledge to family decisions and she might claim some measure of influence over the allocation of family resources since her wages were part of those resources. The other side of independence, however, was vulnerability. Working girls earned low wages and their employment was often unstable. The loss of protections once provided by family, village community, and church increased a girl's economic and sexual vulnerability.

Gradually, despite the continuity of family values among rural and urban working families, changes in the organization of production and in the structure of occupational opportunity for women altered the relationships between parents and daughters during the nineteenth century. The results were both more choice and more risk for young women.

The availability in cities of jobs for women meant that girls were not restricted to domestic service. Often service was only the first step, a means of entry into the city. When a girl lost one job, she pursued others. Many a young woman moved back and forth between domestic service and the numerous unskilled trades in a city. Many of the garment trades were seasonal, too, forcing girls to seek other kinds of work in slack periods. When Charles Benoist reported on women's work in the Parisian garment industry, he wrote:

> Yes, indeed, her budget balances. But with winter comes cold, with unemployment hunger and with sickness death. Irresistibly, the question arises, How do these women who number in the thousands in Paris, how do they live? Live! Ask rather

how they keep from dying.

. . . The existence of alternatives also meant that girls could reject the physically more demanding work of a farm, for example, and remain in the city, an option which earlier had not been available on the scale it was in the nineteenth century. Le Play's account of the experiences of the daughter of a small propertied peasant in the countryside of Champagne captures the process as it affected one family in 1856.

> For the past two years, the oldest daughter has been sent to Châlons for part of each year, as an apprentice in a *maison de lingerie*. She is not paid, but receives her food free. After her apprenticeship is finished, she will be a domestic in a house in some nearby city. When she is at home, she helps her mother with her needlework and replaces her in caring for the household. [The mother was a seamstress and her earnings were "one of the principal resources of the family."] . . . But since she began going to the city, she does certain farm chores only with great repugnance. Despite her resistance, however, she is forced to thresh and to collect manure along the road.

One cannot but conclude that, for this daughter, permanent departure was only a matter of time.

Another aspect of women's occupations, of course, was that, except in textile factories, wages were low and employment was unstable. Accumulating enough money to send home must have been impossible for many girls. Their consequent inability to help their families undoubtedly diminished contacts and ties with their former homes.

Whether or not they maintained contact, rural girls increasingly did not return home. The migration of the domestic servant, which in the past was often temporary, increasingly tended to become permanent. Even when a girl did keep in touch with her parents, the fact that she did not intend to return home loosened family ties. Rural girls no longer used their work as a means of gaining resources which would enable them to become farm wives. Instead they became permanent urban residents.

The life of Jeanne Bouvier, born in the department of Isère in 1865, provides an interesting example of this urban migration. Bouvier entered the gamut of female occupations, ultimately settling in Paris as a seamstress. As a child, she lived on a farm, which her father had inherited from his parents. He was both a farmer and a barrelmaker. Jeanne helped her mother in the fields, but her particular job was to watch the cows. Since that chore left her hands idle, her mother made her knit as well. When she was ten, her parents sent her to a convent for ten months to learn her catechism. She also learned to read and sew there. When she was eleven, in 1876, her father's trade was ruined. Phylloxera, the disease of grapevines, devastated wine production in southern France and hence the barrel trade. M. Bouvier could not support his family with the farm alone. All family members now had to earn wages, so Jeanne's mother found her a job in a silk-spinning factory, where she worked thirteen hours a day spinning the silk threads that supplied the Lyons silk-weaving industry.

After a time, she was sent back to the country to live with her maternal grandfather, then to another silk factory. The work made her ill, so a cousin in Vienne found her a job with some truck farmers. There she was a maid of all work, caring for their children, their cows, and the vegetable gardens. During a visit to her godmother, Jeanne complained of her unhappiness, and the godmother told her not to go back to the farm. The next day she helped the fourteen-year-old Jeanne find a job in a silk factory. This one housed its employees, so Jeanne had a place to live as well. From her wages she bought her own food. (She does not say whether she sent money to her mother, or whether she was expected to do this.) Then her mother wrote and told Jeanne that she had to come with her to Paris. The girl resisted, but her godfather reminded her of her obligation to obey (though her mother had no means of enforcing the demand). "If your mother wants to take you to Paris," he told her, "you must go with her. If you had no parents, you would not have to go."

Jeanne's mother had found jobs for them both with a brush manufacturer in Paris. (Small businesses of this kind proliferated in cities.) Jeanne was an apprentice, her mother a maid of all work. After eight days, both mother and daughter were fired and received no pay. Some cousins helped get them jobs, first as domestic servants. Then they found Jeanne a position as a hatmaker. Family auspices of this type were important for Jeanne during the early stages of her working life. Without the network of kin and godparents, she would have had great difficulty finding work.

Jeanne lived with her cousins for a while, paying fifteen francs a week for room and board. She felt they spent too much on food, so she saved some money, bought a bed, and rented a room. From this point on, Jeanne Bouvier was on her own. She had fewer contacts with her family and rarely saw her mother. She made friends with some other girls her age who rented rooms in the same building, and she basked in the warmth of the friendships they established. When the hat trade foundered, she sought another job. She took on piecework and sewed garments in her room, but found that paid too little. So she entered a shop as a seamstress, gradually working her way up to the highest levels of skill. By this time Jeanne Bouvier had become a Parisian.

Permanent migration of this kind was encouraged not only by expanded opportunities for women to work in cities, but also by changes in families themselves. When families became wage-earning instead of producing units, family members no longer shared a common interest in the property which guaranteed their livelihood. Of course, daughters often had left home in the past and so had not always worked on the land or in the shop. But the resources owned by their parents had had an important influence on their futures in the form of dowries or marriage settlements. When parents had no resources but their own and their children's labor power, they had few long-term material holds on the loyalties of their children. Of course, material considerations were not the only basis of parent-child relationships. The values of the family could and did transcend the conditions which gave rise to them. (Jeanne Bouvier accompanied her mother to Paris simply because she was her mother.) Membership in a family also provided many nonmaterial benefits. Again, Bouvier's experiences are il-

lustrative. Family ties helped her find jobs and negotiate difficulties whenever she moved. But the absence of property often meant there was no reason to return home; indeed, it precluded such a return even if a child desired it.

Even when daughters remained at home, as happened more often in urban families, or when whole families migrated to textile towns, the fact that they earned wages had important effects on family relationships. Family members were no longer bound inseparably to a family enterprise. Instead, the goal became earning enough money to support the minimal needs of the group. The family wage was the sum total of individual members' contributions. Inevitably, in this situation, contributions became individualized. One might work with other family members, but this was not necessary. Children earned wages in textile factories, whether or not they worked alongside their parents. Spinners could hire children who were not their own as reelers and piecers. Ultimately, the wage (however low or unfair) represented remuneration for an individual's labor.

The family now required a financial contribution from each member instead of simply his or her work for the household. Although evidence indicates that children followed the rules of the older family economy, parents had no ultimate means of forcing them to do so. Of course, social and emotional pressures existed, and many a mother must have embarrassed her delinquent child in the manner of the young French barrel-maker's mother who demanded in 1866 that the union punish his employer for underpaying her son. An investigation revealed that the boy had not given his mother all his wages, and he was surely ridiculed, if not condemned for his action, by his peers as well as by neighbors and relatives. In addition, parents could order their children out of the house, thereby depriving them of some of the services, as well as the food and shelter, for which their contributions paid only in part. (There were great advantages to living at home. Mothers, particularly, performed important services for family members that would have cost more if provided by strangers.) But the need of parents for their children's wages made this a risky course. Indeed, parents seem to have tried to keep wage-earning children at home as long as possible, even if this sometimes meant caring for a daughter's illegitimate child (until the costs of its care outweighed the advantages of her contributions).

A teen-aged child's ability to earn wages and, particularly in textiles, the importance of those wages for the family meant that children were no longer as dependent as they once had been on their parents. In fact, the roles might sometimes reverse, with parents depending increasingly on their children. In textile towns, for example, where work was most plentiful and most remunerative for young people in their late teens and early twenties, according to Michael Anderson "children's high wages allowed them to enter into relational bargains with their parents on terms of more or less precise equality." "The children that frequent the factories make almost the purse of the family," observed a contemporary, "and by making the purse of the family, they share in the ruling of it. . . ." In France, an observer at a later period bemoaned the decline of apprenticeship training and the easy availability of wage labor for children. As their wages increased and some-

times surpassed their parents', he wrote, children assumed they had the right to a say in family matters. "When the father earns more than his children, he still has the right to his authority; from the day they earn as much as he does, they no longer recognize his right to command." Furthermore, by earning wages a child established a measure of potential independence. She could move elsewhere and still earn her keep. Hence, while the ability to earn wages increased the importance to a family of a daughter's labor, it also created the potential for a daughter to leave home at an early age.

After reading this selection and the previous one, consider these questions:

1. What were the conditions of children working in the mines and factories of Great Britain?
2. What, according to Tilly and Scott, prompted the increase in women factory workers?
3. How did working-class families change in early industrialization?

# SELECTION 3:

# Women, Work, and Opportunity

*H*istorians Marilyn Boxer and Jean Quataert *discuss the changing roles of women in the workplace and at home through the early phases of the Industrial Revolution to the beginning of the twentieth century. They point to the new opportunities, as well as the new pressures and problems, that young women in particular faced within the new industrial cities of Europe and America. They correct the long-standing view that early industrialization tore the family apart as women and children spent more and more time away from home and became breadwinners within the household. Not only did many textile-manufacturing families continue to work together as a unit in the early factory, but those women who sought employment independently were often young and single. Relatively few mar-*

*ried women were employed outside their homes—17 percent in Lancaster, England—while three-quarters of such working women were single. Boxer and Quataert then turn to the various social and political movements that women either founded or participated in as a response to these changing conditions.*

The increasing employment of women, which in the view of [Friedrich] Engels "unsexes the man and takes from the woman all womanliness," scarcely turned the workers' world topsy-turvy. Such images were overdrawn, often created by social reformers intent upon convincing lawmakers to abandon their laissez-faire principles and pass protective legislation. Joan W. Scott and Louise A. Tilly, in an important study that draws upon occupational and demographic data from systematic samples of urban households in England and France, demonstrate that throughout the nineteenth century, traditional forms of female employment continued to dominate women's wage-earning activity. In 1851, the largest group of female wage-earners in England, fully 40 percent, worked as domestic servants. In 1866, 40 percent of the female labor force in France was employed in agriculture. Moreover, no more than one-fifth of the total female labor force in England, and one-tenth in France, worked in textile manufacturing. Outside of textiles, tobacco, and food processing, relatively few women worked in factories at all. Furthermore, in the major cloth-manufacturing centers such as Roubaix, France, where in 1872 over half the labor force worked in textiles, relatively few *married* women were employed outside their homes—about 17 percent. In the textile center of Lancashire, England, three-quarters of women workers were single.

Although factory work, then, was not *typical* female employment in the nineteenth century, women's lives were altered by the processes that reorganized their work, whether removing the work to factories or . . . providing increased opportunities for wage-earning employment at home.

In the first place, the symbiosis of married women's labor in production and reproduction, whereby women provided the daily necessities for family survival and gave birth to new generations of producers as well, was distorted by the redefinition of work that spread with the growing dominance of factory production. Work was recognized solely as "paid labor" and much of women's work remained unpaid. This enhanced the economic value and increased the autonomy of single women who found work outside the home, but it marginalized married women's work at home, even that done for wages. Second, factory manufacturing increasingly displaced much of the production done at home for the family's own use. In the course of time, mass production of soaps, yarns, and cloth, for example, encouraged their consumption "ready-made." New industries for ready-made goods proliferated in all European cities. In late nineteenth-century Britain and Germany, hundreds of thousands of women did "slop work" (low-skilled, repetitive piece work) in "sweatshops." In France, half of the female industrial labor force remained "isolated," that is, homeworkers. Domestic industry allowed women to continue contributing to family survival, but even in these households, family schedules were increasingly regulated by the factory whistle. Berlin home industry garment-makers in the last third of the nineteenth century organized the rhythm of family life according to their husbands' work schedules, ensuring men leisure time even if it meant for themselves sewing for pay well into the wee hours of the morning.

While the internal cohesion of the preindustrial family and village should not be exaggerated, in the long run the advent of agricultural and industrial reorganization, with its increasing scale of production and growth in market economies and market mentalities, led to a slackening of kinship ties and community solidarity. It also restructured family roles. The movement of traditional women's work out of the home created a conflict between the two primary facets of women's lives—one that remains today as a problem for "working mothers" and "dual-career families." Furthermore, as early as the eighteenth century, men had begun to encroach on the domain of women's work. In textile factories a roomful of female operatives might be supervised by one or two men. Even in the countryside, the shift to market-oriented production narrowed the traditional female economy. In Bavaria, for instance, to the extent that dairy farming centered on the needs of the household, women obtained the necessary know-how on the farm itself. But market production required the mastery of new knowledge not necessarily related to the work processes themselves. And this was acquired by men from trade associations and agricultural institutes that were set up in rural areas. In short, industrialization and commoditization accelerated the process whereby the labor of women became subsidiary to that of men, even in work traditionally deemed feminine. . . .

The process of change in women's familial roles was uneven and complex. Bourgeois women in the north of France maintained a "premodern" view of their roles up to the end of the nineteenth century, emphasizing ties to church and family bloodlines. For these Catholic and convent-educated daughters of the propertied classes, marriage was a "solemn duty." According to historian Bonnie G. Smith, they had "no illusions of love and romance." They recognized the economic basis of marriage and clung to the power they derived from their role in reproduction and sexuality, in supplying the "cord of life" that bound together the generations—and their estates—even though frequent childbearing exacted a high price in chronic illness and maternal mortality.

For most women of all classes, marriage continued to be the only honorable—indeed often the only available—career throughout the nineteenth century. But slowly its purposes and significance was changing. Facing the fateful decision of choosing a mate—a decision that would determine, in a real sense, her life course—a twenty-one-year-old Frenchwoman, Stéphanie Jullien, wrote to her brother in 1833, "This is not child's play, this is a matter of my whole life, of my fu-

ture, of my happiness. . . . To decide my fate once and for all, my whole destiny! I don't dare do it." She worried lest her prospective young husband fail to establish himself sufficiently and she questioned the nature of *his* character and *his* commitment. "Who can assure me that he will succeed? And if he loves me now, how do I know that he will always love me in the same way? Perhaps I'll be paving the way for lots of trouble if I accept, but if I refuse, what will I do? . . . I don't have any calling, nor could I have one."

Despite the idealization of domesticity, most women of all but the wealthiest classes continued to find marriage essential for economic (not emotional) security. For the urban poorer classes, often kept from legal wedlock by poverty (as well as state intervention where laws prohibited the marriage of indigents), "common-law" marriage was commonplace in the nineteenth century. Middle-class moralists, however, disapproved, and some philanthropic groups, such as the Society of Saint Vincent de Paul, were formed to encourage poor people to marry and "legitimize" their offspring. And marriage rates increased as the century progressed. For the spinsters, however, destined by demographic imbalance or lack of dowry never to marry, other solutions were required. No longer able for the most part to retire to convents, less likely than single men to emigrate to the New World, unable to find respectable or remunerative employment, single women sought alternative forms of domesticity. Large numbers entered domestic service. A study of spinsters in mid-Victorian England shows that about 25 percent of single women in all age groups up to thirty-five to forty-four were employed as live-in servants. Older spinsters tended to live with siblings, especially spinster sisters and bachelor brothers. Sometimes spinsters formed what we today call "surrogate families," or cooperative living groups.

The difficulties of earning a living made life alone precarious for single women. In addition, they faced the societal disdain that Charlotte Brontë illustrates in her mid-nineteenth century novel *Shirley*: "Old maids, like the houseless and unemployed poor, should not ask for a place and an occupation in the world." They were not wanted by married relatives. Furthermore, all social life was closed to unescorted women. The French man of letters Jules Michelet felt that "the worst fate for a woman was to live alone. . . . She could hardly go out in the evening; she would be taken for a prostitute. . . . If she were late, far from home, and became hungry, she would not dare enter a restaurant. . . . She would make a spectacle of herself." As single women and widows in the nineteenth century led efforts to provide aid to unwed mothers, to care for foundlings, to rehabilitate prostitutes, to improve opportunities for education and employment for their sex, they also created a new social role for themselves. Some women, moreover, chose spinsterhood because they preferred the company of their own sex. Lifelong, emotionally as well as economically supportive, relationships among women provided them a not uncommon alternative to marriage. These "romantic friendships" also offered an important outlet for their erotic impulses.

Most women, however, preferred to marry. Typically, they entered matrimony later than we might expect, usually only well into their twenties, on average about twenty-four or twenty-five, though with many specific variations. In rural areas, where young people still often had to await both parental permission and economic resources, women might not marry until their intended groom could convince his father to deed him a share of the family plot. Some parents resisted their children's marriages because the departure of grown children from the household meant the loss of labor power or wages essential to family survival. In 1835, when Villermé, while investigating working conditions visited cottage workers in the region of Tarare (near Lyons), he found that men married on average at the age of thirty, women at twenty-seven. Not only age at marriage but even the chance to marry at all depended on occupation. Thus, at mid-century in the textile cities of Roubaix, France (1861) and Preston, England (1851), all but 12 and 10 percent, respectively, of women married. But in the artisanal and commercial cities of Amiens, France, and York, England, 24 percent and 16 percent of women remained unmarried at fifty. Some women, of course, formed long-lasting "free unions," also called "concubinage" and "Parisian marriages,"

and contributed to the rising number of "illegitimate" children. Burgeoning rates of illegitimacy reflected the vulnerability of young women attracted to new urban centers by opportunities for employment. Particularly if they came from communities where premarital pregnancy routinely led to a wedding, they were very susceptible to promises of love and marriage. Separated from family and community, which in earlier times exerted pressure on reluctant bridegrooms, they might find themselves "with child" and deserted by their partner who, in an urban setting with considerable occupational mobility, could easily evade his responsibility.

Marital fertility, illegitimacy, and infant mortality have been the subject of extensive recent research by historical demographers. Social historians, including historians of women, find these records pregnant with meaning for the quality of women's lives. Using crude birthrates (births per 1,000 inhabitants), fertility ratios (number of children under five per number of married women, aged fifteen to forty-four), and infant mortality rates (deaths of infants under one year per 1,000 live births), they have reconstructed a world of reproduction in which women gave birth to numerous offspring and—especially in the working classes—saw half of them die. Birthrates and fertility rates declined steadily throughout the nineteenth century, a token perhaps of new attitudes about human control over their lives. Infant mortality, however, diminished only after the development of public health measures such as the purification of water and pasteurization of milk in the early twentieth century. The latter was particularly significant in reducing recourse to wet-nursing. The sending of the newborn to a rural cottage to be breast-fed diminished among the upper classes after the eighteenth century—at least partly because of the admonitions of Enlightenment philosophers. During the nineteenth century, however, this custom spread among the urban lower-middle classes. Wet nurses were also used by officials charged with the care of foundlings, the thousands of infants abandoned by their unwed or married, but impoverished, mothers. Many destitute women preferred abandoning their children to watching them suffer or die of hunger. This measure was in earlier ages a common recourse of poor families. "Abandonment," states Rachel Fuchs, "was a socially acceptable means to cope with an unwelcome child in an era without safe birth control or abortion, and without an effective program of aid to dependent children." Twenty percent of all babies born in Paris in the early nineteenth century (and over half of the illegitimate) were abandoned.

If the care of abandoned children created a widespread social problem, in France wet-nursing became so prevalent that it constituted a major "business," subject to regulation by law and government agency. Because mortality among nurslings reached scandalous heights—over 50 percent in some cases, up to 80 percent among foundlings—the government in 1874 adopted the Roussel Law, which put all infants nursed outside their homes for pay under state protection. Across the Channel, in 1871 an Infant Life Protection Society was formed, to combat the similar practice of "baby-farming." In 1911, legislation prohibited employment of mothers within four weeks of delivery—but enforcement was lax. These responses of the state offer early examples of a new role for government in family matters.

In the development of the modern family perhaps the most significant change has been the deliberate reduction of the number of children born to the average woman and a concurrent intensification of emotional ties between generations. Beginning with France in the late eighteenth century, followed by Sweden at mid-nineteenth century and much of Europe after the 1870s, most populations in the Western world have employed deliberate means to limit their fertility. It has been suggested that the ability to limit births, and

hence to reduce economic obligations, has contributed to earlier as well as to increased rates of marriage. The source of these changes was not a new technology, as is sometimes assumed. Effective artificial contraceptive devices were not available until the twentieth century. Large-scale production of the condom, which was known in the sixteenth century, and the pessary and diaphragm, both invented in the nineteenth, was indeed possible after the discovery of the vulcanization of rubber in the 1840s, but widespread distribution came many decades later in the era of World War I. Therefore, some historians have assumed an increased practice of *coitus interruptus,* or withdrawal before ejaculation, a male-controlled method known since biblical days but not employed earlier on a scale large enough to affect overall population growth. More recently, historians . . . have pointed to female agency in control of family size, through abortion as well as infanticide and abandonment or neglect. In the nineteenth century, it appears, the mainspring of change was a new secularized attitude justifying human intervention in events previously attributed to nature or to God.

After reading this selection, consider these questions:

1. What types of occupations were most working-class women engaged in during the early industrial era?
2. According to Boxer and Quataert, what were the hopes of these European women?
3. What impact did industrialization have on the family?

# SELECTION 4:

# Working-Class Consciousness

*The type of working-class consciousness among the very first generation of factory workers is illustrated by the following selection. It was written in 1818 by a journeyman cotton spinner who resented the growing economic and political power of the new factory owners. This piece was published in the radical democratic newspaper the* Black Dwarf. *This paper was only one of a handful of such workers' newspapers at the time. In 1820 it had a remarkably wide circulation of over twelve thousand. The* Times *of London, by contrast, then had a circulation of only seven thousand.*

First, then, as to the employers: with very few exceptions, they are a set of men who have sprung from the cotton-shop without education or address, except so much as they have acquired by their intercourse with the little world of merchants on the exchange at Manchester; but to counterbalance that deficiency, they give you enough of appearances by an ostentatious display of elegant mansions, equipages, liveries, parks, hunters, hounds, &c. which they take care to shew off to the merchant stranger in the most pompous manner. Indeed their houses are gorgeous palaces, far surpassing in bulk and extent the neat charming retreats you see round London . . . but the chaste observer of the beauties of nature and art combined will observe a woeful deficiency of taste. They bring up their families at the most costly schools, determined to give their offspring a double portion of what they were so deficient in themselves. Thus with scarcely a second idea in their heads, they are literally petty monarchs, absolute and despotic, in their own particular districts; and to support all this, their whole time is occupied in contriving how to get the greatest quantity of work turned off with the least expence. . . . In short, I will venture to say,

without fear of contradiction, that there is a greater distance observed between the master there and the spinner, than there is between the first merchant in London and his lowest servant or the lowest artisan. Indeed there is no comparison. I know it to be a fact, that the greater part of the master spinners are anxious to keep wages low for the purpose of keeping the spinners indigent and spiritless . . . as for the purpose of taking the surplus to their own pockets.

The master spinners are a class of men unlike all other master tradesmen in the kingdom. They are ignorant, proud, and tyrannical. What then must be the men or rather beings who are the instruments of such masters? Why, they have been for a series of years, with their wives and their families, patience itself—bondmen and bondwomen to their cruel taskmasters. It is in vain to insult our common understandings with the observation that such men are free; that the law protects the rich and poor alike, and that a spinner can leave his master if he does not like the wages. True; so he can: but where must he go? why to another, to be sure. Well: he goes; he is asked where did you work last: 'did he discharge you?' No; we could not agree about wages. Well I shall not employ you nor anyone who leaves his master in that manner. Why is this? Because there is an abominable *combination existing amongst the masters,* first established at Stockport in 1802, and it has since become so general, as to embrace

From untitled article by a cotton spinner, published anonymously in the September 30, 1818, issue of the *Black Dwarf*.

all the great masters for a circuit of many miles round Manchester, though not the little masters: they are excluded. They are the most obnoxious beings to the great ones that can be imagined. . . . When the combination first took place, one of their first articles was, that no master should take on a man until he had first ascertained whether his last master had discharged him. What then is the man to do? If he goes to the parish, that grave of all independence, he is there told—We shall not relieve you; if you dispute with your master, and don't support your family, we will send you to prison; so that the man is bound, by a combination of circumstances, to submit to his master. He cannot travel and get work in any town like a shoe-maker, joiner, or taylor; he is confined to the district.

The workmen in general are an inoffensive, unassuming, set of well-informed men, though how they acquire their information is almost a mystery to me. They are docile and tractable, if not goaded too much; but this is not to be wondered at, when we consider that they are trained to work from six years old, from five in a morning to eight and nine at night. Let one of the advocates for obedience to his master take his stand in an avenue leading to a factory a little before five o'clock in the morning, and observe the squalid appearance of the little infants and their parents taken from their beds at so early an hour in all kinds of weather; let him examine the miserable pittance of food, chiefly composed of water gruel and oatcake broken into it, a little salt, and sometimes coloured with a little milk, together with a few potatoes, and a bit of bacon or fat for dinner; would a London mechanic eat this? There they are, (and if late a few minutes, a quarter of a day is stopped in wages) locked up until night in rooms heated above the hottest days we have had this summer, and allowed no time, except three-quarters of an hour at dinner in the whole day: whatever they eat at any other time must be as they are at work. The negro slave in the West Indies, if he works under a scorching sun, has probably a little breeze of air sometimes to fan him: he has a space of ground, and time allowed to cultivate it. The English spinner slave has no enjoyment of the open atmosphere and breezes of heaven. Locked up in factories eight stories high, he has no relaxation till the ponderous engine stops, and then he goes home to get refreshed for the next day; no time for sweet association with his family; they are all alike fatigued and exhausted. This is no over-drawn picture: it is literally true. I ask again, would the mechanics in the South of England submit to this?

When the spinning of cotton was in its infancy, and before those terrible machines for superseding the necessity of human labour, called steam engines, came into use, there were a great number of what were then called *little masters*; men who with a small capital, could procure a few machines, and employ a few hands, men and boys (say to twenty or thirty), the produce of whose labour was all taken to Manchester central mart, and put into the hands of brokers. . . . The brokers sold it to the merchants, by which means the master spinner was enabled to stay at home and work and attend to his workmen. The cotton was then always given out in its raw state from the bale to the wives of the spinners at home, when they heat and cleansed it ready for the spinners in the factory. By this they could earn eight, ten, or twelve shillings a week, and cook and attend to their families. But none are thus employed now; for all the cotton is broke up by a machine, turned by the steam engine, called a devil: so that the spinners wives have no employment, except they go to work in the factory all day at what can be done by children for a few shillings, four or five per week. If a man then could not agree with his master, he left him, and could get employed elsewhere. A few years, however, changed the face of things. Steam engines came into use, to purchase which, and to erect buildings sufficient to contain them and six or seven hundred hands, required a great capital. The engine power produced a more marketable (though not a better) article than the little master could at the same price. The consequence was their ruin in a short time; and the overgrown capitalists triumphed in their fall; for they were the only obstacle that stood between them and the complete controul of the workmen.

Various disputes then originated between the workmen and masters as to the fineness of the work, the workmen being paid according to the number of hanks or yards of thread he produced from a given quantity of cotton, which was always to be proved by the overlooker, whose interest made it imperative on him to lean to his master, and call the material coarser than it was. If the workman would not submit *he must summon his employer before a magistrate;* the whole of the acting magistrates in that district, with the exception of two worthy clergymen, being gentlemen who have sprung from the *same* source with the master cotton spinners. The employer generally contented himself with sending his overlooker to answer any such summons, thinking it beneath him to meet his servant. The magistrate's decision was generally in favour of the master, though on the statement of the overlook-

er only. The workman dared not appeal to the sessions on account of the expense. . . .

These evils to the men have arisen from that dreadful monopoly which exists in those districts where wealth and power are got into the hands of the few, who, in the pride of their hearts, think themselves the lords of the universe.

After reading this selection, consider these questions:
1. Who were the master spinners?
2. According to the newspaper article, what were the complaints of the master spinners?
3. How should we characterize this type of consciousness?

# SELECTION 5:

# Marx Explains Socialism

*After the failures of the 1848 revolutions, Karl Marx moved to London. He remained there for the rest of his life, researching his major work,* Das Kapital *(the first volume of which was published in 1867). Twelve years after the publication of the first volume of* Das Kapital, *Marx was interviewed in London by a correspondent of the* Chicago Tribune. *In this newspaper interview, Marx gives his opinion on the problems of modern society and proposes ways in which to resolve them.*

In a little villa at Haverstock Hill, the northwest portion of London, lives Karl Marx, the cornerstone of modern socialism. He was exiled from his native country—Germany—in 1844, for propagating revolutionary theories. In 1848, he returned, but in a few months was again exiled. He then took up his abode in Paris, but his political theories procured his expulsion from that city

in 1849, and since that year his headquarters have been in London. His convictions have caused him trouble from the beginning. Judging from the appearance of his home, they certainly have not brought him affluence. Persistently during all these years he has advocated his views with an earnestness which undoubtedly springs from a firm belief in them, and, however much we may deprecate their propagation, we cannot but respect to a certain extent the self-denial of the now venerable exile.

Your correspondent has called upon him twice or thrice, and each time the Doctor was found in

From an interview of Karl Marx by the London correspondent of the *Chicago Tribune,* published in the January 5, 1879, edition.

his library, with a book in one hand and a ciga-
rette in the other. He must be over seventy years
of age. [Marx was sixty.] His physique is well
knit, massive, erect. He has the head of a man of
intellect, and the features of a cultivated Jew. His
hair and beard are long, and iron-gray in color.
His eyes are glittering black, shaded by a pair of
bushy eyebrows. To a stranger he shows extreme
caution. A foreigner can generally gain admission; but the ancient-looking German woman
[Helene Demuth] who waits upon visitors has instructions to admit none who hail from the Fatherland, unless they bring letters of introduction.
Once into his library, however, and having fixed
his one eyeglass in the corner of his eye, in order
to take your intellectual breadth and depth, so to
speak, he loses that self-restraint, and unfolds to
you a knowledge of men and things throughout
the world apt to interest one. And his conversation does not run in one groove, but is as varied
as are the volumes upon his library shelves. A
man can generally be judged by the books he
reads, and you can form your own conclusions
when I tell you a casual glance revealed Shake-
speare, Dickens, Thackeray, Molière, Racine,
Montaigne, Bacon, Goethe, Voltaire, Paine; English, American, French blue books; works political and philosophical in Russian, German, Spanish, Italian, etc., etc. During my conversation I
was struck with his intimacy with American
questions which have been uppermost during the
past twenty years. His knowledge of them, and
the surprising accuracy with which he criticized
our national and state legislation, impressed upon
my mind the fact that he must have derived his
information from inside sources. But, indeed, this
knowledge is not confined to America, but is
spread over the face of Europe. When speaking
of his hobby—socialism—he does not indulge in
those melodramatic flights generally attributed to
him, but dwells upon his utopian plans for "the
emancipation of the human race" with a gravity
and an earnestness indicating a firm conviction in
the realization of his theories, if not in this century, at least in the next.

Perhaps Dr. Karl Marx is better known in
America as the author of *Capital*, and the founder
of the International Society, or at least its most
prominent pillar. In the interview which follows,
you will see what he says of this Society as it at
present exists. . . .

"This platform," I remarked, "applies only to
Germany and one or two other countries."

"Ah!" he returned, "if you draw your conclusions from nothing but this, you know nothing of
the activity of the party. Many of its points have
no significance outside of Germany. Spain, Russia, England, and America have platforms suited
to their peculiar difficulties. The only similarity
in them is the end to be attained."

"And that is the supremacy of labor?"

"That is the emancipation of labor."

"Do European socialists look upon the movement in America as a serious one?"

"Yes: it is the natural outcome of the country's
development. It has been said that the movement
has been improved by foreigners. When labor
movements became disagreeable in England, fifty
years ago, the same thing was said; and that was
long before socialism was spoken of. In America,
since 1857 only has the labor movement become
conspicuous. Then trade unions began to flourish;
then trades assemblies were formed, in which the
workers in different industries united; and after
that came national labor unions. If you consider
this chronological progress, you will see that socialism has sprung up in that country without the
aid of foreigners, and was merely caused by the
concentration of capital and the changed relations
between the workmen and employers."

"Now," asked your correspondent, "what has
socialism done so far?"

"Two things," he returned. "Socialists have
shown the general universal struggle between
capital and labor—the cosmopolitan chapter, in
one word—and consequently tried to bring about
an understanding between the workmen in the
different countries, which became more necessary as the capitalists became more cosmopolitan
in hiring labor, pitting foreign against native
labor not only in America, but in England,
France, and Germany. International relations
sprang up at once between workingmen in the
three different countries, showing that socialism
was not merely a local, but an international problem, to be solved by the international action of

workmen. The working classes move spontaneously, without knowing what the ends of the movement will be. The socialists invent no movement, but merely tell the workmen what its character and its ends will be."

"Which means the overthrowing of the present social system," I interrupted.

"This system of land and capital in the hands of employers, on the one hand," he continued, "and the mere working power in the hands of the laborers to sell a commodity, we claim is merely a historical phase, which will pass away and give place to a higher social condition.

We see everywhere a division of society. The antagonism of the two classes goes hand in hand with the development of the industrial resources of modern countries. From a socialistic standpoint the means already exist to revolutionize the present historical phase. Upon trade unions, in many countries, have been built political organizations. In America the need of an independent workingmen's party has been made manifest. They can no longer trust politicians. Rings and cliques have seized upon the legislatures, and politics has been made a trade. But America is not alone in this, only its people are more decisive than Europeans. Things come to the surface quicker. There is less cant and hypocrisy that there is on this side of the ocean."

I asked him to give me a reason for the rapid growth of the socialistic party in Germany, when he replied: "The present socialistic party came last. Theirs was not the utopian scheme which made headway in France and England. The German mind is given to theorizing, more than that of other peoples. From previous experience the Germans evolved something practical. This modern capitalistic system, you must recollect, is quite new in Germany in comparison to other states. Questions were raised which had become almost antiquated in France and England, and political influences to which these states had yielded sprang into life when the working classes of Germany had become imbued with socialistic theories. Therefore, from the beginning almost of modern industrial development, they have formed an independent political party.

They had their own representatives in the Ger-

man parliament. There was no party to oppose the policy of the government, and this devolved upon them. To trace the course of the party would take a long time; but I may say this: that, if the middle classes of Germany were not the greatest cowards, distinct from the middle classes of America and England, all the political work against the government should have been done by them."

I asked him a question regarding the numerical strength of the Lassallians [devotees to Marx's disciple and fellow socialist Ferdinand Lassalle] in the ranks of the Internationalists.

"The party of Lassalle," he replied, "does not exist. Of course there are some believers in our ranks, but the number is small. Lassalle anticipated our general principles. When he commenced to move after the [German revolution] of 1848, he fancied that he could more successfully revive the movement by advocating cooperation of the workingmen in industrial enterprises. It was to stir them into activity. He looked upon this merely as a means to the real end of the movement. I have letters from his to this effect."

"You would call it his nostrum?"

"Exactly. He called upon [Chancellor Otto von] Bismarck, told him what he designed, and Bismarck encouraged Lassalle's course at that time in every possible way."

"What was his object?"

"He wished to use the working classes as a set-off against the middle classes who instigated the troubles of 1848."

"It is said that you are the head and front of socialism, Doctor, and from your villa here pull the wires of all the associations, revolutions, etc., now going on. What do you say about it?"

The old gentleman smiled: "I know it. It is very absurd, yet it has a comic side. For two months previous to the attempt of Hoedel,[1] Bismarck complained in his *North German Gazette* that I was in league with Father Beck, the leader of the Jesuit movement, and that we were keeping the socialist movement in such a condition that he could do nothing with it."

"But your International Society in London di-

1. Plumber's assistant Emil Hoedel fired two shots at the carriage of Kaiser Wilhelm I on May 11, 1878.

rects the movement?"

"The International Society has outlived its usefulness and exists no longer. It did exist and direct the movement; but the growth of socialism of late years has been so great that its existence has become unnecessary. Newspapers have been started in the various countries. These are interchanged. That is about the only connection the parties in the different countries have with one another. The International Society, in the first instance, was created to bring the workmen together, and show the advisability of effecting organization among their various nationalities. The interests of each party in the different countries have no similarity. This specter of the Internationalist leaders sitting at London is a mere invention. It is true that we dictated to foreign societies when the Internationalist organization was first accomplished. We were forced to exclude some sections in New York, among them one in which Madam Woodhull [an American feminist of the 1870s] was conspicuous. That was in 1871. There are several American politicians—I will not name them—who wish to trade in the movement. They are well known to American socialists."

"You and your followers, Dr. Marx, have been credited with all sorts of incendiary speeches against religion. Of course you would like to see the whole system destroyed, root and branch."

"We know," he replied after a moment's hesitation, "that violent measures against religion are nonsense; but this is an opinion: as socialism grows, religion will disappear. Its disappearance must be done by social development, in which education must play a part."

"The Reverend Joseph Cook, of Boston—you know him—"

"We have heard of him, a very badly informed man upon the subject of socialism."

"In a lecture lately upon the subject, he said, 'Karl Marx is credited now with saying that, in the United States, and in Great Britain, and perhaps in France, a reform of labor will occur without bloody revolution, but that blood must be shed in Germany, and in Russia, and in Italy, and in Austria.'"

"No socialist," remarked the Doctor, smiling, "need predict that there will be a bloody revolution in Russia, Germany, Austria, and possibly Italy if the Italians keep on in the policy they are now pursuing. The deeds of the French Revolution may be enacted again in those countries. That is apparent to any political student. But those revolutions will be made by the majority. No revolution can be made by a party, but by a nation."

"The reverend gentleman alluded to," I remarked, "gave an extract from a letter which he said you addressed to the Communists of Paris in 1871. [A reference to the Paris Commune of 1870–1871. Few if any of its readers can accurately be described as "communists."] Here it is: 'We are as yet but 3,000,000 at most. In twenty years we shall be 50,000,000—100,000,000 perhaps. Then the world will belong to us, for it will be not only Paris, Lyon, Marseilles, which will rise against odious capital, but Berlin, Munich, Dresden, London, Liverpool, Manchester, Brussels, St. Petersburg, New York—in short, the whole world. And before this new insurrection, such as history has not yet known, the past will disappear like a hideous nightmare; for the popular conflagration, kindled at a hundred points at once, will destroy even its memory!' Now, Doctor, I suppose you admit the authorship of that extract?"

"I never wrote a word of it. I never write such melodramatic nonsense. I am very careful what I do write. That was put in Le Figaro, over my signature, about that time. There were hundreds of the same kind of letters flying about them. I wrote to the London Times and declared they were forgeries; but if I denied everything that has been said and written of me, I would require a score of secretaries."

"But you have written in sympathy with the Paris Communists?"

"Certainly I have, in consideration of what was written of them in leading articles; but the correspondence from Paris in English papers is quite sufficient to refute the blunders propagated in editorials. The Commune killed only about sixty people; Marshal MacMahon [president of the French Republic from 1873–1879] and his slaughtering army killed over 60,000. There has never been a movement so slandered as that of the Commune."

"Well, then, to carry out the principles of socialism do its believers advocate assassination and bloodshed?"

"No great movement," Karl answered, "has ever been inaugurated without bloodshed. The independence of America was won by bloodshed, Napoleon captured France through a bloody process, and he was overthrown by the same means. Italy, England, Germany, and every other country gives proof of this, and as for assassination," he went on to say, "it is not a new thing, I need scarcely say. [Italian revolutionary Felice] Orsini tried to kill Napoleon; kings have killed more than anybody else; the Jesuits have killed; the Puritans killed at the time of [Oliver] Cromwell. These deeds were all done or attempted before socialism was born. Every attempt, however, now made upon a royal or state individual is attributed to socialism. The socialists would regret very much the death of the German Emperor at the present time. He is very useful where he is; and Bismarck has done more for the cause than any other statesman, by driving things to extremes."

After reading this selection, consider these questions:
1. What, according to Marx, are the goals of socialism?
2. What was the situation of socialism at the time of the interview?
3. How has socialism progressed in various countries, according to Marx?

# CHAPTER 9
# Darwin, Nietzsche, and Freud

$B$y the middle of the nineteenth century, there was a wide acceptance of utilitarian ethics, empiricism, and liberal political and social ideals. These three modes of thought were interrelated and connected in their fundamental understanding of the individual as a free agent, of society as based on equality, and of government founded on rights and constitutions. In theory, then, early nineteenth-century Europe remained true to the principles of the Enlightenment; and this acceptance shows to what extent Denis Diderot's project of changing "the common way of thinking" had succeeded. In practice as well, liberalism in the broad sense provided the basic structure of governments in postrevolutionary Europe. All European states now legitimated their power in terms of the nation, although such legitimation was institutionalized and put into practice in different ways.

The early nineteenth century also witnessed the emergence of additional principles that modified and, in several instances, transformed these fundamental principles. On the one hand, these components included nationalism and the strong belief that the state should serve, protect, and promote the national culture; conservatism, the position that state and society should honor traditions inherited from the past; and Christianity, the basis of religious belief and moral values. On the other hand, various forms of socialism, although challenging the dominant economic, social, and political status quo, still shared with liberalism a basic belief in the idea of individual freedom and social equality. But socialism also looked to the collective activities of men and women and not the liberal model of the autonomous, rational individual. Given this starting point, socialism called for increased political participation by larger sections of society, for a society based more clearly on an equality of condition, and for an economy managed for the good of society. Socialism also shared with liberalism, but not all forms of conservatism, the idea that the sciences, both natural and social, should move forward, bringing about further progress.

These various political principles were supported by the dominant philosophy of the day, positivism. Developed by the comte de Saint-Simon's secretary, Auguste Comte (1798–1857), positivism provided a more secure scientific foundation for the Enlightenment's progressive view of history. Like the philosophes (and the English utilitarians), Comte insisted that all truth derived from experience or observation of the physical world. Metaphysics, which claimed that there is knowledge beyond observation and that this knowledge provides the answers about the ultimate meaning of things, was at best an earlier and now outmoded way of knowing. Positivists asserted that all that we can know is how things happen. The task of thinking, therefore, is limited to organizing these observations according to the laws of the relations among phenomena. All knowledge was "positive"—that is, factual, scientific knowledge. Comte applied his theory of knowledge to the understanding of society. From the development of the scientific method in the natural sciences, Comte, like his eighteenth-century predecessors, projected a science of society that he called "social physics." Under the leadership of the new positivist philosophers and aided by the further economic exploitation of nature, society should be reorganized according to the laws of social physics. The positivists, as they came to be called, saw that this development to a "positive society" would entail conflict with older moral and social ideals. Not just metaphysical notions but also religious ideas (originating from the "religious stage," which preceded the "metaphysical stage") would have to be overthrown in order that belief and misguided thought be replaced with provable "facts."

In the second half of the nineteenth century, however, a number of ideas emerged that seriously challenged positivism, the Enlightenment heritage, and thus the modern foundations of Western thought and institutions. Though not always revolutionary in intent or even political in definition, these ideas would influence the thought of the second half of the nineteenth century and would have a great impact on twentieth-century culture. The writings of Charles Darwin (1809–1882), Friedrich Nietzsche (1844–1900), and Sigmund Freud (1856–1939) would undermine the notion that the individual is at base or in principle free and rational and that society is capable of imposing just laws upon itself. Darwin, Nietzsche, and Freud all argued that human beings are less distinct from animals than previously assumed. Their ideas were recognized as radical in the second half of the nineteenth and first half of the twentieth centuries, resulting in heated debates over the role of reason in human life, the meaning of religion, and the nature of society. They are still very much part of our modern Western heritage.

Few historians would disagree with including Darwin in the list of the most influential thinkers of the mid to late nineteenth century. Darwin was a naturalist rather than a trained biologist; but he combined a dedication to close observation and a healthy skepticism about theorizing beyond what could be observed. A number of factors came together in his life that proved to be fortuitous to his research. He was a student and friend of the geologist Charles Lyle, who helped him understand that the history of the world was much older than most scientists then believed. This idea allowed Darwin to understand the history of animal species afresh. The relationship between modern species and the fossil record of extinct plants and animal forms indicated not a series of breaks and new starts, as others believed, but a continuum from ancient to present-day forms through a process of slow evolution. In addition, the young Darwin had the opportunity in 1831 to travel around the world as the official naturalist on a government-sponsored scientific expedition. The expedition of HMS *Beagle* lasted for nearly five years and took Darwin to parts of the globe in which the processes of evolutionary diversity could be observed with remarkable clarity. Especially in the Galapagos Islands off Ecuador, Darwin observed both the changes within species distinct to the islands and their variations from similar species on the west coast of South America. Finally, through marriage Darwin secured an income sufficient to allow him to live a quiet life, totally devoted to his research and writing.

In 1859 Darwin published *The Origin of Species,* in which he finally presented his theory of evolution. In itself, evolutionary theory was not entirely new. The idea that the species were not fixed for all time and that they were interrelated and developed over time into what they are today had been debated in antiquity. More recently, eighteenth- and early nineteenth-century biologists and naturalists such as Georges-Louis Leclerc de Buffon and Johann von Goethe had proposed similar ideas. The problem with these earlier notions, however, was that they lacked a reason for why evolution worked. The question was not *whether* but *how* species change. Before Darwin, the most advanced idea on this issue was offered by the French biologist Jean Lamarck. At the beginning of the nineteenth century, Lamarck argued that differing environmental pressures resulted in structural changes within animal forms and that these acquired traits could be handed down biologically from generation to generation. Lamarck's hypothesis was widely criticized at the time, both by those who believed in divine creation and by scientists who found the notion of acquired traits highly improbable.

Although the idea of evolution was not original to Darwin, what Darwin did contribute to the acceptance of this idea was the theory of natural selection. This theory was the key to unlocking the mystery of how and why species change over time. Darwin argued that as the environment changes, it "selects" those individuals and species that are able to adapt to new environments and to continue to produce offspring. Within every generation of a given species, there is some diversity—some have longer horns and others sharper claws. But only those individuals who meet the demands placed on them by the environment survive long enough to reproduce. In reproducing, they accentuate their particular characteristics. Darwin's theory draws the obvious conclusion from these observable phenomena: Given enough time, natural variation and natural selection brings about the development of entirely new species.

While English naturalist Darwin argued that human beings developed over hundreds of thousands of millennia, thus redrawing the line dividing human beings from animals, the Austrian psychologist Sigmund Freud argued that the behavior of men and women was in large measure motivated by underlying urges and drives. These drives were for the most part unconscious and often in conflict with the demands of conscience and even of civilized social existence. Like Darwin, Freud developed his theory of the unconscious from a reassessment of the ways in which human beings are tied to nature. Beginning with a therapeutic method of psychoanalysis, Freud evolved a general theory of human consciousness. Consciousness rested on the unconscious. The unconscious tied individuals directly to nature through the basic urges of power, self-preservation, and sex. Consciousness (the ego) but also society (represented by conscience, or the superego) attempted to control and deny these urges. Efforts of denial resulted, according to Freud, in driving them back into the unconscious, where they lingered on as repressed desires. Though submerged, they often surfaced in altered forms within dreams, lapses of memory, and (more perniciously) in fears, obsessions, and other forms of abnormal behavior.

German philosopher Friedrich Nietzsche took an even more radical position than Freud. He argued that all of reality is an irrational play of powers—sexual, individual, social, and natural. Likewise, Nietzsche was neither a follower of Darwin nor a Social Darwinist. He did not agree with Darwin's theory of natural selection; underneath it, he argued, lay a middle-class notion of functionalism—a variation on utilitarianism. Instead of "survival of the fittest," Nietzsche spoke of the "will to power." The will to power evidenced no law of selection and no pattern of evolution. The will to power was simply struggle, the bare natural energy to produce more and more life—not a process of fitting into an environment or a survival of the fittest. Nietzsche thus did not accept the Social Darwinist idea that history demonstrates that the "best" has always triumphed or that currently existing societies were the winners in the struggle for survival. In opposition to the Social Darwinists, Nietzsche explained that those societies, races, nations, and civilizations that have supposedly triumphed were the weak ones—in Nietzsche's language, the "degenerate" ones. From this framework, Nietzsche criticized all of the much-vaunted claims of European superiority. He attacked democracy, socialism, science, art, and especially Christian morals. He thus emerged as the most thoroughgoing critic of the modern West.

The will to power is the basic reality of organic life, beyond all theories, including biological ones. In contrast to Darwin's evolutionary biology and to Freudian psychology, Nietzsche argued that the will to power is neither understandable in scientific terms nor comprehensible through any other mode of consciousness. Only the symptoms of the will to power could be interpreted. Unknowable in itself, the will to power called only for multiple interpretations. Cultures and various historical epochs within cultures were these interpretations. According to Nietzsche, these interpretations were either "healthy" or "unhealthy"—they either encouraged or discouraged life. The will to power was not the will of the individual. In fact, according to Nietzsche, the traditional notions of the will centered on a false understanding of the individual's freedom of the will. Accepting the will to power, in fact, entailed accepting the fact that one's life, one's body, and one's existence were fully part of nature—were involved in natural processes that exceeded all conscious control and even rational comprehension. Accepting the will to power entailed a renunciation of this traditional notion of the individual will.

Acceptance of the will to power depended not on scientific knowledge but on the powers of art. Nietzsche always considered his greatest work to be *Thus Spoke Zarathustra* (1883), in which he hoped to lead individuals to an alternative set of values and the creation of a new human type. What he called the "overman" was not a "superman" but an individual who had overcome the false morality of the modern West. This older morality was reactive, based on a Christian rejection of nature, and in disguised form was perpetuated in modern art, modern science, modern philosophy, and modern civilization as a whole. The believers in this morality reacted to what was perceived as a goalless, purposeless, and meaningless existence by creating a totally meaningful counter-world. The overman did not reject this world of meaningless competing powers but fully accepted it and then interpreted it creatively. In *Thus Spoke Zarathustra*, Nietzsche proposed that a creative, more life-enhancing set of values and a new culture could be made by channeling the destructive will to power into the culture-building "thought of eternal recurrence," much as the ancient Greeks had created a superior civilization through the notion of the *agon* (contest and struggle).

# SELECTION 1:

# Positivism

Auguste Comte's positive philosophy would prove to be highly influential, providing one of the central ways in which Enlightenment ideas were conveyed into the nineteenth and twentieth centuries. John Stuart Mill not only translated Comte's writing into English but also popularized these ideas in his own utilitarian philosophy. The following selection is taken from Comte's major work, The Course of Positive Philosophy (1830–1842).

In order to understand the true value and character of the positive philosophy, we must take a brief general view of the progressive course of the human mind regarded as a whole, for no conception can be understood otherwise than through its history.

From the study of the development of human intelligence, in all directions, and through all times, the discovery arises of a great fundamental law, to which it is necessarily subject, and which has a solid foundation of proof, both in the facts of our organization and in our historical experience. The law is this: that each of our leading conceptions—each branch of our knowledge—passes successively through three different theoretical conditions: the theological, or fictitious; the metaphysical, or abstract; and the scientific, or positive. In other words, the human mind, by its nature, employs in its progress three methods of philosophizing, the character of which is essentially different, and even radically opposed: namely, the theological method, the metaphysical, and the positive. Hence arise three philosophies, or general systems of conceptions on the aggregate of phenomena, each of which excludes the others. The first is the necessary point of departure of the human understanding, and the third is its fixed and definitive state. The second is merely a state of transition.

In the theological state, the human mind, seeking the essential nature of beings, the first and final causes (the origin and purpose) of all effects—in short, absolute knowledge—supposes all phenomena to be produced by the immediate action of supernatural beings.

In the metaphysical state, which is only a modification of the first, the mind supposes, instead of supernatural beings, abstract forces, veritable entities (that is, personified abstractions) inherent in all beings, and capable of producing all phenomena. What is called the explanation of phenomena is, in this stage, a mere reference of each to its proper entity.

In the final, the positive, state, the mind has given over the vain search after absolute notions, the origin and destination of the universe, and the causes of phenomena, and applies itself to the study of their laws—that is, their invariable relations of succession and resemblance. Reasoning and observation, duly combined, are the means of this knowledge. What is now understood when we speak of an explanation of facts is simply the establishment of a connection between single phenomena and some general facts, the number of which continually diminishes with the progress of science. . . .

There is no science that, having attained the positive stage, does not bear marks of having passed through the others. Some time back, it was (whatever it might be) composed, as we can now perceive, of metaphysical abstractions; and, further back in the course of time, it took its form from theological conceptions. We shall have only too much occasion to see, as we proceed, that our most advanced sciences still bear very evident marks of the two earlier periods through which they have passed.

The progress of the individual mind is not only an illustration, but an indirect evidence of that of the general mind. The point of departure of the individual and of the race being the same, the phases of the mind of a man correspond to the epochs of the mind of the race. Now, each of us is aware, if he looks back upon his own history, that he was a theologian in his childhood, a metaphysician in his youth, and natural philosopher in his manhood. All men who are up to their age can verify this for themselves.

Besides the observation of facts, we have theoretical reasons in support of this law.

After reading this selection, consider these questions:

1. What does Comte mean by *positive philosophy*?
2. How does Comte argue that positive philosophy is the result of intellectual progress?
3. How is positive philosophy related to the thought of the philosophes of the eighteenth century?

From *Auguste Comte and Positivism: Selected Writings*, edited by Gertrud Lenzer (New York: Harper & Row, 1975).

# SELECTION 2:

# The Origin of Species

*Unlike Jean Lamarck's transmission of acquired characteristics, Darwin showed that nature itself, in providing for individual variations within species and with challenging the survival of species within changing environments, was the "cause" of changes within species and the origins of new species. In* The Origin of Species *(1859), Darwin did not deal directly with the species Homo sapiens, but others drew the simple conclusion that what applied to animals also applied to human beings. Darwin himself made the point explicit in his second great book,* The Descent of Man *(1871). In this work, he argued that human beings evolved from some apelike ancestor, long since extinct, that was a common forebear of the existing apes and humans. In chapter 15 of* The Origin of Species, *Darwin recapitulated his arguments and drew his conclusions. This chapter also illustrates Darwin's readable style and his careful use of evidence.*

As this whole volume is one long argument, it may be convenient to the reader to have the leading facts and inferences briefly recapitulated.

That many and serious objections may be advanced against the theory of descent with modification through variation and natural selection, I do not deny. I have endeavored to give to them their full force. Nothing at first can appear more difficult to believe than that the more complex organs and instincts have been perfected, not by means superior to, though analogous with, human reason, but by the accumulation of innumerable slight variations, each good for the individual possessor. Nevertheless, this difficulty, though appearing to our imagination insuperably great, cannot be considered real if we admit the following propositions, namely, that all parts of the organization and instincts offer, at least, individual differences—that there is a struggle for existence leading to the preservation of profitable deviations of structure or instinct—and, lastly, that gradations in the state of perfection of each organ may have existed, each good of its kind. The truth of these propositions cannot, I think, be disputed. . . .

As geology plainly proclaims that each land has undergone great physical changes, we might have expected to find that organic beings have varied under nature, in the same way as they have varied under domestication. And if there has been any variability under nature, it would be an unaccountable fact if natural selection had not come into play. It has often been asserted, but the assertion is incapable of proof, that the amount of variation under nature is a strictly limited quantity. Man, though acting on external characters alone and often capriciously, can produce within a short period a great result by adding up mere individual differences in his domestic productions; and every one admits that species present individual differences. But, beside such differences, all naturalists admit that natural varieties exist, which are considered sufficiently distinct to be worthy of record in systematic works. No one has drawn any clear distinction between individual differences and slight varieties; or between more plainly marked varieties and sub-species and species. On separate continents, and on different

From *The Origin of Species*, by Charles Darwin, vol. 2 (New York: Books Inc., 1900).

parts of the same continent, when divided by barriers of any kind, and on out-lying islands, what a multitude of forms exist, which some experienced naturalists rank as varieties, others as geographical races or sub-species, and others as distinct though closely allied species!

If, then, animals and plants do vary, let it be ever so slightly or slowly, why should not variations or individual differences, which are in any way beneficial, be preserved and accumulated through natural selection, or the survival of the fittest? If man can by patience select variations useful to him, why, under changing and complex conditions of life, should not variations useful to nature's living products often arise, and be preserved or selected? What limit can be put to this power, acting during long ages and rigidly scrutinizing the whole constitution, structure, and habits of each creature, favoring the good and rejecting the bad? I can see no limit to this power, in slowly and beautifully adapting each form to the most complex relations of life. The theory of natural selection, even if we look no further than this, seems to be in the highest degree probable. I have already recapitulated, as fairly as I could, the opposed difficulties and objections: now let us turn to the special facts and arguments in favor of the theory.

On the view that species are only strongly marked and permanent varieties, and that each species first existed as a variety, we can see why it is that no line of demarcation can be drawn between species, commonly supposed to have been produced by special acts of creation, and varieties which are acknowledged to have been produced by secondary laws. On this same view we can understand how it is that in a region where many species of a genus have been produced, and where they now flourish, these same species should present many varieties; for where the manufactory of species has been active, we might expect, as a general rule, to find it still in action; and this is the case if varieties be incipient species. Moreover, the species of the larger genera, which afford the greater number of varieties or incipient species, retain to a certain degree the character of varieties; for they differ from each other by a less amount of difference than do the species of smaller genera. The closely allied species also of a larger genera apparently have restricted ranges, and in their affinities they are clustered in little groups round other species—in both respects resembling varieties. These are strange relations on the view that each species was independently created, but are intelligible if each existed first as a variety.

As each species tends by its geometrical rate of reproduction to increase inordinately in number; and as the modified descendants of each species will be enabled to increase by as much as they become more diversified in habits and structure, so as to be able to seize on many and widely different places in the economy of nature, there will be a constant tendency in natural selection to preserve the most divergent offspring of any one species. Hence, during a long-continued course of modification, the slight differences characteristic of varieties of the same species, tend to be augmented into the greater differences characteristic of the species of the same genus. New and improved varieties will inevitably supplant and exterminate the older, less improved, and intermediate varieties; and thus species are rendered to a large extent defined and distinct objects. Dominant species belonging to the larger groups within each class tend to give birth to new and dominant forms; so that each large group tends to become still larger, and at the same time more divergent in character. But as all groups cannot thus go on increasing in size, for the world would not hold them, the more dominant groups beat the less dominant. This tendency in the large groups to go on increasing in size and diverging in character, together with the inevitable contingency of much extinction, explains the arrangement of all the forms of life in groups subordinate to groups, all within a few great classes, which has prevailed throughout all time. This grand fact of the grouping of all organic beings under what is called the Natural System, is utterly inexplicable on the theory of creation.

As natural selection acts solely by accumulating slight, successive, favorable variations, it can produce no great or sudden modifications; it can act only by short and slow steps. Hence, the canon of "Natura non facit saltum" ["Nature does not make a leap"], which every fresh addition to our knowledge tends to confirm, is on this theory intelligible. We can see why throughout nature the same general end is gained by an almost infinite diversity of means, for every peculiarity when once acquired is long inherited, and structures already modified in many different ways have to be adapted for the same general purpose. We can, in short, see why nature is prodigal in variety, though niggard in innovation. But why this should be a law of nature if each species has been independently created, no man can explain.

Many other facts are, as it seems to me, explicable on this theory. How strange it is that a bird, under the form of a woodpecker, should prey on insects on the ground; that upland geese, which rarely or never swim, should possess webbed feet; that a thrush-like bird should dive and feed on sub-aquatic insects; and that a petrel should have the habits and structure fitting it for the life of an auk! and so in endless other cases. But on the view of each species constantly trying to increase in number, with natural selection always ready to adapt the slowly varying descendants of each to any unoccupied or ill-occupied place in nature, these facts cease to be strange, or might even have been anticipated. . . .

As natural selection acts by competition, it adapts and improves the inhabitants of each country only in relation to their coinhabitants; so that we need feel no surprise at the species of any one country, although on the ordinary view supposed to have been created and specially adapted for that country, being beaten and supplanted by the naturalized productions from another land. Nor ought we to marvel if all the contrivances in nature be not, as far as we can judge, absolutely perfect, as in the case even of the human eye; or if some of them be abhorrent to our ideas of fitness. We need not marvel at the sting of the bee, when used against an enemy, causing the bee's own death; at drones being produced in such great numbers for one single act, and being then slaughtered by their sterile sisters; at the aston-

ishing waste of pollen by our fir-trees; at the instinctive hatred of the queen bee for her own fertile daughters; at ichneumonidae feeding within the living bodies of caterpillars; or at other such cases. The wonder, indeed, is, on the theory of natural selection, that more cases of the want of absolute perfection have not been detected. . . .

It is interesting to contemplate a tangled bank, clothed with many plants of many kinds, with birds singing on the bushes, with various insects flitting about, and with worms crawling through the damp earth, and to reflect that these elaborately constructed forms, so different from each other, and dependent upon each other in so complex a manner, have all been produced by laws acting around us. These laws, taken in the largest sense, being Growth with reproduction; Inheritance which is almost implied by reproduction; Variability from the indirect and direct action of the conditions of life, and from use and disuse: a Ratio of Increase so high as to lead to a Struggle for Life, and as a consequence to Natural Selection, entailing Divergence of Character and the Extinction of less improved forms. Thus, from the war of nature, from famine and death, the most exalted object which we are capable of conceiving, namely, the production of the higher animals, directly follows. There is grandeur in this view of life with its several powers, having been originally breathed by the Creator into a few forms or into one; and that, while this planet has gone circling on according to the fixed law of gravity, from so simple a beginning endless forms most beautiful and most wonderful have been, and are being evolved.

After reading this selection, consider these questions:
1. What is Darwin's theory of natural selection?
2. How does he understand the process of adaptation?
3. What is the struggle for existence?

# SELECTION 3:

# Social Darwinism

*The impact of Charles Darwin's ideas was neither limited to the sciences of biology and geology nor threatening only to believers in traditional forms of Christianity. From its earliest appearance, Darwinism (as it came to be called) was extended to a new understanding of humans as moral and social beings. No one was more influential in extending Darwinian theories of biology to a general theory of human existence than the English philosopher Herbert Spencer (1820–1903). He argued that nations and races, like animal species, were locked in a struggle for existence in which only the fittest survived. Spencer's claim rested on the claim that "evolution" in human society was based on the law of competition among individuals. He championed individualism and condemned all forms of social or state assistance. These would frustrate all further social progress and even undermine the individuals themselves in their struggle for existence. Spencer, in fact, coined the phrase* survival of the fittest. *Although Darwin disliked the extension of his theory of evolution to human values and human history, he was so taken with Spencer's phrase that he adopted it himself. The following selection is taken from Spencer's "Progress: Its Law and Causes."*

The current conception of Progress is somewhat shifting and indefinite. Sometimes it comprehends little more than simple growth—as of a nation in the number of its members and the extent of territory over which it has spread. Sometimes it has reference to quantity of material products—as when the advance of agriculture and manufactures is the topic. Sometimes the superior quality of these products is contemplated; and sometimes the new or improved appliances by which they are produced. When again we speak of moral or intellectual progress, we refer to the state of the individual or people exhibiting it; whilst, when the progress of Knowledge, of Science, of Art, is commented upon, we have in view certain abstract results of human thought and action. Not only, however, is the current conception of Progress more or less vague, but it is in great measure erroneous. It takes in not so much the reality of Progress as its accompaniments—not so much the substance as the shadow. That progress in intelligence which takes place during the evolution of the child into the man, or the savage into the philosopher, is commonly regarded as consisting in the greater number of facts known and laws understood: whereas the actual progress consists in the produce of a greater quantity and variety of articles for the satisfaction of men's wants; in the increasing security of person and property; in the widening freedom of action enjoyed whereas, rightly understood, social progress consists in those changes of structure in the social organism which have entailed these consequences. The current conception is a teleological one. The phenomena are contemplated solely as bearing on human happiness. Only those changes are held to constitute progress which directly or indirectly

From "Progress: Its Law and Causes," by Herbert Spencer, *Westminster Review*, April 1857.

tend to heighten human happiness. And they are thought to constitute progress simply *because* they tend to heighten human happiness. But rightly to understand Progress, we must inquire what is the nature of these changes, considered apart from our interests. Ceasing, for example, to regard the successive geological modifications that have taken place in the Earth, as modifications that have gradually fitted it for the habitation of Man, and as therefore a geological progress, we must seek to determine the character common to these modifications—the law to which they all conform. And similarly in every other case. Leaving out of sight concomitants and beneficial consequences, let us ask what Progress is in itself. . . .

In its primary stage, every germ consists of a substance that is uniform throughout, both in texture and chemical composition. The first step in its development is the appearance of a difference between two parts of this substance; or, as the phenomenon is described in physiological language—a differentiation. Each of these differentiated divisions presently begins itself to exhibit some contrast of parts; and by these secondary differentiations become as definite as the original one. This progress is continuously repeated—is simultaneously going on in all parts of the growing embryo; and by endless multiplication of these differentiations there is ultimately produced that complex combination of tissues and organs constituting the adult animal or plant. This is the course of evolution followed by all organisms whatever. It is settled beyond dispute that organic progress consists in a change from the homogeneous to the heterogeneous.

Now, we propose in the first place to show, that this law of organic progress is the law of all progress. Whether it be in the development of the Earth, in the development of Life upon its surface, the development of Society, of Government, of Manufactures, of Commerce, of Language, Literature, Science, Art, this same evolution of the simple into the complex, through a process of continuous differentiation, holds throughout. From the earliest traceable cosmical changes down to the latest results of civilization, we shall find that the transformation of the homogeneous into the heterogeneous, is that in which Progress

essentially consists. . . .

Whether an advance from the homogeneous to the heterogeneous is or is not displayed in the biological history of the globe, it is clearly enough displayed in the progress of the latest and most heterogeneous creature—Man. It is alike true that, during the period in which the Earth has been peopled, the human organism has become more heterogeneous among the civilized divisions of the species—and that the species, as a whole, has been growing more heterogeneous in virtue of the multiplication of races and the differentiation of these races from each other. . . .

In the course of ages, there arises, as among ourselves, a highly complex political organization of monarch, ministers, lords and commons, with their subordinate administrative departments, courts of justice, revenue offices, &c., supplemented in the provinces by municipal governments, county governments, parish or union governments—all of them more or less elaborated. By its side there grows up a highly complex religious organization, with its various grades of officials from archbishops down to sextons, its colleges, convocations, ecclesiastical courts, &c.; to all which must be added the ever-multiplying independent sects, each with its general and local authorities. And at the same time there is developed a highly complex aggregation of customs, manners, and temporary fashions, enforced by society at large, and serving to control those minor transactions between man and man which are not regulated by civil and religious law. Moreover it is to be observed that this ever-increasing heterogeneity in the governmental appliances of each nation, has been accompanied by an increasing heterogeneity in the governmental appliances of different nations all of which are more or less unlike in their political systems and legislation in their creeds and religious institutions, in their customs and ceremonial usages.

Simultaneously there has been going on a second differentiation of a still more familiar kind; that, namely, by which the mass of the community has become segregated into distinct classes and orders of workers. While the governing part has been undergoing the complex development above described, the governed part has been undergoing an equally complex development, which has resulted in that minute division of labour characterizing advanced nations. It is needless to trace out this progress from its first stages, up through the caste divisions of the East and the incorporated guilds of Europe, to the elaborate producing and distributing organization existing among ourselves. Political economists have made familiar to all, the evolution which, beginning with a tribe whose members severally perform the same actions each for himself, ends with a civilized community whose members severally perform different actions for each other; and they have further explained the evolution through which the solitary producer of any one commodity, is transformed into a combination of producers who united under a master, take separate parts in the manufacture of such commodity. But there are yet other and higher phases of this advance from the homogeneous to the heterogeneous in the industrial structure of the social organism. Long after considerable progress has been made in the division of labour among different classes of workers, there is still little or no division of labour among the widely separated parts of the community: the nation continues comparatively homogeneous in the respect that in each district the same occupations are pursued. But when roads and other means of transit become numerous and good, the different districts begin to assume different functions, and to become mutually dependent. The calico manufacture locates itself in this county, the woollen-cloth manufacture in that; silks are produced here, lace there; stockings in one place, shoes in another; pottery, hardware, cutlery, come to have their special towns; and ultimately every locality becomes more or less distinguished from the rest by the leading occupation carried on in it. Nay, more, this subdivision of functions shows itself not only among the different parts of the same nation, but among different nations. That exchange of commodities which free-trade promises so greatly to increase, will ultimately have the effect of specializing, in a greater or less degree, the industry of each people. So that beginning with a barbarous tribe, almost if not quite homogeneous in the functions of its members, the progress has

been, and still is, towards an economic aggregation of the whole human race, growing ever more heterogeneous in respect of the separate functions assumed by separate nations, the separate functions assumed by the local sections of each nation, the separate functions assumed by the many kinds of makers and traders in each town, and the separate functions assumed by the workers united in producing each commodity.

Not only is the law thus clearly exemplified in the evolution of the social organism, but it is exemplified with equal clearness in the evolution of all products of human thought and action; whether concrete or abstract, real or ideal. . . .

We might trace out the evolution of Science; beginning with the era in which it was not yet differentiated from Art, and was, in union with Art, the handmaid of Religion; passing through the era in which the sciences were so few and rudimentary, as to be simultaneously cultivated by the same philosophers; and ending with the era in which the genera and species are so numerous that few can enumerate them, and no one can adequately grasp even one genus. Or we might do the like with Architecture, with the Drama, with Dress. But doubtless the reader is already weary of illustrations; and our promise has been amply fulfilled. We believe we have shown beyond question, that that which the German physiologists have found to be the law of organic development, is the law of all development. The advance from the simple to the complex, through a process of successive differentiations, is seen alike in the earliest changes of the Universe to which we can reason our way back, and in the earliest changes which we can inductively establish; it is seen in the geologic and climatic evolution of the Earth, and of every single organism on its surface; it is seen in the evolution of Humanity, whether contemplated in the civilized individual, or in the aggregation of races; it is seen in the evolution of Society in respect both of its political and economical organization; and it is seen in the evolution of all those endless concrete and abstract products of human activity which constitute the environment of our daily life. From the remotest past which Science can fathom, down to the novelties of yesterday, that in which Progress essentially consists, is the transformation of the homogeneous into the heterogeneous.

After reading this selection, consider these questions:

1. How does Spencer define *progress*?
2. What does he mean by *heterogeneity*?
3. How does Spencer relate progress in nature to progress in society?

## SELECTION 4:

# An Attack on Western Morals

*Friedrich Nietzsche was a scholar who taught for eleven years at the University of Basel in Switzerland. For medical reasons, he had to take early retirement and thereafter devoted himself to writing. Fascinated with the philosophy of Arthur Schopenhauer and a young protégé of the composer Richard Wagner, Nietzsche was concerned with the problem of the cultural renewal of the West. By the mid-1870s he had broken with Schopenhauer and his notion that art is an escape from the harshness of existence; Nietzsche also rejected Wagnerianism after personally witnessing the self-satisfied, nationalistic values it encouraged. He then devoted himself to developing a new cultural ideal, one that spoke from a reinterpretation of Western civilization.*

*Whatever one makes of Nietzsche's attempts to remold the West upon early Greek rather than late Christian values, his continuing impact on modernity has centered on his criticism of Western values and institutions. In two major works,* Beyond Good and Evil *(1886) and* On the Genealogy of Morals *(1887), Nietzsche undertook to expose the misconceptions behind the notions of modern values and theories of knowledge. In* On the Genealogy of Morals *in particular, Nietzsche made a direct attack on both Christian moralism and Social Darwinism with its progressive notions of the emergence of values. In the following selections from* On the Genealogy of Morals, *Nietzsche introduces two opposing personality types—the priest and the warrior—and the basic values that they embody.*

Above all, there is no exception (though there are opportunities for exceptions) to this rule, that the idea of political superiority always resolves itself into the idea of psychological superiority, in those cases where the highest caste is at the same time the *priestly* caste, and in accordance with its general characteristics confers on itself the privilege of a title which alludes specifically to its priestly function. It is in these cases, for instance, that "clean" and "unclean" confront each other for the first time as badges of class distinction; here again there develops a "good" and a "bad," in a sense which has ceased to be merely social. Moreover, care should be taken not to take these ideas of "clean" and "unclean" too seriously, too

From *On the Genealogy of Morals*, by Friedrich Nietzsche, translated by Horace B. Samuel (New York: Boni & Liveright, 1921).

broadly, or too symbolically: all the ideas of ancient man have, on the contrary, got to be understood in their initial stages, in a sense which is, to an almost inconceivable extent, crude, coarse, physical, and narrow, and above all essentially *unsymbolical*. The "clean man" is originally only a man who washes himself, who abstains from certain foods which are conducive to skin diseases, who does not sleep with the unclean women of the lower classes, who has a horror of blood—not more, not much more! On the other hand, the very nature of a priestly aristocracy shows the reason why just at such an early juncture there should ensure a really dangerous sharpening and intensification of opposed values: it is, in fact, through these opposed values that gulfs are cleft in the social plane, which a veritable Achilles of free thought would shudder to cross. There is from the outset a certain *diseased taint* in such sacerdotal aristocracies, and in the habits which prevail in such societies—habits which, *averse* as they are to action, constitute a compound of introspection and explosive emotionalism, as a result of which there appears that introspective morbidity and [emotional and psychic disorder] neurasthenia, which adheres almost inevitably to all priests at all times: with regard, however, to the remedy which they themselves have invented for this disease—the philosopher has no option but to state, that it has proved itself in its effects a hundred times more dangerous than the disease, from which it should have been the deliverer. Humanity itself is still diseased from the effects of the naïvetés of this priestly cure. Take, for instance, certain kinds of diet (abstention from flesh), fasts, sexual continence, flight into the wilderness . . . ; consider too the whole metaphysic of the priests, with its war on the senses, its enervation, its hair-splitting; consider its self-hypnotism on the fakir and Brahman principles (it uses Brahman as a glass disc and obsession), and that climax which we can understand only too well of an unusual satiety with its panacea of *nothingness* (or God:—the demand for a *unio mystica* [mystical union] with God is the demand of the Buddhist for nothingness, Nirvana—and nothing else!). In sacerdotal societies *every* element is on a more dangerous scale, not

merely cures and remedies, but also pride, revenge, cunning, exaltation, love, ambition, virtue, morbidity:—further, it can fairly be stated that it is on the soil of this *essentially dangerous* form of human society, the sacerdotal form, that man really becomes for the first time an *interesting animal*, that it is in this form that the soul of man has in a higher sense attained *depths* and become *evil*—and those are the two fundamental forms of the superiority which up to the present man has exhibited over every other animal.

The reader will have already surmised with what ease the priestly mode of valuation can branch off from the knightly aristocratic mode, and then develop into the very antithesis of the latter: special impetus is given to this opposition, by every occasion when the castes of the priests and warriors confront each other with mutual jealousy and cannot agree over the prize. The knightly-aristocratic "values" are based on a careful cult of the physical, on a flowering, rich, and even effervescing healthiness, that goes considerably beyond what is necessary for maintaining life, on war, adventure, the chase, the dance, the tourney—on everything, in fact, which is contained in strong, free, and joyous action. The priestly-aristocratic mode of valuation is—we have seen—based on other hypotheses: it is bad enough for this class when it is a question of war! Yet the priests are, as is notorious, *the worst enemies*—why? Because they are the weakest. Their weakness causes their hate to expand into a monstrous and sinister shape, a shape which is most crafty and most poisonous. The really great haters in the history of the world have always been priests, who are also the cleverest haters—in comparison with the cleverness of priestly revenge, every other piece of cleverness is practically negligible. Human history would be too fatuous for anything were it not for the cleverness imported into it by the weak . . . who, in opposition to the aristocratic equation (good = aristocratic = beautiful = happy = loved by the gods), dared with a terrifying logic to suggest the contrary equation, and indeed to maintain with the teeth of the most profound hatred (the hatred of weakness) this contrary equation, namely, "the wretched are alone the good; the poor, the weak, the lowly, are alone the good; the suffering, the needy, the sick, the loathsome, are the only ones who are pious, the only ones who are blessed, for them alone is salvation—but you, on the other hand, you aristocrats, you men of power, you are to all eternity the evil, the horrible, the covetous, the insatiate, the godless: eternally also shall you be the unblessed, the cursed, the damned!". . .

The revolt of the slaves in morals begins in the very principle of *resentment* becoming creative and giving birth to values—a resentment experienced by creatures who, deprived as they are of the proper outlet of action, are forced to find their compensation in an imaginary revenge. While every aristocratic morality springs from a triumphant affirmation of its own demands, the slave morality says "no" from the very outset to what is "outside itself," "different from itself," and "not itself": and this "no" is its creative deed. This volte-face of the valuing standpoint—this *inevitable* gravitation to the objective instead of back to the subjective—is typical of "resentment": the slave-morality requires as the condition of its existence an external and objective world, to employ physiological terminology, it requires objective stimuli to be capable of action at all—its action is fundamentally a reaction. The contrary is the case when we come to the aristocrat's system of values: it acts and grows spontaneously, it merely seeks its antithesis in order to pronounce a more grateful and exultant "yes" to its own self;—its negative conception, "low," "vulgar," "bad," is merely a pale late-born foil in comparison with its positive and fundamental conception (saturated as it is with life and passion), of "we aristocrats, we good ones, we beautiful ones, we happy ones."

When the aristocratic morality goes astray and commits sacrilege on reality, this is limited to that particular sphere with which it is *not* sufficiently acquainted—a sphere, in fact, from the real knowledge of which it disdainfully defends itself. It misjudges, in some cases, the sphere which it despises, the sphere of the common vulgar man and the low people: on the other hand, due weight should be given to the consideration that in any case the mood of contempt, of disdain, of superciliousness, even on the supposition that it *falsely* portrays the object of its contempt, will always be

far removed from that degree of falsity which will always characterise the attacks—in effigy, of course—of the vindictive hatred and revengefulness of the weak in onslaughts on their enemies. In point of fact, there is in contempt too strong an admixture of nonchalance, of casualness, of boredom, of impatience, even of personal exultation, for it to be capable of distorting its victim into a real caricature or a real monstrosity. Attention again should be paid to the almost benevolent *nuances* which, for instance, the Greek nobility imports into all the words by which it distinguishes the common people from itself; note how continuously a kind of pity, care, and consideration imparts its honeyed *flavour,* until at last almost all the words which are applied to the vulgar man survive finally as expressions for "unhappy," "worthy of pity". . .—and how, conversely, "bad," "low," "unhappy" have never ceased to ring in the Greek ear with a tone in which "unhappy" is the predominant note: this is a heritage of the old noble aristocratic morality, which remains true to itself even in contempt. . . . The "well-born" simply *felt* themselves the "happy"; they did not have to manufacture their happiness artificially through looking at their enemies, or in cases to talk and lie themselves into happiness (as is the custom with all resentful men); and similarly, complete men as they were, exuberant with strength, and consequently *necessarily* energetic, they were too wise to dissociate happiness from action—activity becomes in their minds necessarily counted as happiness . . .—all in sharp contrast to the "happiness" of the weak and the oppressed, with their festering venom and malignity, among whom happiness appears essentially as a narcotic, a deadening, a quietude, a peace, a "Sabbath," an enervation of the mind and relaxation of the limbs,—in short, a purely *passive* phenomenon. While the aristocratic man lived in confidence and openness with himself . . . , the resentful man, on the other hand, is neither sincere nor naïf, nor honest and candid with himself. His soul *squints*; his mind loves hidden crannies, tortuous paths and backdoors, everything secret appeals to him as *his* word, *his* safety, *his* balm; he is past master in silence, in not forgetting, in waiting, in provisional self-depreciation and self-abasement. A race of such *resentful* men will of necessity eventually prove more *prudent* than any aristocratic race, it will honour prudence on quite a distinct scale, as, in fact, a paramount condition of existence, while prudence among aristocratic men is apt to be tinged with a delicate flavour of luxury and refinement; so among them it plays nothing like so integral a part as that complete certainty of function of the governing *unconscious* instincts, or as indeed a certain lack of prudence, such as a vehement and valiant charge, whether against danger or the enemy, or as those ecstatic bursts of rage, love, reverence, gratitude, by which at all times noble souls have recognised each other. When the resentment of the aristocratic man manifests itself, it fulfils and exhausts itself in an immediate reaction, and consequently instills no *venom*: on the other hand, it never manifests itself at all in countless instances, when in the case of the feeble and weak it would be inevitable. An inability to take seriously for any length of time their enemies, their disasters, their *misdeeds*—that is the sign of the full strong natures who possess a superfluity of moulding plastic force, that heals completely and produces forgetfulness: a good example of this in the modern world is Mirabeau [an early political leader of the French Revolution], who had no memory for any insults and meannesses which were practised on him, and who was only incapable of forgiving because he forgot. Such a man indeed shakes off with a shrug many a worm which would have buried itself in another; it is only in characters like these that we see the possibility (supposing, of course, that there is such a possibility in the world) of the real "*love* of one's enemies." What respect for his enemies is found, forsooth, in an aristocratic man—and such a reverence is already a bridge to love! He insists on having his enemy to himself as his distinction. He tolerates no other enemy but a man in whose character there is nothing to despise and *much* to honour! On the other hand, imagine the "enemy" as the resentful man conceives him—and it is here exactly that we see his work, his creativeness; he has conceived "the evil enemy," the "evil one," and indeed that is the root idea from which he now evolves as a contrasting and corresponding figure a "good one," himself—his very self! . . .

I cannot refrain at this juncture from uttering a sign and one last hope. What is it precisely which I find intolerable? That which I alone cannot get rid of, which makes me choke and faint? Bad air! Bad air! That something misbegotten comes near me; that I must inhale the odour of the entrails of a misbegotten soul!—That excepted, what can one not endure in the way of need, privation, bad weather, sickness, toil, solitude? In point of fact, one manages to get over everything, born as one is to a burrowing and battling existence; one always returns once again to the light, one always lives again one's golden hour of victory—and then one stands as one was born, unbreakable, tense, ready for something more difficult, for something more distant, like a bow stretched but the tauter by every strain. But from time to time do ye grant me—assuming that "beyond good and evil" there are goddesses who can grant—one glimpse, grant me but one glimpse only, of something perfect, fully realised, happy, mighty, triumphant, of something that still gives cause for fear! A glimpse of a man that justifies the existence of man, a glimpse of an incarnate human happiness that realises and redeems, for the sake of which one may hold fast to *the belief in man!* For the position is this: in the dwarfing and levelling of the European man lurks *our* greatest peril, for it is this outlook which fatigues—we see today nothing which wishes to be greater, we surmise that the process is always still backwards, still backwards towards something more attenuated, more inoffensive, more cunning, more comfortable, more mediocre, more indifferent, more Chinese, more Christian—man, there is no doubt about it, grows always "better"—the destiny of Europe lies even in this—that in losing the fear of man, we have also lost the hope in man, yea, the will to be man. The sight of man now fatigues.—What is present-day Nihilism if it is not *that*?—We are tired of *man*.

After reading this selection, consider these questions:

1. What is the distinction between "good and evil" and "good and bad"?
2. Why is Nietzsche concerned with resentment?
3. What is the result of the acceptance of priestly values?

# SELECTION 5:
# The Origins of Depth Psychology

*Not unlike the theories of Charles Darwin and the Social Darwinists, and similar to Friedrich Nietzsche's interpretations of the individual and the relation of the individual to the will to power, Sigmund Freud's depth psychology called for a reevaluation of our traditional moral codes and for a rethinking of our notions of reason. As Freud himself made clear, the mind was no longer in control of itself. Freud was trained as a physician in Vienna and further studied psychology in France. Returning to Vienna at the end of the nineteenth century, he had to face a long struggle for personal success and the acceptance of his ideas among the doctors and scientists of the age. In the following selection from his* An Autobiographical Study, *Freud explains both the bases of his ideas and the problems he had in finding public acceptance of them.*

The theories of resistance and of repression, of the unconscious, of the aetiological [causal] significance of sexual life and of the importance of infantile experiences—these form the principal constituents of the theoretical structure of psychoanalysis. In these pages, unfortunately, I have been able to describe only the separate elements and not their interconnections and their bearing upon one another. But I am obliged now to turn to the alterations which gradually took place in the technique of the analytic method.

The means which I first adopted for overcoming the patient's resistance, by pressing and encouraging him, had been indispensable for the purpose of giving me a first general survey of what was to be expected. But in the long run it proved to be too much of a strain upon both sides, and further it seemed open to certain obvious criticisms. It therefore gave place to another

method which was in one sense its opposite. Instead of urging the patient to say something upon some particular subject, I now asked him to abandon himself to a process of *free association, i.e.* to say whatever came into his head, while ceasing to give any conscious direction to his thoughts. It was essential, however, that he should bind himself to report literally everything that occurred to his self-perception. . . .

With the help of the method of free association and of the closely related art of interpretation, psychoanalysis succeeded in achieving one thing which appeared to be of no practical importance but which in fact necessarily led to a fresh attitude and a fresh scale of values in scientific thought. It became possible to prove that dreams have a meaning and to discover it. In classical antiquity great importance was attached to dreams as foretelling the future; but modern science would have nothing to do with them, it handed them over to superstition, declaring them to be purely "somatic" processes—a kind of spasm occurring in a mind that is otherwise asleep. It seemed quite inconceivable that anyone who had done serious scientific work could make his appearance as an "interpreter of dreams." But by disregarding the excommunication pronounced upon dreams, by treating them as unexplained neurotic symptoms, as delusional or obsessional ideas, by neglecting their apparent content and by making their separate component images into subjects for free association, psychoanalysis arrived at a different conclusion. The numerous associations produced by the dreamer led to the discovery of a mental structure which could no longer be described as absurd or confused, which was on an equality with any other product of the mind, and of which the *manifest* dream was no more than a distorted, abbreviated, and misunderstood translation, and usually a translation into visual images. These *latent dream-thoughts* contained the meaning of the dream, while its manifest content was simply a make-believe, a façade, which could serve as a starting-point for the associations but not for the interpretation.

There were now a whole series of questions to be answered, among the most important of them being whether there was a motive for the formation of dreams, under what conditions it took place, by what methods the dream-thoughts (which are invariably full of sense) become converted into the dream (which is often senseless), and others besides. I attempted to solve all of these problems in *The Interpretation of Dreams*, which I published in the year 1900. I can only find space here for the briefest abstract of my investigation. When the latent dream-thoughts that are revealed by the analysis of a dream are examined, one of them is found to stand out from among the rest, which are intelligible and well known to the dreamer. These latter thoughts are residues of waking life (the *day's residues*, as they are called technically); but the isolated thought is found to be an impulse in the form of a wish, often of a very repellent kind, which is foreign to the waking life of the dreamer and is consequently disavowed by him with surprise or indignation. This impulse is the actual constructor of the dream: it provides the energy for its production and makes use of the day's residues as material; the dream which thus originates represents a situation in which the impulse is satisfied, it is the fulfilment of the wish which the impulse contains. It would

not be possible for this process to take place without being favoured by the presence of something in the nature of a state of sleep. The necessary mental pre-condition of sleep is the concentration of the ego upon the wish to sleep and the withdrawal of psychical energy from all the interests of life; since at the same time all the paths of approach to motility are blocked, the ego is also able to reduce the expenditure of energy by which at other times it maintains the repressions. The unconscious impulse makes use of this nocturnal relaxation of repression in order to push its way into consciousness with the dream. But the repressive resistance of the ego is not abolished in sleep but merely reduced. Some of it remains in the shape of a *censorship of dreams* and forbids the unconscious impulse to express itself in the forms which it would properly assume. In consequence of the severity of the censorship of dreams, the latent dream-thoughts are obliged to submit to being altered and softened so as to make the forbidden meaning of the dream unrecognizable. This is the explanation of *dream-distortion,* which accounts for the most striking characteristic of the manifest dream. We are therefore justified in asserting that *a dream is the (disguised) fulfilment of a (repressed) wish.* It will now be seen that dreams are constructed like a neurotic symptom: they are compromises between the demands of a repressed impulse and the resistance of a censoring force in the ego. Since they have a similar origin they are equally unintelligible and stand in equal need of interpretation.

There is no difficulty in discovering the general function of dreaming. It serves the purpose of warding off, by a kind of soothing action, external or internal stimuli which would tend to arouse the sleeper, and thus of securing sleep against interruption. External stimuli are warded off by being given a new interpretation and by being woven into some harmless situation; internal stimuli, caused by the pressure of instincts, are given free play by the sleeper and allowed to find satisfaction in the formation of dreams, so long as the latent dream-thoughts submit to the control of the censorship. But if they threaten to break free and the meaning of the dream becomes too plain, the sleeper cuts short the dream and awakens in terror. (Dreams of this class are known as *anxiety-dreams*.) A similar failure in the function of dreaming occurs if an external stimulus becomes too strong to be warded off. (This is the class of *arousal-dreams*.) I have given the name of *dream-work* to the process which, with the co-operation of the censorship, converts the latent thoughts into the manifest content of the dream. It consists of a peculiar way of treating the pre-conscious material of thought, so that its component parts become *condensed*, its mental emphasis becomes *displaced*, and the whole of it is translated into visual images or *dramatized*, and filled out by a deceptive *secondary elaboration*. The dream-work is an excellent example of the processes occurring in the deeper, unconscious layers of the mind, which differ considerably from the familiar normal processes of thought. It also displays a number of archaic characteristics, such as the use of a *symbolism* (in this case of a predominantly sexual kind) which it has since also been possible to discover in other spheres of mental activity.

We have explained that the unconscious impulse which causes the dream connects itself with part of the day's residues, with some unexhausted interest of waking life; this lends the dream which is thus brought into being a double value for the work of analysis. It is true that on the one hand a dream that has been analysed reveals itself as the fulfilment of a repressed wish; but on the other hand it will be a continuation of some preconscious activity of the day before and will contain subject-matter of some kind or other, whether it gives expression to a determination, a warning, a reflection, or once more to the fulfilment of a wish. Analysis exploits the dream in both directions, as a means of obtaining knowledge alike of the patient's conscious and of his unconscious processes. It also profits from the fact that dreams have access to the forgotten material of childhood, and so it happens that infantile amnesia is for the most part overcome in connection with the interpretation of dreams. In this respect dreams achieve a part of what was previously the task of hypnotism. On the other hand, I have never maintained the assertion which has so often been ascribed to me that dream-interpretation shows that all dreams have a sexual content or are derived from sexual motive forces. It is easy to see that hunger, thirst, or the need to excrete, can produce dreams of satisfaction just as well as any repressed sexual or egoistic impulse. The case of young children affords us a convenient test of the validity of our theory of dreams. In them the various psychical systems are not yet sharply divided and the repressions have not yet grown deep, so that we often come upon dreams which are nothing more than undisguised fulfilments of impulses left over from waking life. Under the influence of imperative needs, adults may also produce dreams of this infantile type.

After reading this selection, consider these questions:

1. What does Freud mean by *resistance*?
2. Why did Freud turn to the interpretation of dreams?
3. What happens in dreams, according to Freud?

# CHAPTER 10
# Christianity in the Modern World

The various modern forms of the Christian faith had to face a number of challenges in recent centuries. The Enlightenment of the eighteenth century and its nineteenth-century evolution into utilitarianism, positivism, and liberal political, social, and economic institutions were all either avowedly anti-Christian or conceived of Christianity as an outmoded set of beliefs. Christian faith in general, and the various established churches in particular—Anglicanism in England; Lutheranism in northern Germany and Scandinavia; Catholicism in France, Spain, Italy, and Austria; and Orthodoxy in Russia—most often aligned with those forces of the anti-Enlightenment that emerged in the course of the nineteenth century. What was generally referred to as "the Alliance of Throne and Altar" in post-Napoleonic Europe found most forms of Christianity on the side of the conservatives and in some cases of the reactionaries.

# SELECTION 1:

# The Origins of Liberal Protestantism

*Although often understood in opposition to the dominant forms of thought of the day, Christianity—especially as defined by a number of important thinkers—nonetheless proved to be innovative and even dynamic in the recent modern period. The Protestant minister and theologian Friedrich Schleiermacher (1768–1834), for instance, took up the challenge of the anti-Christian attitudes of the Enlightenment. In* Religion: Speeches to Its Cultured Despisers *(1799), Schleiermacher moved beyond Christian dogma and the simple affirmation of faith to rethink the foundation of Christianity. He discovered this foundation within the individual's "feeling" of dependence on something greater than oneself. This dependence is absolute and points to the existence of a monotheistic God. In this way, Schleiermacher founded religion on the individual's experience of God and not on the affirmation of a system of beliefs or a church doctrine. In his later works, including* Christian Faith *(1821–1822), he expanded this idea into a regrounding of traditional interpretations of Christ and the major doctrines of the Protestant faith. Schleiermacher was clearly one of the founders of what has come to be called liberal Protestantism. The following selection is taken from* Religion: Speeches to Its Cultured Despisers.

Let us . . . examine whence exactly religion has its rise. Is it from some clear intuition, or from some vague thought? Is it from the different kinds and sects of religion found in history, or from some general idea which you have perhaps conceived arbitrarily? Some doubtless will profess the latter view. But here as in other things the ready judgment may be without ground, the matter being superficially considered and no trouble being taken to gain an accurate knowledge. Your general idea turns on fear of an eternal being, or, broadly, respect for his influence on the occurrences of this life called by you providence, on expectation of a future life after this one, called

by you immorality. These two conceptions which you have rejected, are, you consider, in one way or another, the hinges of all religion. But say, my dear sirs, how you have found this; for there are two points of view from which everything taking place in man or proceeding from him may be regarded. Considered from the centre outwards, that is according to its inner quality, it is an expression of human nature, based in one of its necessary modes of acting or impulses or whatever else you like to call it, for I will not now quarrel with your technical language. On the contrary, regarded from the outside, according to the definite attitude and form it assumes in particular cases, it is a product of time and history. From what side have you considered religion that great spiritual phenomenon, that you have reached the idea that everything called by this name has a common content? You can hardly affirm that it is by re-

From *On Religion*, by Friedrich Schleiermacher, translated by John Oman (New York: Harper & Row, 1958).

garding it from within. If so, my good sirs, you would have to admit that these thoughts are at least in some way based in human nature. And should you say that as now found they have sprung only from misinterpretations or false references of a necessary human aim, it would become you to seek in it the true and eternal, and to unite your efforts to ours to free human nature from the injustice which it always suffers when aught in it is misunderstood or misdirected.

By all that is sacred, and according to that avowal, something must be sacred to you, I adjure you, do not neglect this business, that mankind, whom with us you honour, do not most justly scorn you for forsaking them in a grave matter. If you find from what you hear that the business is as good as done, even if it ends otherwise than you expect, I venture to reckon on your thanks and approval.

But you will probably say that your idea of the content of religion is from the other view of this spiritual phenomenon. You start with the outside, with the opinions, dogmas and usages, in which every religion is presented. They always return to providence and immortality. For these externals you have sought an inward and original source in vain. Wherefore religion generally can be nothing but an empty pretence which, like a murky and oppressive atmosphere, has enshrouded part of the truth. Doubtless this is your genuine opinion. But if you really consider these two points the sum of religion in all the forms in which it has appeared in history, permit me to ask whether you have rightly observed all these phenomena and have rightly comprehended their common content? If your idea has had its rise in this way you must justify it by instances. If anyone says it is wrong and beside the mark, and if he points out something else in religion not hollow, but having a kernel of excellent quality and extraction, you must first hear and judge before you venture further to despise. Do not grudge, therefore, to listen to what I shall say to those who, from first to last, have more accurately and laboriously adhered to observation of particulars.

You are doubtless acquainted with the histories of human follies, and have reviewed the various structures of religious doctrine from the senseless fables of wanton peoples to the most refined Deism, from the rude superstition of human sacrifice to the ill-put together fragments of metaphysics and ethics now called purified Christianity, and you have found them all without rhyme or reason. I am far from wishing to contradict you. Rather, if you really mean that the most cultured religious system is no better than the rudest, if you only perceive that the divine cannot lie in a series that ends on both sides in something ordinary and despicable, I will gladly spare you the trouble of estimating further all that lies between. Possibly they may all appear to you transitions and stages towards the final form. Out of the hand of its age each comes better polished and carved, till at length art has grown equal to that perfect plaything with which our century has presented history. But this consummation of doctrines and systems is often anything rather than consummation of religion. Nay, not infrequently, the progress of the one has not the smallest connection with the other. I cannot speak of it without indignation. All who have a regard form what issues from within the mind, and who are in earnest that every side of man be trained and exhibited, must bewail how the high and glorious is often turned from its destination and robbed of its freedom in order to be held in despicable bondage by the scholastic spirit of a barbarian and cold time. What are all these systems, considered in themselves, but the handiwork of the calculating understanding, wherein only by mutual limitation each part holds its place? What else can they be, these systems of theology, these theories of the origin and the end of the world, these analyses of the nature of an incomprehensible Being, wherein everything runs to cold argufying, and the highest can be treated in the tone of a common controversy? And this is certainly—let me appeal to your own feeling—not the character of religion.

If you have only given attention to these dogmas and opinions, therefore, you do not yet know religion itself, and what you despise is not it. Why have you not penetrated deeper to find the kernel of this shell? I am astonished at your voluntary ignorance, ye easy-going inquirers, and at the all too quiet satisfaction with which you linger by the first thing presented to you. Why do you not regard the religious life itself, and first those pious exaltations of the mind in which all other known activities are set aside or almost suppressed, and the whole soul is dissolved in the immediate feeling of the Infinite and Eternal? In such moments the disposition you pretend to despise reveals itself in primordial and visible form. He only who has studied and truly known man in these emotions can rediscover religion in those outward manifestations. He will assuredly perceive something more in them than you. Bound up in them all something of that spiritual matter lies, without which they could not have arisen. But in the hands of those who do not understand how to unbind it, let them break it up and examine it as they may, nothing but the cold dead mass remains.

This recommendation to seek rather in those scattered and seemingly undeveloped elements your object that you have not yet found in the developed and the complete to which you have hitherto been directed, cannot surprise you who have more or less busied yourselves with philosophy, and are acquainted with its fortunes. With philosophy, indeed, it should be quite otherwise. From its nature it must strive to fashion itself into the closest connection. That special kind of knowledge is only verified and its communication assured by its completeness, and yet even here you must commence with the scattered and incomplete. Recollect how very few of those who, in a way of their own, have penetrated into the secrets of nature and spirit, viewing and exhibiting their mutual relation and inner harmony in a light of their own, have put forth at once a system of their knowledge. In a finer, if more fragile form, they have communicated their discoveries.

On the contrary, if you regard the systems in all schools, how often are they mere habitations and nurseries of the dead letter. With few exceptions, the plastic spirit of high contemplation is too fleeting and too free for those rigid forms whereby those who would willingly grasp and retain what is strange, believe they are best helped. Suppose that any one held the architects of those great edifices of philosophy, without distinction, for true philosophers! Suppose he would learn from them the spirit of their research! Would you not advise him thus, "See to it, friend, that you have not lighted upon those who merely follow, and collect, and rest satisfied with what another has furnished; with them you will never find the spirit of that art: to the discoverers you must go, on whom it surely rests." To you who seek religion I must give the same advice. It is all the more necessary, as religion is as far removed, by its whole nature, from all that is systematic as philosophy is naturally disposed to it.

After reading this selection, consider these questions:

1. Who are the "cultured despisers" Schleiermacher addresses?
2. What, according to Schleiermacher, is the basis of faith?
3. What results from this faith?

# Selection 2:

# The Essence of Christianity

**B**oth the more traditional forms of Christianity and the new theological thought of Friedrich Schleiermacher did not go unchallenged. In the first half of the nineteenth century there developed a more philosophical critique of religion than had prevailed earlier. Particularly in Germany from the 1820s to the 1840s, debates arose over the truth and meaning of Chris-

*tianity in the modern world. The more radical followers of the nineteenth-century German philosopher Georg Wilhelm Friedrich Hegel (1770–1831)—known as the "left-wing" Hegelians (as opposed to the more conservative "right-wing" Hegelians)—found in these debates a means of criticizing the social, economic, political, and religious beliefs of their times. Karl Marx himself began as a left-wing Hegelian. In developing his own views, however, Marx had to show the limitations of this position.*

*The most radical of these left-wing Hegelians was Ludwig Feuerbach (1804–1872). Feuerbach redefined Hegel's idealist position in terms of a thoroughgoing materialism. Although materialism, as we have seen, dates back to the radical wing of the eighteenth-century French Enlightenment, Feuerbach articulated the first fully materialist philosophy. He stated that human beings, as well as their forms of consciousness, are shaped by the material conditions in which they find themselves. Their actions and goals are defined by their constant material needs. In other words, Feuerbach undermined the idea that human beings are spiritual entities. Reason, Feuerbach argued, should be based on a knowledge of these material conditions. In* The Essence of Christianity (1841), *Feuerbach argues that religion is "illusionistic," the projection of an idealized image of man onto a nonexistent being (God), from which human beings in turn define their own existence and values. In place of the circular arguments of religion, Feuerbach argues for a more naturalistic, humanistic ethic. His materialism became the basis of what throughout the nineteenth century was called "free thinking." The following selection comes from the central chapter of his most important work,* The Essence of Christianity.

When religion—consciousness of God—is designated as the self-consciousness of man, this is not to be understood as affirming that the religious man is directly aware of this identity; for, on the contrary, ignorance of it is fundamental to the peculiar nature of religion. To preclude this misconception, it is better to say, religion is man's earliest and also indirect form of self-knowledge. Hence, religion everywhere precedes philosophy, as in the history of the race, so also in that of the individual. Man first of all sees his nature as if *out of* himself, before he finds it in himself. His own nature is in the first instance contemplated by him as that of another being. Religion is the childlike condition of humanity; but the child sees his nature—man—out of himself; in childhood a man is an object to himself, under the form of another man. Hence the historical progress of religion consists in this: that what by an earlier religion was regarded as objective, is now recognised as subjective; that is, what was formerly contemplated and worshipped as God is now perceived to be something *human*. What was at first religion becomes at a later period idolatry; man is seen to have adored his own nature. Man has given objectivity to himself, but has not recognised the object as his own nature: a later religion takes this forward step; every advance in religion is therefore a deeper self-knowledge. But every particular religion, while it pronounces its predecessors idolatrous, excepts itself—and necessarily so, otherwise it would no longer be religion—from the fate, the common nature of all religions: it imputes only to other religions what is the fault, if fault it be, of religion in general. Because it has a different object, a different tenor, because it has transcended the ideas of preceding religions, it erroneously supposes itself exalted above the necessary eternal laws which constitute

From *The Essence of Christianity*, by Ludwig Feuerbach, translated by George Eliot (New York: Blanchard, 1855).

the essence of religion—it fancies its object, its ideas, to be superhuman. But the essence of religion, thus hidden from the religious, is evident to the thinker, by whom religion is viewed objectively, which it cannot be by its votaries [followers]. And it is our task to show that the antithesis of divine and human is altogether illusory, that it is nothing else than the antithesis between the human nature in general and the human individual; that, consequently, the object and contents of the Christian religion are altogether human.

Religion, at least the Christian, is the relation of man to himself, or more correctly to his own nature (*i.e.,* his subjective nature); but a relation to it, viewed as a nature apart from his own. The divine being is nothing else than the human being, or, rather, the human nature purified, freed from the limits of the individual man, made objective—*i.e.,* contemplated and revered as another, a distinct being. All the attributes of the divine nature are, therefore, attributes of the human nature.

In relation to the attributes, the predicates, of the Divine Being, this is admitted without hesitation, but by no means in relation to the subject of these predicates. The negation of the subject is held to be irreligion, nay, atheism; though not so the negation of the predicates. But that which has no predicates or qualities, has no effect upon me; that which has no effect upon me has no existence for me. To deny all the qualities of a being is equivalent to denying the being himself. A being without qualities is one which cannot become an object to the mind, and such a being is virtually non-existent. Where man deprives God of all qualities, God is no longer anything more to him than a negative being. To the truly religious man, God is not a being without qualities, because to him he is a positive, real being. The theory that God cannot be defined, and consequently cannot be known by man, is therefore the offspring of recent times, a product of modern unbelief.

As reason is and can be pronounced finite only where man regards sensual enjoyment, or religious emotion, or aesthetic contemplation, or moral sentiment, as the absolute, the true; so the proposition that God is unknowable or undefinable, can only be enunciated and become fixed as a dogma, where this object has no longer any interest for the intellect; where the real, the positive, alone has any hold on man, where the real alone has for him the significance of the essential, of the absolute, divine object, but where at the same time, in contradiction with this purely worldly tendency, there yet exist some old remains of religiousness. On the ground that God is unknowable, man excuses himself to what is yet remaining of his religious conscience for his forgetfulness of God, his absorption in the world: he denies God practically by his conduct,—the world has possession of all his thoughts and inclinations,—but he does not deny him theoretically, he does not attack his existence; he lets that rest. But this existence does not affect or incommode him; it is a merely negative existence, an existence without existence, a self-contradictory existence,—a state of being which, as to its effects, is not distinguishable from non-being. The denial of determinate, positive predicates concerning the divine nature is nothing else than a denial of religion, with, however, an appearance of religion in its favour, so that it is not recognised as a denial; it is simply a subtle, disguised atheism. The alleged religious horror of limiting God by positive predicates is only the irreligious wish to know nothing more of God, to banish God from the mind. Dread of limitation is dread of existence. All real existence, *i.e.*, all existence which is truly such, is qualitative, determinative existence. He who earnestly believes in the Divine existence is not shocked at the attributing even of gross sensuous qualities to God. He who dreads an existence that may give offence, who shrinks from the grossness of a positive predicate, may as well renounce existence altogether. A God who is injured by determinate qualities has not the courage and the strength to exist. Qualities are the fire, the vital breath, the oxygen, the salt of existence. An existence in general, an existence without qualities, is an insipidity, an absurdity. But there can be no more in God than is supplied by religion. Only where man loses his taste for religion, and thus religion itself becomes insipid, does the existence of God become an insipid existence—an existence without qualities. . . .

Now, when it is shown that what the subject is lies entirely in the attributes of the subject; that is, that the predicate is the true subject; it is also proved that if the divine predicates are attributes of the human nature, the subject of those predicates is also of the human nature. But the divine predicates are partly general, partly personal. The general predicates are the metaphysical, but these serve only as external points of support to religion; they are not the characteristic definitions of religion. It is the personal predicates alone which constitute the essence of religion—in which the Divine Being is the object of religion. Such are, for example, that God is a Person, that he is the moral Lawgiver, the Father of mankind, the Holy One, the Just, the Good, the Merciful. It is, however, at once clear, or it will at least be clear in the sequel, with regard to these and other definitions, that, especially as applied to a personality, they are purely human definitions, and that consequently man in religion—in his relation to God— is in relation to his own nature; for to the religious sentiment these predicates are not mere conceptions, mere images, which man forms of God, to be distinguished from that which God is in himself, but truths, facts, realities. Religion knows nothing of anthropomorphisms; to it they are not anthropomorphisms. It is the very essence of religion, that to it these definitions express the nature of God. They are pronounced to be images only by the understanding, which reflects on religion, and which while defending them yet before its own tribunal denies them. But to the religious sentiment God is a real Father, real Love and Mercy; for to it he is a real, living, personal being, and therefore his attributes are also living and personal. Nay, the definitions which are the most sufficing to the religious sentiment are precisely those which give the most offence to the understanding, and which in the process of reflection on religion it denies. Religion is essentially emotion; hence, objectively also, emotion is to it necessarily of a divine nature. Even anger appears to it an emotion not unworthy of God, provided only there be a religious motive at the foundation of this anger.

But here it is also essential to observe, and this phenomenon is an extremely remarkable one, characterising the very core of religion, that in proportion as the divine subject is in reality human, the greater is the apparent difference between God and man; that is, the more, by reflection on religion, by theology, is the identity of the divine and human denied, and the human, considered as such, is depreciated. The reason of this is, that as what is positive in the conception of the divine being can only be human, the conception of man, as an object of consciousness, can only be negative. To enrich God, man must become poor; that God may be all, man must be nothing. But he desires to be nothing in himself, because what he takes from himself is not lost to him, since it is preserved in God. Man has his being in God; why then should he have it in himself? Where is the necessity of positing the same thing twice, of having it twice? What man withdraws from himself, what he renounces in himself, he only enjoys in an incomparably higher and fuller measure in God.

After reading this selection, consider these questions:

1. What does Feuerbach identify as the attributes ("the predicates") of God?
2. What is the source of these predicates?
3. What, according to Feuerbach, is the result upon man of his belief in God?

# SELECTION 3:

# The Beginnings of Christian Existentialism

*Radical forms of Protestant thought also developed in the middle years of the nineteenth century. Foremost among such theologies was the position developed by the Danish pastor Søren Kierkegaard (1813–1855). Kierkegaard was disturbed by the dominant middle-class attitudes toward Christianity. He found in liberal forms of Protestantism an active avoidance of the fundamental conditions of human existence and the truth of the Christian faith. He was particularly angered by the ways in which Protestant moralism had become merely a salve for the conscience of individuals involved with moneymaking and other workaday activities. Like Ludwig Feuerbach, Kierkegaard developed his own thoughts in direct opposition to those of Georg Hegel. But unlike Feuerbach, he did not move to materialism; rather, Kierkegaard sought to find in individual existence a new relation to God. Through an "existential dialectic," the individual, according to Kierkegaard, moves from the aesthetic stage to the ethical stage and finally to the religious one. This movement results in despair as the individual comes to recognize the disparity between mortal life and the eternal truths of religion. To find God, reason is unsuitable; one must have the courage to make a "leap of faith" through which one's life becomes completely transformed. In this way Kierkegaard broke from one of the basic tenets of the Enlightenment and from the liberal Protestant position. Science and knowledge, technological progress, and social improvement could not improve the moral condition of human society. The individual's relation to God and his or her moral stance lay in an entirely different sphere of activity. The following selection is taken from one of Kierkegaard's essays, "The Present Age," in which he identifies the weakness of the generally accepted values of his times.*

It has often been said that a reformation should begin with each man reforming himself. That, however, is not what actually happened, for the Reformation produced a hero who paid God high enough for his position as hero. By joining up with him directly people buy cheap, indeed at bargain prices, what he had paid for so dearly; but they do not buy the highest of all things. The abstract principle of leveling, on the contrary, like the biting east wind, has no personal relation to any individual, but has only an abstract relationship which is the same for everyone. There no hero suffers for others, or helps them; the taskmaster of all alike is the leveling process, which itself takes on their education. And the man who learns most from the leveling and himself becomes greatest does not become an out-

From "On the Present Age," by Søren Kierkegaard, in *A Kierkegaard Anthology*, edited by Robert Bretall (New York: Modern Library, 1946).

standing man or a hero—that would only impede the leveling process, which is rigidly consistent to the end; he himself prevents that from happening because he has understood the meaning of leveling: he becomes a man and nothing else, in the complete equalitarian sense. That is the idea of religion. But, under those conditions, the equalitarian order is severe and the profit is seemingly very small; seemingly, for unless the individual learns in the reality of religion and before God to be content with himself, and learns, instead of dominating others, to dominate himself, content as priest to be his own audience, and as author his own reader—if he will not learn to be satisfied with that as the highest, because it is the expression of the equality of all men before God and of our likeness to others, then he will not escape from reflection. It may be that for one deceptive moment it will seem to him, in relation to his gifts, as though he were leveling, but in the end he will sink down beneath the leveling process. There is no good calling upon a Holger Danske [a Danish folk hero] or a Martin Luther; their day is over, and at bottom it is only the individual's laziness which makes a man long to have them back, a worldly impatience which prefers to buy something cheap, second-hand, rather than to buy the highest of all things very dear and first-hand. It is worse than useless to found society after society, because negatively speaking there is something above them, even though the short-sighted member of the society cannot see it.

The principle of individuality in its *immediate* and beautiful formation symbolizes the generation in the outstanding and eminent individual; it groups subordinate individualities around the representative. This principle of individuality, in its *eternal* truth, uses the abstraction and equality of the generation to level down, and in that way co-operates in developing the individual religiously into a real man. For the leveling process is as powerful where temporary things are concerned as it is impotent where eternal things are concerned. Reflection is a snare in which one is caught but, once the "leap" of enthusiasm has been taken, the relation is a different one and it becomes a noose which drags one into eternity. Reflection is and re-mains the hardest creditor in existence; hitherto it has cunningly bought up all the possible views of life, but it cannot buy the essentially religious and eternal view of life; on the other hand, it can tempt people astray with its dazzling brilliance and dishearten them by reminding them of all the past. But, by leaping into the depths, one learns to help oneself, learns to love others as much as oneself, even though one is accused of arrogance and pride—because one will not accept help—or of selfishness, because one will not cunningly deceive people by helping them, i.e. by helping them to escape their highest destiny. . . .

In order that everything should be reduced to the same level it is first of all necessary to procure a phantom, a spirit, a monstrous abstraction, an all-embracing something which is nothing, a mirage—and that phantom is *the public*. It is only in an age which is without passion, yet reflective, that such a phantom can develop itself with the help of the Press which itself becomes an abstraction. In times of passion and tumult and enthusiasm, even when a people desire to realize a fruitless idea and lay waste and destroy everything—even then there is no such thing as a public. There are parties and they are concrete. The Press, in times such as those, takes on a concrete character according to the division of parties. But just as sedentary professional people are the first to take up any fantastic illusion which comes their way, so a passionless, sedentary, reflective age, in which only the Press exhibits a vague sort of life, fosters this phantom. The public is, in fact, the real leveling-master rather than the actual leveler, for whenever leveling is only approximately accomplished it is done by something, but the public is a monstrous nothing. . . .

The public is a host, more numerous than all the peoples together, but it is a body which can never be reviewed; it cannot even be represented, because it is an abstraction. Nevertheless, when the age is reflective and passionless and destroys everything concrete, the public becomes everything and is supposed to include everything. And that again shows how the individual is thrown back upon himself.

The real moment in time and the real situation of being simultaneous with real people, each of whom is something—that is what helps to sustain the individual. But the existence of a public produces neither a situation nor simultaneity. The individual reader of the Press is not the public, and even though little by little a number of individuals or even all of them should read it, the simultaneity is lacking. Years might be spent gathering the public together, and still it would not be there. This abstraction, which the individuals so illogically form, quite rightly repulses the individual instead of coming to his help. The man who has no opinion of an event at the actual moment accepts the opinion of the majority or, if he is quarrelsome, of the minority. But it must be remembered that both majority and minority are real people, and that is why the individual is assisted by adhering to them. A public, on the contrary, is an abstraction. . . .

A generation, a people, an assembly of the people, a meeting, or a man are responsible for what they are and can be made ashamed if they are inconstant and unfaithful; but a public remains a public. A people, an assembly or a man can change to such an extent that one may say: they are no longer the same; a public on the other hand can become the very opposite and still be the same—a public. But it is precisely by means of this abstraction and this abstract discipline that the individual will be formed (insofar as the individual is not already formed by his inner life), if he does not succumb in the process: taught to be content, in the highest religious sense, with himself and his relation to God, to be at one with himself instead of being in agreement with a public which destroys everything that is relative, concrete and particular in life; educated to find peace within himself and with God, instead of counting hands; and the absolute difference between the modern world and antiquity will be: that the totality is not concrete and is therefore unable to support the individual, or to educate him as the concrete should (though without developing him absolutely), but is an abstraction which by its abstract equality repels him and thus helps him to be educated absolutely—unless he succumbs in the process. . . .

A public is neither a nation, nor a generation, nor a community, nor a society, nor these particular men, for all these are only what they are through the concrete. . . .

A public is everything and nothing, the most dangerous of all powers and the most insignificant: one can speak to a whole nation in the name of the public and still the public will be less than a single real man, however unimportant. . . .

If I tried to imagine the public as a particular person. . . . I should perhaps think of one of the Roman emperors, a large well-fed figure, suffering from boredom, looking only for the sensual intoxication of laughter, since the divine gift of wit is not earthly enough. And so for a change he wanders about, indolent rather than bad, but with a negative desire to dominate. Everyone who has read the classical authors knows how many things a Caesar could try out in order to kill time. In the same way the public keeps a dog to amuse it. That dog is literary scum. If there is some one superior to the rest, perhaps even a great man, the dog is set on him and the fun begins. The dog goes for him, snapping and tearing at his coattails, allowing itself every possible ill-mannered familiarity—until the public tires, and says it may stop. That is an example of how the public levels. Their betters and superiors in strength are mishandled—and the dog remains a dog which even the public despises. The leveling is therefore done by a third party; a non-existent public leveling with the help of a third party which in its insignificance is less than nothing, being already more than leveled. And so the public is unrepentant, for it was after all not the public that acted, but the dog; just as one says to children—the cat's mother did it. The public is unrepentant—it was not really belittling anyone; it just wanted a little amusement. . . .

The public is unrepentant, for it is not they who own the dog—they only subscribe. They neither set the dog on anyone, nor whistle it off—directly. If asked, they would answer: the dog is not mine, it has no master. And if the dog had to be killed, they would say: it was really a good thing that bad-tempered dog was put away, everyone wanted it killed—even the subscribers.

Perhaps someone, familiarizing himself with such a case, and inclined to fix his attention upon the outstanding individual who suffered at the hands of the public, may be of the opinion that such an ordeal is a great misfortune. I cannot at all agree with such an opinion, for anyone who really wishes to be helped to attain the highest is in fact benefited by undergoing such a misfortune, and must rather desire it, even though people may be led to revolt. The really terrible thing is the thought of the many lives that are or easily may be wasted. I will not even mention those who are lost, or at any rate led completely astray—those who play the part of the dog for money—but the many who are helpless, thoughtless and sensual, who live superior lazy lives and never receive any deeper impression of existence than this meaningless grin, and all those bad people who are led into further temptation because in their stupidity they even become self-important by commiserating with the one who is attacked, without even understanding that in such a position the person attacked is always the stronger, without understanding that in this case the terrible and ironical truth applies: Weep not over him, but over yourselves.

That is the leveling process at its lowest, for it always equates itself to the divisor by means of which everyone is reduced to a common denominator. Eternal life is also a sort of leveling, and yet that is not so, because the unity is that everyone should really and essentially be a man in a religious sense. . . .

And so when the generation, which itself desired to level and to be emancipated, to destroy authority and at the same time itself, has, through the skepticism of the principle "association," started the hopeless forest fire of abstraction; when as a result of leveling with this skepticism, the generation has rid itself of the individual and of everything organic and concrete, and put in its place "humanity" and the numerical equality of man and man; when the generation has, for a moment, delighted in this unlimited panorama of abstract infinity, unrelieved by even the smallest eminence, undisturbed by even the slightest interest, a sea of desert: then the time has come for work to begin, for every individual must work for himself, each for himself. No longer can the individual, as in former times, turn to the great for help when he grows confused. That is past; he is either lost in the dizziness of unending abstraction or saved forever in the reality of religion. . . .

For the development is, in spite of everything, a progress, because all the individuals who are saved will receive the specific weight of religion, its essence at first hand, from God himself. Then it will be said: "Behold, all is in readiness: see how the cruelty of abstraction makes the true form of worldliness only too evident, the abyss of eternity opens before you, the sharp scythe of the leveler makes it possible for every one individually to leap over the blade—and behold, it is God who waits. Leap, then, into the arms of God."

After reading this selection, consider these questions:
1. How does Kierkegaard define "the public"?
2. Why can't the individual break from the public?
3. How does Kierkegaard introduce the need for a "leap of faith"?

# SELECTION 4:

# Catholicism in the Modern World

Modern Catholicism advanced a response to the problems of modernity that differed from both liberal Protestantism and Søren Kierkegaard's existentialism. The stronger institutional basis of Catholicism made the declared position of the pope essential in helping Catholics define their way in the modern world. Pope Pius IX took the lead in defining the modern Catholic response. Beginning as a liberal and a supporter of many of the modernizing tendencies of the early nineteenth century, Pius was appalled by what he came to see as the excesses of the revolutions of 1848. He thereafter turned against the entire modern world. In 1864, for instance, he issued a Syllabus of Errors condemning what he regarded as the principal religious and philosophical "errors" of the times. Among them were materialism, free thought, and "indifferentism" (the idea that one religion is as good as another). In 1869 he also invoked a general council of the church to reevaluate the relation of Catholicism to the modern world. This was the first general council since the Council of Trent in the mid-sixteenth century. Subsequently known as Vatican I, this council reconfirmed the traditions of the church. The one issue at Vatican I that did arouse controversy within the Catholic world was that of papal infallibility. According to this church teaching, when the pope speaks ex cathedra—that is, in his capacity as "pastor and doctor of all Christians"—he is absolutely and unchallengeably correct in all matters of faith and morals. Although accepted by most Catholics, this position roused a storm of protest among the leaders of a number of Catholic nations throughout Europe. The governments of France, Spain, and Italy openly denounced it both as a challenge to their power and as a misinterpretation of the Catholic tradition.

Although the Catholic Church under Pius IX clearly positioned itself against the tendencies of the age, his successors gradually modified this position. (At the Vatican II council in 1961, the church in many ways reversed its earlier stance.) Reaction against Vatican I, however, began almost immediately. With Pius's successor, a more accommodating attitude began to prevail. Pope Leo XIII was ready to concede that there was "good" as well as "evil" in modern civilization. He also added a scientific staff to the Vatican bureaucracy to deal with the questions raised by modern knowledge. Although Leo still opposed liberalism, socialism, and all forms of anticlericalism, he hoped to improve the relation between capitalists and workers. In the encyclical Rerum Novarum (1891), Leo restated the position of the church in regard to organized labor. This document became the basis of Christian socialism.

The foremost duty, therefore, of the rulers of the State should be to make sure that the laws and institutions, the general character and administration of the commonwealth, shall be such as of themselves to realize public well-being and private prosperity. This is the proper scope of wise statesmanship and the work of the heads of the State. Now a State chiefly prospers and thrives through moral rule, well-regulated family life, respect for religion and justice, the moderation and fair imposing of public taxes, the progress of the arts and of trade, the abundant yield of the land—through everything, in fact, which makes the citizens better and happier. Hereby, then, it lies in the power of a ruler to benefit every class in the State, and amongst the rest to promote to the utmost the interests of the poor; and this in virtue of his office, and without being open to suspicion of undue interference—since it is the province of the State to consult the common good. And the more that is done for the benefit of the working classes by the general laws of the country, the less need will there be for special means to relieve them. . . .

Whenever the general interest or any particular class suffers, or is threatened with harm, which can in no other way be met, the public authority must step in to deal with it.

Now, it is to the interests of the State, as well as of the individual, that peace and good order should be maintained; that family life should be carried on in accordance with God's laws and those of nature; that Religion should be reverenced and obeyed; that a high standard of morality should prevail, both in public and private life; that justice should be held sacred and that no one should injure another with impunity; that the members of the commonwealth should grow up to man's estate strong and robust, and capable, if need be, of guarding and defending their country. If by a strike, or other combination of workmen, there should be imminent danger of disturbance to the public peace; or if circumstances were such

as that among the working class the ties of family life were relaxed; if Religion were found to suffer through the workers not having time and opportunity afforded them to practise its duties; if in workshops and factories there were danger to morals through the mixing of the sexes or from other harmful occasions of evil; or if employers laid burdens upon their workmen which were unjust, or degraded them with conditions repugnant to their dignity as human beings; finally, if health were endangered by excessive labor, or by work unsuited to sex or age—in such cases, there can be no question but that, within certain limits, it would be right to invoke the aid and authority of the law. The limits must be determined by the nature of the occasion which calls for the law's interference—the principle being that the law must not undertake more, nor proceed further, than is required for the remedy of the evil or the removal of the mischief.

Rights must be religiously respected wherever they exist; and it is the duty of the public authority to prevent and to punish injury, and to protect every one in the possession of his own. Still, when there is question of defending the rights of individuals, the poor and badly-off have a claim to especial consideration. The richer class have many ways of shielding themselves, and stand less in need of help from the State; whereas the mass of the poor have no resources of their own to fall back upon, and must chiefly depend upon the assistance of the State. And it is for this reason that wage-earners, since they mostly belong to that class, should be specially cared for and protected by the Government.

Here, however, it is expedient to bring under special notice certain matters of moment. The chief thing is the duty of safeguarding private property by legal enactment and protection. Most of all it is essential, where the passion of greed is so strong, to keep the people within the line of duty; for if all may justly strive to better their condition, neither justice nor the common good allows any individual to seize upon that which belongs to another, or, under the futile and shallow pretext of equality, to lay violent hands on other people's possessions. Most true it is that by far the larger part of the workers prefer to better

From *Rerum Novarum*, by Leo XIII (1891), translated by the Catholic Truth Society, London.

themselves by honest labor rather than by doing any wrong to others. But there are not a few who are imbued with evil principles and eager for revolutionary change, whose main purpose is to stir up disorder and incite their fellows to acts of violence. The authority of the State should intervene to put restraint upon such firebrands, to save the working classes from being led astray by their manoeuvres, and to protect lawful owners from spoliation [being plundered].

When work-people have recourse to a strike, it is frequently because the hours of labor are too long, or the work too hard, or because they consider their wages insufficient. The grave inconvenience of this not uncommon occurrence should be obviated by public remedial measures; for such paralysing of labor not only affects the masters and their work-people alike, but is extremely injurious to trade and to the general interests of the public; moreover, on such occasions, violence and disorder are generally not far distant, and thus it frequently happens that the public peace is imperilled. The laws should forestall and prevent such troubles from arising; they should lend their influence and authority to the removal in good time of the causes which lead to conflicts between employers and employed. . . .

If We turn now to things external and material, the first thing of all to secure is to save unfortunate working people from the cruelty of men of greed, who use human beings as mere instruments for money-making. It is neither just nor human so to grind men down with excessive labor as to stupefy their minds and wear out their bodies. . . .

In all agreements between masters and work-people there is always the condition expressed or understood that there should be allowed proper rest for soul and body. To agree in any other sense would be against what is right and just; for it can never be just or right to require on the one side, or to promise on the other, the giving up of those duties which a man owes to his God and to himself.

We now approach a subject of great importance, and one in respect of which, if extremes are to be avoided right notions are absolutely necessary. Wages, as we are told, are regulated by free consent, and therefore the employer, when he pays what was agreed upon, has done his part and

seemingly is not called upon to do any thing beyond. The only way, it is said, in which injustice might occur would be if the master refused to pay the whole of the wages, or if the workman should not complete the work undertaken; in such cases the State should intervene, to see that each obtains his due; but not under any other circumstances.

To this kind of argument a fair-minded man will not easily or entirely assent: it is not complete, for there are important considerations which it leaves out of account altogether. To labor is to exert oneself for the sake of procuring what is necessary for the various purposes of life, and chief of all for self-preservation. *In the sweat of thy face thou shalt eat bread (Gen. iii, 19).* Hence a man's labor necessarily bears two notes or characters. First of all, it is personal, inasmuch as the force which acts is bound up with the personality and is the exclusive property of him who acts, and, further, was given to him for his advantage. Secondly, man's labor is necessary; for without the result of labor a man cannot live; and self-preservation is a law of nature, which it is wrong to disobey. Now, were we to consider labor merely in so far as it is personal, doubtless it would be within the workman's right to accept any rate of wages whatsoever; for in the same way as he is free to work or not, so is he free to accept a small wage or even none at all. But our conclusion must be very different if together with the personal element in a man's work we consider the fact that work is also necessary for him to live: these two aspects of his work are separable in thought, but not in reality. The preservation of life is the bounden duty of one and all, and to be wanting therein is a crime. It necessarily follows that each one has a natural right to procure what is required in order to live; and the poor can procure that in no other way than by what they can earn through their work.

Let the working man and the employer make free agreements, and in particular let them agree freely as to wages; nevertheless there underlies a dictate of natural justice more imperious and ancient than any bargain between man and man, namely that wages ought not to be insufficient to support a frugal and well behaved wage-earner. If through necessity or fear of a worse evil the workman accepts harder conditions because an employer or contractor will afford him no better, he is made the victim of force and injustice. In these and similar questions however,—such as, for example, the hours of labor in different trades, the sanitary precautions to be observed in factories and workshops, etc.—in order to supersede undue interference on the part of the State, especially as circumstances, times and localities differ so widely, it is advisable that recourse be had to Societies or Boards such as we shall mention presently, or to some other mode of safeguarding the interests of the wage-earners; the State being appealed to, should circumstances require, for its sanction and protection. . . .

Many excellent results will follow from this; and first of all, property will certainly become more equitably divided. For the result of civil change and revolution has been to divide society into two widely differing castes. On the one side there is the party which holds power because it holds wealth; which has in its grasp the whole of labor and trade; which manipulates for its own benefit and its own purposes all the sources of supply, and which is even represented in the councils of the State itself. On the other side there is the needy and powerless multitude, sick and sore in spirit and ever ready for disturbance. If working people can be encouraged to look forward to obtaining a share in the land, the consequence will be that the gulf between vast wealth and sheer poverty will be bridged over, and the respective classes will be brought nearer to one another. A further consequence will result in the greater abundance of the fruits of the earth. Men always work harder and more readily when they work on that which belongs to them; nay, they learn to love the very soil that yields in response to the labor of their hands, not only food to eat, but an abundance of good things for themselves and those dear to them. That such a spirit of willing labor would add to the produce of the earth and to the wealth of the community is self-evident. And a third ad-

vantage would spring from this: men would cling to the country in which they were born; for no one would exchange his country for a foreign land if his own afforded him the means of living a decent and happy life. These three important benefits, however, can be reckoned on only provided that a man's means be not drained and exhausted by excessive taxation. The right to possess private property is derived from nature, not from man; and the State has the right to control its use in the interest of the public good alone, but by no means to absorb it altogether. The State would therefore be unjust and cruel if under the name of taxation it were to deprive the private owner of more than is fair. . . .

The most important of all organizations are Workingmen's Unions; for these virtually include all the rest. History attests what excellent results were brought about by the Artificers' Guilds of olden times. They were the means of affording not only many advantages to the workmen, but in no small degree of promoting the advancement of art, as numerous monuments remain to bear witness. Such Unions should be suited to the requirements of this our age—an age of wider education, of different habits, and of far more numerous requirements in daily life. It is gratifying to know that there are actually in existence not a few associations of this nature, consisting either of workmen alone, or of workmen and employers together; but it were greatly to be desired that they should become more numerous and more efficient.

After reading this selection, consider these questions:
1. What position does the encyclical take on labor strikes?
2. What is the correct relation between employer and employee?
3. What is the notion of "natural justice"?

# SELECTION 5:

# Neo-Reformation Theology

*One of the most influential movements within twentieth-century Protestantism was founded by the Swiss theologian Karl Barth (1886–1968). Barth held various chairs of theology in Germany until 1935, when he was expelled by the Nazi regime as an undesirable alien. Barth returned to his native Switzerland, where he assumed the chair of theology at the University of Basel. Barth was the founder of what has variously been labeled "dialectical theology" or "theology of the word" because he defined the central concern of theology to be the word of God and God's revelation in Jesus Christ. Barth contended that this revelation was the only means for God to reveal himself to humans, who must listen in awe, trust, and obedience. Barth's theology has also been called "Neo-Orthodox" and "Neo-Reformation" since he also returned to the main tenets of Martin Luther's position. Like Luther, Barth contended that man and God are separated by an infinite gulf, which only faith in the word can bridge. Also like Luther, Barth turned to the works of Paul, especially* The Epistle to the Romans, *as expressing the essence of this faith. As the following selection from* The Word of God and the Word of Man *shows, Barth positioned himself against the liberal theology of Friedrich Schleiermacher.*

"The voice of him that crieth in the wilderness, Prepare ye the way of the Lord, make straight in the desert a highway for our God. Every valley shall be exalted, and every mountain and hill shall be made low; and the crooked shall be made straight, and the rough places plain; and the glory of the Lord shall be revealed!" This is the voice of our conscience, telling us of the righteousness of God. And since conscience is the perfect interpreter of life, what it tells us is no question, no riddle, no problem, but a fact—the deepest, innermost surest fact of life: God is righteous. Our only question is what attitude toward the fact we ought to take.

We shall hardly approach the fact with our critical reason. The reason sees the small and the larger but not the large. It sees the preliminary but not the final, the derived but not the original, the complex but not the simple. It sees what is human but not what is divine.

We shall hardly be taught this fact by men. . . .

For we suffer from unrighteousness. We dread it. All that is within us revolts against it. We know more about it, it is true, than we do about righteousness. We have constantly before us, in the great and small occurrences of life, in our own conduct and in that of others, another kind of will, a will which knows no dominant and inflexible idea but is grounded upon caprice, vagary, and self-seeking—a will without faithfulness, logic, or correlation, disunited and distraught within itself. The more sharply we look, the more clearly we see it. Of such are we, of such is life, of such is the world. The critical reason may come and prove to us that it has always been so and always must be so. But we have before our eyes the consequences of this unrighteous will—

From *The Word of God and the Word of Man*, by Karl Barth, translated by Douglas Horton (London: Hodder & Stoughton, 1935).

disquiet, disorder, and distress in forms minute and gross, obscure and evident. We have before us the fiendishness of business competition and the world war, passion and wrongdoing, antagonism between classes and moral depravity within them, economic tyranny above and the slave spirit below. . . .

Oppressed and afflicted by his own unrighteousness and the unrighteousness of others, man—every man—lifts up from the depths of his nature the cry for righteousness, the righteousness of God. . . .

But now comes a remarkable turn in our relation with the righteousness of God. The trumpet of conscience sounds; we start with apprehension; we feel the touch of holiness upon us—but at first we do not dream of appealing beyond ourselves for help in our need and anxiety. Quite the opposite. "They said one to another, Go to, let us make brick, and burn them throughly. Let us build us a city and a tower whose top may reach unto heaven; and let us make a name, lest we be scattered abroad upon the face of the whole earth!" We come to our own rescue and build the tower of Babel. . . .

Shall we call this pride on our part? There is, as a matter of fact, something of pride in it. We are inwardly resentful that the righteousness we pant after is God's and can come to us only from God. We should like to take the mighty thing into our own hands and under our own management, as we have done with so many other things. It seems quite desirable that the righteousness without which we cannot exist should be controlled by our own will, whatever kind of will that may really be. We arrogate to ourselves, unquestioningly, the right to take up the tumultuous question, What shall we *do?* as if that were in any case the first and most pressing problem. Only let us be quick to put our hand to reform, sanitation, methods, cultural and religious endeavors of all sorts! Only to do "real work"! And before we know it, the trumpet blast of conscience has lost its disturbing tone. The anxiety in which we found ourselves when confronted by the dominant world-will has been gently changed into a prosperous sense of normality, and we have arrived again at reflection, criticism, construction,

and organization. The longing for a new world has lost all its bitterness, sharpness, and restlessness, has become the joy of development, and now blossoms sweetly and surely in orations, donor's tablets, committee meetings, reviews, annual reports, twenty-five-year anniversaries, and countless mutual bows. The righteousness of God itself has slowly changed from being the surest of facts into being the highest among various high ideals, and is now at all events our very own affair. This is evident in our ability now to hang it gayly out of the window and now to roll it up again, somewhat like a flag. *Eritis sicut Deus* [You shall be like God]! You may act as if you were God, you may with ease take his righteousness under your own management. This is certainly pride. . . .

Does it not make us blind and impenitent toward the deep real needs of existence? Is it not remarkable that the greatest atrocities of life—I think of the capitalistic order and of the war—can justify themselves on purely moral principles? The devil may also make use of morality. He laughs at the tower of Babel which we erect to him.

The righteousness of the state and of the law. A wonderful tower! A most necessary and useful substitute to protect us in some measure from certain unpleasant results of our unrighteous will! Very suitable for quieting the conscience! But what does the state really do for us? It can order and organize the self-seeking and capricious vagaries of the human will. It can oppose certain hindrances to this will by its regulations and intimidations. It can set up certain institutions—schools, for instance—for the refining and ennobling of it. A vast amount of respectable work goes into all of this; for the building of this one tower of the state, millions of valuable lives are offered and consumed—to what end? The righteousness of the state, for all its variety of form, fails to touch the inner character of the world-will at any point. By this will it is indeed dominated. The war again provides the striking illustration: were it really possible for the state to make men out of wild animals, would the state find it necessary by a thousand arts to make wild animals out of men? The devil may laugh at this tower of Babel, also. . . .

In the question, Is God righteous? our whole tower of Babel falls to pieces. In this now burning question it becomes evident that we are looking for a righteousness without God, that we are looking, in truth, for a god without God and against God—and that our quest is hopeless. It is clear that such a god is not God. He is not even righteous. He cannot prevent his worshipers, all the distinguished European and American apostles of civilization, welfare, and progress, all zealous citizens and pious Christians, from falling upon one another with fire and sword to the amazement and derision of the poor heathen in India and Africa. This god is really an unrighteous god, and it is high time for us to declare ourselves thorough-going doubters, sceptics, scoffers and atheists in regard to him. It is high time for us to confess freely and gladly: this god, to whom we have built the tower of Babel, is not God. He is an idol. He is dead.

God himself, the real, the living God, and his love which comes in glory! These provide the solution. We have not yet begun to listen quietly to what the conscience asks when it reminds us, in our need and anxiety, of the righteousness of God. We have been much too eager to do something ourselves. . . .

In the Bible this humility and this joy are called—faith. Faith means seeking not noise but quiet, and letting God speak within—the righteous God, for there is no other. And then God works in us. Then begins in us, as from a seed, but an unfailing seed, the new basic something which overcomes unrighteousness. Where faith is, in the midst of the old world of war and money and death, there is born a new spirit out of which grows a new world, the world of the righteousness of God. . . .

It remains to be seen whether the quaking of the tower of Babel which we are now experiencing will be violent enough to bring us somewhat nearer to the way of *faith*. Opportunity offers. We may take the new way. Or we may not. Sooner or later we shall. There is no other. . . .

Let me conclude this part of our discussion with a historical note. Those who accept the thoughts I have brought forward as germane to the essential facts thereby acknowledge themselves descendents of an ancestral line which runs back through [Søren] *Kierkegaard* to *Luther* and [John] *Calvin,* and so to *Paul* and *Jeremiah.* . . .

And to leave nothing unsaid, I might explicitly point out that this ancestral line—which I commend to you—does *not include Schleiermacher.* With all due respect to the genius shown in his work, I can *not* consider Schleiermacher a good teacher in the realm of theology because, so far as I can see, he is disastrously dim-sighted in regard to the fact that man as man is not only in *need* but beyond all hope of saving himself; that the whole of so-called religion, and not least the Christian religion, *shares* in this need; and that one can *not* speak of God simply by speaking of man in a loud voice. There are those to whom Schleiermacher's peculiar excellence lies in his having discovered a conception of religion by which he overcame Luther's so-called dualism and connected earth and heaven by a much needed bridge, upon which we may reverently cross. Those who hold this view will finally turn their backs, if they have not done so already, upon the considerations I have presented. I ask only that they do not appeal *both* to Schleiermacher *and* the Reformers, *both* to Schleiermacher *and* the New Testament, *both* to Schleiermacher *and* the Old Testament prophets, but that from Schleiermacher back they look for another ancestral line. In such a line the next previous representative might possibly be [the German scholar and religious reformer Philipp] *Melanchthon.* The very names Kierkegaard, Luther, Calvin, Paul, and Jeremiah suggest what Schleiermacher never possessed, a clear and direct apprehension of the truth that man is made to serve *God* and not God to serve man.

After reading this selection, consider these questions:

1. How does Barth define the "unrighteousness" of man?
2. What is faith for Barth?
3. Why is Barth critical of Schleiermacher?

# UNIT 3

# The Contemporary West

## CONTENTS

Maps     194

**CHAPTER 11:**
Mass Democracy and World War I     195

**CHAPTER 12:**
Nazism and the Holocaust     220

**CHAPTER 13:**
From the Russian Revolution to the Fall of the Soviet Union     243

**CHAPTER 14:**
The Embattled Enlightenment Tradition     263

**CHAPTER 15:**
The West Within the World     276

# Europe After World War I

## Europe During the Cold War

## Post Cold War Europe

# CHAPTER 11
# Mass Democracy and World War I

Historians of modern Europe often refer to the period from 1870 to the present as the era of mass society or the age of mass democracies. During this period, a number of major changes overtook the various nations of the West, altering and reinterpreting the Western heritage, especially as it had come to be defined in the modern period. These changes were often quantitative rather than qualitative, yet they were of such magnitude that they effected qualitative changes. The world that we experience and understand as our own—the contemporary West—is clearly identified with the age of the masses.

Perhaps the most obvious quantitative change that bore qualitative results has been the vast increase in population. The reasons for this rapid increase in population were complex. One central factor in the case of modern Europe is clear. There was a precipitous fall in the rate of mortality. From 1870 on, this decrease can be attributed to advances in preventive medicine. Diseases such as cholera, typhoid, and smallpox—hitherto seemingly unavoidable—were understood and controlled. The curtailing of diseases and the general improvements in living conditions also caused a rapid fall in infant mortality. These advances and improvements were clearly evidenced in urban centers. With the exception of population growth in rural eastern Europe, the increases in population occurred in towns and cities. In 1870 some seventy European cities had at least 100,000 inhabitants; by 1900 they boasted nearly 200,000 inhabitants. Berlin, Vienna, Moscow, and St. Petersburg joined London and Paris as cities with populations of over 1 million.

Patterns of life and labor within these large metropolises were necessarily intertwined. Between 1870 and 1914 (the year of the outbreak of World War I), the industrialization characteristic of Britain and Belgium took hold throughout the continent. Factory production increased; and besides the textile industry and the production of iron and coal, there now evolved new types of manufacture in steel, new sources of energy in electricity, and ever-widening markets for consumer goods. New types of transportation, including the bicycle and the automobile, became widespread. The telephone and radio facilitated communication. These changes definitely resulted in advances in the material and physical conditions of living, but they also brought on their own problems. Although more products were being produced for the consumption of individuals of all classes, these products tended to be more uniform. In general, life in the growing cities of the West became more standardized and anonymous. Health conditions improved and more consumer goods were available, but there was little beyond popular entertainment and spectator sports to relieve the individual and collective psychological strains and the pressures of the new urban, commercialized environment.

Only in the second half of the nineteenth century did quantitative changes result in qualitative transformations. The sheer growth of industry encouraged the integration of manufacturing processes, the enlargement in the average size of factory units, and the amalgamation of firms into great new complexes and monopolies. This expansion of industrial capacity, joined to the fuller exploitation of world agricultural potential, soon caused severe bouts of overproduction. For two decades after 1873, there was a depression in prices, a crisis in profits and investments, a high incidence of commercial failures, and consequential unemployment and labor unrest. Although these setbacks did not alter the overall picture of economic growth, they still caused new tensions among competing firms, between workers and employers, and among nations.

New ideologies arose to speak to the conditions of the new mass societies. Perhaps the most influential of these ideologies was a new type of nationalism, which was popular in France. The Revolution of 1848 established the Second French Republic, of which Louis-Napoléon was elected president. Louis Napoléon (1808–1873) was the nephew of Emperor Napoléon I. After his election as president in 1848, Louis-Napoléon consolidated his powers and united conservative elements behind him. On December 2, 1851, in imitation of his uncle, he staged a coup d'état and dissolved the legislative assembly. Louis-Napoléon issued a new constitution in January 1852, declaring himself Emperor Napoléon III. Again imitating Napoléon I, this new arrangement was confirmed by an overwhelming vote in a national plebiscite. In his first eight years of rule, Napoléon III proved very popular. In large measure his popularity depended on his policies of active government intervention in the development of French industries, the expansion of the railway system, and the rebuilding of the cities of France. In both the form of government and the policies he initiated, Napoléon III represented a new type of political leader. He based his powers on the support of conservative politicians and industrialists as well as the consent of the mass of the politically passive population. In this way, Napoléon III surmounted the political institutions and political machinations of the liberal, essentially middle-class parties of France. By bringing economic progress at home and an aggressive foreign policy abroad, Napoléon won favor with almost all sections of French society. When the French economy began to suffer after 1860, his popularity waned. Ever resilient,

Napoléon changed course and ushered in the so-called Liberal Empire, in which he began to cooperate more fully with the National Assembly and the liberal parties. When his foreign policies brought him into direct confrontation with Otto von Bismarck's plans to reunite Germany, Napoléon found himself at war with Prussia in 1870. The emperor himself was captured in the decisive Battle of Sedan (1870) and lived out the rest of his life in exile in England. After his fall, France established the Third Republic.

The 1870s also witnessed the development of other mass democracies. The reunification of Germany under Prussian leadership offered a spectacular example of state building. Reunification instantly made the new German Empire the major political and military power on the continent, and economic dominance soon followed. Through a series of complex alliances, Bismarck consolidated Germany's position and ensured that the surrounding states would accept the empire's new position. Internally, Bismarck cooperated with the liberals in drawing up a constitution based on universal manhood suffrage and guaranteed basic civil liberties. But although founded on liberal principles, in practice, a number of built-in constitutional features ensured that power remained with the chancellor, the state of Prussia, and the traditional agricultural and new industrial elites. After 1880 Bismarck would increasingly turn conservative and curtail the power of the Catholic Center Party and the growing Social Democratic Party.

After the fall of Bismarck (1890) and the end of his system of interlocking treaties, which had guaranteed peace on the continent, the European states coalesced into two competing camps. The two great coalitions finally went to war to resolve their differences in August 1914.

Not all wars are of equal historical significance, nor can their significance be measured by the numbers of death and the amount of devastation or even by the shifts in political and military power that they bring about. World War I (1914–1918) was important in all these terms, but its true significance lies in its lasting impact on the history of the West. In addition to the destruction that it caused and the resulting rise, and especially the fall, of a number of the great nation-states of modern Europe, the war had profound social consequences and psychological effects. Perhaps more significantly, the war set in motion a number of long-term processes. World War I and its aftermath would eventually end European colonial domination of the globe. In addition, both in the attitudes that brought it about as well as in the devastation that it wrought, World War I initiated a process of self-reflection and of self-criticism of the basic meaning and values of the West.

Historians have been debating the specific causes of the war ever since its end, but even today no consensus has been reached. Did Germany's plans for extending and consolidating its dominant position on the continent and challenging Britain on the high seas cause the war? Did the alliance systems themselves—the Triple Alliance (Germany, Austria-Hungary, and Italy) and the Triple Entente (France, Russia, and Britain)—set the conditions for an eventual confrontation? Or did the arms race among the nations of Europe mean that some type of war was inevitable? Expenditures on armaments rose dramatically in the prewar decades. In 1910 Austria-Hungary had the lowest expenditures, with only 10 percent of its annual budget devoted to the armed forces and armaments; Germany had the highest, with a remarkable 45 percent.

Was the war the result of inept leadership, especially among the diplomats of the various nations, who seemed out of touch with the realities of an industrial and economically interconnected world? When retracing the steps that led to the outbreak of war, it is obvious that the national rivalries in Europe and the global contest for colonies played an important part. Unnecessary confrontations, missed opportunities for reconciliations, and simply inept policies all contributed significantly to intensifying antagonisms among the great powers. Perhaps the greatest miscalculation of German prewar diplomacy was the basic assumption that Britain would never reconcile its imperial rivalries with France and Russia. British tensions with these other powers were real enough, but German policymakers did not understand that Britain would never just busy itself with consolidating its overseas holdings while Germany expanded its military and political dominance over the European continent.

On its side, Britain sought friendlier relations with Germany, but Germany rejected them by making the price for an alliance too high—namely, British membership in the Triple Alliance of Germany, Austria-Hungary, and Italy. Germany responded to this rebuff by countering British expansion (notably in the Boer War in South Africa) and by constructing a first-class high seas fleet. Begun in 1898, this fleet-building policy directly challenged Britain's dominance of the seas both militarily and commercially. These challenges led Britain to seek improved relations with France, which resulted in the Entente Cordiale in 1904. Germany responded by increasing its pressure on the British Empire and by a renewed commitment to expanding its fleet. In 1907 Britain finally reconciled its differences with Russia and formally joined the Dual Entente of France and Russia, changing it into the Triple Entente. The encirclement of Germany became complete, leaving the major European powers divided into two competitive and combative groups.

All of these factors, as well as others, were at play in the decades before the outbreak of the war in 1914. There were also less tangible reasons for the war. The prewar years were also ones of feverish nationalistic intensity, both within and among the great powers of Europe. The new nationalism, along with the drive for economic dominance and imperialistic dreams, created an atmosphere in which political and social stability at home was often achieved at the cost of overly aggressive policies abroad.

# SELECTION 1:

# The Age of the Masses

*An interrelated series of changes—population growth, increased indus-trialization, and economic booms and busts—brought forth a whole series of unintended consequences. These can most clearly be seen in the defin-itions of government and the relation between the state and the individual; but they are also witnessed in changes in social relations and ideology. The twentieth-century historian Michael D. Biddiss traces several of these consequences through the late nineteenth century and then relates them to the outbreak of World War I. Biddiss begins this selection with a discus-sion of the higher degree of social mobility afforded by the breakdown of more traditional forms of social order.*

The mobility of social status was unprecedented in scope and speed of action. With aristocratic values receding before the advance of bourgeois ones, the broad principles of stratification be-came those appropriate to a market hierarchy that had progressively smaller reference to "orders" or "estates." This trend, though understandably productive of much tension in the socially and politically backward areas dominated by Ot-toman, Romanov, and Habsburg rule, was clear-est in Western and parts of Central Europe. It was there that social divisions were becoming struc-tured most rapidly in terms of essentially eco-nomic "class," not least as between the owners of industrial and commercial capital and the labour-ing mass of wage-earners. While the expropria-tion of the former by the latter was the aim of many resentful of bourgeois society, there were no fewer workers who accepted as an economic and ethical postulate that by striving, saving, and self-help they might more readily than ever be-fore aspire rather to be assimilated within the ranks of the middle classes. What was most sig-nificantly common to both cases was a sense of

acceleration in the beat of time, a feeling of greater proximity to the moment at which hope might be fulfilled. This is one of the keys to ap-preciating the urgency that radiates from the so-cial thinking of the age.

These aspirations and confrontations were as-sociated too with the processes of political de-mocratization. By the 1870s parliamentary insti-tutions in some form or other had been adopted by most European countries, but they had sub-stantial checking effects on executive power only in Britain, France, and Belgium. Moreover, al-though there was general acceptance of the prin-ciple of equality before the law, there was still much opposition to political egalitarianism. Every franchise arrangement embodied discrimi-nation on grounds of sex and normally also of property. However, on balance and in despite of a number of ingenious and quite successful stalling actions by conservative rearguards fearful of an incompatibility between democracy and order, there was during the period firm general advance towards mass politics through extensions both of parliamentary functions and of popular voting rights. For present purposes it will suffice to sug-gest the stages in the triumph of universal man-hood suffrage—though we have to remember that it varied in actual significance as between countries according to its place within a total

From *The Age of the Masses: Ideas and Society in Europe Since 1870*, by Michael D. Biddiss (Hassocks: Harvester Press, 1977). Copyright © 1977 by Michael D. Biddiss. Reprinted with permission.

context of constitutional provisions referring, for example, to age qualifications, plural voting, or the composition and powers of a second less democratic chamber.

All male Germans were enfranchised in 1871, for national Reichstag elections at least. Universal manhood suffrage was reintroduced in France in the same year, and implemented by Switzerland in 1874, by Spain, Belgium, and Norway in the 1890s, and by Sweden, Austria, and Portugal too before 1914. Over the same period, the British, Dutch, and Italian electorates were also enlarged; Russia and Turkey, albeit only in the aftermath of revolutions, introduced for the first time some form of parliament and franchise in 1905 and 1908 respectively; and between 1907 and 1913 the first European victories for female suffrage were registered in Finland, Norway, and Denmark. The political thinkers of the time interpreted these developments variously, but none could deny their immense significance either for better or worse. The progress of democracy, and of parliamentarianism, was certainly not tantamount to an unequivocal triumph for liberalism. As we shall see, the ability of this political creed to respond adequately to needs that were changing so rapidly was severely questioned through much of the speculation of the epoch. Some of the acutest criticism came from liberals themselves, but there were also explicit assaults from those standing either to right or left of a moderate tradition increasingly endangered by the passions of mass politics. In principle franchise extension, like enlargement of educational opportunities, had potential for intensifying popular involvement and responsibility in society. But in certain contexts it was also available to élites as an instrument for manipulating the populace on a scale hitherto unknown. Certainly it hastened the evolution of a more demagogic political style, adapted not merely to wider electorates but also to conditions of denser urbanization and of improved literacy and communications.

The development of this style was accompanied by the emergence, on a mass basis, of firmly institutionalized and relatively disciplined political parties whose organization and functions provided contemporary theorists with much food for thought. For instance, in the Marxist setting the heightening of such concerns was one of the chief features of contrast between [Vladimir] Lenin's generation and the preceding one. The most outstanding example of a mass party was that of the German Social Democrats which was more than a million strong by 1914. As foci for a sense of loyalty and belonging amidst the flux of mass society, the party organizations have to be viewed within the broader context of a general boom in the popularity of a whole range of voluntary associations organized for economic, social, or cultural purposes. Such bodies as credit associations, women's leagues, sporting organizations, and youth movements—with or without explicit political affiliations—burgeoned profusely in the period. Perhaps most notable was growth amongst trade unions, which by 1890 had gained in Britain, France, Austria, Germany, and Spain some form of legal recognition and were progressing towards federation at the national and international levels. . . .

National rivalries and racial confrontations also had relevance in an extra-European setting. In the long history of European colonial imperialism there is for sheer explosive expansion no period comparable to the thirty years from 1870. The main force was in the direction of Eastern Asia and still more especially of the African continent which by 1895 had been within a generation carved up into European colonies. There the British and French made vast extensions from their previous holdings, while on a lesser scale Germany, Belgium, and Italy sought for the first time to establish African empires of their own. In the same setting the Portuguese consolidated their existing influence, and this was also the case with the Dutch in Asia. However, in the latter continent it was the growth of Russian claims and the competing challenge from Japan which stood out. There were some conscious efforts to ensure that these expansionist developments did not unduly aggravate antagonism between the powers. Most notably, the Berlin Conference of 1884–5 attempted to establish working rules for the peaceful dissection of Africa. But it became increasingly unrealistic to separate colonial confrontations from national rivalries and other tensions within the politics of the European continent itself. The Anglo-French Fashoda episode of 1898, the British fears of German influence in South Africa and of Russian influence in Persia, and the successive crises arising from Franco-German antagonism over the future of Morocco were all clear examples of this interrelationship. It also had much to do with that naval race, principally as between Germany and Britain, which so stirred the popular imagination. More generally still, colonial issues were part of the fabric of that system of alliances and confrontations between the powers which was developed in the ten years or so before 1914. When major war came between Germany and Austria on one side and Britain, France, and Russia upon the other it could scarcely fail to have certain truly global dimensions.

The motivations behind imperialism were immensely complex and cannot be pursued here. Yet it must be said that the commonest error has been to depict them too predominantly in economic terms. Factors such as the search for new markets, the investigation of openings where surplus capital might be invested, or the demand for raw materials are all noteworthy. But explanation primarily on these lines, though it has a certain plausibility overall, normally becomes severely inadequate when a particular area of expansion is examined in detail. Competition for naked political power was no less significant, nor can the wellsprings of imperialism be traced adequately without substantial reference to the realms of cultural and even spiritual mission. In short, any sweeping generalization about the overall relationship between, for example, trade, flag, and Bible is perilous. It is however quite indisputable that, in political, economic, and cultural contexts alike, imperialism emerged from and then itself intensified a long-established sense of European superiority. In ages past this feeling had contributed to the fundamental painlessness of such modes of self-criticism as those reliant upon contrast with noble savagery and primitive virtue. Here too—on a scale of continental self-flattery—by the end of the nineteenth century supremacy was being expressed, to a degree hitherto unknown, in terms of innate racial hierarchization. This was now one of the chief symptoms of belief in the essential timelessness and im-

mutability of European hegemony. In the years around 1900 the healthy continuance of such supremacy seemed to most people unquestionable. With hindsight we can clearly see their error. In political terms at the very least, Europe had reached a point of apogee beyond which extended a curve of decline. The victory of Abyssinians over an Italian expeditionary army at Adowa in 1896, the Boxer Rebellion of 1900 in China, the defeat of Russia by Japanese land and sea forces in the war of 1904–5, and the growing involvement of the United States in Central and South America, the Pacific, and the Far East were all straws in a wind of change.

Those who perceived the real significance of these varied external challenges to hegemony were a minority. So too were those who fully appreciated the self-destructive potential growing within European civilization itself. Yet the importance of this minority is out of all proportion to its number once we seek to trace the history of intellectual developments. For there it must be emphasized that disaffection, doubt, and despair, manifested in modes ranging from passive gloom to active denunciation, characterized many of Europe's acutest minds in the generation before the First World War. But certainly until Armageddon itself their prophecies went generally unhonoured amongst those masses which were now more self-conscious and socially self-assertive than ever before. Even the outbreaks of anarchist violence, or the nationalistic fevers running high nearly everywhere from the Balkans to Ireland, or the multiplication of armaments had not dissolved the popular adherence to certain vague ideas of progress. The masses had the clearest vested interests in the continued plausibility of beliefs about the inexorable forward march of civilization. This creed had given consolation, had enlarged aspirations, and indeed—in the mode of self-fulfilling prophecy—had inspired real gains. Eventually the manifestations of progress even came to be regarded as matters less of faith than of the most ordinary everyday experience.

It was only when there were massive reverses at this very level of the mundane, amidst the carnage and waste of the Great War, that more general disillusionment set in. Not until then did the symbiosis between material growth and the advance of civilization become, for a time at least, the object of widespread scepticism. Its previous dominance over the popular mind had been related in no small way to the contemporary worship of natural science, both as a model of cumulative knowledge and as a dramatic contributor to general welfare. But this was an image with important areas of superficiality, not least because, in the very generation before 1914, science was a sphere essentially of dissolving certainties. Ironically, it was becoming—at least for experts and perceptive laymen—in many respects a paradigm of doubt. For understanding the relationship between ideas and society in and beyond this period there is no more significant point of departure than an examination of the course of this truly revolutionary transformation.

After reading this selection, consider these questions:

1. What, according to Biddiss, were the major social changes during the nineteenth century?
2. What were the consequences of social mobility?
3. What were the consequences of extending the franchise?

# SELECTION 2:

# The New Nationalism

*In his recent book* Nations and Nationalism since 1780, *the eminent British historian E.J. Hobsbawm traces the changing conception of the nation from the French Revolution to the present. Within this two hundred-year period, Hobsbawm points to the period from 1880 to World War I as making a major break. He argues that both the activities of the state and the idea of nationhood changed radically in these decades. He begins by comparing this new nationalism with that of Giuseppe Mazzini (see Selection 5 from Chapter 6).*

The nationalism of 1880–1914 differed in three major respects from the Mazzinian phase of nationalism. First, it abandoned the "threshold principle" which, as we have seen, was central to nationalism in the Liberal era. Henceforth *any* body of people considering themselves a "nation" claimed the right to self-determination which, in the last analysis, meant the right to a separate sovereign independent state for their territory. Second, and in consequence of this multiplica-tion of potential "unhistorical" nations, ethnicity and language became the central, increasingly the decisive or even the only criteria of potential nationhood. Yet there was a third change which affected not so much the non-state national movements, which now became increasingly numerous and ambitious, but national sentiments within the established nation-states: a sharp shift to the political right of nation and flag, for which the term "nationalism" was actually invented in the last decade(s) of the nineteenth century. . . .

At the same time—roughly, in the second half of the century—ethnic nationalism received enormous reinforcements, in practice from the increasingly massive geographical migrations of peoples,

From *Nations and Nationalism Since 1780*, by E.J. Hobsbawm. Copyright © E.J. Hobsbawm 1990. Reprinted by permission of Cambridge University Press.

and in theory by the transformation of that central concept of nineteenth-century social science, "race." On the one hand the old-established division of mankind into a few "races" distinguished by skin colour was now elaborated into a set of "racial" distinctions separating peoples of approximately the same pale skin, such as "Aryans," and "Semites," or, among the "Aryans," Nordics, Alpines and Mediterraneans. On the other hand Darwinian evolutionism, supplemented later by what came to be known as genetics, provided racism with what looked like a powerful set of "scientific" reasons for keeping out or even, as it turned out, expelling and murdering strangers. All this was comparatively late. Anti-Semitism did not acquire a "racial" (as distinct from a religio-cultural) character until about 1880, the major prophets of German and French racism (Vacher de Lapouge, Houston Stewart Chamberlain) belong to the 1890s, and "Nordics" do not enter the racist or any discourse until about 1900.

The links between racism and nationalism are obvious. "Race" and language were easily confused as in the case of "Aryans" and "Semites," to the indignation of scrupulous scholars like Max Muller who pointed out that "race," a genetic concept, could not be inferred from language, which was not inherited. Moreover, there is an evident analogy between the insistence of racists on the importance of racial purity and the horrors of miscegenation, and the insistence of so many—one is tempted to say of most—forms of linguistic nationalism on the need to purify the national language from foreign elements. In the nineteenth century the English were quite exceptional in boasting of their mongrel origins (Britons, Anglo-Saxons, Scandinavians, Normans, Scots, Irish, etc.) and glorying in the philological mixture of their language. However, what brought "race" and "nation" even closer was the practice of using both as virtual synonyms, generalizing equally wildly about "racial"/"national" character, as was then the fashion. Thus before the Anglo-French Entente Cordiale of 1904, a French writer observed, agreement between the two countries had been dismissed as impossible because of the "hereditary enmity" between the two races. Linguistic and ethnic nationalism thus reinforced each other.

It is hardly surprising that nationalism gained ground so rapidly from the 1870s to 1914. It was a function of both social and political changes, not to mention an international situation that provided plenty of pegs on which to hang manifestos of hostility to foreigners. Socially three developments gave considerably increased scope for the development of novel forms of inventing "imagined" or even actual communities as nationalities: the resistance of traditional groups threatened by the onrush of modernity, the novel and quite non-traditional classes and strata now rapidly growing in the urbanizing societies of developed countries, and the unprecedented migrations which distributed a multiple diaspora of peoples across the globe, each strangers to both natives and other migrant groups, none, as yet, with the habits and conventions of coexistence. The sheer weight and pace of change in this period would be enough to explain why under such circumstances occasions for friction between groups multiplied, even if we were to overlook the tremors of the "Great Depression" which so often, in these years, shook the lives of the poor and the economically modest or insecure. All that was required for the entry of nationalism into politics was that groups of men and women who saw themselves, in whatever manner, as Ruritanians [an imaginary name of a nationality, used here for illustrative purposes], or were so seen by others, should become ready to listen to the argument that their discontents were in some way caused by the inferior treatment (often undeniable) of Ruritanians by, or compared with, other nationalities, or by a non-Ruritanian state or ruling class. At all events by 1914 observers were apt to be surprised at European populations which still seemed completely unreceptive to any appeal on the grounds of nationality, though this did not necessarily imply adherence to a nationalist programme. US citizens of immigrant origins did not demand any linguistic or other concessions to their nationality by the Federal Government, but nevertheless every Democratic city politician knew perfectly well that appeals to the Irish as Irish, to Poles as Poles, paid off.

As we have seen, the major political changes which turned a potential receptivity to national appeals into actual reception, were the democratization of politics in a growing number of states, and the creation of the modern administrative, citizen-mobilizing and citizen-influencing state. And yet, the rise of mass politics helps us to reformulate the question of popular support for nationalism rather than to answer it. What we need to discover is what precisely national slogans meant in politics, and whether they meant the same to different social constituencies, how they changed, and under what circumstances they combined or were incompatible with other slogans that might mobilize the citizenry, how they prevailed over them or failed to do so. . . .

Among the lesser middle strata nationalism thus mutated from a concept associated with liberalism and the left, into a chauvinist, imperialist and xenophobic movement of the right, or more precisely, the radical right, a move already observable in the ambiguous usage of such terms as "patrie" and "patriotism" round 1870 in France. The term "nationalism" itself was coined to reflect the emergence of this tendency, notably in France and a little later in Italy, where Romance language lent itself to this formation. At the end of the century it seemed quite novel. However, even where there was continuity, as in the "Turner," the mass gymnastic organisations of German nationalism, the shift to the right of the 1890s can be measured by tracking the spread of anti-Semitism from Austria into the German branches, and the substitution of the imperial (black-white-red) tricolour for the Liberal-national (black-red-gold) tricolour of 1848, and the new enthusiasm for imperial expansionism. How high up in the middle-class scale we find the centre of gravity of such movements—e.g. of "that rebellion of groups of the lower and middle urban bourgeoisie against what they saw as a hostile and rising proletariat," which drove Italy into World War I, may be a matter of debate. But work on the social composition of Italian and German fascism leaves no doubt that these movements drew their strength essentially from the middle strata.

Moreover, while in established nation-states and powers the patriotic zeal of these intermediate strata was more than welcome to governments engaged in imperial expansion and national rivalry against other such states, we have seen that such sentiments were autochthonous [indigenous], and therefore not entirely manipulable from above. Few governments, even before 1914, were as chauvinist as the nationalist ultras who urged them on. And, as yet, there were no governments which had been created by the ultras.

Nevertheless, if governments could not entirely control the new nationalism, and it could not yet control governments, identification with the state was essential to the nationalist petty-bourgeoisie and lesser middle classes. If they had no state as yet, national independence would give them the position they felt they deserved. To preach the return of Ireland to its ancient language would no longer be a propagandist slogan for men and women studying elementary Gaelic in Dublin evening classes and teaching what they had just learned to other militants. As the history of the Irish Free State was to demonstrate, it would become the qualification for all but the most subaltern civil service jobs and passing examinations in Irish would therefore be the criterion of belonging to the professional and intellectual classes. If they already lived in a nation-state, nationalism gave them the social identity which proletarians got from their class movement. One might suggest that the self-definition of the lower middle classes—both that section which was helpless as artisans and small shop-keepers and social strata which were largely as novel as the workers, given the unprecedented expansion of higher education white-collar and professional occupations—was not so much as a class, but as the body of the most zealous and loyal, as well as the most "respectable" sons and daughters of the fatherland.

Whatever the nature of the nationalism which came to the fore in the fifty years before 1914, all versions of it appeared to have something in common: a rejection of the new proletarian socialist movements, not only because they were proletarian but also because they were, consciously and militantly *internationalist,* or at the very least non-nationalist. Nothing seems more logical, therefore, than to see the appeals of nationalism and socialism as mutually exclusive, and the advance of one as equivalent to the retreat of the other. And the canonical view among historians is indeed that in this period mass nationalism triumphed against rival ideologies, notably class-based socialism, as demonstrated by the outbreak of war in 1914 which revealed the hollowness of socialist internationalism, and by the overwhelming triumph of the "principle of nationality" in the post-1918 peace settlements.

After reading this selection, consider these questions:
1. How does Hobsbawm define the new nationalism?
2. What is the relation between nationalism and race?
3. To what social groups did nationalism appeal?

# SELECTION 3:

# Vienna and the New Politics

*The development of mass politics in the Austrian Empire (after 1867, the Austro-Hungarian Empire) were more complex. As a direct result of the international economic crisis of the 1870s, the liberals were finally called into power, but from the start their power and leadership were compromised. Unlike France and Germany, Austria faced a fundamental problem: The empire consisted of more than a dozen major national groups, speaking different languages and with different national traditions. Although united in their support of the imperial family and in their acceptance of the Catholic faith, these divisions limited the extension of a national liberal program throughout the empire as well as the formation of a strong transnational liberal party.*

*In a brilliant interpretation, the twentieth-century historian Carl E. Schorske shows how, within these conditions of weak liberalism and nationalist divisions, a new type of politics evolved in the Austro-Hungarian Empire. Mass politics produced leaders who actively sought popular support by evoking the deepest fears and hatreds of the largest segments of the population—the industrial workers and the peasants. Schorske also shows how new cultural forms—what would become the culture of "modernism"—also evolved within Austria and especially in Vienna in the 1880s and 1890s. Modernism, in Schorske's interpretation, represented a rejection of and withdrawal from the failure of liberalism and the grossness of the new mass democracy. In the following selection from his book* Fin-de-Siècle Vienna, *Schorske portrays the various types of mass politics and their leaders in the 1880s.*

From "Politics and the Psyche in Fin-de-siècle Vienna: Schnitzler and Hofmannsthal," by Carl E. Schorske, *American Historical Review,* July 1961. Reprinted by permission of the author.

Austrian liberalism, like that of most European nations, had its heroic age in the struggle against aristocracy and baroque absolutism. This ended in the stunning defeat of 1848. The chastened liberals came to power and established a constitutional régime in the 1860's almost by default. Not their own internal strength, but the defeats of the old order at the hands of foreign enemies brought the liberals to the helm of state. From the first, they had to share their power with the aristocracy and the imperial bureaucracy. Even during their two decades of rule, the liberals' social base remained weak, confined to the middle-class Germans and German Jews of the urban centers. Increasingly identified with capitalism, they maintained parliamentary power by the undemocratic device of the restricted franchise.

Soon new social groups raised claims to political participation: the peasantry, the urban artisans and workers, and the Slavic peoples. In the 1880's these groups formed mass parties to challenge the liberal hegemony—anti-Semitic Christian Socials and Pan-Germans, Socialists, and Slavic nationalists. Their success was rapid. In 1895, the liberal bastion, Vienna itself, was engulfed in a Christian Social tidal wave. Emperor Francis Joseph, with the support of the Catholic hierarchy, refused to sanction the election of Karl Lueger, the anti-Semitic Catholic mayor. Sigmund Freud, the liberal, smoked a cigar to celebrate the action of the autocratic savior of the Jews. Two years later, the tide could no longer be stemmed. The emperor, bowing to the electorate's will, ratified Lueger as mayor. The Christian Social demagogues began a decade of rule in Vienna which combined all that was anathema to classical liberalism: anti-Semitism, clericalism, and municipal socialism. On the national level as well, the liberals were broken as a parliamentary political power by 1900, never to revive. They had been crushed by modern mass movements, Christian, anti-Semitic, socialist, and nationalist.

This defeat had profound psychological repercussions. The mood it evoked was one not so much of decadence as of impotence. Progress seemed at an end. The *Neue Freie Presse* saw the expected rational course of history as cruelly altered. The "culture-hostile mass" was victorious before the prerequisites of political enlightenment had been created. In the Mardi Gras of 1897, wrote the *Neue Freie Presse,* the liberals

could wear "a false nose [only] to conceal an anxious face. . . . Instead of the gay waltz, one hears only the cries of an excited brawling mob, and the shouts of police trying to disperse [political] antagonists." Anxiety, impotence, a heightened awareness of the brutality of social existence: these features assumed new centrality in a social climate where the creed of liberalism was being shattered by events.

The writers of the nineties were children of this threatened liberal culture. What were the values which they had inherited, and with which they would now have to face the crisis? Two groups of values can, I think, be loosely distinguished in the liberal culture of the last half of the century: one moral and scientific, the other aesthetic.

The moral and scientific culture of Vienna's *haute bourgeoisie* can scarcely be distinguished from garden-variety Victorianism elsewhere in Europe. Morally, it was secure, righteous, and repressive; politically, it was concerned for the rule of law, under which both individual rights and social order were subsumed. It was intellectually committed to the rule of the mind over the body and to a latter-day Voltairism: to social progress through science, education, and hard work. The achievements resulting in a few short decades from the application of these values to Austria's legal, educational, and economic life are too often underestimated. But neither the values nor the progress made under them gave the Austrian upper middle class a unique character.

More significant for our concern is the evolution of the aesthetic culture of the educated bourgeoisie after the mid-century, for out of it grew the peculiar receptivity of a whole class to the life of art, and, concomitantly at the individual level, a sensitivity to psychic states. By the beginning of our century, the usual moralistic culture of the European bourgeoisie was in Austria both overlaid and undermined by an amoral *Gefühlskultur* ["culture of feeling"]. This development has not been closely studied, and I can only suggest its outline.

Two basic social facts distinguish the Austrian from the French and English bourgeoisie: it did not succeed either in destroying or in fully fusing with the aristocracy; and because of its weakness, it remained both dependent upon and deeply loyal to the emperor as a remote but necessary father-protector. The failure to acquire a monopoly of power left the bourgeois always something of an outsider, seeking integration with the aristocracy. The numerous and prosperous Jewish element in Vienna, with its strong assimilationist thrust, only strengthened this trend.

Direct social assimilation to the aristocracy occurred rarely in Austria. Even those who won a patent of nobility were not admitted, as in Germany, to the life of the imperial court. But assimilation could be pursued along another, more open road: that of culture. This too had its difficulties. The traditional culture of the Austrian aristocracy was far removed from the legalistic, puritanical culture of both bourgeois and Jew. Profoundly Catholic, it was a sensuous, plastic culture. Where traditional bourgeois culture saw nature as a sphere to be mastered by imposing order under divine law, Austrian aristocratic culture viewed nature as a scene of joy, a manifestation of divine grace to be glorified in art. Traditional Austrian culture was not, like that of the German north, moral, philosophical, and scientific, but primarily aesthetic. Its greatest achievements were in the applied and performing arts: architecture, the theater, and music. The Austrian bourgeoisie, rooted in the liberal culture of reason and law, thus confronted all older aristocratic culture of sensuous feeling and grace. The two elements . . . could only form a most unstable compound.

The first phase in the assimilation to aristocratic culture was purely external, almost mimetic. The new Vienna built by the ascendant bourgeoisie of the sixties illustrates it in stone. The liberal rulers, in an urban reconstruction which dwarfed that of Napoleon III's Paris, tried to design their way into a history, a pedigree, with grandiose buildings inspired by a Gothic, Renaissance, or Baroque past that was not their own.

A second avenue to aristocratic culture, even more striking than the building spree, lay through the patronage of the traditionally strong performing arts. This form of aristocratic tradition penetrated deeper into the middle-class consciousness than did architecture, for the traditional Viennese folk theater had prepared the ground for it. Vien-

na's new *haute bourgeoisie* may have begun its sponsorship of classical theater and music in emulation of the Lobkowitzes and Rasoumowskys [important aristocratic patrons of Beethoven in Vienna at the beginning of the nineteenth century], but no witness denies that, by the end of the century, it manifested more genuine enthusiasm for these arts than its counterparts in any other city in Europe. By the 1890's the heroes of the upper middle class were no longer political leaders, but actors, artists, and critics. The number of professional scriveners and amateur literati increased rapidly. . . .

Karl Lueger (1844–1910) had much in common with the Knight of Rosenau [Georg von Schönerer, founder of the Pan-German Party]. Both men began as liberals, both criticized liberalism initially from a social and democratic viewpoint, and both ended as apostates, espousing explicitly anti-liberal creeds. Both used anti-Semitism to mobilize the same unstable elements in the population: artisans and students. And—crucial for our purposes—both developed the techniques of extra-parliamentary politics, the politics of the rowdy and the mob. Here the similarities end.

Schönerer's central positive accomplishment was to metamorphose a tradition of the Old Left into an ideology of the New Right: he transformed democratic, *grossdeutsch* nationalism ["Great Germany" nationalists sought the incorporation of German Austria into the German Reich] into racist Pan-Germanism. Lueger did the opposite: he transformed an ideology of the Old Right—Austrian political Catholicism—into an ideology of a New Left, Christian Socialism. Schönerer began as a master organizer in his country constituency and ended as an agitator with a small, fanatical following in the city. Lueger began as an agitator in the city, conquered the city, and then organized a great party with its stable base in the countryside. Our concern will be with Lueger militant, not with Lueger triumphant. After 1900, the mature national politician shepherded his once unruly flock into the homely stall of the Hofburg [the imperial palace in Vienna]. We shall focus rather on Lueger the tribune, Lueger the partner and competitor of

Schönerer as composer in the new key; for this is the Lueger who yoked "backward" and "forward," "above" and "below," who brought together the ancient and modern enemies of liberalism for a successful political assault on its central bastion, the city of Vienna. In the year 1897, when the reluctant emperor finally ratified Lueger's election as mayor, the era of classical liberal ascendancy in Austria reached its formal close. . . .

Even while Lueger was being impelled toward Schönerer by his lower-middle-class and artisan followers, possibilities for a less nationalistic mass politics were quietly opening up in a most unexpected quarter—namely, in the Catholic community. Catholicism offered Lueger an ideology that could integrate the disparate anti-liberal elements which had been moving in contradictory directions as his career developed: democracy, social reform, anti-Semitism, and Habsburg loyalty. Conversely, Lueger could give Catholicism the political leadership to weld together its shattered social components into an organization strong enough to make its way in the modern secular world.

Until the emergence of Lueger's Christian Social party in about 1889, Austrian Catholicism, both political and ecclesiastical, had been languishing in anachronism. Both intellectually and sociologically, the Catholic leadership remained committed to an order which the liberal ascendancy had forever destroyed. The chief political leaders of Catholicism were federalist Bohemian noblemen and provincial conservatives from the Alpine lands. Their parliamentary clubs were . . . small groups of notables. Modernity and all its works and pomps alarmed them; they could only look back wistfully to the vanished days when religion provided the basis of a deferential society in which the landed aristocracy predominated. For protection in the living present, they leaned . . . on the emperor, even though he had since 1860 evidently become a prisoner of the liberals.

The hierarchy, whose highest prelates tended to be drawn from the nobiliar families, likewise offered little resistance to the dismantling of the Church's traditional authority. Both bishops and priests, like the Vatican itself, were overwhelmed by the collapse of neo-absolutism. The Austrian emperor, first son and last protector of the Church Universal, had been defeated in the field by the Piedmontese apostates in 1860 and the Prussian Protestants in 1866. "Casca il mondo!" ["The world has collapsed!"] exclaimed Pius IX's secretary of state when he heard of Austria's defeat at Königgrätz. The words were as prophetic for the fate of baroque Catholicism in a liberal era as they were expressive of the limited, frightened outlook of its ecclesiastics. For now liberalism celebrated its triumph in Austria not only by instituting constitutional government but by denouncing the Concordat between Empire and Papacy, introducing school reform, and cheering while the pope lost Rome and immured himself in the Vatican. . . .

Between 1875 and 1888, while Lueger was drawing away from his liberal origins and vacillating uneasily between secular democracy and nationalist anti-Semitism, the elements of a political Catholicism capable of fulfilling these tasks slowly emerged. The contributors to the new movement came from sectors of society smarting in varying degrees under liberal capitalist rule: aristocrats and Catholic intellectuals, businessmen, clergymen, and artisans. . . .

In both the ecclesiastical and the political sphere, the program of Christian social-democratic action encountered the opposition of the older and more cautious generation. The new program involved throwing the gauntlet down to the establishment, hence to incur risk, never popular with the chastened leaders of the Catholic world. The sharper key, with all its ruthlessness, appeared within the Catholic fold in the late eighties and nineties just as clearly as it did in the Liberal Vienna city council when . . . Lueger unleashed [his] democratic opposition, or in the Reichsrat when Schönerer embarked upon his crusade against the Jew. The radical Catholics manifested many of the signs of cultural alienation that characterized the Pan-Germans, the Social Democrats, and the Zionists. They established their own press, they organized sport clubs, they developed, like the Pan-German nationalists, a school association to free their community of dependence on state education. And they took to the streets in rowdy mass demonstrations, as shocking to the old guard Catholic hierarchy as they were alarming to the liberals. The younger Catholics of the new style, like the younger nationalists, seemed to feel the need to manifest their alienation from the established order as the necessary prelude to redemption. Whether their salvation should lie in a withdrawal from the state or in its conquest, the psychological premise of success would seem to have been the clear profession of minority status, frank self-definition as an oppressed social subgroup. This was as true for the new Catholics as for the new nationalists and the Zionists.

The political chemist who fused the elements of Catholic social disaffection into an organization of the first magnitude was Karl Lueger. Although not particularly religious, Lueger knew how to use the new Catholic social theory as a catalyst in his political experiment. Having secured the support of the Schönerer forces by professions of anti-Semitism, he was able, thanks to Schönerer's imprisonment, to lead most of his Vienna artisan following into the Christian Social fold.

In the city of Vienna, Lueger's following increased from election to election until, in 1895, he acquired the majority in the city council needed to elect him mayor. His public persona contained all the colors of his multi-hued constituency. *Der schöne Karl* ["Handsome Karl"] commanded that fine, almost dandyish presence which . . . arises as an effective attribute of political leadership in "periods of transition when democracy is not yet all-powerful and aristocracy is only partially tottering. . . ." His elegant, almost cool manner demanded deference from the masses, while his capacity to speak to them in Vienna's warm folk dialect won their hearts. A *Volksmann* ["man of the people"] with an aristocratic veneer, Lueger also had some attributes to draw the Viennese middle class to his banner. He loved the city with a true passion and worked to enhance it. Yet he criticized his predecessors ruthlessly for their needless expenditures and kept his critical tongue at the ready for all signs of waste. Thus Lueger made steady inroads into

the following of the Liberals until, in March of 1895, he captured the prosperous second curia of voters. Only the richest property holders remained true to liberalism.

Lueger's victory at the polls in Vienna in 1895 opened a two-year period of deadlock which may be regarded as the last stand of Viennese liberalism. Although Lueger had been duly elected mayor by the necessary majority of the city council, the emperor refused to ratify his taking office. A trinity of pressures was brought to bear on the emperor against him: the Liberals and Conservatives in the coalition government, and the higher clergy. The government, through the personal mediation of Franz Cardinal Schönborn, tried in vain to secure papal intervention against the movement. The Viennese went to the polls to reaffirm their choice. The emperor persisted in his refusal until 1897. . . .

The imperial veto could not be sustained in an age of mass politics. On Good Friday 1897, the emperor capitulated, and *der schöne Karl* entered the Rathaus in triumph. At the same time, the Austrian government entered a profound crisis over the language ordinances in the Czech lands. Thus, just as the old liberal bastion fell to the Christian anti-Semites, the Reichsrat fell into such hopeless discord that the emperor had to dissolve it and establish government by decree. The liberals could, however ruefully, only welcome the change. Their salvation lay henceforward in . . . an avoidance not only of democracy but even of representative parliamentary government, which seemed to lead to only two results: to general chaos or to the triumph of one or another of the anti-liberal forces.

After reading this selection, consider these questions:
1. Who was Karl Lueger, and why was he significant?
2. How did Lueger found a new mass political party?
3. To what groups did Christian socialism appeal?

# SELECTION 4:

# The New Imperialism

*One very popular aspect of the new mass democracies of the late nineteenth century was the rapid growth of colonialism. In what is generally referred to as "the new imperialism"—the colonial expansion of the 1870s, 1880s, and 1890s—Western states assumed dominance over all parts of the globe. This dominance took the form both of direct control over colonies and of indirect political, military, and economic hegemony. Competition among the states of Europe (and increasingly with the United States), and economic expansions (as a quest for both raw materials and markets) played their parts. But the overwhelming popularity of expansionist policies led the leaders of these states to support empire building. Government and party leaders found in imperial expansion and the competition for world empires a means of guaranteeing continued approval from the mass, whatever the fate of their other policies.*

*In her study of the evolution of totalitarianism in the twentieth century, German-born American political philosopher Hannah Arendt points to this alliance between governments and mass politics in imperialism. Imperialism, she argues, seemed to offer a panacea for all troubles. The following selection is taken from her classic work,* The Origins of Totalitarianism.

When imperialism entered the scene of politics with the scramble for Africa in the [1880s], it was promoted by businessmen, opposed fiercely by the governments in power, and welcomed by a surprisingly large section of the educated classes. To the last it seemed to be God-sent, a cure for all evils, an easy panacea for all conflicts. And it is true that imperialism in a sense did not disappoint these hopes. It gave a new lease on life to political and social structures which were quite obviously threatened by new social and political forces and which, under other circumstances, without the interference of imperialist developments, would hardly have needed two world wars to disappear.

As matters stood, imperialism spirited away

all troubles and produced that deceptive feeling of security, so universal in pre-war Europe, which deceived all but the most sensitive minds. [Writers Charles-Pierre] Péguy in France and [Gilbert] Chesterton in England knew instinctively that they lived in a world of hollow pretense and that its stability was the greatest pretense of all. Until everything began to crumble, the stability of obviously outdated political structures was a fact, and their stubborn unconcerned longevity seemed to give the lie to those who felt the ground tremble under their feet. The solution of the riddle was imperialism. The answer to the fateful question: why did the European comity of nations allow this evil to spread until everything was destroyed, the good as well as the bad, is that all governments knew very well that their countries were secretly disintegrating, that the body politic was being destroyed from within, and that they lived on borrowed time.

Innocently enough, expansion appeared first as

the outlet for excess capital production and offered a remedy, capital export. The tremendously increased wealth produced by capitalist production under a social system based on maldistribution had resulted in "oversaving"—that is, the accumulation of capital which was condemned to idleness within the existing national capacity for production and consumption. This money was actually superfluous, needed by nobody though owned by a growing class of somebodies. The ensuing crises and depressions during the decades preceding the era of imperialism had impressed upon the capitalists the thought that their whole economic system of production depended upon a supply and demand that from now on must come from "outside of capitalist society." Such supply and demand came from inside the nation, so long as the capitalist system did not control all its classes together with its entire productive capacity. When capitalism had pervaded the entire economic structure and all social strata had come into the orbit of its production and consumption system, capitalists clearly had to decide either to see the whole system collapse or to find new markets, that is, to penetrate new countries which were not yet subject to capitalism and therefore could provide a new noncapitalistic supply and demand.

The decisive point about the depressions of the sixties and seventies, which initiated the era of imperialism, was that they forced the bourgeoisie to realize for the first time that the original sin of simple robbery, which centuries ago had made possible the "original accumulation of capital" (Marx) and had started all further accumulation, had eventually to be repeated lest the motor of accumulation suddenly die down. In the face of this danger, which threatened not only the bourgeoisie but the whole nation with a catastrophic breakdown in production, capitalist producers understood that the forms and laws of their production system "from the beginning had been calculated for the whole earth."

The first reaction to the saturated home market, lack of raw materials, and growing crises, was export of capital. The owners of superfluous wealth first tried foreign investment without expansion and without political control, which resulted in an unparalleled orgy of swindles, financial scandals, and stock-market speculation, all the more alarming since foreign investments grew much more rapidly than domestic ones. Big money resulting from oversaving paved the way for little money, the product of the little fellow's work. Domestic enterprises, in order to keep pace with high profits from foreign investment, turned likewise to fraudulent methods and attracted an increasing number of people who, in the hope of miraculous returns, threw their money out of the window. The Panama scandal in France, the *Gründungsschwindel* in Germany and Austria, became classic examples. Tremendous losses resulted from the promises of tremendous profits. The owners of little money lost so much so quickly that the owners of superfluous big capital soon saw themselves left alone in what was, in a sense, a battlefield. Having failed to change the whole society into a community of gamblers they were again superfluous, excluded from the normal process of production to which, after some turmoil, all other classes returned quietly, if somewhat impoverished and embittered.

Export of money and foreign investment as such are not imperialism and do not necessarily lead to expansion as a political device. As long as the owners of superfluous capital were content with investing "large portions of their property in foreign lands," even if this tendency ran "counter to all past traditions of nationalism," they merely confirmed their alienation from the national body on which they were parasites anyway. Only when they demanded government protection of their investments (after the initial stage of swindle had opened their eyes to the possible use of politics against the risks of gambling) did they re-enter the life of the nation. In this appeal, however, they followed the established tradition of bourgeois society, always to consider political institutions exclusively as an instrument for the protection of individual property. Only the fortunate coincidence of the rise of a new class of property holders and the industrial revolution had made the bourgeoisie producers and stimulators of production. As long as it fulfilled this basic function in modern society, which is essentially a community of producers, its wealth had an important function for the nation as a whole. The owners of superfluous capital were the first section of the class to want profits without fulfilling some real social function—even if it was the function of an exploiting producer—and whom, consequently, no police could ever have saved from the wrath of the people.

Expansion then was an escape not only for superfluous capital. More important, it protected its owners against the menacing prospect of remaining entirely superfluous and parasitical. It saved the bourgeoisie from the consequences of maldistribution and revitalized its concept of ownership at a time when wealth could no longer be used as a factor in production within the national framework and had come into conflict with the production ideal of the community as a whole.

Older than the superfluous wealth was another by-product of capitalist production: the human debris that every crisis, following invariably upon each period of industrial growth, eliminated permanently from producing society. Men who had become permanently idle were as superfluous to the community as the owners of superfluous wealth. That they were an actual menace to society had been recognized throughout the nineteenth century and their export had helped to populate the dominions of Canada and Australia as well as the United States. The new fact in the imperialist era is that these two superfluous forces, superfluous capital and superfluous working power, joined hands and left the country together. The concept of expansion, the export of government power and annexation of every territory in which nationals had invested either their wealth or their work, seemed the only alternative to increasing losses in wealth and population. Imperialism and its idea of unlimited expansion seemed to offer a permanent remedy for a permanent evil.

Ironically enough, the first country in which superfluous wealth and superfluous men were brought together was itself becoming superfluous. South Africa had been in British possession since the beginning of the century because it assured the maritime road to India. The opening of the Suez Canal, however, and the subsequent administrative conquest of Egypt, lessened considerably the importance of the old trade station on the Cape. The British would, in all probability, have withdrawn from Africa just as all European nations had done whenever their possessions and trade interests in India were liquidated.

The particular irony and, in a sense, symbolical circumstance in the unexpected development of South Africa into the "culture-bed of Imperialism" lies in the very nature of its sudden attractiveness when it had lost all value for the Empire proper: diamond fields were discovered in the seventies and large gold mines in the eighties. The new desire for profit-at-any-price converged for the first time with the old fortune hunt. Prospectors, adventurers, and the scum of the big cities emigrated to the Dark Continent along with capital from industrially developed countries. From now on, the mob, begotten by the monstrous accumulation of capital, accompanied its begetter on those voyages of discovery where nothing was discovered but new possibilities for investment. The owners of superfluous wealth were the only men who could use the superfluous men who came from the four corners of the earth. Together they established the first paradise of parasites whose lifeblood was gold. Imperialism, the product of superfluous money and superfluous men, began its startling career by producing the most superfluous and unreal goods.

It may still be doubtful whether the panacea of expansion would have become so great a temptation for non-imperialists if it had offered its dangerous solutions only for those superfluous forces which, in any case, were already outside the nation's body corporate. The complicity of all parliamentary parties in imperialist programs is a matter of record. The history of the British Labor Party in this respect is an almost unbroken chain of justifications of [British colonial administrator and financier] Cecil Rhodes' early prediction: "The workmen find that although the Americans are exceedingly fond of them, and are just now exchanging the most brotherly sentiments with them yet are shutting out their goods. The workmen also find that Russia, France and Germany locally are doing the same, and the workmen see that if they do not look out they will have no place in the world to trade at all. And so the workmen have become Imperialist and the Liberal Party are following." In Germany, the liberals (and not the Conservative Party) were the actual promoters of that famous naval policy which contributed so heavily to the outbreak of the first World War. The Socialist Party wavered between active support of the imperialist naval policy (it repeatedly voted funds for the building of a German navy after 1906) and complete neglect of all questions of foreign policy. Occasional warnings against the *Lumpenproletariat* [A very negative but not easily translated term, referring to the boorish and stupid members of the lower urban class. "Slobs" would be an idiomatic English equivalent], and the possible bribing of sections of the working class with crumbs from the imperialist table, did not lead to a deeper understanding of the great appeal which the imperialist programs had to the rank and file of the party. In Marxist terms the new phenomenon of an alliance between mob and capital seemed so unnatural, so obviously in conflict with the doctrine of class struggle, that the actual dangers of the imperialist attempt—to divide mankind into master races and slave races, into higher and lower breeds, into colored peoples and white men, all of which were attempts to unify the people on the basis of the mob—were completely overlooked. Even the breakdown of international solidarity at the outbreak of the first World War did not disturb the complacency of the socialists and their faith in the proletariat as such. Socialists were still probing the economic laws of imperialism when imperialists had long since stopped obeying them, when in overseas countries these laws had been sacrificed to the "imperial factor" or to the "race factor," and when only a few elderly gentlemen in high finance still believed in the inalienable rights of the profit rate.

The curious weakness of popular opposition to imperialism, the numerous inconsistencies and outright broken promises of liberal statesmen, frequently ascribed to opportunism or bribery, have other and deeper causes. Neither opportunism nor bribery could have persuaded a man like [William] Gladstone to break his promise, as the leader of the Liberal Party, to evacuate Egypt when he became Prime Minister. Half consciously and hardly articulately, these men shared with the people the conviction that the national body itself was so deeply split into classes, that class struggle was so universal a characteristic of modern political life, that the very cohesion of the nation was jeopardized. Expansion again appeared as a lifesaver, if and insofar as it could provide a common interest for the nation as a whole, and it is mainly for this reason that imperialists were allowed to become "parasites upon patriotism."

Partly, of course, such hopes still belonged with the old vicious practice of "healing" domestic conflicts with foreign adventures. The difference, however, is marked. Adventures are by their very nature limited in time and space; they may succeed temporarily in overcoming conflicts, although as a rule they fail and tend rather to sharpen them. From the very beginning the imperialist adventure of expansion appeared to be an eternal solution, because expansion was conceived as unlimited. Furthermore, imperialism was not an adventure in the usual sense, because it depended less on nationalist slogans than on the seemingly solid basis of economic interests. In a society of clashing interests, where the common good was identified with the sum total of individual interests, expansion as such appeared to be a possible common interest of the nation as a whole. Since the owning and dominant classes had convinced everybody that economic interest and the passion for ownership are a sound basis for the body politic, even nonimperialist statesmen were easily persuaded to yield when a common economic interest appeared on the horizon.

These then are the reasons why nationalism developed so clear a tendency toward imperialism, the inner contradiction of the two principles notwithstanding. The more ill-fitted nations were for the incorporation of foreign peoples (which contradicted the constitution of their own body politic), the more they were tempted to oppress them. In theory, there is an abyss between nationalism and imperialism; in practice, it can and has been bridged by tribal nationalism and outright racism. From the beginning, imperialists in all countries preached and boasted of their being "beyond the parties," and the only ones to speak for the nation as a whole. This was especially true of the Central and Eastern European countries with few or no overseas holdings; there the alliance between mob and capital took place at home and resented even more bitterly (and attacked much more violently) the national institutions and all national parties.

The contemptuous indifference of imperialist politicians to domestic issues was marked everywhere, however, and especially in England. While "parties above parties" like the Primrose League were of secondary influence, imperialism was the chief cause of the degeneration of the two-party system into the Front Bench system, which led to a "diminution of the power of opposition" in Parliament and to a growth of "power of the Cabinet as against the House of Commons." Of course this was also carried through as a policy beyond the strife of parties and particular interests, and by men who claimed to speak for the nation as a whole. Such language was bound to attract and delude precisely those persons who still retained a spark of political idealism. The cry for unity resembled exactly the battle cries which had always led peoples to war; and yet, nobody detected in the universal and permanent instrument of unity the germ of universal and permanent war. . . .

The alliance between capital and mob is to be found at the genesis of every consistently imperialist policy. In some countries, particularly in Great Britain, this new alliance between the much-too-rich and the much-too-poor was and remained confined to overseas possessions. The so-called hypocrisy of British policies was the result of the good sense of English statesmen who drew a sharp line between colonial methods and normal domestic policies, thereby avoiding with considerable success the feared boomerang effect of imperialism upon the homeland. In other countries, particularly in Germany and Austria, the alliance took effect at home in the form of pan-movements, and to a lesser extent in France, in a so-called colonial policy. The aim of these "movements" was, so to speak, to imperialize the whole nation (and not only the "superfluous" part of it), to combine domestic and foreign policy in such a way as to organize the nation for the looting of foreign territories and the permanent degradation of alien peoples.

After reading this selection, consider these questions:

1. What does Arendt mean by the claim that imperialism was a panacea?
2. With what classes was imperialism most popular?
3. Why did imperialism appeal to these classes?

# SELECTION 5:

# War as a Shaper of Consciousness

*In his study of the various responses to the war, the American literary historian Paul Fussell shows how the experience of witnessing human slaughter on such a massive scale altered the European experience of reality. As a result of the war, the sense of innocence and the belief in fair play were permanently lost. In his 1975 book* The Great War and Modern Memory, *Fussell examines the ways the English expressed the experience at the front. By looking at how the war was written about and in what ways language was altered to convey these experiences, Fussell exposes the depths of the psychological consequences of total war.*

Irony is the attendant of hope, and the fuel of hope is innocence. One reason the Great War was more ironic than any other is that its beginning was more innocent. "Never such innocence again," observes Philip Larkin, who has found himself curiously drawn to regard with a wondering tenderness not the merely victimized creatures of the nearby Second World War but the innocents of the remote Great War, those sweet, generous people who pressed forward and all but solicited their own destruction. In "MCMXIV," written in the early [1960s], Larkin contemplates a photograph of the patient and sincere lined up in early August outside a recruiting station:

> Those long uneven lines
> Standing as patiently
> As if they were stretched outside
> The Oval or Villa Park,
> The crowns of hats, the sun
> On moustached archaic faces
> Grinning as if it were all
> An August Bank Holiday lark. . . .

The shops are shut, and astonishingly, the Defense of the Realm Act not yet having been thought of,

>                     . . . the pubs
> Wide open all day. . . .

The class system is intact and purring smoothly:

> The differently-dressed servants
> With tiny rooms in huge houses,
> The dust behind limousines. . . .

"Never such innocence," he concludes:

> Never before or since,
> As changed itself to past
> Without a word—the men
> Leaving the gardens tidy,
> The thousands of marriages

> Lasting a little while longer:
> Never such innocence again.

Far now from such innocence, instructed in cynicism and draft-dodging by the virtually continuous war since 1936, how can we forbear condescending to the eager lines at the recruiting stations or smiling at news like this, from the *Times* of August 9, 1914:

> At an inquest on the body of Arthur Sydney Evelyn Annesley, aged 49, formerly a captain in the Rifle Brigade, who committed suicide by flinging himself under a heavy van at Pimlico, the Coroner stated that worry caused by the feeling that he was not going to be accepted for service led him to take his life.

But our smiles are not appropriate, for that was a different world. The certainties were intact. Britain had not known a major war for a century, and on the Continent, as A.J.P. Taylor points out, "there had been no war between the Great Powers since 1871. No man in the prime of life knew what war was like. All imagined that it would be an affair of great marches and great battles, quickly decided."

Furthermore, the Great War was perhaps the last to be conceived as taking place within a seamless, purposeful "history" involving a coherent stream of time running from past through present to future. The shrewd recruiting poster depicting a worried father of the future being asked by his children, "Daddy, what did *you* do in the Great War?" assumes a future whose moral and social pressures are identical with those of the past. Today, when each day's experience seems notably *ad hoc,* no such appeal would shame the most stupid to the recruiting office. But the Great War took place in what was, compared with ours, a static world, where the values appeared stable and where the meanings of abstractions seemed permanent and reliable. Everyone knew what Glory was, and what Honor meant. It was not until eleven years after the war that Hemingway could declare in *A Farewell to Arms* that "abstract words such as glory, honor, courage, or hallow were obscene beside the concrete names of villages, the numbers of roads, the names of rivers, the numbers of regiments and the dates." In the summer of 1914 no one would have understood what on earth he was talking about.

Certainly the author of a personal communication in the *Times* two days before the declaration of war would not have understood:

> Pauline—Alas, it cannot be. But I will dash into the great venture with all that pride and spirit an ancient race has given me. . . .

The language is that which two generations of readers had been accustomed to associate with the quiet action of personal control and Christian self-abnegation ("sacrifice"), as well as with more violent actions of aggression and defense. The tutors in this special diction had been the boys' books of George Alfred Henty; the male-romances of Rider Haggard; the poems of Robert Bridges; and especially the Arthurian poems of Tennyson and the pseudo-medieval romances of William Morris. We can set out this "raised," essentially feudal language in a table of equivalents:

| | |
|---|---|
| A friend is a | *comrade* |
| Friendship is | *comradeship,* or *fellowship* |
| A horse is a | *steed,* or *charger* |
| The enemy is | *the foe,* or *the host* |
| Danger is | *peril* |
| To conquer is to | *vanquish* |
| To attack is to | *assail* |
| To be earnestly brave is to be | *gallant* |
| To be cheerfully brave is to be | *plucky* |
| To be stolidly brave is to be | *staunch* |
| Bravery considered after the fact is | *valor* |
| The dead on the battlefield are | *the fallen* |
| To be nobly enthusiastic is to be | *ardent* |
| To be unpretentiously enthusiastic is to be | *keen* |
| The front is | *the field* |
| Obedient soldiers are | *the brave* |
| Warfare is | *strife* |
| Actions are | *deeds* |
| To die is to | *perish* |
| To show cowardice is to | *swerve* |
| The draft-notice is | *the summons* |
| To enlist is to | *join the colors* |
| Cowardice results in | *dishonor* |
| Not to complain is to be | *manly* |
| To move quickly is to be | *swift* |
| Nothing is | *naught* |
| Nothing but is | *naught, save* |
| To win is to | *conquer* |
| One's chest is one's | *breast* |
| Sleep is | *slumber* |
| The objective of an attack is | *the goal* |
| A soldier is a | *warrior* |
| One's death is one's | *fate* |
| The sky is | *the heavens* |
| Things that glow or shine are | *radiant* |
| The army as a whole is | *the legion* |
| What is contemptible is | *base* |
| The legs and arms of young men are | *limbs* |
| Dead bodies constitute | *ashes,* or *dust* |
| The blood of young men is | *"the red/Sweet wine of youth"*—R. Brooke. |

This system of "high" diction was not the least of the ultimate casualties of the war. But its staying power was astonishing. As late as 1918 it was still possible for some men who had actually fought to sustain the old rhetoric. Thus Sgt. Reginald Grant writes the Dedication of his book *S.O.S. Stand To* (1918):

> In humble, reverent spirit I dedicate these pages to the memory of the lads who served with me in the "Sacrifice Battery," and who gave their lives that those behind might live, and, also, in brotherly affection and esteem to my brothers, Gordon and Billy, who are still fighting the good fight and keeping the faith.

Another index of the prevailing innocence is a curious prophylaxis of language. One could use with security words which a few years later, after the war, would constitute obvious *double entendres.* One could say *intercourse,* or *erection,* or *ejaculation* without any risk of evoking a smile or a leer. Henry James's innocent employment of the word *tool* is as well known as Browning's artless misapprehensions about the word *twat.* Even the official order transmitted from British headquarters to the armies at 6:50 on the morning of November 11, 1918, warned that "there will be no intercourse of any description with the enemy." Imagine daring to promulgate that at the end of the Second War! In 1901 the girl who was to become [American writer] Christopher Isherwood's mother and whose fiancé was going to be killed in the war could write in her diary with no self-consciousness: "Was bending over a book when the whole erection [a toque hat she had been trimming] caught fire in the candles and was ruined. So vexed!" She was an extraordinarily shy, genteel, proper girl, and neither she nor her fiancé read anything funny or anything not entirely innocent and chaste into the language of a telegram he once sent her after a long separation: "THINKING OF YOU HARD." In this world "he ejaculated breathlessly" was a tag in utterly innocent dialogue rather than a moment in pornographic description.

Indeed, the literary scene is hard to imagine. There was no *Waste Land,* with its rats' alleys, dull canals, and dead men who have lost their bones: it would take four years of trench warfare to bring these to consciousness. There was no *Ulysses* [James Joyce's master novel], no *Mauberley* [Ezra Pound's 1920 poem], no *Cantos* [the collection of poems by Ezra Pound], no Kafka, no Proust, no Waugh, no Auden, no Huxley, no Cummings. . . . There was no "Valley of Ashes" in *The Great Gatsby.* One read Hardy and Kipling and Conrad and frequented worlds of traditional moral action delineated in traditional moral language. . . .

For the modern imagination that last summer [before the war] has assumed the status of a permanent symbol for anything innocently but irrecoverably lost. Transferred meanings of "our summer of 1914" retain the irony of the original, for the change from felicity to despair, pastoral to anti-pastoral, is melodramatically unexpected. Elegizing the "Old South" in America, which could be said to have disappeared around 1950, David Lowe writes in 1973:

> We never thought that any of this would change; we never thought of change at all. But we were the last generation of the Old South; that spring in the early fifties was our summer of 1914. . . . Like those other generations who were given to witness the guillotining of a world, we never expected it. And like that of our counterparts, our world seemed most beautiful just before it disappeared.

Out of the world of summer, 1914, marched a unique generation. It believed in Progress and Art and in no way doubted the benignity even of technology. The word *machine* was not yet invariably coupled with the word *gun.*

It was not that "war" was entirely unexpected during June and July of 1914. But the irony was that trouble was expected in Ulster rather than in Flanders. It was expected to be domestic and embarrassing rather than savage and incomprehensible. Of the diary his mother kept during 1914, Christopher Isherwood notes that it has "the morbid fascination of a document which records, without the dishonesty of hindsight, the day-by-day approach to a catastrophe by an utterly unsuspecting victim. Meanwhile, as so often happens, this victim expects and fears a different catastrophe—civil war in Ulster—which isn't going to take place." Kathleen Isherwood writes in her diary on July 13: "The papers look fearfully serious. . . . Sir Edward Carson says 'if it be not peace with honor it must be war with honor.'" The rhetoric seems identical with that of the early stages of the war itself. I have omitted only one sentence in the middle: "Ulster is an armed camp." Alec Waugh remembers the farewell address of his school headmaster: "There were no clouds on my horizon during those long July evenings, and when the Chief in his farewell speech spoke of the bad news in the morning papers, I thought he was referring to the threat of civil war in Ireland." Even in a situation so potent with theatrical possibilities as the actual war was to become, for ironic melodrama it would be hard to improve on the Cabinet meeting of July 24, with the map of Ireland spread out on the big table. "The fate of nations," says John Terraine, "appeared to hang upon parish boundaries in the counties of Fermanagh and Tyrone." To them, enter [England's secretary of state for foreign affairs] Sir Edward Grey ashen-faced, in his hand the Austro-Hungarian ultimatum to Servia: *coup de théâtre* [an unexpected or dramatic event that overturns a situation].

In nothing, however, is the initial British innocence so conspicuous as in the universal commitment to the sporting spirit. Before the war, says Osbert Sitwell, we were still in the trough of peace that had lasted a hundred years between two great conflicts. In it, such wars as arose were not general, but only a brief armed version of the Olympic Games. You won a round; the enemy won the next. There was no more talk of extermination, or of Fights to a Finish, than would occur in a boxing match.

It is this conception of war as strenuous but entertaining that permeates Rupert Brooke's letters home during the autumn and winter of 1914–15. "It's all great fun," he finds. The classic equation between war and sport—cricket, in this case—had been established by Sir Henry Newbolt in his poem "Vitaï Lampada," a public-school [prep school] favorite since 1898:

> There's a breathless hush in the Close
>     tonight—
>     Ten to make and the match to win—
> A bumping pitch and a blinding light,
>     An hour to play and the last man in.
> And it's not for the sake of a ribboned coat,
>     Or the selfish hope of a season's fame,
> But his Captain's hand on his shoulder
>     smote—
>     "Play up! play up! and play the game!"

In later life, the former cricket brave exhorts his colonial troops beset by natives:

> The sand of the desert is sodden red—
>     Red with the wreck of a square that broke;
> The Gatling's jammed and the Colonel dead,
>     And the regiment blind with dust and smoke;
> The river of death has brimmed his banks,
>     And England's far, and Honor a name;
> But the voice of a schoolboy rallies the ranks:
>     "Play up! Play up! and play the game!"

The author of these lines was a lifetime friend of Douglas Haig [the British commander on the Western Front during World War I, much criticized for his willingness to allow vast numbers of soldiers to perish in assaults on the German line]. They had first met when they were students together at Clifton College, whose cricket field provides the scene of Newbolt's first stanza. Much later Newbolt wrote, "When I looked into Douglas Haig I saw what is really great—perfect ac-

ceptance, which means perfect faith." This version of Haig brings him close to the absolute ideal of what Patrick Howarth has termed *homo newboltiensis,* or "Newbolt Man": honorable, stoic, brave, loyal, courteous—and unaesthetic, unironic, unintellectual and devoid of wit. To Newbolt, the wartime sufferings of such as Wilfred Owen [a great English poet killed during World War I in which he served as a frontline officer] were tiny—and whiny—compared with Haig's: "Owen and the rest of the broken men," he says, "rail at the Old Men who sent the young to die: they have suffered cruelly, but in the nerves and not the heart—they haven't the experience or the imagination to know the extreme human agony. . . ." Only Newbolt Man, skilled in games, can know that.

Cricket is fine for implanting the right spirit, but football is even better. Indeed, the English young man's fondness for it was held to be a distinct sign of his natural superiority over his German counterpart. That was Lord Northcliffe's conclusion in a quasi-official and very popular work of propaganda, *Lord Northcliffe's War Book:*

> Our soldiers are individual. They embark on little individual enterprises. The German . . . is not so clever at these devices. He was never taught them before the war, and his whole training from childhood upwards has been to obey, and to obey in numbers.

The reason is simple:

> He has not played individual games. Football, which develops individuality, has only been introduced into Germany in comparatively recent times.

The English tank crews, Lord Northcliffe finds, "are young daredevils who, fully knowing that they will be a special mark for every kind of Prussian weapon, enter upon their task in a sporting spirit with the same cheery enthusiasm as they would show for football." One thing notable about Prussians is that they have an inadequate concept of playing the game. Thus Reginald Grant on the first German use of chlorine gas: "It was a new device in warfare and thoroughly illustrative of the Prussian idea of playing the game."

One way of showing the sporting spirit was to

kick a football toward the enemy lines while attacking. This feat was first performed by the 1st Battalion of the 18th London Regiment at Loos in 1915. It soon achieved the status of a conventional act of bravado and was ultimately exported far beyond the Western Front. Arthur ("Bosky") Borton, who took part in an attack on the Turkish lines near Beersheba in November, 1917, proudly reported home: "One of the men had a football. How it came there goodness knows. Anyway we kicked off and rushed the first [Turkish] guns, dribbling the ball with us." But the most famous football episode was Captain W.P. Nevill's achievement at the Somme attack. Captain Nevill, a company commander in the 8th East Surreys, bought four footballs, one for each platoon, during his last London leave before the attack. He offered a prize to the platoon which, at the jump-off, first kicked its football up to the German front line. Although J.R. Ackerley remembered Nevill as "the battalion buffoon," he may have been shrewder than he looked: his little sporting contest did have the effect of persuading his men that the attack was going to be, as the staff had been insisting, a walkover. A survivor observing from a short distance away recalls zero hour:

> As the gun-fire died away I saw an infantryman climb onto the parapet into No Man's Land, beckoning others to follow. [Doubtless Captain Nevill or one of his platoon commanders.] As he did so he kicked off a football. A good kick. The ball rose and travelled well towards the German line. That seemed to be the signal to advance.

Captain Nevill was killed instantly. Two of the footballs are preserved today in English museums.

After reading this selection, consider these questions:
1. What does Fussell mean by the "irony" created by the war?
2. What does the "high diction" indicate about British attitudes at the beginning of the war?
3. How do images from sports give meaning to the war experience?

# CHAPTER 12
# Nazism and the Holocaust

A general armistice for World War I was finally concluded in November 1918, and the need for a major peace conference was obvious to everyone. Beginning in 1919 the major and minor powers of Europe (as well as delegates from the European colonies) met in Versailles, outside Paris. One great exception was Germany, another was Russia. Although the armistice simply put a stop to the fighting, Germany's exclusion from the conference indicated that the Allies considered themselves victors in a war that Germany had started. The terms of the Treaty of Versailles also branded Germany as a defeated and guilty nation. Territory was taken away, the size of its armed forces was severely limited, and worst of all a huge indemnity was imposed. Only after the major provisions of the treaty had been decided were representatives of the newly organized Weimar Republic (which replaced the Second Reich) allowed to attend the conference, and then they were basically forced to accept the treaty under threat of renewed conflict. The consequences on future German history were unforeseen and disastrous. Not only was the infant Weimar Republic and its leaders saddled with accepting humiliating and economically devastating terms, for which the republic itself was always identified in some Germans' minds, but the terms of the treaty and its continuing aftereffects gave opponents of the government powerful weapons to condemn the entire republican political structure.

The worldwide economic crisis of the 1930s, sparked in large measure by the Wall Street stock market crash of 1929, intensified social grievances that had festered in Europe since the end of World War I. The crisis brought financial failures, industrial breakdown, and unprecedented unemployment. As established governments failed to improve conditions, popular protests erupted and strikes broke out throughout the industrial areas of Europe and North America. Reaction to this crisis brought to the fore a number of alternatives not just to capitalism, which had brought on the crisis, but also to the political system with which this system was associated. Liberal democracy as it had evolved from the French Revolution through the nineteenth century was, in other words, challenged in new and threatening ways. Almost all of these alternative regimes were dictatorial and rightist, though in ways unknown to the nineteenth century. They arose and took power in states as diverse as Spain and Portugal, Germany and Italy, and Hungary, Romania, and Poland. This does not mean that all types of mass politics were eliminated, for a direct appeal of leaders like Adolf Hitler in Germany, Benito Mussolini in Italy, and even to a degree and with a different ideology Joseph Stalin in the Soviet Union relied on some direct—though noninstitutionalized—dependence on the will of the masses.

The rise of the National Socialists in Germany provides the most dramatic and the most consequential of these new dictatorships. In a time of economic crisis and infighting among the German political elite, Hitler was given the chancellorship of a coalition government in January 1933. He moved quickly to consolidate his position. In February 1933, when the Reichstag building was gutted by fire, Hitler blamed the Communists and used the event to justify imposing press censorship, prohibiting political meetings of his opponents, and assuming dictatorial powers. In March 1933 he added to this the Enabling Act. Passed by the Reichstag with only the Social Democrats voting against it, this act essentially put an end to parliamentary government in Germany and suspended the constitution for four years, which Hitler maintained would boost the nation out of its crisis. In May 1933 the government outlawed all labor unions and seized their property. Upon President Paul von Hindenburg's death in August 1934, Hitler assumed the position of president as well as chancellor and conferred upon himself the new title of Reichsführer—the leader of the Reich. There was no political opposition left by the summer of 1934.

The Nazis attempted to reorganize all of German society in the mid-1930s, and they eventually plunged the world into another war in 1939. Hitler's goals, however, were not merely to achieve control of the state. The real goal was to unite the people in a unity greater than had been ever achieved in liberal democracies or under Soviet Communism. This new community was called the *Volksgemeinschaft*—the folk community. The *Volksgemeinschaft* was to be achieved by merging society with the state and the Nazi Party. In other words, the type of control that had proved successful in the reorganization of the party now had to lead to the more highly controlled organization of the state and the extension of the state and party over all aspects of the lives of individual German men and women. In the mid-1930s this policy was carried out by creating a whole series of new organizations that all types of professionals, bureaucrats, students, housewives, and children were forced to join. Workers, for instance, were organized into the National Labor Front. This organization functioned less as a union than as a means for the party to control workers and direct factory procedures. Government officials classified jobs, determined work procedures, and set pay levels. The National Labor Front also initiated a program called *Kraft durch Freude* ("Strength Through Joy"), which rewarded workers and their families with free concerts, vacation trips, and at least the promise of an automobile. Economically, the mid-1930s were good for most German workers. As the rest of Europe and large parts of the world were suffering from overwhelming unemployment, Germany experienced underemployment, especially when the government proclaimed the Four-Year Plan in 1936. The secret aim of this plan was to prepare Germany for war by 1940. Government officials allocated raw materials, sponsored the production of synthetics, and intensified labor management. By 1938 government expenditures on defense soared over 50 percent. The Nazi regime was thus prepared for war when it began with the German invasion of Poland on September 1, 1939.

# SELECTION 1:

# The Party Program

*The origins of the National Socialists were modest. Organized soon after World War I by former soldiers Anton Drexler and Gottfried Feder as a very small, extra-political group, the German Workers' Party was only one of a score of such disgruntled "political" groups that existed in Munich in these years. Adolf Hitler joined the party in 1920, was soon made head of propaganda, and by 1921 became the party's sole leader. In 1920 the German Workers' Party—soon to change its name to the National Socialist German Workers' Party (NSDAP)—announced its platform in a list of twenty-five principles penned by Drexler, Feder, and Hitler. Within these points, the party at this time combined socialist projects with extreme nationalist and anti-Semitic pronouncements. Once in power in 1933, the party leadership did not follow these principles in any detail and in fact renounced them. Still, the program provides a good indication of what the party stood for in its formative stage and suggests to what type of individuals it was intended to appeal. The party still thought the program significantly important to reissue it in the party yearbook of 1941, from which the following selection has been taken.*

The Programme of the German Workers' Party is limited as to period. The leaders have no intention, once the aims announced in it have been achieved, of setting up fresh ones, merely in order to increase the discontent of the masses artificially, and so ensure the continued existence of the Party.

1. We demand the union of all Germans to form a Great Germany on the basis of the right of

From Gottfried Feder, "The Programme of the Party of Hitler," translated by F.T.S. Dugdale, in U.S. Department of State, *National Socialsim: Basic Principles* (Washington, DC: U.S. Government Printing Office, 1943).

the self-determination enjoyed by nations.

2. We demand equality of rights for the German People in its dealings with other nations, and abolition of the Peace Treaties of Versailles and St. Germain.

3. We demand land and territory (colonies) for the nourishment of our people and for settling our superfluous population.

4. None but members of the nation may be citizens of the State. None but those of German blood, whatever their creed, may be members of the nation. No Jew, therefore, may be a member of the nation.

5. Anyone who is not a citizen of the State may live in Germany only as a guest and must be regarded as being subject to foreign laws.

6. The right of voting on the State's government and legislation is to be enjoyed by the citizen of the State alone. We demand therefore that all official appointments, of whatever kind, whether in the Reich, in the country, or in the smaller localities, shall be granted to citizens of the State alone.

We oppose the corrupting custom of Parliament of filling posts merely with a view to party considerations, and without reference to character or capability.

7. We demand that the State shall make it its first duty to promote the industry and livelihood of citizens of the State. If it is not possible to nourish the entire population of the State, foreign nationals (non-citizens of the State) must be excluded from the Reich.

8. All non-German immigration must be prevented. We demand that all non-Germans, who entered Germany subsequent to August 2nd, 1914, shall be required forthwith to depart from the Reich.

9. All citizens of the State shall be equal as regards rights and duties.

10. It must be the first duty of each citizen of the State to work with his mind or with his body. The activities of the individual may not clash with the interests of the whole, but must proceed within the frame of the community and be for the general good.

We demand therefore:

11. Abolition of incomes unearned by work.

12. In view of the enormous sacrifice of life and property demanded of a nation by every war, personal enrichment due to a war must be regarded as a crime against the nation. We demand therefore ruthless confiscation of all war gains.

13. We demand nationalization of all businesses which have been up to the present formed into companies (Trusts).

14. We demand that the profits from wholesale trade shall be shared out.

15. We demand extensive development of provision for old age.

16. We demand creation and maintenance of a healthy middle class, immediate communalisation of wholesale business premises, and their lease at a cheap rate to small traders, and that extreme consideration shall be shown to all small purveyors to the State, district authorities and smaller localities.

17. We demand land-reform suitable to our national requirements, passing of a law for confiscation without compensation of land for communal purposes; abolition of interest on land loans, and prevention of all speculation in land.

18. We demand ruthless prosecution of those whose activities are injurious to the common interest. Sordid criminals against the nation, usurers, profiteers, etc. must be punished with death, whatever their creed or race.

19. We demand that the Roman Law, which serves the materialistic world order, shall be replaced by a legal system for all Germany.

20. With the aim of opening to every capable and industrious German the possibility of higher education and of thus obtaining advancement, the State must consider a thorough re-construction of our national system of education. The curriculum of all educational establishments must be brought into line with the requirements of practical life. Comprehension of the State idea (State sociology) must be the school objective, beginning with the first dawn of intelligence in the pupil. We demand development of the gifted children of poor parents, whatever their class or occupation, at the expense of the State.

21. The State must see to raising the standard of health in the nation by protecting mothers and infants, prohibiting child labour, increasing bodily efficiency by obligatory gymnastics and sports laid

down by law, and by extensive support of clubs engaged in the bodily development of the young.

22. We demand abolition of a paid army and formation of a national army.

23. We demand legal warfare against conscious political lying and its dissemination in the Press. In order to facilitate creation of a German national Press we demand:

(a) that all editors of newspapers and their assistants, employing the German language, must be members of the nation;

(b) that special permission from the State shall be necessary before non-German newspapers may appear. These are not necessarily printed in the German language;

(c) that non-Germans shall be prohibited by law from participation financially in or influencing German newspapers, and that the penalty for contravention of the law shall be suppression of any such newspaper, and immediate deportation of the non-German concerned in it.

It must be forbidden to publish papers which do not conduce to the national welfare. We demand legal prosecution of all tendencies in art and literature of a kind likely to disintegrate our life as a nation, and the suppression of institutions which militate against the requirements above-mentioned.

24. We demand liberty for all religious denominations in the State, so far as they are not a danger to it and do not militate against the moral feelings of the German race.

The Party, as such, stands for positive Christianity, but does not bind itself in the matter of creed to any particular confession. It combats the Jewish-materialist spirit within us and without us, and is convinced that our nation can only achieve permanent health from within on the principle:

THE COMMON INTEREST BEFORE SELF

25. That all the fore-going may be realised we demand the creation of a strong central power of the State. Unquestioned authority of the politically centralized Parliament over the entire Reich and its organizations; and formation of Chambers for classes and occupations for the purpose of carrying out the general laws promulgated by the Reich in the various States of the confederation.

The leaders of the Party swear to go straight forward—if necessary to sacrifice their lives—in securing fulfilment of the foregoing Points.

*Munich, February 24th, 1920*

After reading this selection, consider these questions:

1. What lingering consequences of losing World War I can be seen in the party program?
2. What socialist aspects are found in the National Socialist program?
3. How does anti-Semitism enter into the program?

# SELECTION 2:

# The Nazi Seizure of Power

Adolf Hitler's assumption of the chancellorship in 1933 showed him both to be extremely lucky and a master of exploiting a crisis. The economic crisis and the sharp rise in unemployment resulted in the complete breakdown of parliamentary government by 1930. Germany was ruled by extraordinary, yet still constitutional, means through the appointment of chancellors by the president. Even these measures failed to bring about a parliamentary majority and the revival of democratic government. Elec-

*tions to the Reichstag (national parliament) continued but these increasingly brought success to the parties from the extremes of the political spectrum as well as the destruction of the more centrist and liberal parties. Although the left-wing Independent Socialists and the Communists gained support in ways they had not previously achieved, the Nazi Party quickly won over many voters. The Nazis received little more than 2 percent of the national vote in 1928. By 1930 they received almost 20 percent. In the 1932 national election they won a plurality in the Reichstag. Together with their allies in the Nationalist Party, the Nazis commanded a majority. Against his basic instincts and better judgment, President Paul von Hindenburg was finally persuaded to accept Hitler as chancellor in January 1933.*

*The historian Karl Dietrich Bracher provides one of the finest analyses of Hitler's infighting and political maneuvering from his assumption of the chancellorship to his acquisition of full dictatorial powers in the summer of 1934. In* The German Dictatorship *(1969), Bracher shows how Hitler's seizure of power—though he swore to uphold the constitution and work within established political forms—was definitely unconstitutional.*

The victory of National Socialism, the alarmingly rapid triumphant march of an apparently irrevocable totalitarian system of government in Germany, was consolidated in less than two years, between 30 January 1933 and August 1934. By the summer of 1933, totalitarian one-party rule had become a reality. A comparison of events in Germany with those which ten years earlier in Italy and fifteen years earlier in Russia had led to the installation of totalitarian systems points up many differences. Though the Bolshevik seizure of power was accomplished as rapidly, it was the result of a planned, armed *coup d'état*, and moreover, the revolutionary Soviet Government turned into a totalitarian dictatorship only after some years. And it took Italian Fascism, in appearance and aims more closely related to National Socialism, six years to overwhelm the opposition completely and establish its one-party dictatorship, and even then not in the same total, exclusive fashion as Hitler's Third Reich. Whereas Hitler, as Leader and Chancellor, formally retained all power in his hands, in Italy the King and monar-

chy, however insignificant their weight, continued their existence alongside and above [dictator Benito] Mussolini. To be sure, in all three cases we are dealing with the seizure of power by a violent minority. The methods they used had many similarities, and in many respects they even copied from each other; the Communist coup tactics undoubtedly served as an example in the planning of the Fascist seizure, and the Fascist example in turn played a role in the National Socialist takeover. Yet considerable differences remain.

If nothing else, the preconditions differed. In Russia, the revolution took place against the background of an absolutistic state and agrarian, feudal society of an "underdeveloped" country. In the "semideveloped" Italy, parliamentary democracy was unable to cope with the explosive force of the transition to industrialism. Germany, on the other hand, was faced with the political and psychological problems of the unresolved defeat of 1918, and above all with internal structural crises of its already highly developed industrial mass society. These factors underlie all explanations of the unique course and success of the National Socialist seizure of power. Essential to any such attempt is the stress laid on the individual components of the development.

In addition to the ideological and sociological reflections according to which the totalitarian state

From *The German Dictatorship*, by Karl Dietrich Bracher, translated by Jean Steinberg. Copyright © 1969 Verlag Kiepenheuer & Witsch, Köln, Berlin. English translation copyright © Praeger Publishers, Inc., 1970. Reproduced by permission of Greenwood Publishing Group, Westport, Connecticut.

was the product of an almost unstoppable series of historical and socio-economic causal factors, there is the political analysis which considers the immediate process of the seizure of power in the light of the special conditions of our time. Though taking account of historical and sociological factors, it nonetheless confines itself to the concrete, differentiated facts of the event itself. This type of analysis maintains that only an in-depth study of the specific development, of the special technique and tactics of the seizure of power, can avoid the pitfalls of erroneous generalizations and, out of the welter of historical and sociological determinism, sift and classify the causes.

The slogan of legal revolution offers the key to the character and development of the National Socialist power seizure. National Socialist propagandists, politicians, and constitutional experts all along emphasized that although Hitler's takeover was the beginning of a revolution that would profoundly affect all aspects of life, it was a completely legal, constitutional process. The paradoxical concept of a "legal revolution" artificially linked two contradictory axioms of political action and behaviour. The significance of this legality tactic with revolutionary aspirations was in fact more than a mere propaganda gimmick and should not be underestimated. In examining specific components of the political process, we find that this tactic played a decisive role in surrounding this new type of totalitarian power seizure with its seductive aura of effectiveness and made all legal, political, or even intellectual resistance so difficult, and, in the opinion of many, well-nigh impossible.

This holds true of the earlier preconditions as well. The abortive putsch of 1923 had convinced Hitler that any direct attack on the existing order was doomed. Neither the Government nor the Army had been caught napping in 1923; the defences of the democratic parties, including the unions, proved strong enough to withstand a putsch, despite all the internal and external problems of the Republic. Above all, the very respect for authority and bureaucracy which so strained the fabric of the Weimar Republic at the same time proved a considerable obstacle to all coup attempts. However great the sympathies for the critics and enemies of the Republic, it seems that holding fast to legality, legitimacy, and the values of law and order (if not freedom) were among the traditions of the authoritarian state in Germany. That is why the 1918 revolution did not spread, why the Kapp Putsch of 1920 failed, and why, despite all dictatorial aspirations of the Army and of [general-turned-politician Hans von] Seeckt, the Republic survived in 1923.

These factors prescribed the road of the reorganized NSDAP [the National Socialist German Workers' Party] after Hitler's release from prison, a road to which he kept despite impatient revolutionaries in his party and the SA [Sturmabteilung, Nazi storm troopers], despite the seeming weakness and hopelessness of his position in a parliamentary democracy. Yet at the same time, the German people's deeply rooted aversion to and mistrust of overt revolution opened up a new possibility to the tactician of legal revolution: the road via Presidential dictatorship.

A double defect of the Weimar Constitution made this possible. First, in the overwhelming opinion of scholars, the Constitution did not preclude the erosion and abrogation of its substance by constitutional means. This basically is what had been happening since 1930, and particularly after 1932; the process was completed in 1933 with the Reichstag fire decree and the Enabling Act. Hitler spelled out the possibility of the legal dismemberment of the Constitution in unmistakable terms in his legality oath at the 1930 Leipzig Reichswehr trial, when he told the court: "The Constitution only maps out the arena of battle, not the goal. We enter the legal agencies and in that way will make our party the determining factor. However, once we possess the constitutional power, we will mould the state into the shape we hold to be suitable."

At that time the NSDAP was of course still far from playing a decisive role in parliament. And even at the moment of its greatest expansion, in the summer of 1932, it held little more than one third of the parliamentary seats; the legal road via a majority party remained blocked to Hitler, particularly when the elections of November 1932 showed a clear decline in National Socialist strength.

But here a second weakness of the Weimar constitutional and governmental system offered a way out of the seemingly insurmountable dilemma created by the legality strategy, namely the possibility of a Presidential government without and even against the will of parliament and of democratic public opinion. The gist of the growing body of literature on this theme is that the Presidential dictatorial powers under the famous-infamous Article 48 of the Weimar Constitution, intended specifically to protect the democratic order against radical efforts to overthrow it in the early postwar years, now, under a President with a different orientation, served diametrically opposite purposes. In the days of the [Heinrich] Brüning Government (1930), and certainly during the authoritarian [Franz von] Papen and [Kurt von] Schleicher Cabinets (1932), it became apparent that the possibility of an extra- let alone anti-parliamentary government would inevitably paralyse parliament and parties. The ever-present possibility of invoking emergency powers offered a convenient escape-hatch from political responsibility, and at the same time prepared the population for the type of authoritarian ideas of government which were being bandied about with growing force by propagandists and in the universities. The catastrophic repercussions of the world-wide economic crisis, together with the public esteem enjoyed by a President receptive to such authoritarian concepts, turned the possibility of throttling democracy by authoritarianism into reality. Out of the confusing welter of political and personal factors leading to Hitler's Chancellorship, one fact emerges clearly: in the course of the negotiations, Hitler adhered to the basic demand that as the head of a Presidential government he, too, must be granted the extraordinary dictatorial emergency powers. Hitler gained "legitimate" control of the Government not as the head of a parliamentary coalition, as a misleading apologia still suggests, but through this authoritarian loophole in the Weimar Constitution. On 30 January 1933, the new Chancellor found himself in a position to reap the fruit of his successful legality strategy—swearing formal allegiance to a Constitution which he immediately set about to destroy. With that, the real seizure of power got under way; now it was demonstrated how the tactic of gaining

power by legal means could be brought into line with the strategy of revolution and blended with the technique of seizing power by overtaking, eliminating, and levelling all political, social, and intellectual safeguards and counter-forces. To do this, another magic formula was needed to confuse the mind, deflect the opponents, and deceive or seduce Hitler's allies. The name of this magic formula was "national revolution."

This was the slogan under which the so-called legal revolution unfolded in the first seven weeks of Hitler's Presidential rule—up to the remoulding of the basis of government through passage of the Enabling Act on 23 March 1933. Ever since the anti-Young Plan[1] campaign, and particularly since the establishment of the Harzburg Front,[2] Hitler had courted industry, the military, and large landholders to join in a national opposition of right-wing parties, but now no longer as a mere drummer and pioneer whom his conservative-national partners could discard. In this, too, he had learned the lesson of 1923 well. In the years that followed, the alliance with the reactionary Right served merely as a political tool in the battle against the Republic. Wherever this alliance was put to the test, it fell apart, as during the Presidential elections of 1932, when Hitler on his own tried to run against Hindenburg and Düsterberg.[3] But at the end of 1932, once his conservative partners—the German Nationals with Papen and [Alfred] Hugenberg, the Stahlhelm[4] and its industrial and agrarian backers—indicated their willingness to accept a government under National Socialist direction, Hitler readily accepted Papen's offer to revive the alliance. The result was the reappearance of the Harzburg Front, at the very moment

1. The Young Plan was a restructuring of German reparation payments set by the Treaty of Versailles. The Plan, worked out by an international committee headed by the American financier Owen D. Young, was accepted by the German government in 1930. Both before and after its adoption, the Young Plan led to opposition both by the right and the left.   2. The projected alliance of rightist nationalists in 1931 in opposition to the government of Chancellor Heinrich Brüning.   3. Theodor Düsterberg, a former officer of the General Staff, along with Franz Seldte, a reserve officer, founded the Stahlhelm (Steel Helmet) at the end of WWI on December 23, 1918.   4. A nationalist ex-servicemen's organization, formed in 1918. The purpose of the organization was to prevent a German revolution which would bring about a more liberal or socialist form of government.

when the NSDAP faced grave internal problems, when the economy stood on the brink of recovery, and when the Schleicher Government was about to institute determined counter-measures.

It became apparent during the formation of the new Government that the National Socialists, in making their power claims by donning the programmatic garb of the "above-party" national revolution, also acquired an unrivalled ideological framework for the constitutional implementation of their legal revolution. The Government was composed of only three National Socialists and eight conservatives, who in addition to the Vice Chancellorship held such important Ministries as Defence, Economics, and Foreign Affairs; moreover, the conservatives felt confident of the President and the Army. To all appearances, this was surely a coalition Cabinet capable of containing National Socialist ambitions: "We have engaged him [Hitler]," Vice Chancellor Papen, the initiator of the Government, stated triumphantly, in view of his own firm ties to Hindenburg. And he told a conservative critic, Ewald von Kleist-Schmenzin, who later joined the resistance: "What do you want? I have Hindenburg's confidence. Within two months we will have pushed Hitler so far into a corner that he'll squeak." In fact, however, it was not the National Socialists but their self-assured partners who were roped in. Even before the swearing-in of this "Government of the national concentration" on 30 January, the dominating power of Chancellor Hitler, who in contrast to his partners knew what he wanted, became apparent: when, in opposition to Hugenberg, he was able to win his fight to have the Reichstag dissolved once again, the non–National Socialist front in the Cabinet was already broken. This breakthrough was to be repeated time and again in Cabinet sessions. No resistance on this level ever materialized, even though the National Socialists took over the majority of ministry posts only at a much later date.

This, however, was not only a consequence of the delusions and opportunism with which the German Nationals entered into the alliance, confident of their prestige and their influence in economic life, society, and Army. It was a consequence as well of the unequal distribution of

power in the Government and in the political arena as a whole, all external appearances to the contrary. As it turned out, possession of the Chancellorship and of the Interior Ministries in the Reich and in Prussia (posts held by [Wilhelm] Frick and [Hermann] Göring, respectively) was all that was needed to turn the national revolution into a National Socialist takeover. Reich Defence Minister [Werner von] Blomberg's ready susceptibility to the blandishments of the National Socialists and their promises to rearm the military was yet another contributing factor. A series of emergency laws based on the ill-fated Article 48 and enacted in February 1933, to which Hindenburg, blinded by Hitler's conservative, Christian-national promises, agreed, laid the foundations for the power through which the National Socialists were able almost at will to control and oppress the country.

This, however, could not be accomplished without doing some injury to legal process. Thus, a decree passed on 6 February 1933 giving Göring practically full control over Prussia was in clear violation of the findings of the State Court in the Prussian conflict of 1932. Also, the rigorous limitation on freedom of the press and assembly, and above all the utilization of the Reichstag fire in the permanent abrogation of all basic civil rights, on which the Third Reich based its life-long emergency powers, went far beyond existing constitutional practices. But a façade of legality was preserved insofar as none of the offices responsible or accountable for the preservation of the legal state—from the President and the Army down to the ministries, the state governments, the parties, the trade unions, and the courts—resisted or effectively opposed these power grabs. Their failure helped to erect the façade of a national revolution in the early weeks. Despite substantial evidence to the contrary, Hitler's national partners continued to cling to this fiction until by the end of June they were irrevocably outmanoeuvred. They clung to this legend with almost fearful readiness in the hope that they thereby could ward off the threatening alternative of Nazi autocratic rule. That their behaviour made this possible at all, and without any risk for Hitler, was recognized too late by accomplices like Hugenberg, and by men like Papen never at all.

Thus, the mistaken notion of the legal revolution was able to blossom effectively only with the help of another mistaken notion—that of the national revolution. For when the new Reichstag elections of 5 March, despite the propaganda and the terror, failed to bring Hitler his expected majority, he once more fell back on the national alliance. In a gigantic display at Potsdam on 21 March he repeated the national-conservative pledges of the early days which so deeply impressed the middle class, civil service, and Army, and deflected their attention from the terrorist methods of the Nazi leadership. *"Wo gehobelt wird, fliegen Späne"* (approximately, "You can't make an omelette without breaking eggs") was a frequently heard saying meant to reassure the people about the "unavoidable excesses" of this national "turning point' (thus Papen). That is why, on 21 March 1933, the anniversary of the convocation of [Otto von] Bismarck's Reichstag (1871), [Joseph] Goebbels, the new Propaganda Minister, staged a gigantic, virtuoso show at the tomb of Frederick the Great in Potsdam. In the presence of Hindenburg and the Crown Prince, before a chair set aside for the Emperor [former Kaiser Wilhelm II was still living, but in exile in the Netherlands], the Potsdam "touching comedy" (*Rührkomödie*) successfully distracted monarchists and nationalists from the true nature of the spreading National Socialist dictatorship. The black, red, and gold national colours were replaced by the black, white and red flag of the national revolution, a violation of the Constitution which the German National partners of Hitler could hardly object to, in view of their demand that these colours of Bismarck's Reich replace the flag of the Republic. Here, too, the apparent subjugation of National Socialist ambitions to the common goal was preserved, since the swastika banner was after all only one of the two flags of the national revolution.

But only two days after the Potsdam show, the veil was lifted, and the reality of the National Socialist power-seizure stood nakedly revealed. The bourgeois parties, from the Liberals to the Centre, had been so intimidated by the pressure of accomplished facts and so impressed by the appeal to nationalism that they felt sure they could not withhold their agreement to the Enabling Act. To be sure, this decision of 23 March 1933, in which the Reichstag, against the opposition of the persecuted Left, handed all legislative powers over to the Government, was an outgrowth of the permanent state of emergency proclaimed in the fatal Reichstag fire decree of 28 February. It should also be pointed out that Hitler proceeded to violate the limiting provisions of the Enabling Act on which the bourgeois parties thought they could rely; alone the fact that the act was passed by a Reichsrat (the upper chamber of parliament) which, after the dismemberment of the state governments by coups, unquestionably was not properly constituted must be considered irregular. And the Centre and Liberals probably were motivated also by the hope that in this way the regime could be brought back from government by radical decrees to the area of legislative rule. But precisely this fatal deception effected by the legal revolution enabled National Socialism to consolidate and expand its rule much more rapidly and more totally than Italian Fascism.

The enormous importance of the Enabling Act was rooted in this deception even more than in the concrete powers granted by it. It is true that the sanctions and acts of terror up to and including the brutal suppression and annihilation of the resistance movement were largely based on the radical decrees of the early days before the passage of the Enabling Act. But now the willing collaborators in the civil service and the courts, on which National Socialism, lacking its own specialists, was so dependent, were able to find reassuring legal provisions; after all, given such apparently unexceptional legal foundations, there was no basis for any real objections to a government, however turbulent and violent, and however regrettable some of its "excesses" (which were, however, "exceptions"). Wasn't it a good thing—so state the files of many a high official of that time—that the irresistible revolution was carried out in so legal a fashion? It was therefore only logical to do everything in one's power to assure this legal revolution every technical and administrative success.

After reading this selection, consider these questions:

1. How does Bracher counter the notion of a Nazi "legal revolution"?

2. How did the Weimar constitution allow for "unconstitutional acts"?

3. What groups helped Hitler gain dictatorial power?

# SELECTION 3:

# The Volksgemeinschaft

*As Karl Dietrich Bracher demonstrates in the previous selection, Hitler quickly moved to consolidate his political position in the course of 1933 and 1934. Hitler thought that he had a clearer view of reality because he understood the nature of race and the significance of racial struggle through the course of history. The* Volksgemeinschaft *was clearly to be based on "purity" of race. The word* Volk *is almost impossible to render accurately in English. It means "people" or "folk" but with racial and mystical overtones that are missing from these English equivalents.* Volksgemeinschaft *means a community versus a society based on a racially defined "people" or "folk." The Nazi "movement" was ultimately directed to "purifying" the racial community within Germany and then realizing the racial destiny of the Aryans by dominating non-Aryan races.*

*Most Germans became aware of the ideas of the new "racial" community and its relation to the Nazi Party through Hitler's speeches, delivered both before and after he assumed power in 1933. Hitler had the ability to give rousing speeches. He could whip up his audiences by dramatically portraying the success of "the movement" (as the Nazis referred to the party) and to its high significance in German and, indeed, world history. The following speech was given by Hitler at the annual Party Rally Day of 1937.*

This has in truth nothing to do with that superficial arid patriotism which in past decades posed so often as national strength and yet was only a hollow mockery. What has in this week so often almost broken us down was the confession of faith of a new generation—the confession of faith of a people, based upon a common outlook upon the world. More than once hundreds of thousands

have stood here no longer under the impression produced by a political demonstration, but rather under the spell of a heartfelt prayer. Who would maintain that such an effect is due merely to the form of our gathering? No! the form is but the external shape assumed by the organic activity of an idea. . . . The addition of sports-contests to the programme of the *Parteitag* [Party Day] will help to form the new type of German: here men steeled to hardship, here women with the charm of beauty, in the centuries to come, year by year will meet and by their presence will be the living proof that National Socialism has successfully

From *The Speeches of Adolf Hitler, April 1922–August 1939*, translated and edited by Norman H. Baynes, vol. 1 (Oxford: Oxford University Press, 1942).

NAZISM AND THE HOLOCAUST   231

solved its task. Thus will be refuted the idea held by so many, both within and without Germany, that this is but the old Germany reborn. That which has passed before our eyes this week has never been in Germany before. This is no rebirth of the old, this is something new, something which has never yet been in German history, something unique. For never yet has the aim set before the spirit, never yet has the formation of our nation's will been so closely identified with the natural duty of political self-preservation as they are to-day. . . . Never in the sluggish days of German *bourgeois* world-liberalism would it have been possible to create in our people so gigantic an increase in strength and in the consciousness of a national mission. Just as the human body develops its strongest hold on life at the moment when it resists a threatening illness, so peoples are driven to bring into fullest play the energies slumbering within them only when their existence is threatened or even endangered.

When you see this great demonstration of the strength and force of our Movement and thus of our people, do not all of you, my fellow countrymen, feel that such a mobilization alike of spirit and of body could be only the result and consequence of a compelling motive? How often do not many of us ask ourselves what would have become of Germany if Fate in the year 1914 had granted us an easy, rapid victory? That for which we so earnestly, so passionately strove would possibly, if regarded from a higher point of view, have been only a misfortune for our people. This victory would probably have had very sorry consequences. For in the domestic life of Germany we should, precisely through that victory, have been prevented from recognition of these facts which to-day cause us to shrink back in horror from the road on which the Germany of that day was travelling. Those few men of insight who warned us of the peril would have met with nothing but ridicule. The State, its power based, as it was, only on external military strength and supported only by that military strength, completely ignorant of the significance of those sources of a people's force which lie in its blood, sooner or later, would have become the destroyer of its own existence, of the very foundations of its life. We

should have been in the grasp of those developments which we can observe in other lands—the results of their supposed victory. Instead of being torn back from the abyss which yawned before us, our eyes opened by a catastrophic disaster, we should gradually but all the more surely have fallen a victim to the creeping poison of internal dissolution. For us the truth of a wise old saying has indeed been proved afresh: "Often it is through a chastisement that the deepest love of Providence towards its creatures is displayed."

From the distress of the collapse of that day arose the National Socialist idea and at the same time that political confession of faith in the inner regeneration of the people, not merely in the external reconstruction of a State in the form of a restoration of previous conditions. It was to this same distress that the National Socialist Movement owed its unique organization. Only because it was surrounded by a world of foes could the Party develop into that fighting machine which could ultimately wage the decisive battle which led to power. And only thanks to continuous persecution and oppression did there take place within the Party that first and best process of selection which gave to the nation in place of its former politicians the fanatics of a popular Movement.

Thanks to this distress, again, the Movement not only won supreme power in the State, but could later discover and employ all those forces which were needed for the successful execution of its ideas and projects. In place of the National Socialist Party there now stands the German people led by the National Socialist Party. And the German people is now exposed to the same influences as was formerly the National Socialist Party. The same foe which first called us into life and in the course of the struggle reinforced us time after time—it still threatens us to-day. Any lie and any violence are good enough if they help it to gain its end. This is no longer a fight for paltry dynastic interests, a fight to round off the frontiers of States, a struggle for small economic aims: no! this is the battle against a veritable world sickness which threatens to infect the peoples, a plague which devastates whole peoples, whose special characteristic is that it is an international pestilence. For that we know the reason:

here there is no question of a Russian or a Spanish malady, just as little as in 1918 it was a question of a German malady or in 1919 of a Hungarian or Bavarian malady. Neither Russians nor Germans, neither Hungarians nor Spaniards were or are the source of this malady, the source is to be found in that international parasite upon the life of peoples that has spread itself over the world for centuries in order in our day to attain once more to the full effectiveness of its destructive existence. . . .

There should be no illusions on the point: National Socialism has banished the Bolshevist world peril from the domestic life of Germany: it has taken care that the scum of Jewish writers who are alien to the German people shall no longer play the dictator over the German proletariat, i.e. over the German workman, but that the German people shall at length understand its own mission and find in its own body its leaders. National Socialism has, further, made our people and therefore the Reich immune from a Bolshevist infection. And apart from this it will not hesitate to oppose with the most decisive measures every repetition of those attacks which were formerly made within Germany itself against the sovereignty of our people. It was through our attacks upon this enemy that we National Socialists gained our power. In a struggle lasting more than fifteen years we have in fact annihilated him—intellectually and in his outlook on the world—and neither his countless murders and other acts of violence nor the support which he received from the then Marxist rulers of the Reich could stay our victorious march. To-day we will keep strict watch and ward that never again shall such a danger come upon Germany. But should anyone venture to bring this danger from without to the frontiers of Germany or to introduce this danger into Germany he should know that the National Socialist State has forged for itself those weapons which with lightning speed would crush any such attempt.

That we have been in the past good soldiers—that assuredly the world will not have forgotten. That to-day we are still better soldiers—for that

the world can take our word. But that the National Socialist State will defend and fight for its existence with a very different fanaticism from that of the *bourgeois* Reich of yesterday—that no one should doubt. The period of parliamentary weakness from which the German people suffered is past and it will never return. . . . We have no intention of forcing upon anyone else our conceptions or ideals; we would ask that none should seek to impose their views upon us. . . . Never in German history has the whole German people in one Reich been more united than at the present time.

Formerly there were always differences or reservations founded upon tribe, religious confession, dynasty or, later, on party. The age of these reservations is ended. The millions of our people are to-day devoted unconditionally to National Socialism and the National Socialist State. *Weltanschauung* [worldview] and national discipline meet on one and the same level. The intellectual guidance and the political leadership of the nation find their confirmation in the political will. And that political will has found its necessary complement in the internal and the external attitude of the German. No better proof of this can be found than the *Parteitag* in Nuremberg. For eight days you have had here a living demonstration of the success of a work and an achievement which is truly a part of world-history. . . .

May you be conscious that thus a hope of millennia, the prayer of many generations, the confidence and the faith of countless great men of our nation have become a reality of history. At length it has arisen—the Germanic Empire of German nationality.

After reading this selection, consider these questions:
1. How does Hitler define the goals of the movement?
2. How is the movement related to pre-1914 Germany? To the Weimar years?
3. Who are the enemies of this new Germany?

# SELECTION 4:

# The Racial State

*In Mein Kampf and his speeches, Hitler raged against those German citizens who were not members of the new community of race. He specifically identified German Jews as the source of all of Germany's problems. According to Hitler, the Jews dominated the disruptive national press and the degenerate forms of popular arts; they were behind the movement to beguile the workers through Bolshevism and to rob Germans of their wealth through finance capitalism; and they controlled the disorienting politics of the Weimar Republic and were guilty of the "stab in the back" that caused Germany's defeat in World War I. The image of the Jew in Nazi propaganda—since it had little reference to reality— became the source of all personal, economic, social, and political ills of the nation.*

*The historians Michael Burleigh and Wolfgang Wippermann have reexamined the racial theories underlying Nazi ideology. In the following selection from* The Racial State: Germany, 1933–1945, *Burleigh and Wippermann trace the origins of racial theory and show how the Nazis implemented it as state policy.*

Charles Darwin's *On the Origins of Species by Means of Natural Selection, or the Preservation of Favoured Races in the Struggle for Life* enjoyed massive success after its appearance in 1859. Darwin was a reclusive Victorian gentleman scholar of a liberal, progressive cast of mind. He was opposed to slavery, and strongly supported ideas of human equality by avoiding references to "lower" or "higher" races. He was concerned about poverty and established Friendly Societies in Kent. *The Origins* did not contain racial theories, and was almost exclusively concerned with plants and animals. Nonetheless, Darwin . . . was the involuntary progenitor of racist ideology, for he was responsible for the theory of natural selection as the mechanism of evolution. Selection was to become central to all subsequent racist discourse.

It is important to emphasise here that Darwin himself was too intelligent and responsive to criticism to adhere to a fixed set of ideas, and that his theories themselves were composite and not intended for application to human society in a prescriptive sense. This was the "achievement" of Social Darwinians, who unlike Darwin himself used terms like "betterment" or "progress" in a morally-loaded manner. Contrary to popular belief, Social Darwinism was not an exclusively right-wing concern. Social theorists who were politically antagonistic to each other could call themselves Darwinians simply by referring to different tendencies in Darwin's thought. This, and a generalised belief in science and progress, accounts for the existence of Social Darwinians who could be conservative, liberal, socialist, or Fascist.

According to Darwin, there was a constant struggle for existence in the plant and animal kingdoms. It would be won by those species which demonstrated that they were the most ca-

From *The Racial State: Germany 1933–1945*, by Michael Burleigh and Wolfgang Wippermann. Copyright © Cambridge University 1991. Reprinted by permission of Cambridge University Press.

pable of adaption. These would be capable of reproduction. This process of natural selection would lead to the further development of the individual species. In order to counter criticism of the application of this theory to man, Darwin wrote *The Descent of Man,* in which he accounted for some human attributes by resorting to a theory of sexual selection. He also noted the counterselective effects of modern civilisation, and suggested that breeding could make up for the diminishing impact of natural selection. This shift in his thought reflected the increasing influence upon him of his cousin [the scientist Francis] Galton and the German zoologist Ernst Haeckel.

The extension of Darwin's theories to human society lent an air of scientific legitimisation to the various utopias involving selective breeding which had been propounded from antiquity onwards by . . . Plato, [Thomas] More, and [Tommaso] Campanella. Francis Galton (1822–1911) took the principle of selection further, in the interests of improving the biological health of the *human* race. Healthy parents, by whom he meant members of the middle classes and the learned professions, should be encouraged to marry early and have as many children as possible. These should be issued with certificates of hereditary health. By contrast, those persons who failed this "Passed in Genetics" test were to be encouraged to emigrate to the land of "Cantsayanywhere." Man, in other words, was to take control of his own evolutionary processes. Galton was the founder of hereditary health care, for which in 1883 he coined the term "Eugenics," a programme for improving the human race by genetic means. The prescriptive measures were not confined to the question of "judicious mating," but encompassed education, public health, and welfare. Darwin and Galton's ideas were gradually diffused throughout Europe and North America, where through the mediation of [English philosopher] Herbert Spencer the notion of the "survival of the fittest" was used to legitimise *laissez-faire* capitalism. . . .

These scientific ideas did not unfold in a social void, and nor, as we shall see, were they the exclusive property of professional scientists. The scientists discussed above, and their adherents in applied health care, came from particular social classes, belonged to increasingly ramified professional structures, and lived within societies undergoing profound social and economic change. Specifically, these members of the educated bourgeoisie saw their urban "living space" threatened by hordes of fecund proletarians bearing the physical and psychological imprint of deplorable living and working conditions. Eugenics and racial hygiene were one response to the "social question." While, socialist or otherwise, these responses also undoubtedly reflected genuine concern for suffering humanity, they also mirrored the frustrated modernising arrogance of the educated bourgeoisie towards people apparently impervious to the verities of human betterment and progress, whether espoused by right-wingers or socialists. The debate about the origins and solution of the problem assumed ever narrower forms, while the areas of professional medical competence broadened into schools, prisons, or welfare services. Social Darwinists contributed the identification of low social position with "unfitness," or in other words, the idea that the poor must be "unfit" because they had failed in the "struggle of life." In some circles, concern about differential rates of fertility between the upper and lower social classes was related to the "counter-selective" impact of modern medicine and welfare, a notion which bore the imprint of Darwin as mediated by Galton. Put simply, welfare was obstructing the "natural" elimination of the "unfit." Questions of quality also began to enter the orbit of questions of cost. Long before the health and welfare system faced a financial crisis, some pundits were applying cost:benefit calculations to the "asocial" and "handicapped." For example, in 1911 an essay competition solicited responses to the question: "What do inferior racial elements cost the state and society?" Although eugenicists differed about the comparable merits of "negative" and "positive" measures, the balance of opinion began to tilt towards the former. The North American example, specifically the introduction of a Sterilisation Law in 1907 by the state of Indiana, appeared to lend this questionable practice an air of modern, democratic reasonableness. However, debates in Germany on these questions were overtaken by events. Specifically, the outbreak of the First World War resulted in a renewed emphasis upon population quantity rather than quality. The question of whether or not chronic alcoholics or habitual criminals should be sterilised was hardly the burning issue of 1914–18, when numbers counted. The issue of quality resurfaced in the early 1920s. This was partly because of concern about the perceived "qualitative imbalance" resulting from the war's "mass annihilation of our genetically most valuable elements," partly a reflection of paranoia over the fecundity of neighbouring races. Renewed debate also occurred because interested parties deliberately forced "negative" eugenics on to the political agenda. Specifically, in 1923 the Zwickau District Health Officer, Gerhard Boeters, went public with the information that surgeons in his district were already sterilising the mentally handicapped without legal sanction. Boeters tried to prompt the legislature into retrospective legitimisation through the draft *Lex Zwickau*. Although his draft was rejected by the Reichstag in 1925, the onset of the Depression further reduced the gap between scientific and demographic advocates of "negative" eugenics and those engaged in the making of policy in an austere financial climate. Mass unemployment and a corresponding fall in tax receipts at all levels of government raised questions concerning the allocation of resources. Questions of cost served to lower the ethical threshold of politicians, who were also confronted by the "weight" of professional scientific opinion and the irrefutably gloomy prognostications of their own statisticians and demographic planners. By July 1932, the Prussian government had formulated a draft Reich Sterilisation Law, which it forwarded to the Reich government that winter. By the time it arrived, the Reich government was in the hands of Adolf Hitler. . . .

Did the Third Reich pursue modern rather than profoundly reactionary policies? This question is among the most important posed by recent research. If the Third Reich was a modern and modernising regime, then it can hardly be said to have been the culmination of a German separate road of historical development, but rather is to be compared to other modern regimes, whether Communist, Fascist, or democratic. Questions concerning

whether Hitler or other agencies and individuals were responsible for particular policies pale into insignificance beside the implications of this thesis. If the modernising theory is correct, then not only do the crimes of Nazi Germany cease to be singular, but they become comparable with the crimes of other regimes, or indeed part of the "pathology" of advanced societies in general. Just as the highly dubious Milgram psychological tests apparently "prove" that we are all capable of torture, so the modernisation theorists would like us to believe that all our societies are latently like Nazi Germany. Of course this is not so. Vacuous notions like "body fascism" and the indiscriminately inflationary use of the term "fascist" to describe anyone who happens to disagree with a particular point of view compound this (discomforting) delusion.

Although in our opinion the question of the modern or anti-modern character of the Nazi regime is of central importance, it has received relatively little attention in the existing secondary literature, firstly because there has been no comprehensive treatment of Nazi racial and social policy, and secondly because the inner relationships between the different areas of policy have been neglected. Finally, it is often overlooked that social policy was designed to achieve a global remodelling of society in accordance with racial criteria.

The essential elements of the resulting barbaric utopia had been considered long before Hitler achieved political power. Racial ideologies were not solely concerned with a return to some imagined past social order. They also reflected the desire to create a future society based upon the alleged verities of race. Hitler took over existing ideas and converted them into a comprehensive programme for a racial new order. Without doubt, racial anti-Semitism was the key element in a programme designed to achieve the "recovery" of the "Aryan Germanic race." Various racial-hygienic measures were designed to achieve this goal. These ranged from compulsory sterilisation to murdering the sick, the "asocial," and those designated as being of "alien race." The extermination of the Jews was crucial to these policies. In Hitler's mind they were not only "racial aliens," but also a threat to his plans for the "racial recovery" of the German people. They were both a "lesser race" and one bent upon destroying the "racial properties" of Hitler's "Aryans."

Under the Third Reich, this racial-ideological programme became the official dogma and policy of the State. Racism replaced the Weimar Republic's imperfect experiment in political pluralism. Along with the political parties and trade unions, the Nazis also endeavoured to destroy the existing social structure. Although there were undoubtedly social classes in Nazi Germany, it was a society organised increasingly upon racial rather than class lines. The regime's racial policies struck at people whether they were rich or poor, bourgeois, peasants, or workers.

As we have seen, this racial new order was based upon the "purification of the body of the nation" of all those categorised as being "alien," "hereditarily ill," or "asocial." That meant Jews, Sinti and Roma [Gypsies], the mentally and physically handicapped, "community aliens," and homosexuals. Obviously there were major quantitative and qualitative differences in the degree of persecution to which these groups were subjected. Jews, as the racial group whom the Nazis regarded as the greatest threat, undoubtedly constituted the largest single group of victims and were persecuted in the most intensive and brutal manner. Persecution undoubtedly had different specificities. This should not result in attempts either to relativise or to overlook the sufferings of others, let alone a ghoulish and profoundly inhuman competition to claim the right to having been most persecuted. All of these people were persecuted for the same reasons, although the degree of persecution was bound up with how threatening the regime perceived them to be.

The regime's "national community" was based upon the exclusion and extermination of all those deemed to be "alien," "hereditarily ill," or "asocial." These "elements" were subject to constant and escalating forms of selection. The "national community" itself was categorised in accordance with racial criteria. The criteria included not merely "racial purity" but also biological health and socio-economic performance. Members of the "national community" were also compelled to

reproduce through a series of measures ranging from financial inducements to criminal sanctions. The inducements contained in the regime's social legislation were also conditional upon an individual's racial "value," health, and performance.

For biological reasons, women were particularly affected by the regime's attempts at racial selective breeding. Women's worth was assessed in terms of their ability to produce as many Aryan, healthy, and capable children as possible. Women were therefore reduced to the status of mere "reproductive machines." Racially-motivated anti-feminism represented a significant departure from traditional Christian-Conservative anti-feminism. The Nazis' hierarchically organised, racist society, with healthy, "Aryan" German man at the apex, began to rival the existing social order. However, it failed to supersede it for a variety of reasons. The first is that changes on this scale required longer than twelve years to be realised, a fact which makes any generalisations concerning the impact of the regime on German society difficult. Secondly, there were disagreements within the ruling cartel about the forms, radicalism, and tempo with which a consensually approved racial programme should be implemented. Finally, political and military considerations forced the regime to establish priorities and to postpone some of its plans until the post-war period. In other words, social policy was heavily influenced by military, economic, and domestic-political considerations, not least by the desire to integrate and pacify the population in a wartime crisis.

The main object of social policy remained the creation of a hierarchical racial new order. Everything else was subordinate to this goal, including the regime's conduct of foreign affairs and the war. In the eyes of the regime's racial politicians, the Second World War was above all a racial war, to be pursued with immense brutality until the end, that is until the concentration camps were liberated by invading Allied armies. All of these points draw attention to the specific and singular character of the Third Reich. It was not a form of regression to past times, although the regime frequently instrumentalised various ahistorical myths to convey the idea of historical normalcy. Its objects were novel and *sui generis:* to realise an ideal future world, without "lesser races," without the sick, and without those who they decreed had no place in the "national community." The Third Reich was intended to be a racial rather than a class society. This fact in itself makes existing theories, whether based upon modernisation, totalitarianism, or global theories of Fascism, poor heuristic devices for a greater understanding of what was a singular regime without precedent or parallel.

After reading this selection, consider these questions:

1. What were the origins of "scientific" racial theory?
2. How did racial theories relate to questions of sterilization?
3. According to Burleigh and Wippermann, how should an understanding of racial theory change our interpretation of Nazi Germany?

# SELECTION 5:

# The "Final Solution" of the Jewish Question

*These racial theories had their most drastic consequences in the Nazi policies toward German Jews. Once Hitler came to power, the new regime drove Jews from many aspects of public life and restricted their private and professional lives. In 1935 the Nuremberg Laws deprived Jews of full German citizenship. Their political rights were denied, and they were classified as "subjects" of the new regime. The Nazis continued to harass German Jews. On the night of November 9, 1938, Jewish businesses were destroyed and synagogues burned. Although organized by the government, Kristallnacht (as this event became known, due to the broken glass in the streets) was blamed on the Jews themselves. For incurring the rage of the German people, the argument went, they had to pay for all damages. In this way, money and property were extorted from Jews.*

*With the outbreak of war in 1939 and the German occupation of Poland, a new stage was reached in Nazi policy. There were millions of Polish Jews, and the Germans tried resettlement plans, ghettoization in the larger cities, and then internment in work camps. Finally, with the war definitely going against them, the upper echelons of the leadership evolved a well-coordinated policy of extermination. This policy was worked out at the Wannsee Conference in Berlin. Held on January 20, 1942, the conference was called by Reinhard Heydrich, the second in command of the Schutzstaffel (SS) under Heinrich Himmler, and it included top Nazi bureaucrats from all sections of German-occupied Europe. It is clear from the minutes of the meeting that the Nazis at this time planned to exterminate all European Jews.*

At the beginning of the discussion Chief of the Security Police and of the SD [Sicherheitsdienst, the intelligence branch of the SS], SS-Obergruppenführer [general] Heydrich, reported that the Reich Marshal [Hermann Göring] had appointed him delegate for the preparations for the final solution of the Jewish question in Europe and pointed out that this discussion had been called for the purpose of clarifying fundamental questions. The wish of the Reich Marshal to have a draft sent to him concerning organizational, factual and material interests in relation to the final solution of the Jewish question in Europe makes necessary an initial common action of all central offices immediately concerned with these questions in order to bring their general activities into line.

The Reichsführer-SS and the Chief of the German Police (Chief of the Security Police and the SD) was entrusted with the official central handling of the final solution of the Jewish question without regard to geographic borders.

The Chief of the Security Police and the SD then gave a short report of the struggle which has been carried on thus far against this enemy, the essential points being the following:

a) the expulsion of the Jews from every sphere of life of the German people,

b) the expulsion of the Jews from the living space of the German people.

In carrying out these efforts, an increased and planned acceleration of the emigration of the Jews from Reich territory was started, as the only possible present solution.

By order of the Reich Marshal, a Reich Central Office for Jewish Emigration was set up in January 1939 and the Chief of the Security Police and SD was entrusted with the management. Its most important tasks were

a) to make all necessary arrangements for the preparation for an increased emigration of the Jews,

b) to direct the flow of emigration,

c) to speed the procedure of emigration in each individual case.

The aim of all this was to cleanse German living space of Jews in a legal manner.

All the offices realized the drawbacks of such enforced accelerated emigration. For the time being they had, however, tolerated it on account of the lack of other possible solutions of the problem.

The work concerned with emigration was, later on, not only a German problem, but also a problem with which the authorities of the countries to which the flow of emigrants was being directed would have to deal. Financial difficulties, such as the demand by various foreign governments for increasing sums of money to be presented at the time of the landing, the lack of shipping space, increasing restriction of entry permits, or the cancelling of such, increased extraordinarily the difficulties of emigration. In spite of these difficulties, 537,000 Jews were sent out of the country between the takeover of power and the deadline of 31 October 1941. Of these

• approximately 360,000 were in Germany proper on 30 January 1933

• approximately 147,000 were in Austria (Ostmark) on 15 March 1939

• approximately 30,000 were in the Protectorate of Bohemia and Moravia on 15 March 1939.

The Jews themselves, or their Jewish political organizations, financed the emigration. In order to avoid impoverished Jews' remaining behind, the principle was followed that wealthy Jews have to finance the emigration of poor Jews; this was arranged by imposing a suitable tax, i.e., an emigration tax, which was used for financial arrangements in connection with the emigration of poor Jews and was imposed according to income.

Apart from the necessary Reichsmark exchange, foreign currency had to be presented at the time of landing. In order to save foreign exchange held by Germany, the foreign Jewish financial organizations were—with the help of Jewish organizations in Germany—made responsible for arranging an adequate amount of foreign currency. Up to 30 October 1941, these foreign Jews donated a total of around 9,500,000 dollars.

In the meantime the Reichsführer-SS and Chief

From the minutes of the Wannsee Conference, January 20, 1942, Berlin, Germany.

of the German Police had prohibited emigration of Jews due to the dangers of an emigration in wartime and due to the possibilities of the East.

Another possible solution of the problem has now taken the place of emigration, i.e. the evacuation of the Jews to the East, provided that the Führer gives the appropriate approval in advance.

These actions are, however, only to be considered provisional, but practical experience is already being collected which is of the greatest importance in relation to the future final solution of the Jewish question.

Approximately 11 million Jews will be involved in the final solution of the European Jewish question, distributed as follows among the individual countries:

| Country | Number |
|---|---|
| A. Germany proper | 131,800 |
| Austria | 43,700 |
| Eastern territories | 420,000 |
| General Government (German-occupied Poland) | 2,284,000 |
| Bialystok | 400,000 |
| Protectorate Bohemia and Moravia | 74,200 |
| Estonia      —free of Jews— | |
| Latvia | 3,500 |
| Lithuania | 34,000 |
| Belgium | 43,000 |
| Denmark | 5,600 |
| France / occupied territory | 165,000 |
| unoccupied territory | 700,000 |
| Greece | 69,600 |
| Netherlands | 160,800 |
| Norway | 1,300 |
| B. Bulgaria | 48,000 |
| England | 330,000 |
| Finland | 2,300 |
| Ireland | 4,000 |
| Italy including Sardinia | 58,000 |
| Albania | 200 |
| Croatia | 40,000 |
| Portugal | 3,000 |
| Rumania including Bessarabia | 342,000 |
| Sweden | 8,000 |
| Switzerland | 18,000 |
| Serbia | 10,000 |
| Slovakia | 88,000 |
| Spain | 6,000 |
| Turkey (European portion) | 55,500 |
| Hungary | 742,800 |
| USSR | 5,000,000 |
| Ukraine | 2,994,684 |
| White Russia excluding Bialystok | 446,484 |

Total over 11,000,000

The number of Jews given here for foreign countries includes, however, only those Jews who still adhere to the Jewish faith, since some countries still do not have a definition of the term "Jew" according to racial principles.

The handling of the problem in the individual countries will meet with difficulties due to the attitude and outlook of the people there, especially in Hungary and Rumania. Thus, for example, even today the Jew can buy documents in Rumania that will officially prove his foreign citizenship.

The influence of the Jews in all walks of life in the USSR is well known. Approximately five million Jews live in the European part of the USSR, in the Asian part scarcely 1/4 million.

The breakdown of Jews residing in the European part of the USSR according to trades was approximately as follows:

| | |
|---|---|
| Agriculture | 9.1% |
| Urban workers | 14.8% |
| In trade | 20.0% |
| Employed by the state | 23.4% |
| In private occupations such as medical profession, press, theater, etc. | 32.7% |

Under proper guidance, in the course of the final solution the Jews are to be allocated for appropriate labor in the East. Able-bodied Jews, separated according to sex, will be taken in large work columns to these areas for work on roads, in the course of which action doubtless a large portion will be eliminated by natural causes.

The possible final remnant will, since it will undoubtedly consist of the most resistant portion, have to be treated accordingly, because it is the product of natural selection and would, if released, act as the seed of a new Jewish revival (see the experience of history).

In the course of the practical execution of the final solution, Europe will be combed through from west to east. Germany proper, including the Protectorate of Bohemia and Moravia, will have to be handled first due to the housing problem and additional social and political necessities.

The evacuated Jews will first be sent, group by group, to so-called transit ghettos, from which they will be transported to the East.

SS-Obergruppenführer Heydrich went on to say that an important prerequisite for the evacuation as such is the exact definition of the persons involved.

It is not intended to evacuate Jews over 65 years old, but to send them to an old-age ghetto—Theresienstadt is being considered for this purpose.

In addition to these age groups—of the approximately 280,000 Jews in Germany proper and Austria on 31 October 1941, approximately 30% are over 65 years old—severely wounded veterans and Jews with war decorations (Iron Cross I) will be accepted in the old-age ghettos. With this expedient solution, in one fell swoop many interventions will be prevented.

The beginning of the individual larger evacuation actions will largely depend on military developments. Regarding the handling of the final solution in those European countries occupied and influenced by us, it was proposed that the appropriate expert of the Foreign Office discuss the matter with the responsible official of the Security Police and SD.

In Slovakia and Croatia the matter is no longer so difficult, since the most substantial problems in this respect have already been brought near a solution. In Rumania the government has in the meantime also appointed a commissioner for Jewish affairs. In order to settle the question in Hungary, it will soon be necessary to force an adviser for Jewish questions onto the Hungarian government.

With regard to taking up preparations for dealing with the problem in Italy, SS-Obergruppenführer Heydrich considers it opportune to contact the chief of police with a view to these problems.

In occupied and unoccupied France, the registration of Jews for evacuation will in all probability proceed without great difficulty.

Under Secretary of State [Martin] Luther calls attention in this matter to the fact that in some countries, such as the Scandinavian states, difficulties will arise if this problem is dealt with thoroughly and that it will therefore be advisable to defer actions in these countries. Besides, in view of the small numbers of Jews affected, this deferral will not cause any substantial limitation.

The Foreign Office sees no great difficulties for southeast and western Europe.

SS-Gruppenführer [Lieutenant General Otto] Hofmann plans to send an expert to Hungary from the Race and Settlement Main Office for general orientation at the time when the Chief of the Security Police and SD takes up the matter there. It was decided to assign this expert from the Race and Settlement Main Office, who will not work actively, as an assistant to the police attaché.

In the course of the final solution plans, the Nuremberg Laws should provide a certain foundation, in which a prerequisite for the absolute solution of the problem is also the solution to the problem of mixed marriages and persons of mixed blood.

The Chief of the Security Police and the SD discusses the following points, at first theoretically, in regard to a letter from the chief of the Reich chancellery:

1) *Treatment of Persons of Mixed Blood of the First Degree.* Persons of mixed blood of the first degree will, as regards the final solution of the Jewish question, be treated as Jews.

From this treatment the following exceptions will be made:

a) Persons of mixed blood of the first degree married to persons of German blood if their marriage has resulted in children (persons of mixed blood of the second degree). These persons of mixed blood of the second degree are to be treated essentially as Germans.

b) Persons of mixed blood of the first degree, for whom the highest offices of the Party and State have already issued exemption permits in any sphere of life. Each individual case must be examined, and it is not ruled out that the decision may be made to the detriment of the person of mixed blood.

The prerequisite for any exemption must always be the personal merit of the person of mixed blood. (Not the merit of the parent or spouse of German blood.)

Persons of mixed blood of the first degree who are exempted from evacuation will be sterilized in order to prevent any offspring and to eliminate the problem of persons of mixed blood once and for all. Such sterilization will be voluntary. But it is required to remain in the Reich. The sterilized "person of mixed blood" is thereafter free of all restrictions to which he was previously subjected.

*2) Treatment of Persons of Mixed Blood of the Second Degree.* Persons of mixed blood of the second degree will be treated fundamentally as persons of German blood, with the exception of the following cases, in which the persons of mixed blood of the second degree will be considered as Jews:

a) The person of mixed blood of the second degree was born of a marriage in which both parents are persons of mixed blood.

b) The person of mixed blood of the second degree has a racially especially undesirable appearance that marks him outwardly as a Jew.

c) The person of mixed blood of the second degree has a particularly bad police and political record that shows that he feels and behaves like a Jew.

Also in these cases exemptions should not be made if the person of mixed blood of the second degree has married a person of German blood.

*3) Marriages Between Full Jews and Persons of German Blood.* Here it must be decided from case to case whether the Jewish partner will be evacuated or whether, with regard to the effects of such a step on the German relatives, [this mixed marriage] should be sent to an old-age ghetto.

*4) Marriages Between Persons of Mixed Blood of the First Degree and Persons of German Blood.*

a) Without Children.
If no children have resulted from the marriage, the person of mixed blood of the first

degree will be evacuated or sent to an old-age ghetto (same treatment as in the case of marriages between full Jews and persons of German blood, point 3.)

b) With Children.
If children have resulted from the marriage (persons of mixed blood of the second degree), they will, if they are to be treated as Jews, be evacuated or sent to a ghetto along with the parent of mixed blood of the first degree. If these children are to be treated as Germans (regular cases), they are exempted from evacuation as is therefore the parent of mixed blood of the first degree.

*5) Marriages Between Persons of Mixed Blood of the First Degree and Persons of Mixed Blood of the First Degree or Jews.* In these marriages (including the children) all members of the family will be treated as Jews and therefore be evacuated or sent to an old-age ghetto.

*6) Marriages Between Persons of Mixed Blood of the First Degree and Persons of Mixed Blood of the Second Degree.* In these marriages both partners will be evacuated or sent to an old-age ghetto without consideration of whether the marriage has produced children, since possible children will as a rule have stronger Jewish blood than the Jewish person of mixed blood of the second degree.

SS-Gruppenführer Hofmann advocates the opinion that sterilization will have to be widely used, since the person of mixed blood who is given the choice whether he will be evacuated or sterilized would rather undergo sterilization.

State Secretary Dr. [Wilhelm] Stückart maintains that carrying out in practice of the just mentioned possibilities for solving the problem of mixed marriages and persons of mixed blood will create endless administrative work. In the second place, as the biological facts cannot be disregarded in any case, State Secretary Dr. Stückart proposed proceeding to forced sterilization.

Furthermore, to simplify the problem of mixed marriages possibilities must be considered with the goal of the legislator saying something like: "These marriages have been dissolved."

With regard to the issue of the effect of the evacuation of Jews on the economy, State Secretary [Erich] Neumann stated that Jews who are working in industries vital to the war effort, provided that no replacements are available, cannot be evacuated.

SS-Obergruppenführer Heydrich indicated that these Jews would not be evacuated according to the rules he had approved for carrying out the evacuations then underway.

State Secretary Dr. [Joseph] Bühler stated that the General Government would welcome it if the final solution of this problem could be begun in the General Government, since on the one hand transportation does not play such a large role here nor would problems of labor supply hamper this action. Jews must be removed from the territory of the General Government as quickly as possible, since it is especially here that the Jew as an epidemic carrier represents an extreme danger and on the other hand he is causing permanent chaos in the economic structure of the country through continued black market dealings. Moreover, of the approximately 2½ million Jews concerned, the majority is unfit for work.

State Secretary Dr. Bühler stated further that the solution to the Jewish question in the General Government is the responsibility of the Chief of the Security Police and the SD and that his ef-

forts would be supported by the officials of the General Government. He had only one request, to solve the Jewish question in this area as quickly as possible.

In conclusion the different types of possible solutions were discussed, during which discussion both Gauleiter [Nazi Party Area Leader Alfred] Dr. Meyer and State Secretary Dr. Bühler took the position that certain preparatory activities for the final solution should be carried out immediately in the territories in question, in which process alarming the populace must be avoided.

The meeting was closed with the request of the Chief of the Security Police and the SD to the participants that they afford him appropriate support during the carrying out of the tasks involved in the solution.

After reading this selection, consider these questions:
1. What was the purpose of the Wannsee Conference?
2. What was to be done with the Jews in Germany and occupied Europe?
3. How did the Nazis define degrees of Jewishness?

# CHAPTER 13
## From the Russian Revolution to the Fall of the Soviet Union

<p>

**O**f equal and perhaps of more long-lasting significance than the consequences of World War I on Germany was the Bolshevik Revolution in Russia and the establishment of the Soviet Union. Without Russia's participation in World War I, there would not have been a revolution and thus no creation of a major Communist state. And without World War II, it is questionable whether the Soviet Union would have been able to reconstitute a rather economically and socially backward Russia into one of the world's two great powers in the half-century after World War II.

World War I thus set in motion a number of unforeseen occurrences that would have been impossible, even inconceivable, without the war. Had the war not occurred, there would have been no chance for a tiny group (the Bolsheviks) within the rather small Social Democratic Party of Russia to take over and give direction to a successful revolution against the Russian imperial government. Yet this was exactly what happened. This is not to say that the revolution was entirely a result of Russia's losses in the war. The roots of the Russian Revolution of 1917 ran deep. Protests against the authoritarian czarist government and its economic policies occurred throughout the last decades of the nineteenth century. As a result of a revolution in 1905, Czar Nicholas II had accepted a plan for establishing a national assembly, the Duma. But even with this superficially liberal move, the czar and his bureaucracy continued to dominate both domestic and foreign policy. The failure to bring about real reforms eroded support for the regime across a wide range of politically active individuals and groups.

Even with growing political unrest at home, it still was the disastrous ways in which the czar's government handled World War I that brought on the revolution of 1917. Russia's industrial and economic backwardness resulted in poorly armed and ill-supplied armies. Germany's much smaller forces easily defeated the armies the czar sent against them, resulting in devastating Russian casualties. As the front collapsed, the situation within Russia itself reached a crisis state. Unable to exchange their produce for consumer goods, peasants withheld crops from the market, causing the price of food in the cities to rise nearly 800 percent. In February 1917 (March by the old Russian calendar) crowds of working women in Petrograd (St. Petersburg) turned an International Woman's Day march into a demonstration against the government. The women demanded economic relief. They looted shops in search of food and called on the soldiers guarding the capital to join them. The result was general rioting, which then spread among the soldiers at the front, causing the collapse of the army.

Realizing that the situation was hopeless, Nicholas II abdicated. The leaders of the Duma immediately set up a provisional government under generally liberal auspices. Even with the overthrow of the czar and the formation of a new government in 1917, rioting continued. Protests mounted as workers, women, students, liberal politicians, and soldiers made demands on the new government. In the face of these challenges, the provisional government sought to establish its credibility by granting a general amnesty, proposing a new constitution, and improving economic conditions. They did not, however, promise the much-needed redistribution of land and initially said nothing about the continuation of the war. The decision to continue the war ultimately proved disastrous for the new regime. By not remaining faithful to its prewar alliances and its commitment to the war effort, the head of the new government, Alexander Kerensky, feared that Russia would lose all international credibility. With this decision, as well as with the impossibility of immediately changing the harsh economic conditions or meeting the growing expectations of so many protesting groups, the provisional government found itself in a very precarious position by the last months of 1917.

Actual power soon devolved to the soviets—that is, the spontaneously elected councils of workers and soldiers. Soviets had originally been formed during the revolution of 1905 and sprang up almost immediately again in 1917. The meetings of the numerous soviets were lively, giving members of the lower classes opportunities to express their demands and hopes. Thus, the soviets presented a sharp contrast to what appeared to be the aimless and ineffectual debates by the middle-class members of the Duma. In November 1917 (October by the old calendar), a Bolshevik-led coup d'état in Petrograd deposed the provisional government and purportedly turned over all power to the soviets. Actually, the Bolsheviks took control in Petrograd, Moscow, and other cities, and a cabinet (the Council of People's Commissars) was set up with Vladimir Lenin as chairman. This gave Lenin virtually dictatorial power. Workers' control was established in factories, banks were nationalized, and an economic council was founded. The Cheka (political police) was created to eliminate all opposition. The Bolshevik takeover was thus achieved. After a bitter civil war, Bolshevik rule was consolidated in Russia and the neighboring Soviet republics, which in 1924 united to form the Soviet Union.

In 1941 Nazi Germany invaded the Soviet Union. Despite widespread personal suffering, gruesome material devastation, and massive loss of life (up to 25 million), the Soviet Union retained its formidable military power after its victory in 1945, extending its hegemony over all of east Central Europe. The end of World War II and the victory of the Allies did not bring about the more peaceful world for which so many had hoped. Rather, ideological differences, submerged for the purposes of the war effort, quickly resurfaced to reassert themselves in a variety of forms. The United States, whose territories had remained virtually untouched by the war, emerged after World War II as the preeminent military power and the unchallenged master of the world's economy. It and the Soviet Union became locked in an all-out struggle for domination that was to last for nearly half a century. Originally, the confrontation emerged over elections in Poland, the civil war in Greece, and the survival of divided Berlin within a divided Germany. But the conflict soon spread to the entirety of Eastern Europe as the Soviet Union consolidated its hegemony; then, it moved to Western Europe as these countries realized their need for U.S. aid to rebuild their postwar economies. By the 1950s the contest became global, encompassing Asia, Africa, and Latin America. Although limited armed conflicts occurred in a number of places, this Cold War, as it was called by the late 1940s, was primarily fought out diplomatically, ideologically, and through economic aid packages to foreign states deemed strategically important. Within this tense situation, which divided much of the globe between the two superpowers, the threat of another total world war was always close at hand.

Although a world power in the postwar years, the Soviet Union continued to experience economic difficulties. After 1929 the economy was forced into rapid industrialization under Joseph Stalin (1879–1953). To compete with other nations both militarily and economically, Stalin intensified rapid development through a series of economic plans, which emphasized heavy industry. World War II demanded even more intensified economic development. After the war, Stalin decided not to curtail further intensified industrialization or to direct it to the manufacture of consumer goods. The Cold War continued to make heavy industry and the production of armaments paramount: Between 15 and 20 percent of the gross national product continued to pour into the armaments industries. By the 1980s, however, the Soviet economy was in decline. Years of stagnation and negative growth finally resulted in a deteriorating standard of living for most Soviet citizens.

By the mid-1980s, a new leadership took control of the Soviet Union. In 1985 Mikhail Gorbachev launched a program of reinvigorating the economy. Called perestroika (restructuring), it aimed at streamlining production and management and introducing free-floating prices and the profit motive. Along with perestroika, Gorbachev introduced a policy of glasnost (openness), by which he meant truth in the way the government spoke to the people and the freedom of people to speak themselves. Throughout the Soviet Union, however, perestroika failed to revitalize the economy and, in fact, had disastrous consequences. Prices soared, causing an even greater scarcity of goods than before. Satellite states that were resentful of Soviet domination took advantage of the reorganization of the Soviet government and the lessening of tensions between the Soviet Union and the United States. In 1989 Poland, Hungary, and Czechoslovakia held free elections and effectively ended Soviet domination. In the spring of 1990, the Eastern European freedom movement spread to the republics of the Soviet Union itself. They demanded the end of centralized economic control and the freedom to develop their own economies. To stave off further disintegration, in the autumn of 1990 Gorbachev proclaimed the end of the socialist economy. The state would sell off property, gradually end price controls, allow collective farmers to decide their own fate, and devalue the ruble in accordance with its price in the world currency markets.

But all of this came too late. Lithuania—a state that had been incorporated into the Soviet Union in 1940—declared its independence. While Gorbachev was willing to give up Soviet rule over Eastern Europe, he could not allow the breakup of the Soviet Union itself. He placed an immediate embargo on all essential imports to Lithuania. This move failed, too. Pressure from the republics for more freedom increased to such a degree that the Soviet Union as an association of soviet republics was officially dissolved on January 1, 1992. Even before this date, eleven of the fifteen former republics had banded together in a Commonwealth of Independent States on December 8, 1991.

# SELECTION 1:

# The Bolsheviks Take Control

*An associate of Vladimir Lenin and the future organizer of the Red Army, Leon Trotsky (1879–1940) wrote the best-known history of the Russian Revolution. Penned after Joseph Stalin had forced him into exile, this account is full of the vitality and partisan politics that dominated the early years of the revolution. The following selection picks up the story of the October Revolution from Lenin's return to Petrograd and his first speeches before the Petrograd Bolsheviks.*

On April 4, Lenin appeared at the party conference. His speech, developing his "theses," passed over the work of the conference like the wet sponge of a teacher erasing what had been written on the blackboard by a confused pupil.

"Why didn't you seize the power?" asked Lenin. At the Soviet conference not long before that, Steklov[1] had confusedly explained the reasons for abstaining from the power: the revolution is bourgeois—it is the first stage—the war, etc. "That's nonsense," Lenin said. "The reason is that the proletariat was not sufficiently conscious and not sufficiently organized. That we have to acknowledge. The material force was in the hands of the proletariat, but the bourgeoisie was conscious and ready. That is the monstrous fact. But it is necessary to acknowledge it frankly, and say to the people straight out that we did not seize the power because we were unorganized and not conscious."

From the plane of pseudo-objectivism, behind which the political capitulators were hiding, Lenin shifted the whole question to the subjective plane. The proletariat did not seize the power in February because the Bolshevik Party was not equal to its objective task, and could not prevent the Compromisers from expropriating the popular masses politically for the benefit of the bourgeoisie.

The day before that, lawyer Krassikov had said challengingly: "If we think that the time has now come to realize the dictatorship of the proletariat, then we ought to pose the question that way. We unquestionably have the physical force for a seizure of power." The chairman at that time deprived Krassikov of the floor on the ground that practical problems were under discussion, and the question of dictatorship was out of order. But Lenin thought that, as the sole practical question, the question of preparing the dictatorship of the proletariat was exactly in order. "The peculiarity of the present moment in Russia," he said in his theses, "consists in the transition from the first stage of the revolution, which gave the power to the bourgeoisie on account of the inadequate consciousness and organization of the proletariat, to its second stage which must give the power to the proletariat and the poor layers of the peasantry." The conference, following the lead of *Pravda* [the official paper of the Bolshevik Party], had limited the task of the revolution to a democratic transformation to be realized through the Constituent Assembly. As against this, Lenin declared that "life and the revolution will push the Constituent Assembly into the background. A dictatorship of the proletariat exists, but nobody knows what to do with it."

The delegates exchanged glances. They whispered to each other that Ilych [Lenin] had stayed too long abroad, had not had time to look around and familiarize himself with things. But the speech of Stalin on the ingenious division of labor between the government and the Soviet, sank out of sight once and forever. Stalin himself remained silent. From now on he will have to be silent for a long time. [Russian Communist leader Lev] Kamenev alone will man the defenses.

Lenin had already given warning in letters from Geneva that he was ready to break with anybody who made concessions on the question of war, chauvinism and compromise with the bourgeoisie. Now, face to face with the leading circles of the party, he opens an attack all along the line. But at the beginning he does not name a single Bolshevik by name. If he has need of a living model of equivocation and half-wayness, he points his finger at the non-party men, or at Steklov or [Menshevik Party leader Nikolai Semenovich] Cheidze. That was the customary method of Lenin: not to nail anybody down to his position too soon, to give the prudent a chance to withdraw from the battle in good season and thus weaken at once the future ranks of his open enemies. Kamenev and Stalin had thought that in participating in the war after February, the soldiers and workers were defending the revolution. Lenin thinks that, as before, the soldier and the worker take part in the war as the conscripted slaves of capital. "Even our Bolsheviks," he says,

---

1. A non-party socialist in the Petrograd soviet who urged a policy of including liberals in the provisional government.

From *The History of the Russian Revolution*, by Leon Trotsky, translated by Max Eastman (New York: Simon & Schuster, 1932).

narrowing the circle around his antagonists, "show confidence in the government. Only the fumes of the revolution can explain that. That is the death of socialism. . . . If that's your position, our ways part. I prefer to remain in the minority." That was not a mere oratorical threat; it was a clear path thought through to the end.

Although naming neither Kamenev nor Stalin, Lenin was obliged to name the paper: *"Pravda* demands of the government that it renounce annexation. To demand from the government of the capitalists that it renounce annexation is nonsense, flagrant mockery." Restrained indignation here breaks out with a high note. But the orator immediately takes himself in hand: he wants to say no less than is necessary, but also no more. Incidentally and in passing, Lenin gives incomparable rules for revolutionary statesmanship: "When the masses announce that they do not want conquests, I believe them. When Guchkov[2] and Lvov[3] say they do not want conquests, they are deceivers! When a worker says that he wants the defense of the country, what speaks in him is the instinct of the oppressed." This criterion, to call it by its right name, seems simple as life itself. But the difficulty is to call it by its right name in time.

On the question of the appeal of the Soviet "to the people of the whole world"—which caused the liberal paper *Rech* at one time to declare that the theme of pacifism is developing among us into an ideology common to the Allies—Lenin expressed himself more clearly and succinctly: "What is peculiar to Russia is the gigantically swift transition from wild violence to the most delicate deceit."

"This appeal," wrote Stalin concerning the manifesto, "if it reaches the broad masses (of the West), will undoubtedly recall hundreds and thousands of workers to the forgotten slogan 'Proletarians of all Countries Unite!'"

"The appeal of the Soviet," objects Lenin, "— there isn't a word in it imbued with class consciousness. There is nothing to it but phrases."

This document, the pride of the homegrown Zimmerwaldists,[4] is in Lenin's eyes merely one of the weapons of "the most delicate deceit."

Up to Lenin's arrival *Pravda* had never even mentioned the Zimmerwald left. Speaking of the International,[5] it never indicated which International. Lenin called this "the Kautskyanism[6] of *Pravda.*" "In Zimmerwald and Kienthal,"[7] he declared at a party conference, "the Centrists predominated. . . . We declare that we created a left and broke with the center. . . . The left Zimmerwald tendency exists in all the countries of the world. The masses ought to realize that socialism has split throughout the world. . . ."

Three days before that Stalin had announced at that same conference his readiness to live down differences with [Menshevik leader Iraklii Georgevich] Tseretelli on the basis of Zimmerwald-Kienthal—that is, on the basis of Kautskyanism. "I hear that in Russia there is a trend toward consolidation," said Lenin. "Consolidation with the defensists—that is betrayal of socialism. I think it would be better to stand alone like [German Social Democrat Karl] Liebknecht—one against a hundred and ten." The accusation of betrayal of socialism—for the present still without naming names—is not here merely a strong word; it fully expresses the attitude of Lenin toward those Bolsheviks who were extending a finger to the social patriots. In opposition to Stalin who thought it was possible to unite with the Mensheviks, Lenin thought it was unpermissible to share with them any longer the name of Social Democrat. "Personally and speaking for myself alone," he said, "I propose that we change the name of the party, that we call it the Communist Party." "Personally and speaking for myself alone"—that means that nobody, not one of the members of the conference, agreed to that symbolic gesture of ultimate break with the Second International.

"You are afraid to go back on your old memories?" says the orator to the embarrassed, bewildered and partly indignant delegates. But the

---

2. Aleksandr Ivanovich Guchkov was Chairman of the Duma under the Czar and first Minister of War and Navy under the provisional government.   3. Prince Georgii Evgen'evich L'vov formed the Provisional Government after the February Revolution of 1917.

4. Socialists loyal to the principles of internationalism during World War I.   5. The International Socialist Party, of which Karl Marx was a founding member; also the meeting of the party.   6. Karl Kantsky was a major theorist of Marxism after Marx who urged peaceful evolution towards a state of Communism.   7. Swiss sites of conferences

time has come "to change our linen; we've got to take off the dirty shirt and put on clean." And he again insists: "Don't hang on to an old word which is rotten through and through. Have the will to build a new party . . . and all the oppressed will come to you."

Before the enormity of the task not yet begun,

and the intellectual confusion in his own ranks, a sharp thought of the precious time foolishly wasted in meetings, greetings, ritual resolutions, wrests a cry from the orator: "Have done with greetings and resolutions! It's time to get down to business. We must proceed to practical sober work!"

# SELECTION 2:

# The Bolshevik "Program"

*The founder and leader of Bolshevism was Vladimir Ilich Ulyanov, who took the name Lenin (1870–1924). The son of a teacher and educational official, Lenin became a revolutionary after the czarist government executed his brother. He spent several years in exile in Siberia and then wandering outside of Russia. While in exile, he became the leader of the left wing of the Russian Social Democratic Workers' Party and called for an independent socialist party that would maintain a clearly revolutionary program. This call eventually led to the split of the Social Democratic Workers' Party between the Bolshevik (majority) faction and the more moderate Menshevik (minority) one. The Bolsheviks were only temporarily in the majority at the party congress where the split occurred. In fact, the Mensheviks represented a majority within the Russian social democratic movement. After the revolution, the Bolsheviks renamed themselves the Communist Party. In 1899 Lenin wrote "Our Program" to define his position. In it, he clearly states that he was opposed to all forms of socialism that called for policies of gradual reform and were disinclined to put revolutionary activities first.*

International Social-Democracy is at present in a state of ideological wavering. Hitherto the doctrines of Marx and Engels were considered to be the firm foundation of revolutionary theory, but voices are now being raised everywhere to proclaim these doctrines inadequate and obsolete. Whoever declares himself to be a Social-Democrat and intends to publish a Social-Democratic organ

must define precisely his attitude to a question that is preoccupying the attention of the German Social-Democrats and not of them alone.

We take our stand entirely on the Marxist theoretical position: Marxism was the first to transform socialism from a utopia into a science, to lay a firm foundation for this science, and to indicate the path that must be followed in further developing and elaborating it in all its parts. It disclosed the nature of modern capitalist economy by explaining how the hire of the labourer, the purchase of labour-power, conceals the enslavement of millions of propertyless people by a

From *Collected Works*, by V.I. Lenin, vol. 4 (Moscow: Foreign Languages Publishing House, 1960).

handful of capitalists, the owners of the land, factories, mines, and so forth. It showed that all modern capitalist development displays the tendency of large-scale production to eliminate petty production and creates conditions that make a socialist system of society possible and necessary. It taught us how to discern, beneath the pall of rooted customs, political intrigues, abstruse laws, and intricate doctrines—the *class struggle*, the struggle between the propertied classes in all their variety and the propertyless mass, the *proletariat*, which is at the head of all the propertyless. It made clear the real task of a revolutionary socialist party: not to draw up plans for refashioning society, not to preach to the capitalists and their hangers-on about improving the lot of the workers, not to hatch conspiracies, *but to organise the class struggle of the proletariat and to lead this struggle, the ultimate aim of which is the conquest of political power by the proletariat and the organisation of a socialist society.*

And we now ask: Has anything new been introduced into this theory by its loud-voiced "renovators" who are raising so much noise in our day and have grouped themselves around the German socialist [Eduard] Bernstein? *Absolutely nothing.* Not by a single step have they advanced the science which Marx and Engels enjoined us to develop; they have not taught the proletariat any new methods of struggle; they have only retreated, borrowing fragments of backward theories and preaching to the proletariat, not the theory of struggle, but the theory of concession—concession to the most vicious enemies of the proletariat, the governments and bourgeois parties who never tire of seeking new means of baiting the socialists. [Georgy] Plekhanov, one of the founders and leaders of Russian Social-Democracy, was entirely right in ruthlessly criticising Bernstein's latest "critique"; the views of Bernstein have now been rejected by the representatives of the German workers as well (at the Hannover Congress).

We anticipate a flood of accusations for these words; the shouts will rise that we want to convert the socialist party into an order of "true believers" that persecutes "heretics" for deviations from "dogma," for every independent opinion, and so forth. We know about all these fashionable and trenchant phrases. Only there is not a grain of truth or sense in them. There can be no strong socialist party without a revolutionary theory which unites all socialists, from which they draw all their convictions, and which they apply in their methods of struggle and means of action. To defend such a theory, which to the best of your knowledge you consider to be true, against unfounded attacks and attempts to corrupt it is not to imply that you are an enemy of *all* criticism. We do not regard Marx's theory as something completed and inviolable; on the contrary, we are convinced that it has only laid the foundation stone of the science which socialists *must* develop in all directions if they wish to keep pace with life. We think that an *independent* elaboration of Marx's theory is especially essential for Russian socialists; for this theory provides only general *guiding* principles, which, *in particular,* are applied in England differently than in France, in France differently than in Germany, and in Germany differently than in Russia. We shall therefore gladly afford space in our paper for articles on theoretical questions and we invite all comrades openly to discuss controversial points.

What are the main questions that arise in the application to Russia of the programme common to all Social-Democrats? We have stated that the essence of this programme is to organise the class struggle of the proletariat and to lead this struggle, the ultimate aim of which is the conquest of political power by the proletariat and the establishment of a socialist society. The class struggle of the proletariat comprises the economic struggle (struggle against individual capitalists or against individual groups of capitalists for the improvement of the workers' condition) and the political struggle (struggle against the government for the broadening of the people's rights, i.e., for democracy, and for the broadening of the political power of the proletariat). Some Russian Social-Democrats . . . regard the economic struggle as incomparably the more important and almost go so far as to relegate the political struggle to the more or less distant future. This standpoint is utterly false. All Social-Democrats are agreed that it is necessary to organise the economic struggle of the working class, that it is necessary to carry on agitation among the workers on this basis, i.e., to help the workers in their day-to-day struggle against the employers, to draw their attention to every form and every case of oppression and in this way to make clear to them the necessity for combination. But to forget the political struggle for the economic would mean to depart from the basic principle of international Social-Democracy, it would mean to forget what the entire history of the labour movement teaches us. The confirmed adherents of the bourgeoisie and of the government which serves it have even made repeated attempts to organise purely economic unions of workers and to divert them in this way from "politics," from socialism. It is quite possible that the Russian Government, too, may undertake something of the kind, is it has always endeavoured to throw some paltry sops or, rather, sham sops, to the people, only to turn their thoughts away from the fact that they are oppressed and without rights. No economic struggle can bring the workers any lasting improvement, or can even be conducted on a large scale, unless the workers have the right freely to organise meetings and unions, to have their own newspapers, and to send their representatives to the national assemblies, as do the workers in Germany and all other European countries (with the exception of Turkey and Russia). But in order to win these rights it is necessary to wage a *political struggle.* In Russia, not only the workers, but all citizens are deprived of political rights. Russia is an absolute and unlimited monarchy. The tsar alone promulgates laws, appoints officials and controls them. For this reason, *it seems* as though in Russia the tsar and the tsarist government are independent of all classes and accord equal treatment to all. But *in reality* all officials are chosen exclusively from the propertied class and all are subject to the influence of the big capitalists, who make the ministers dance to their tune and who achieve whatever they want. The Russian working class is burdened by a double yoke; it is robbed and plundered by the capitalists and the landlords, and to prevent it from fighting them, the police bind it hand and foot, gag it, and every attempt to defend the rights of the people is persecuted. Every strike against a capitalist results in the military and police being let loose on the workers. Every economic struggle necessarily becomes a political struggle, and Social-Democracy must indissolubly combine the one with the other into a *single class struggle of the proletariat.*

After reading this selection and the previous one, consider these questions:

1. How did Lenin define the Bolshevik "program"?
2. What, according to Trotsky, were Lenin's strengths as a leader?
3. What political action did Lenin call for in the autumn of 1917?

## SELECTION 3:

# How Did the Bolsheviks Take Over the Revolution?

*The American historian Alexander Rabinowitch concludes his study of the revolution,* The Bolsheviks Come to Power *(1972), with an evaluation of the reasons the Bolsheviks succeeded in taking over the government in 1917. He begins by comparing the Bolsheviks to the Kadets (members of the liberal Constitutional Democratic Party and supporters of the provisional government) and the other socialist parties. The Kornilov affair, which Rabinowitch mentions, was a failed attempt to end Bolshevik influence. It backfired and only increased the power of the Bolsheviks.*

The central question of why the Bolsheviks won the struggle for power in Petrograd in 1917 permits no simple answer. To be sure, from the perspective of more than half a century, it is clear that the fundamental weakness of the Kadets and moderate socialists during the revolutionary period and the concomitant vitality and influence of the radical left at that time can be traced to the peculiarities of Russia's political, social, and economic development during the nineteenth century and earlier. The world war also inevitably had a good deal to do with the way the 1917 revolution in Petrograd turned out. Had it not been for the Provisional Government's commitment to pursue the war to victory, a policy which in 1917 enjoyed no broad support, it surely would have been better able to cope with the myriad problems that inevitably attended the collapse of the old order and, in particular, to satisfy popular demands for immediate fundamental reform.

As it was, a major source of the Bolsheviks' growing strength and authority in 1917 was the magnetic attraction of the party's platform as embodied in the slogans "Peace, Land, and Bread" and "All Power to the Soviets." The Bolsheviks conducted an extraordinarily energetic and resourceful campaign for the support of Petrograd factory workers and soldiers and Kronstadt sailors. Among these groups, the slogan "All Power to the Soviets" signified the creation of a democratic, exclusively socialist government, representing all parties and groups in the Soviet and committed to a program of immediate peace, meaningful internal reform, and the early convocation of a Constituent Assembly. In the late spring and summer of 1917, a number of factors served to increase support for the professed goals of the Bolsheviks, especially for transfer of

power to the soviets. Economic conditions steadily worsened. Garrison soldiers became directly threatened by shipment to the front. Popular expectations of early peace and reform under the Provisional Government dwindled. Concomitantly, all other major political groups lost credibility because of their association with the government and their insistence on patience and sacrifice in the interest of the war effort. . . .

That in the space of eight months the Bolsheviks reached a position from which they were able to assume power was due as well to the special effort which the party devoted to winning the support of military troops in the rear and at the front; only the Bolsheviks seem to have perceived the necessarily crucial significance of the armed forces in the struggle for power. Perhaps even more fundamentally, the phenomenal Bolshevik success can be attributed in no small measure to the nature of the party in 1917. Here I have in mind neither Lenin's bold and determined leadership, the immense historical significance of which cannot be denied, nor the Bolsheviks' proverbial, though vastly exaggerated, organizational unity and discipline. Rather, I would emphasize the party's internally relatively democratic, tolerant, and decentralized structure and method of operation, as well as its essentially open and mass character—in striking contrast to the traditional Leninist model.

As we have seen, within the Bolshevik Petrograd organization at all levels in 1917 there was continuing free and lively discussion and debate over the most basic theoretical and tactical issues. Leaders who differed with the majority were at liberty to fight for their views, and not infrequently Lenin was the loser in these struggles. To gauge the importance of this tolerance of differences of opinion and ongoing give-and-take, it is enough to recall that throughout 1917 many of the Bolsheviks' most important resolutions and public statements were influenced as much by the outlook of right Bolsheviks as by that of

From *The Bolsheviks Come to Power: The Revolution of 1917 in Petrograd*, by Alexander Rabinowitch (New York: Norton, 1976). Reprinted by permission of the author.

Lenin. In addition, moderate Bolsheviks . . . were among the party's most articulate and respected spokesmen in key public institutions such as the soviets and the trade unions. . . .

The importance to the Bolshevik success of the dynamic relationship that existed in 1917 within the top Bolshevik hierarchy, as well as between it, the ostensibly subordinate elements of the party, and the masses, was illustrated immediately after the July uprising. At the time, Lenin believed that the Provisional Government was effectively controlled by counterrevolutionary elements; overestimating the government's capacity to damage the left, he was convinced, moreover, that under the influence of the Mensheviks and SRs [a peasant Socialist Party] the existing soviets had been rendered powerless. Hence he demanded that the party abandon its orientation toward a possible peaceful transfer of power to the soviets and shift its attention toward preparations for an armed uprising at the earliest opportunity. Other leaders, many of whom had particularly close ties with workers and soldiers and were also active in the Central Executive Committee and the Petrograd Soviet, refused to discount completely the Mensheviks and SRs as potential allies and the soviets as legitimate revolutionary institutions. While the slogan "All Power to the Soviets" was officially withdrawn by the Sixth Congress in late July, this change did not take hold at the local level. Moreover, the congress did not deemphasize efforts to win the soviets, and they continued to be a major focus of party activity throughout the month of August.

As it turned out, the impact of the post-July days reaction against the left was not nearly as serious as originally feared. To the contrary, the repressive measures adopted by the government, as well as the indiscriminate persecution of leftist leaders and the apparently increasing danger of counterrevolution, served simply to increase resentment toward the [Aleksandr] Kerensky regime among the masses and stimulated them to unite more closely around the soviets in defense of the revolution. . . .

Probably the clearest example of the importance and value of the party's relatively free and flexible structure, and the responsiveness of its

tactics to the prevailing mass mood, came during the second half of September, when party leaders in Petrograd turned a deaf ear to the ill-timed appeals of Lenin, then still in hiding in Finland, for an immediate insurrection. To be sure, on October 10 the Bolshevik Central Committee, with Lenin in attendance, made the organization of an armed insurrection and the seizure of power "the order of the day." Yet in the ensuing days there was mounting evidence that an uprising launched independently of the soviets and in advance of the Second Congress of Soviets would not be supported by the Petrograd masses; that the seizure of power by the Bolsheviks alone would be opposed by all other major political parties, by peasants in the provinces and soldiers at the front, and possibly even by such mass democratic institutions as the soviets and trade unions; and that in any case the party was technically unprepared for an offensive against the government. In these circumstances tactically cautious party leaders in Petrograd, headed by [Leon] Trotsky, devised the strategy of employing the organs of the Petrograd Soviet for the seizure of power; of masking an attack on the government as a defensive operation on behalf of the Soviet; and, if possible, of linking the formal overthrow of the government with the work of the Second Congress of Soviets.

On October 21–23, using as an excuse the government's announced intention of transferring the bulk of the garrison to the front and cloaking every move as a defensive measure against the counterrevolution, the Military Revolutionary Committee of the Petrograd Soviet took control of most Petrograd-based military units, in effect disarming the Provisional Government without a shot. In response, early on the morning of October 24, Kerensky initiated steps to suppress the left. Only at this point, just hours before the scheduled opening of the Congress of Soviets and in part under continuous prodding by Lenin, did the armed uprising that Lenin had been advocating for well over a month actually begin.

The argument has been made that the belated uprising of October 24–25 was of crucial historical importance because, by impelling the main body of Mensheviks and SRs to withdraw from the Second Congress of Soviets, it prevented the creation by the congress of a socialist coalition government in which the moderate socialists might have had a strong voice. In so doing, it paved the way for the formation of a soviet government completely controlled and dominated by the Bolsheviks. The evidence indicates that this was indeed the case. A more crucial point, however, is that only in the wake of the government's direct attack on the left was an armed uprising of the kind envisioned by Lenin feasible. For it bears repeating that the Petrograd masses, to the extent that they supported the Bolsheviks in the overthrow of the Provisional Government, did so not out of any sympathy for strictly Bolshevik rule but because they believed the revolution and the congress to be in imminent danger. Only the

creation of a broadly representative, exclusively socialist government by the Congress of Soviets, which is what they believed the Bolsheviks stood for, appeared to offer the hope of insuring that there would not be a return to the hated ways of the old regime, of avoiding death at the front and achieving a better life, and of putting a quick end to Russia's participation in the war.

After reading this selection, consider these questions:
1. What were the various factors that led to the Bolshevik victory?
2. What, to Rabinowitch, was the most important factor?
3. What was the strategy of the Bolsheviks in 1917?

# SELECTION 4:

# The Cold War

*In the second half of the 1940s, a series of crises and apparent confrontations resulted in the United States developing a global policy designed to thwart Soviet expansionist plans. But once the Soviet Union had consolidated its hold on Eastern Europe, was it still primarily concerned with further expansion or with simply responding to what it perceived as continuing threats from the West? As the Cold War continued into the 1960s and 1970s, scholars in both the East and the West attempted to review the events that led to the confrontation. Several historians and political scientists in the United States devised a revisionist interpretation. Historian Charles S. Maier reviews the revisionists' interpretations and evaluates their validity. The following selection is drawn from Maier's* The Origins of the Cold War and Contemporary Europe *(1978).*

Few historical reappraisals have achieved such sudden popularity as the . . . revisionist critique of American foreign policy and the origins of the

Cold War. Much of this impact is clearly due to Vietnam. Although the work of revision began before the United States became deeply involved in that country, the war has eroded so many national self-conceptions that many assumptions behind traditional Cold War history have been cast into doubt. . . . The Soviet-American conflict was attributed to [Soviet premier Joseph] Stalin's effort to expand Soviet control through revolutionary subversion, or, as in a more recent formulation, to "the logic of his position as the ruler of a totalitarian society and as the supreme head of a movement that seeks security through constant expansion." Revisionist assailants of this view have now found readers receptive to the contrary idea that the United States must bear the blame for the Cold War. The preoccupation with America's historical guilt distinguishes the new authors not only from anti-communist historians but from earlier writers who felt the question of blame was inappropriate. . . . This viewpoint has been preserved in some recent accounts; but since . . . 1961, the revisionists have gone on to indict the United States for long-term antipathy to communism, insensitivity to legitimate Soviet security needs, and generally belligerent behavior after World War II.

The revisionist version of Cold War history includes three major elements: an interpretation of Eastern European developments; an allegation of anti-Soviet motives in the Americans' use of the atomic bomb; and a general Marxian critique of the alleged American search for a world capitalist hegemony. Since these three elements comprise a detailed reassessment of the role of the United States in world politics they deserve to be discussed and evaluated in turn; but in the end one must consider the more fundamental question of the conceptual bases of revisionist history.

The revisionists are divided among themselves about the turning points and the causes of American aggressiveness, but all agree that the traditional description of the crucial events in Eastern Europe must be radically altered. The old version of the roots of the Cold War charged Soviet Russia with progressively tightening totalitarian control from mid-1944. In effect the earlier historians only confirmed the diagnosis of Ambassador Averell Harriman in Moscow, whose cables between late 1943 and early 1945 changed from emphasizing the needs of a functioning wartime alliance to stressing the difficulties of prolonging cooperation in the face of Soviet ambitions. In this evolution of views, the Russian refusal to facilitate Anglo-American supply flights to the Warsaw uprising of August 1944 and Moscow's

backing for its own Polish government later in that year provoked major western disillusionment. It was agreed after 1945 that the germs of the Cold War lay in Stalin's intransigence on the Polish issue.

In contrast to this interpretation, the revisionists charge that the United States forced Stalin into his stubborn Polish policy by backing the excessive aspirations of the exile Polish government in London. Revisionist accounts emphasize how antagonistic the State Department's refusal to sanction any territorial changes during the war must have appeared in Moscow. They point out that the territory that the Soviets had annexed in 1939, and which the Poles were contesting, had restored the 1919 Curzon line of mediation and merely reversed Poland's own acquisitions by war in 1920–1921. At the Teheran Conference in December 1943, Churchill and Roosevelt had loosely consented to Poland's borders being shifted westward. Even Harriman backed the British in counseling the London Poles to accept the terms the Soviets were offering in October 1944. Only when the Russians produced their own so-called Lublin Committee and thereafter Polish government—allegedly out of frustration and bitterness at the unyielding stance of the London Poles—did the focus switch from the question of territory to that of regimes. At the Yalta conference, Stalin agreed to add some Western Poles to the communist-based government and to move toward free elections; and if the United States had continued to accept the Yalta provisions in a generous spirit, the revisionists maintain, the earlier disputes might have been overcome. . . . But Roosevelt's successors, notably President Harry Truman and Secretary of State James Byrnes, put up a harsh fight to reverse this supposed acquiescence in the creation of a basically communist-dominated government.

This American attitude toward Polish issues, the revisionists claim, was typical of a wide range of Eastern European questions where the United States appeared to be set upon frustrating Russia's international security. From the summer of 1945 Truman and Byrnes, it is charged, sought to reverse the pro-Soviet governments in Rumania and Bulgaria by blustering with atomic weapons.

The American opposition to Soviet demands for territorial security and friendly neighboring states allegedly forced the Russians away from their minimal aims of 1943–1945, which envisaged United Front coalition regimes, to the ruthless communization they imposed by 1947–1948. Had the United States not demanded total openness to Western influence, the revisionists imply, Poland, Bulgaria, and Rumania might have survived as Hungary and Czechoslovakia did until 1947–1948 and Finland thereafter. But in fact, they argue, the parties and social groups that Washington desired to entrench could only intensify Stalin's mistrust. In revisionist eyes these groups were either unworthy or unviable: unworthy because they regrouped pre-war reactionary elements who had often been pro-German, unviable because even when democratic they were doomed to fall between the more intransigent right and the Russian-backed left.

Even more fundamental from the revisionist point of view, there was no legitimacy for any American concern with affairs in that distant region. However ugly the results in Eastern Europe, they should not really have worried Washington. Russia should have been willingly accorded unchallenged primacy because of her massive wartime sacrifices, her need for territorial security, and the long history of the area's reactionary politics and bitter anti-bolshevism. Only when Moscow's deserved primacy was contested did Stalin embark upon a search for exclusive control.

These revisionist assessments of the United States' political choices in Eastern Europe are valid in some respects, simplistic in others. It is true that American policymakers sought to establish agrarian democracies and based their hopes upon peasant proprietors and populist-like parties whose adherents had oscillated between left and right before the war. As revisionist accounts suggest, these occupied a precarious middle ground in Polish politics and an even narrower one in the former Axis satellites, Rumania and Bulgaria, where the Russians may have felt entitled to complete hegemony. [England's prime minister Winston] Churchill for one felt that his "percentages" agreement of October 1944 had sanctioned Soviet control over these countries as a *quid pro*

*quo* for the Russians' acceptance of British dominance in Greece. And whatever the effective status of that arrangement, Stalin might well have considered his domination of Rumania no more than the counterpart of Allied exclusion of the Soviets from any effective voice in Italy.

But despite revisionist implications to the contrary, the major offense of the middle- and pro-Western groups in Soviet eyes was not really their collusion with rightists. The Russians themselves, after all, supported the far more fascist-tainted Marshall Badoglio as Italian premier. The major crime of the pro-Western elements seems really to have been the desire to stay independent of Soviet influence in a situation of Soviet-American polarization that made independence seem enmity. Perhaps the pro-Westerners acted imprudently by looking to Washington: [Czech president Edvard] Benes won three years of Czech democracy by collaboration with Moscow—but one might argue from his example that either the collaboration prolonged the Czech respite or that it helped contribute to the final undermining of Prague's independence. In any case the outcome throughout the area was communist dictatorship. Between 1945 and 1947 the peasant party and social democratic leaders were harassed in their assemblies and organizations, tried for treason by communist interior ministries, driven abroad or into silence, and finally, as with the case of Nikola Petkov, the Bulgarian agrarian party leader, executed.

This bleak result naturally undercut those who advocated voluntarily relinquishing United States influence in the area. Opposing the official American rejection of spheres of influence, [former vice president] Henry Wallace on one side, and [former secretary of war] Henry Stimson and [ambassador to Russia] George Kennan on the other, counseled restraint and acceptance of the new status quo; but few contemporary advocates could wholeheartedly celebrate a policy of spheres of influence. It was justified from expedience and as a second-best alternative. As a former advocate recalls, it had always to be advanced as a melancholy necessity, especially as the men for whom Western liberals felt most sympathy were liquidated. To follow a policy of abnegation might indeed have allowed more openness in Eastern Europe; on the other hand, the Stalinist tendencies toward repression might well have followed their own Moscow-determined momentum. . . .

This view produces a more radical interpretation of both American foreign relations and the country's internal history. . . . This critique of United States foreign policy forms only part of a wider reassessment of American liberal institutions. The anti-communist effort is depicted as the natural product of an industrial society in which even major reform efforts have been intended only to rationalize corporate capitalism.

The more the revisionists stress the continuity of American capitalist goals and de-emphasize the importance of the Roosevelt-Truman transition, the more they tend to condemn all of America's earlier policies as contributing to the Cold War. The revisionists in general have stressed the direct pre-1945 clashes with the Soviets. They emphasize the significance of the Allies' delay in opening a Second Front in Europe; and while anti-Soviet historians duly cite Russia's non-aggression pact with Germany, the revisionists usually argue that the Soviets were forced into this arrangement by the Western powers' appeasement policies and their exclusion of Moscow from any common defense plans. Finally, revisionists . . . recall the United States' original hostility to bolshevism and the interventions of 1918–1920. In short, all revisionists are mindful of the Western treatment of the Soviets as a pariah regime.

The more radical revisionists, however, go on to depict all of twentieth-century foreign policy as woven into a large counter-revolutionary fabric of which the Cold War itself is only one portion. Their logic links a hesitant and ineffective anti-Nazi foreign policy with a zealous anti-communism and thus finds that the issues of the 1930's adumbrate Cold War attitudes. Similarly, revisionists who discuss pre-war diplomacy have attacked the usual image of American isolationism by stressing the country's persistent economic stakes abroad. All this vaguely serves to hint that the lateness of United States enlistment against Nazism is no longer explainable in terms of deep internal divisions about involvement in European quarrels: the United States responded only as it perceived threats to foreign economic interests. Receding even further, the revisionists view Woodrow Wilson as a major architect of liberal but counter-revolutionary interventionism. And even before Wilson the roots of the Cold War can be discerned, they feel, in the economic lobbying that backed the Open Door policy and the capitalist expansion of the late nineteenth century. Finally, under the stresses of a market economy, even the otherwise virtuous farmers felt it necessary to seek world markets and back imperialist expansionism. The private economy, for [certain revisionist historians] taints with acquisitiveness the Jeffersonian Eden that America might have been. . . .

The revisionists' approach to international conflict and foreign policy formation is a narrow one. They are interested in certain specific modes of explanation and no others. Rejecting any model of international society that sees crucial impulses to conflict as inherent in the international system itself, they seek explanations in American domestic conditions. But for them all domestic conditions are not equally valid. They are unwilling to accept any description that tends to stress the decentralized nature of decision-making or that envisages the possibility of expansionist policy taking shape by imperceptible commitments and bureaucratic momentum. Above all, they approach history with a value system and a vocabulary that appear to make meaningful historical dialogue with those who do not share their framework impossible.

The revisionists presuppose international harmony as a normal state and have a deep sense of grievance against whatever factors disturb it. This common assumption shapes their work from the outset in terms of both analysis and tone. But is international harmony a normal state? The division of sovereignty among nation-states makes it difficult to eliminate friction and tension, as theorists . . . have pointed out. The disputes of 1944–1945 especially were not easy to avoid. With a power vacuum in Central Europe created by the defeat of Germany and with the expansion of American and Soviet influence into new, overlapping regions, some underlying level of dispute was likely. Angered by the scope that the Cold War finally assumed, the revisionists do not really ask whether conflict might have been totally avoided or what level of residual disagreement was likely to emerge even with the best intentions on both sides.

Once mutual mistrust was unchained—and much already existed—all disputes were burdened by it. The initiatives that would have been required to assuage incipient conflict appeared too risky to venture in terms either of domestic public opinion or international security. By late 1945 the United States and Russia each felt itself to be at a competitive disadvantage in key disputes. Each felt that the other, being ahead, could best afford to make initial concessions, while gestures on its part would entail disproportionate or unilateral sacrifice. Perhaps more far-sighted leaders could have sought different outcomes, but there were pressures on all policy makers to take decisions that would harden conflict rather than alleviate it. Some details on this point are particularly worth considering.

In retrospect there appear to have been several areas of negotiation where compromise might at least have been possible, where accommodation demanded relatively little cost, and where the continued absence of greater concession probably deepened suspicion. Some additional flexibility on the issues of both atomic control and financial assistance might have helped to alleviate the growing estrangement. Innovative and generous as our plans for atomic energy control appeared to Americans at the time, the provisions for holding all United States weapons until controls were complete, as well as the demand that the Russians renounce their United Nations veto on all atomic-energy matters, probably doomed the proposal. With such an imbalance of obligations the Soviet advocates of their own country's atomic arsenal were likely to prevail over those willing to acquiesce in nuclear inferiority for a decade or so. As so often after 1946, the reluctance to give up an advantage that at best could only be transitory led to a further spiral in the arms race.

After reading this selection, consider these questions:

1. According to Maier, what were the main reasons for the development of revisionist histories of the Cold War?
2. What is the revisionist position?
3. According to Maier, what are the weaknesses of the revisionist position?

# Selection 5:

# The Fall of the Soviet Union

*Recognizing that the Cold War arms race was draining economic resources, Mikhail Gorbachev also unilaterally began scaling back Soviet missile production. In February 1988, Gorbachev explained the new policy of perestroika to a plenum session of the Communist Party of the Soviet Union.*

Our Plenum takes place at an important period of perestroika. The democratization of social

From *USSR Documents Annual, 1988: Perestroika—the Second Stage*, edited by J.L. Black. Copyright © 1989 by Academic International Press. Reprinted by permission of Academic International Press.

life and radical economic reform demand from the Party a clear perspective of things to be done. The Politburo is being guided by these considerations in working out a concept for the 19th Party Conference. It is to determine much in the Party's strategic work. . . .

Today, as we have entered the decisive stage of

the effort to translate into life the decisions adopted, as politics has turned into daily practice and perestroika has got under way, the vital interests of tens of millions of people and of all of society are being influenced to an ever greater extent. Issues to which answers seem to have been given have become topical again. People want to understand better the essence and purpose of perestroika, the essence of changes that have begun in our society. They want to understand where we are moving, what heights we are seeking to attain, and what we mean by the new quality of the society which we wish to achieve.

This desire is quite natural: we have started restructuring forms of social life, we are adopting new practices and discarding outdated stereotypes. The change concerns people's consciousness and psychology, their interests, status in society, at work and in the collective. There can be no concealing the fact that many good people got used in the past to abuses and failings, grew indifferent to them and became less active socially. Initially many failed to grasp the essence of the changes started, failed to see that perestroika is opening up new prospects in life and elevating the people themselves, that it is in full accord with their material and intellectual interests. Perestroika makes a special claim on those who enjoyed unearned benefits and were not guided by their conscience, on those who performed poorly at work. I am leaving aside those who violated laws and morality of socialist society.

Such is, I would say, the complex political and ideological situation in which we have to act. The Party has literally to fight for perestroika, both in production and in the spiritual sphere. Of course, this fight does not assume here the form of class antagonisms. But we can see, comrades, how sharp it is. . . .

We say that we support and will support everything that benefits socialism, and reject and will reject everything that injures the people's interests. We see that there is confusion in the minds of some people: are we not retreating from the positions of socialism, especially when we introduce new, unhabitual forms of economic management and social life, are we not revising Marxist-Leninist teaching itself? No wonder that

there have emerged "defenders" of Marxism-Leninism and "mourners" for socialism who believe that both are under threat.

From where is this emanating? What is behind such fears? It seems that perestroika itself is often understood in different ways. Some regard it as a face-lift, as an "adjustment" to the existing mechanism that performs poorly but at least operates somehow, while it is not clear how the new one will work. Others demand the dismantling of the very system of socialism down to its very foundation and claim that the path followed by people for decades was wrong and leading nowhere; they deny offhand the values of socialism and borrow alternatives to them from the arsenal of bourgeois liberalism and nationalism. Still others turn to radical phraseology, calling for skipping the stages of socialist development, ignoring the logic of perestroika.

There is no exaggeration, no deliberate exacerbation of the problem in what I am saying. Yes, all this is taking place. This situation has been engendered by the scope of perestroika, its deepening and its advancement to new frontiers, when the majority have realized that our goals and plans are realistic, that they, using Lenin's expression, are "in earnest and for a long time."

One should not fail to take into account the immense difficulties associated with reorientation of thinking on matters of principle. A similar situation has already occurred in our history. In working out his cooperative plan, Lenin pointed out: ". . .We have to admit that there has been a radical modification in our whole outlook on socialism." But we know what effort the Party had to exert for that. This is evidenced by discussions of those years. It took Lenin's authority and genius for the new approach to socialism to win support in the Party and in the country. We must learn well the lessons of that period. This is of vital importance to us now. . . .

This is why, comrades, the problems of ideological activity, and questions of the theory of socialism and perestroika assume such vast importance. One cannot say that we have overlooked ideological and theoretical matters. . . . It would be impossible to set the tasks of perestroika in the economy, and in the political, social and cultural spheres of society without reliance on theory and without ideological substantiation. . . .

It is the Party, equipped with the scientific knowledge of the past and present, and of the tendencies having real prospects of development, that is to guide the processes of fostering socialist consciousness in society. It is the Party that can and must theoretically elucidate the new stage of socialist construction, taking into account the innovation introduced by perestroika. It is the Party that must choose and put at the service of all of society what really promotes socialism, meets the interests of its development, advances us to socialist, and not some alien, "borrowed" aims.

It is certainly above all the desire to solve the most urgent problems caused by the stagnation of the previous period that made us aware of the need for perestroika. The wider the scale of perestroika, the more understandable its general meaning and importance for the future of socialism become.

Today, there is firm awareness that perestroika is an objectively necessary stage in the development of Soviet society whose essence is a transition to its new qualitative state. We must bring about radical changes in the productive forces and relations of production, and ensure a revolutionary renewal of social and political structures, and the growth of the spiritual, intellectual potential of society. We are striving in the present conditions to revive the Leninist image of the new system, to rid it of crustations and deformations, of everything that shackled society and prevented it from using the potential of socialism in full measure. And, most importantly, we must impart a new quality to socialist society, while taking into account all the realities of the world of today.

The essence of socialism lies in asserting the power of the working people, the priority of the welfare of man, the working class, and the entire people. In the final analysis, the task of socialism is to put an end to the social alienation of man which is characteristic of an exploiter society, his alienation from power, from the means of production, from the results of his work, and from spiritual values.

The October Revolution opened the way to accomplishing this historic task. The establishment of the power of the working people, the abolition of private ownership of the means of production, and the elimination of the exploitation of man by man were steps of fundamental importance. These are the basic gains of socialism.

For over 70 years our Party and people have been inspired by the idea of socialism and have been building it. But because of external and internal factors we have not been able to implement in full the Leninist principles of the new social system. This was seriously hampered by the personality cult, the system of management by injunction that evolved in the thirties, bureaucratic, dogmatic and voluntarist aberrations, arbitrariness, and—in the late seventies and early eighties—by a lack of initiative and hindrances that led to stagnation. These phenomena, and what has remained of them and survived to the present, must become things of the past.

In this lies the answer to those who have fears that we might just be retreating from socialism, from the foundations laid by generations of Soviet people. So, we are not retreating a single step from socialism, from Marxism-Leninism from everything that has been gained and created by the people.

But we decisively reject the dogmatic, bureaucratic and voluntarist legacy because it has nothing in common with either Marxism-Leninism or genuine socialism.

Creative Marxism-Leninism is always an objective, profound scientific analysis of developing reality. It is a critical analysis which does not ignore anything, which does not conceal anything, and which does not fear any truth. Only such an analysis works for socialism. There are no, nor can there be, any limits to a truly scientific search. Questions of theory cannot and must not be decided by decrees. Free competition of minds is needed. Our social thinking stands to gain from this. Its prognosticating capacity will be enhanced and thereby its ability to serve as a reliable basis for working out the Party's policy will increase. . . .

The economic reform is an inalienable part of transforming and renewing socialism as a social system, and of imparting more modern and dynamic forms to it. It should create the necessary preconditions and powerful stimuli for scientific and technological progress, for combining the potential of a planned economy with the personal interests, initiative and enterprise of people, and give public property, methods of management and administration such forms as would make people really feel that they are the true masters of production.

Scientific analysis and practical experience have given us the firm conviction that all these tasks in their organic interconnection and unity can be successfully accomplished by placing the operation of enterprises on the principles of cost-accounting, self-repayment, self-financing and self-management. This is the way of harmonizing the interests of society, the collective and the individual which guarantees the satisfaction of public needs and at the same time ensures the interest of the working people themselves in the end results of production. This is the way of uprooting the practice of levelling and sponging which have inflicted so much damage on us. This is the way of the most rapid solution of social problems, something that directly concerns both the individual and whole collectives, strengthens discipline and raises efficiency. This is a real economic foundation for promoting democracy and enlisting the participation of working people in management, for overcoming the alienation of people from the economic progress and its results.

The question of social justice has acquired still greater acuteness during the extensive implementation of the economic reform. The problem, it would seem, is clear enough—it is essential to advance consistently along the road of strict observance of socialism's main principle, "From each according to his abilities, to each according to his work." All this is so. But in practice and, there can be no denying it, in our perceptions too, we still have a long way to go to rid ourselves of the levelling out psychology.

It is no secret that even now many people get their pay only for reporting to work and hold positions regardless of their actual labor contribution. And the most surprising thing is that this hardly worries anyone. But no sooner had people

in pay-your-own-way collectives got pay rises for achieving better end results than protests and irritated voices could be heard, complaining that those people allegedly were earning too much.

Under socialism, however, the question can only be whether the wages have been earned or not, rather than whether they are high or low. It is another matter that the way of judging the amount and quality of work should be based on scientifically grounded, tried and tested yardsticks.

In general, comrades, we should get down in earnest to eradicating levelling tendencies. This is a highly important social, economic and ideological issue. To all intents and purposes, levelling has a ruinous impact not only on the economy, but also on people's morality and on their entire way of thinking and acting. It detracts from the prestige of conscientious and creative work, spoils discipline, smothers the interest to upgrade skills, and undermines competition at work. We should say bluntly that levelling is a reflection of petty bourgeois views which have nothing to do with Marxism-Leninism or with scientific socialism. And we shall not make progress or be able to cope with the tasks of perestroika, if we don't knock the levelling attitudes out wherever they still persist.

Yes, socialism is a society of social guarantees which does not leave a person to deal with the difficulties of life and adversities all on its own. The social protection of the Soviet people rests on the abolition of private ownership and exploitation and on the power of the working people. The principle of social protection has been written into our laws and confirmed by experience over many years. The most important social guarantees created in the country include the right to housing, full employment, free education and medical services.

Even with all the drawbacks and flaws, the fundamental significance of these gains is indubitable. But the extent of social protection in society depends on the amount of national wealth which, for its part, depends on how correctly and consistently socialism's principle, "From each according to his abilities, to each according to his work" is applied. In keeping with this principle, the individual's well-being, including his living conditions, directly depends on how he uses his aptitudes and talents and contributes to the common effort. This is the basis of socialism's vitality and it depends precisely on the talent and concrete contribution made by every worker to the country's public wealth. At the same time, we must resolutely cut short any money-grabbing inclinations wherever they manifest themselves. It is only honest and conscientious work within the framework of our laws and existing standards that can be highly rewarded materially and get public acclaim.

After reading this selection, consider these questions:

1. How does Gorbachev define *perestroika*?
2. How does he relate perestroika to the history of the Soviet Union since the Russian Revolution?
3. How does Gorbachev plan to revive the economy?

# CHAPTER 14
# The Embattled Enlightenment Tradition

The contemporary cultural and intellectual situation of the West has given rise to a number of fundamental challenges to the dominant trends that have defined the West in the past three hundred years. These challenges have been grouped together under the term *postmodernism*, which emphasizes that the traditions and principles of what we consider "modern" have so changed that we need a new term and historical category to describe them. Aside from its historical significance, however, postmodernism indicates a radical break from the very foundations of knowledge, the definition of the individual, and the notion of reality that has emerged in the West in the recent modern period.

Providing an adequate definition of postmodernism—one that encompasses all of its principles and manifestations—contradicts the very notion of postmodernism. Postmodernism does not attempt to replace the conventional foundations of the modern West with new principles of art or with new definitions of truth. Postmodernism undermines the idea of foundations, principles, and even truth. In the arts, for example, from architecture to the performing arts, postmodernism is a break from traditions and a new appreciation of play within conventional forms and styles and a new play against the hierarchical distinctions between high and low art. In this sense, there is a freedom in dealing with the popular forms of mass culture. Within the various intellectual and academic fields impacted by postmodernism, the organizational principles of the individual, knowing subject, of truth as a form of objectivity, and even of the capacity of language to capture anything outside of itself have all been brought into question. This critique of conventional definitions, again, gives a more open relation between text and critic, the "object" of knowledge and the "knowing subject," the referents of language and the free play of signs.

The same problem of definition arises with the attempt to situate postmodernism historically. Although it is much too soon to evaluate the long-term impact of postmodernism on the history of the West, it is nonetheless clear that postmodernism is challenging modernism and the foundations of scientific knowledge, the notion of an ordered cosmos, and the place and role of the arts that we have inherited from the Enlightenment. This questioning in turn challenges whether the West should be thought of in terms of this Enlightenment tradition. Is the West something other or more than we have come to think of it in the modern period?

## SELECTION 1:

# The Postmodern Condition

*In Knowledge and Postmodernism in Historical Perspective (1996), Joyce Appleby, Elizabeth Covington, David Hoyt, Michael Latham, and Allison Sneider formulate a historical notion of postmodernism as an attack against "the Enlightenment project." Unfortunately, their definition exhibits their biases against postmodernism; nonetheless, it provides a starting point for understanding postmodernism.*

While much in modernism shaped the way contemporary critics think about late-twentieth-century society, it was not until the 1970s that a comprehensive challenge to modernity in all its forms emerged, with its own center of philosophical and aesthetic gravity. The rubric postmodernism announced the passing of the Modern Age, but many postmodernists went well beyond a notice of death to an exhuming of the body itself. Four old Enlightenment bones, in particular, have attracted attention: rational inquiry as a prelude to reform (the critique), the free development of liberated persons (the autonomous individual), the mastery of the cause-and-effect relations that run the world (the idea of progress), and the capacity of language to describe the external world (representation).

The individual was the pivotal force in the Enlightenment project. Postmodernists have been indefatigable in reconstructing the omniscient power of the social. Around these two charged poles have gathered almost all of the filings in this grand dispute about the Enlightenment project. Two French philosophers, Michel Foucault and Jacques Derrida, come to everyone's mind when postmodernism is mentioned. Foucault, who worked primarily with historical materials, used them to detonate a whole gallery of icons: the credibility of reforms effected under the banner of Enlightenment, the independence of individual thinkers, the continuity of human efforts, the idea of progress. Wishing to reveal the arbitrary aspect of Enlightenment science, Foucault reversed Bacon's claim that knowledge is power to make the point that only those with power have the right to say what is knowledge.

The celebrated postmodernist statements about the depriviledging of authors and the death of the subject are basically assertions that the concept of individuality is spurious because men and women are actually the repositories of their cultural systems. We do not speak language, say the postmodernists; language speaks us, imposing as it does a particular logic, aesthetics, and morality, or as Foucault would say, a discourse. Discourses, not impartial scientific investigations, define our world, as it is social constructions of reality, not reality, that we encounter when we speak and act. More concerned with language, Derrida has subjected the texts upon which Western civilization has relied for its understanding of the world to a process called deconstruction, in which imaginative exposures of gaps, transgressive possibilities, or unintended indicators lead to a multiplicity of readings. Having rendered communication unstable, Derrida then answers the classic epistemological question "What can I know?" with "Nothing for certain."

Where modernity promoted rational discourse, postmodernists have rained down upon the claims of rationality showers of ridicule, mockery, neologisms, and word plays. They have felt compelled to upend nearly every modern conviction. Enlightenment hopes were based upon the newly-discovered capacities of scientists to represent the external world, but postmodernists have denied that we have access to objects except through human paradigms and discourses. The social glue of language has become unstuck. Words are now presented as changelings and texts, as the sites for an endless succession of interpretations. Even the universal affirmations of the Enlightenment have been relocated as part of the hypocritical strategies of a small elite in the West.

Just as modern thinkers conceived of time in new ways with their lexicon of process and development, so postmodernists proclaim a new understanding of time as discontinuous, open to rupture and capable of multifarious arrangements. Another striking contrast between the two cultural forms is the way postmodernism parodies the seriousness of the Enlightenment agenda, insisting upon the edification of the trivial and the unintended disclosures of all communication. Not only do postmodernist literary critics rail against the academic establishment's canon of major works of literature or philosophy, but postmodernist social critics insist that marginal observers have as much of value to say as licensed experts. For postmodernists, any effort to fix meaning will and should yield in time to the power of the repressed, the disclosures from the edge, and the surprises that come from the decoded and disinterred. Very much influenced by [Friedrich] Nietzsche's effort to tear the veil of illusion from modern society, postmodernists have returned inquiry to its Baconian [relating to philosopher Francis Bacon] starting point: is the objective world accessible to human inquiry, and are language and reason up to the task of representing such a nature?

Our reliance on posts, as in postindustrial or postmodern, to locate ourselves in cultural times indicates that we still identify ourselves through old beliefs. We have not so much rejected modern values as lost the old certainty about modernization. Like the eighteenth-century *philosophes*, postmodernists often feel a kind of exhilaration in having routed a soul-diminishing absolutism, but unlike our predecessors of [the eighteenth century], we do not have a new program to deflect us from the contemplation of the misery, pain, and failure in the human condition. Postmodernism in this view might be taken as the messenger of our disappointment, and characteristically people have tried to shoot the messenger, blaming postmodernist thought for promoting nihilism and relativism. . . .

The pessimism that the postmodernist critique generates can be mitigated by the defenders of the Enlightenment project. . . . We shall give the last word to these critics and commentators, who have engaged with the issues raised by postmodernists with increasing fervor in the last decade. They have shown what is at stake and what is involved in giving up on the representation of reality and the capacity of people to communicate, in hopes of changing it. What remains to be seen is how much of our world rests on modern footings. Here the American postmodernist philosopher Richard Rorty has posed the critical question: "Can free societies prevail without the philosophical foundation upon which they have rested for two hundred years? Can the Enlightenment project survive Enlightenment fantasies?" We won't know until we move into that unknown future, accepting its unknowability.

After reading this selection, consider these questions:

1. What are the main characteristics of postmodernism?
2. How do they challenge "the Enlightenment project"?
3. What, according to the authors, is the greatest threat of postmodernist thought?

# SELECTION 2:

# Power and Discourse

*Although postmodernism is opposed to all definitions of truth and meaning handed down by our cultural and intellectual traditions, the leading thinkers of postmodernism themselves point to a number of radical thinkers within the recent past who prepared the way for postmodernist thought. Central among these is Friedrich Nietzsche. As we have seen, Nietzsche challenged a number of the foundational ideas of the modern West. The West's supposed scientific and technological advances as well as its supposed social and moral progress, Nietzsche argued, did not lead to freer, more autonomous individuals. The reverse is actually the case. The modern West, he claimed, had produced only mediocrity and a leveling culture. Nietzsche probed the reasons for this in a number of his works, and in the process he made a frontal attack against the scientific notion of truth and against the dominant understanding of goodness. He also sketched out an alternative way of conceiving of knowledge and value through what he called a genealogical approach.*

*From the 1960s to the time of his death in the mid-1980s, the French philosopher and historian Michel Foucault developed this Nietzschean notion of genealogy into a critical method for questioning present-day forms of knowledge and the institutional practices that support them. In such texts as* Discipline and Punish *(1975) and* The History of Sexuality *(1976–1985), Foucault deplored the easy acceptance of such Enlightenment ideas as the free subject, the role of consciousness in ascertaining knowledge, and the progressive development of history. For him, the freedom proffered by the so-called sexual revolution was one more type of liberation movement originating from Enlightenment concepts of the self and freedom has not in fact liberated anything; quite the opposite has actually occurred. Sexuality as it has come to be defined was an all-pervasive and much more subtle form of power—as a way individuals, but more importantly society and institutions, control and limit human beings.*

*The genealogical method, as Foucault came to employ it, focused on the complex interplay between various forms of discourse and the relations of power that these discourses partly illuminate and partly extend. In the following interview, Foucault provides one of the most concise and clearest explanations of the relation between discourse and power.*

[Questioner:] Within this methodological context [the philosophies of Marxism and phenomenology, which dominated French intellectual life when Foucault was a student], how would you situate the genealogical approach? As a questioning of the conditions of possibility, modalities, and constitution of the "objects" and domains you have successively analyzed, what makes it necessary?

[Michel Foucault:] I wanted to see how these problems of constitution could be resolved within a historical framework, instead of referring them back to a constituent object (madness, criminality, or whatever). But this historical contextualization needed to be something more than the simple relativization of the phenomenological subject. I don't believe the problem can be solved by historicizing the subject as posited by the phenomenologists, fabricating a subject that evolves through the course of history. One has to dispense with the constituent subject, to get rid of the subject itself, that's to say, to arrive at an analysis which can account for the constitution of the subject within a historical framework. And this is what I would call genealogy, that is, a form of history which can account for the constitution of knowledges, discourses, domains of objects, etc., without having to make reference to a subject which is either transcendental in relation to the field of events or runs in its empty sameness throughout the course of history.

Q: Marxist phenomenology and a certain kind of Marxism have clearly acted as a screen and an obstacle; there are two further concepts which continue today to act as a screen and an obstacle: ideology, on the one hand, and repression, on the other.

All history comes to be thought of within these categories which serve to assign a meaning to such diverse phenomena as normalization, sexuality, and power. And regardless of whether these two concepts are explicitly utilized, in the end one always comes back, on the one hand to ideology—where it is easy to make the reference back to Marx—and on the other to repression, which is a concept often and readily employed by Freud throughout the course of his career. Hence I would like to put forward the following suggestion. Behind these concepts and among those who (properly or improperly) employ them, there is a kind of nostalgia; behind the concept of ideology, the nostalgia for a quasi-transparent form

of knowledge, free from all error and illusion, and behind the concept of repression, the longing for a form of power innocent of all coercion, discipline, and normalization. On the one hand, a power without a bludgeon and, on the other hand, knowledge without deception. You have called these two concepts, ideology and repression, negative, "psychological," insufficiently analytical. This is particularly the case in *Discipline and Punish*, where, even if there isn't an extended discussion of these concepts, there is nevertheless a kind of analysis that allows one to go beyond the traditional forms of explanation and intelligibility which, in the last (and not only the last) instance, rest on the concepts of ideology and repression. Could you perhaps use this occasion to specify more explicitly your thoughts on these matters? With *Discipline and Punish*, a kind of positive history seems to be emerging, which is free of all the negativity and psychologism implicit in those two universal skeleton-keys.

M.F.: The notion of ideology appears to me to be difficult to make use of, for three reasons. The first is that, like it or not, it always stands in virtual opposition to something else which is supposed to count as truth. Now I believe that the problem does not consist in drawing the line between that in a discourse which falls under the category of scientificity or truth, and that which comes under some other category, but in seeing historically how effects of truth are produced within discourses which in themselves are neither true nor false. The second drawback is that the concept of ideology refers, I think necessarily, to something of the order of a subject. Third, ideology stands in a secondary position relative to something which functions as its infrastructure, as its material, economic determinant, etc. For these three reasons, I think that this is a notion that cannot be used without circumspection.

The notion of repression is a more insidious one, or at all events I myself have had much more trouble in freeing myself of it, insofar as it does indeed appear to correspond so well with a whole range of phenomena which belong among the effects of power. When I wrote *Madness and Civilization*, I made at least an implicit use of this notion of repression. I think, indeed, that I was positing the existence of a sort of living, voluble, and anxious madness which the mechanisms of power and psychiatry were supposed to have come to repress and reduce to silence. But it seems to me now that the notion of repression is quite inadequate for capturing what is precisely the productive aspect of power. In defining the effects of power as repression, one adopts a purely juridical conception of such power; one identifies power with a law which says no; power is taken above all as carrying the force of a prohibition. Now I believe that this is a wholly negative, narrow, skeletal conception of power, one which has been curiously widespread. If power were never anything but repressive, if it never did anything but to say no, do you really think one would be brought to obey it? What makes power hold good, what makes it accepted, is simply the fact that it doesn't only weigh on us as a force that says no, but that it traverses and produces things, it induces pleasure, forms knowledge, produces discourse. It needs to be considered as a productive network which runs through the whole social body, much more than as a negative instance whose function is repression. In *Discipline and Punish*, what I wanted to show was how, from the seventeenth and eighteenth centuries onward, there was a veritable technological take-off in the productivity of power. Not only did the monar-chies of the classical period develop great state apparatuses (the army, the police and fiscal administration), but above all there was established in this period what one might call a new "economy" of power, that is to say, procedures which allowed the effects of power to circulate in a manner at once continuous, uninterrupted, adapted, and "individualized" throughout the entire social body. These new techniques are both much more efficient and much less wasteful (less costly economically, less risky in their results, less open to loopholes and resistances) than the techniques previously employed, which were based on a mixture of more or less forced tolerances (from recognized privileges to endemic criminality) and costly ostentation (spectacular and discontinuous interventions of power, the most violent form of which was the "exemplary," because exceptional, punishment).

After reading this selection, consider these questions:

1. How does Foucault define *genealogy*?
2. How does genealogy differ from Marxist ideology critique and Freudian psychoanalysis?
3. What does Foucault mean by the phrase *economy of power*?

# SELECTION 3:

# "The Question Concerning Technology"

*The other leading figure within postmodern theory is Jacques Derrida. Instead of historical analysis and the interplay between knowledge and power, Derrida has focused on the ways in which language inherently limits the possibility of capturing truth about the world. Drawing on structuralist linguistics but challenging its foundational claims, Derrida shows how language functions as a "decentering center," as an "anti-structural structure." Like Michel Foucault, Derrida draws heavily on the writings of Friedrich Nietzsche, especially those aspects of his thought that question whether the subject has or can form an identity and whether language has or can provide knowledge of the world. In a more direct manner than Foucault, Derrida relies heavily on the philosophy of Martin Heidegger (1889–1976). The radicalism of Heidegger's thinking, especially as he adopted a highly critical stance toward the Western tradition of philosophy, had led Derrida to question the limitations of the logic and concept formation as well as the priority we traditionally give to them. With differing emphases, both Heidegger and Derrida rethink this philosophical tradition and the often hidden ways it continues to influence our everyday notions of reality, truth, and knowledge.*

*Heidegger himself directed his thinking into areas that neither Derrida nor Foucault (who also acknowledges his debt to Heidegger) have followed. Beginning in the 1950s, Heidegger began to think through the problem of modernity in terms of the growing dominance of technology. By* technology *he meant less the actual physical objects we usually think of when we use the term or the development of a technological civilization in a historical sense. Rather, Heidegger perceived the notion of an "essence" of technology—the concepts beyond human control that make technology possible. The following selection is taken from his essay "The Question Concerning Technology." Here, Heidegger speaks of truth as a form of "revealing" and the differences between the truth or the essence of modern technology and the ancient Greek notion of "making" (poiēsis).*

What is modern technology? It too is a revealing. Only when we allow our attention to rest on this fundamental characteristic does that which is new in modern technology show itself to us.

And yet the revealing that holds sway throughout modern technology does not unfold into a bringing-forth in the sense of *poiēsis*. The revealing that rules in modern technology is a challenging, which puts to nature the unreasonable demand that it supply energy that can be extracted and stored as such. But does this not hold true for the old windmill as well? No. Its sails do indeed turn in the wind; they are left entirely to the wind's blowing. But the windmill does not unlock energy from the air currents in order to store it.

In contrast, a tract of land is challenged into the putting out of coal and ore. The earth now reveals itself as a coal mining district, the soil as a mineral deposit. The field that the peasant formerly cultivated and set in order appears differently than it did when to set in order still meant to take care of and to maintain. The work of the peasant does not challenge the soil of the field. In the sowing of the grain it places the seed in the keeping of the forces of growth and watches over its increase. But meanwhile even the cultivation of the field has come under the grip of another kind of setting-in-order, which *sets* upon nature. It sets upon it in the sense of challenging it. Agriculture is now the mechanized food industry. Air is now set upon to yield nitrogen, the earth to yield ore, ore to yield uranium, for example; uranium is set upon to yield atomic energy, which can be released either for destruction or for peaceful use.

This setting-upon that challenges forth the energies of nature is an expediting, and in two ways. It expedites in that it unlocks and exposes. Yet that expediting is always itself directed from the beginning toward furthering something else, i.e., toward driving on to the maximum yield at the minimum expense. The coal that has been hauled out in some mining district has not been supplied in order that it may simply be present somewhere or other. It is stockpiled; that is, it is on call, ready to deliver the sun's warmth that is stored in it. The sun's warmth is challenged forth for heat, which in turn is ordered to deliver steam whose pressure turns the wheels that keep a factory running.

The hydroelectric plant is set into the current of the Rhine. It sets the Rhine to supplying its hydraulic pressure, which then sets the turbines turning. This turning sets those machines in motion whose thrust sets going the electric current for which the long-distance power station and its network of cables are set up to dispatch electricity. In the context of the interlocking processes pertaining to the orderly disposition of electrical energy, even the Rhine itself appears as something at our command. The hydroelectric plant is not built into the Rhine River as was the old wooden bridge that joined bank with bank for hundreds of years. Rather the river is dammed up into the power plant. What the river is now, namely, a water power supplier, derives from out of the essence of the power station. In order that we may even remotely consider the monstrousness that reigns here, let us ponder for a moment the contrast that speaks out of the two titles, "The Rhine" as dammed up into the *power* works, and "The Rhine" as uttered out of the *art* work, in [German poet Friedrich] Hölderlin's hymn by that name. But, it will be replied, the Rhine is still a river in the landscape, is it not? Perhaps. But how? In no other way than as an object on call for inspection by a tour group ordered there by the vacation industry.

The revealing that rules throughout modern technology has the character of a setting-upon, in the sense of a challenging-forth. That challenging happens in that the energy concealed in nature is unlocked, what is unlocked is transformed, what is transformed is stored up, what is stored up is, in turn, distributed, and what is distributed is switched about ever anew. Unlocking, transforming, storing, distributing, and switching about are ways of revealing. But the revealing never simply comes to an end. Neither does it run off into the

indeterminate. The revealing reveals to itself its own manifoldly interlocking paths, through regulating their course. This regulating itself is, for its part, everywhere secured. Regulating and securing even become the chief characteristics of the challenging revealing.

What kind of unconcealment is it, then, that is peculiar to that which comes to stand forth through this setting-upon that challenges? Everywhere everything is ordered to stand by, to be immediately at hand, indeed to stand there just so that it may be on call for a further ordering. Whatever is ordered about in this way has its own standing. We call it the standing-reserve. The word expresses here something more, and something more essential, than mere "stock." The name "standing-reserve" assumes the rank of an inclusive rubric. It designates nothing less than the way in which everything presences that is wrought upon by the challenging revealing. Whatever stands by in the sense of standing-reserve no longer stands over against us as object.

Yet an airliner that stands on the runway is surely an object. Certainly. We can represent the machine so. But then it conceals itself as to what and how it is. Revealed, it stands on the taxi strip only as standing-reserve, inasmuch as it is ordered to ensure the possibility of transportation. For this it must be in its whole structure and in every one of its constituent parts, on call for duty, i.e., ready for takeoff. (Here it would be appropriate to discuss [Georg] Hegel's definition of the machine as an autonomous tool. When applied to the tools of the craftsman, his characterization is correct. Characterized in this way, however, the machine is not thought at all from out of the essence of technology within which it belongs. Seen in terms of the standing-reserve, the machine is completely unautonomous, for it has its standing only from the ordering of the orderable.)

The fact that now, wherever we try to point to modern technology as the challenging revealing, the words "setting-upon," "ordering," "standing-reserve," obtrude and accumulate in a dry, monotonous, and therefore oppressive way, has its basis in what is now coming to utterance.

Who accomplishes the challenging setting-upon through which what we call the real is revealed as standing-reserve? Obviously, man. To what extent is man capable of such a revealing? Man can indeed conceive, fashion, and carry through this or that in one way or another. But man does not have control over unconcealment itself, in which at any given time the real shows itself or withdraws. The fact that the real has been showing itself in the light of Ideas ever since the time of Plato, Plato did not bring about. The thinker only responded to what addressed itself to him.

Only to the extent that man for his part is already challenged to exploit the energies of nature can this ordering revealing happen. If man is challenged, ordered, to do this, then does not man himself belong even more originally than nature within the standing-reserve? The current talk about human resources, about the supply of patients for a clinic, gives evidence of this. The forester who, in the wood, measures the felled timber and to all appearances walks the same forest path in the same way as did his grandfather is today commanded by profit-making in the lumber industry, whether he knows it or not. He is made subordinate to the orderability of cellulose, which for its part is challenged forth by the need for paper, which is then delivered to newspapers and illustrated magazines. The latter, in their turn, set public opinion to swallowing what is printed, so that a set configuration of opinion becomes available on demand. Yet precisely because man is challenged more originally than are the energies of nature, i.e., into the process of ordering, he never is transformed into mere standing-reserve. Since man drives technology forward, he takes part in ordering as a way of revealing. But the unconcealment itself, within which ordering unfolds, is never a human handiwork, any more than is the realm through which man is already passing every time he as a subject relates to an object.

Where and how does this revealing happen if it is no mere handiwork of man? We need not look far. We need only apprehend in an unbiased way That which has already claimed man and has done so, so decisively that he can only be man at any given time as the one so claimed. Wherever man opens his eyes and ears, unlocks his heart, and gives himself over to meditating and striving, shaping and working, entreating and thanking, he finds himself everywhere already brought into the unconcealed. The unconcealment of the unconcealed has already come to pass whenever it calls man forth into the modes of revealing allotted to him. When man, in his way, from within unconcealment reveals that which presences, he merely responds to the call of unconcealment even when he contradicts it. Thus when man, investigating, observing, ensnares nature as an area of his own conceiving, he has already been claimed by a way of revealing that challenges him to approach nature as an object of research, until even the object disappears into the objectlessness of standing-reserve.

Modern technology as an ordering revealing is, then, no merely human doing. Therefore we must take that challenging that sets upon man to order the real as standing-reserve in accordance with the way in which it shows itself. That challenging gathers man into ordering. This gathering concentrates man upon ordering the real as standing-reserve.

After reading this selection, consider these questions:
   1. What does Heidegger mean by *standing-reserve*?
   2. How does Heidegger claim that technology is not the creation of man?
   3. What is the "truth" of modern technology?

# SELECTION 4:

# Postmodern Feminism

*Within the general and expansive term* postmodernism, *and generating new and creative modes of thinking within it, there has arisen a distinctive type of French feminist writing. This feminist writing, as it is generally called, both undermines the conventional definitions of the feminine coming from society and psychiatry and goes beyond definitions of feminism that focus on women's liberation in terms of sexual, legal, and economic equality. Feminist writing defines the feminine in its multiple ways through the act of writing itself. In her provocative essay "The Laugh of the Medusa," Hélène Cixous (1937– ) in a brilliant manifesto of feminist writing, challenges all notions of a bipolar opposition of "masculine" and "feminine" as artificial and stereotyped.*

I shall speak about women's writing: about *what it will do*. Woman must write her self: must write about women and bring women to writing, from which they have been driven away as violently as from their bodies—for the same reasons, by the same law, with the same fatal goal. Woman must put herself into the text—as into the world and into history—by her own movement.

The future must no longer be determined by the past. I do not deny that the effects of the past are still with us. But I refuse to strengthen them by repeating them, to confer upon them an irremovability the equivalent of destiny, to confuse the biological and the cultural. Anticipation is imperative.

Since these reflections are taking shape in an area just on the point of being discovered, they necessarily bear the mark of our time—a time during which the new breaks away from the old, and, more precisely, the (feminine) new from the old (*la nouvelle de l'ancien*). Thus as there are no grounds for establishing a discourse, but rather an arid millennial ground to break, what I say has at least two sides and two aims: to break up, to destroy; and to foresee the unforeseeable, to project.

I write this as a woman, toward women. When I say "woman," I'm speaking of woman in her inevitable struggle against conventional man; and of a universal woman subject who must bring women to their senses and to their meaning in history. But first it must be said that in spite of the enormity of the repression that has kept them in the "dark"— that dark which people have been trying to make them accept as their attribute—there is, at this time, no general woman, no one typical woman. What they have *in common* I will say. But what strikes me is the infinite richness of their individual constitutions: you can't talk about *a* female sexuality, uniform, homogeneous, classifiable into codes—any more than you can talk about one unconscious resembling another. Women's imaginary is inexhaustible, like music, painting, writing: their stream of phantasms is incredible.

I have been amazed more than once by a description a woman gave me of a world all her own which she had been secretly haunting since early childhood. A world of searching, the elaboration of a knowledge, on the basis of a systematic experimentation with the bodily functions, a passionate and precise interrogation of her erotogeneity. This practice, extraordinarily rich and in-

From "Laugh of the Medusa," by Hélène Cixous, translated by Keith Cohen and Paula Cohen, *Signs: Journal of Women in Culture and Society*, vol. 1, no. 4 (1976). Copyright © 1976 by The University of Chicago. Reprinted by permission of the University of Chicago Press.

ventive, in particular as concerns masturbation, is prolonged or accompanied by a production of forms, a veritable aesthetic activity, each stage of rapture inscribing a resonant vision, a composition, something beautiful. Beauty will no longer be forbidden.

I wished that that woman would write and proclaim this unique empire so that other women, other unacknowledged sovereigns, might exclaim: I, too, overflow; my desires have invented new desires, my body knows unheard-of songs. Time and again I, too, have felt so full of luminous torrents that I could burst—burst with forms much more beautiful than those which are put up in frames and sold for a stinking fortune. And I, too, said nothing, showed nothing; I didn't open my mouth, I didn't repaint my half of the world. I was ashamed. I was afraid, and I swallowed my shame and my fear. I said to myself: You are mad! What's the meaning of these waves, these floods, these outbursts? Where is the ebullient, infinite woman who, immersed as she was in her naiveté, kept in the dark about herself, led into self-disdain by the great arm of parental-conjugal phallocentrism, hasn't been ashamed of her strength? Who, surprised and horrified by the fantastic tumult of her drives (for she was made to believe that a well-adjusted normal woman has a . . . divine composure), hasn't accused herself of being a monster? Who, feeling a funny desire stirring inside her (to sing, to write, to dare to speak, in short, to bring out something new), hasn't thought she was sick? Well, her shameful sickness is that she resists death, that she makes trouble.

And why don't you write? Write! Writing is for you, you are for you; your body is yours, take it. I know why you haven't written. (And why I didn't write before the age of twenty-seven.) Because writing is at once too high, too great for you, it's reserved for the great—that is, for "great men"; and it's "silly." Besides, you've written a little, but in secret. And it wasn't good, because it was in secret, and because you punished yourself for writing, because you didn't go all the way; or because you wrote, irresistibly, as when we would masturbate in secret, not to go further, but to attenuate the tension a bit, just enough to take the edge off. And then as soon as we come, we go

and make ourselves feel guilty—so as to be forgiven; or to forget, to bury it until the next time.

Write, let no one hold you back, let nothing stop you: not man; not the imbecilic capitalist machinery, in which publishing houses are the crafty, obsequious relayers of imperatives handed down by an economy that works against us and off our backs; and not *yourself*. Smug-faced readers, managing editors, and big bosses don't like the true texts of women—female-sexed texts. That kind scares them.

I write woman: woman must write woman. And man, man. So only an oblique consideration will be found here of man; it's up to him to say where his masculinity and femininity are at: this will concern us once men have opened their eyes and seen themselves clearly.

Now women return from afar, from always: from "without," from the heath where witches are kept alive; from below, from beyond "culture"; from their childhood which men have been trying desperately to make them forget, condemning it to "eternal rest." The little girls and their "ill-mannered" bodies immured, well-preserved, intact unto themselves, in the mirror. Frigidified. But are they ever seething underneath! What an effort it takes—there's no end to it—for the sex cops to bar their threatening return. Such a display of forces on both sides that the struggle has for centuries been immobilized in the trembling equilibrium of a deadlock.

Here they are, returning, arriving over and again, because the unconscious is impregnable. They have wandered around in circles, confined to the narrow room in which they've been given a deadly brainwashing. You can incarcerate them, slow them down, get away with the old Apartheid routine, but for a time only. As soon as they begin to speak, at the same time as they're taught their name, they can be taught that their territory is black: because you are Africa, you are black. Your continent is dark. Dark is dangerous. You can't see anything in the dark, you're afraid. Don't move, you might fall. Most of all, don't go into the forest. And so we have internalized this horror of the dark.

Men have committed the greatest crime against women. Insidiously, violently, they have led them to hate women, to be their own enemies, to mobilize their immense strength against themselves, to be the executants of their virile needs. They have made for women an antinarcissism! A narcissism which loves itself only to be loved for what women haven't got! They have constructed the infamous logic of antilove.

We the precocious, we the repressed of culture, our lovely months gagged with pollen, our wind knocked out of us, we the labyrinths, the ladders, the trampled spaces, the bevies—we are black and we are beautiful. . . .

It is time to liberate the New Woman from the Old by coming to know her—by loving her for getting by, for getting beyond the Old without delay, by going out ahead of what the New Woman will be, as an arrow quits the bow with a movement that gathers and separates the vibrations musically, in order to be more than her self.

I say that we must, for, with a few rare exceptions, there has not yet been any writing that inscribes femininity; exceptions so rare, in fact, that, after plowing through literature across languages, cultures, and ages, one can only be startled at this vain scouting mission. It is well known that the number of women writers (while having increased very slightly from the nineteenth century on) has always been ridiculously small. This is a useless and deceptive fact unless from their species of female writers we do not first deduct the immense majority whose workmanship is in no way different from male writing, and which either obscures women or reproduces the classic representations of women (as sensitive—intuitive—dreamy, etc.) . . .

Nearly the entire history of writing is confounded with the history of reason, of which it is at once the effect, the support, and one of the privileged alibis. It has been one with the phallocentric tradition. It is indeed that same self-admiring, self-stimulating, self-congratulatory phallocentrism.

With some exceptions, for there have been failures—and if it weren't for them, I wouldn't be writing (I-woman, escapee)—in that enormous machine that has been operating and turning out its "truth" for centuries. There have been poets who would go to any lengths to slip something by at odds with tradition—men capable of loving love and hence capable of loving others and of wanting them, of imagining the woman who would hold out against oppression and constitute herself as a superb, equal, hence "impossible" subject, untenable in a real social framework. Such a woman the poet could desire only by breaking the codes that negate her. Her appearance would necessarily bring on, if not revolution—for the bastion was supposed to be immutable—at least harrowing explosions. . . .

But only the poets—not the novelists, allies of representationalism. Because poetry involves gaining strength through the unconscious and because the unconscious, that other limitless country, is the place where the repressed manage to survive: women, or . . . fairies.

She must write her self, because this is the invention of a *new insurgent* writing which, when the moment of her liberation has come, will allow her to carry out the indispensable ruptures and transformations in her history, first at two levels that cannot be separated.

*a*) Individually. By writing her self, woman will return to the body which has been more than confiscated from her, which has been turned into the uncanny stranger on display—the ailing or dead figure, which so often turns out to be the nasty companion, the cause and location of inhibitions. Censor the body and you censor breath and speech at the same time.

Write your self. Your body must be heard. Only then will the immense resources of the unconscious spring forth. Our naphtha will spread, throughout the world, without dollars—black or gold—nonassessed values that will change the rules of the old game.

To write. An act which will not only "realize" the decensored relation of woman to her sexuality, to her womanly being, giving her access to her native strength; it will give her back her goods, her pleasures, her organs, her immense bodily territories which have been kept under seal; it will tear her away from the superegoized structure in which she has always occupied the place reserved for the guilty (guilty of everything, guilty at every turn: for having desires, for not having any; for being frigid, for being "too hot"; for not being both at once; for being too motherly and not enough; for having children and for not having any; for nursing and for not nursing . . .)—tear her away by means of this research, this job of analysis and illumination, this emancipation of the marvelous text of her self that she must urgently learn to speak. A woman without a body, dumb, blind, can't possibly be a good fighter. She is reduced to being the servant of the militant male, his shadow. We must kill the false woman who is preventing the live one from breathing. Inscribe the breath of the whole woman.

*b*) An act that will also be marked by woman's *seizing* the occasion to *speak*, hence her shattering entry into history, which has always been based *on her suppression*. To write and thus to forge for herself the antilogos weapon. To become *at will* the taker and initiator, for her own right, in every symbolic system, in every political process.

It is time for women to start scoring their feats in written and oral language.

Every woman has known the torment of getting up to speak. Her heart racing, at times entirely lost for words, ground and language slipping away—that's how daring a feat, how great a transgression it is for a woman to speak—even just open her mouth—in public. A double distress, for even if she transgresses, her words fall almost always upon the deaf male ear, which hears in language only that which speaks in the masculine.

It is by writing, from and toward women, and by taking up the challenge of speech which has been governed by the phallus, that women will confirm women in a place other than that which is reserved in and by the symbolic, that is, in a place other than silence. Women should break out of the snare of silence. They shouldn't be conned into accepting a domain which is the margin or the harem.

Listen to a woman speak at a public gathering (if she hasn't painfully lost her wind). She doesn't "speak," she throws her trembling body forward; she lets go of herself, she flies; all of her passes into her voice, and it's with her body that she vitally supports the "logic" of her speech. Her flesh speaks true. She lays herself bare. In fact, she physically materializes what she's thinking; she signifies it with her body. In a certain way she *inscribes* what she's saying, because she doesn't deny her drives the intractable and impassioned part they have in speaking. Her speech, even when "theoretical" or political, is never simple or linear or "objectified," generalized: she draws her story into history.

There is not that scission, that division made by the common man between the logic of oral speech and the logic of the text, bound as he is by his antiquated relation—servile, calculating—to mastery. From which proceeds the niggardly lip service which engages only the tiniest part of the body, plus the mask.

In women's speech, as in their writing, that element which never stops resonating, which, once we've been permeated by it, profoundly and imperceptibly touched by it, retains the power of moving us—that element is the song: first music from the first voice of love which is alive in every woman. Why this privileged relationship with the voice? Because no woman stockpiles as many defenses for countering the drives as does a man. You don't build walls around yourself, you don't forego pleasure as "wisely" as he. Even if phallic mystification has generally contaminated good relationships, a woman is never far from "mother" (I mean outside her role functions: the "mother" as nonname and as source of goods). There is always within her at least a little of that good mother's milk. She writes in white ink.

After reading this selection, consider these questions:

1. According to Cixous, why must women write?
2. What is the "crime" men have perpetrated against women?
3. How does Cixous understand history?

# CHAPTER 15
# The West Within the World

One of the most significant developments in the history of the West since the middle of the twentieth century has been the decline of colonial empires and the end of at least direct control of the world by the West. Beginning in the fifteenth century, European states began taking control over and establishing colonies outside of Europe. These processes intensified in the seventeenth and eighteenth centuries and culminated in the second half of the nineteenth century. By 1890 the West (including the United States and Russia) effectively controlled either directly or indirectly—that is, politically influenced or economically dominated—all parts of the globe. With the possible exception of Japan, the few states that did not come under direct Western domination were either so small and isolated or of such limited economic potential that they are hardly worth mentioning.

European nations gave up control of India and the Middle East in the late 1940s. China threw off Western hegemony with the Communist Revolution of 1949. In the 1960s almost all of the various colonial empires throughout sub-Saharan Africa and Southeast Asia were freed from European domination. Although the end of imperialism brought an end to the political domination and, for the most part, the economic exploitation of the former colonies, decades and sometimes centuries of forced Western contact had left indelible marks. This impact varied from country to country; and it also varied in what features of Western civilization continued to survive. In some places it was the legal system, in others the economic organization, and in still others class relations. In almost all cases, the non-Western states that emerged were defined territorially by older colonial boundaries. Almost all of these states also adopted modern European notions of politics and the organization of the political domain.

The end of colonialism raised other problems as well. The former colonies needed to create a sense of their own identities in the modern world. The heritage of colonialism has set to work a complex series of interrelationships between the West and the rest of the world. In some cases, this identity took the form of reaffirming religious identities, as throughout most of the Islamic world; in others, it entailed enfolding an understanding of the colonial past within a new sense of national identity, as in India and Pakistan. However resolved, the continued relations between the West and the rest of the world involves not just diplomatic and economic relations but also an ongoing series of discussions about the definitions of the various non-Western nations. In an interesting turn, the identity of the West itself comes into question.

# Selection 1:

# The Clash of Civilizations

*In an attempt to consider what the future of the West and its relation to the non-Western world might be, the American social scientist Samuel P. Huntington points out that diverse moral systems may well prove to be the decisive factor. The following selection is taken from his book* The Clash of Civilizations. *Huntington begins by exploring the possible lines of demarcation of a future war.*

In the [twenty-first century], in short, the avoidance of major intercivilizational wars requires core states to refrain from intervening in conflicts in other civilizations. This is a truth which some states, particularly the United States, will undoubtedly find difficult to accept. This *abstention rule* that core states abstain from intervention in conflicts in other civilizations is the first requirement of peace in a multicivilizational, multipolar world. The second requirement is the *joint mediation rule* that core states negotiate with each other to contain or to halt fault line wars between states or groups from their civilizations.

Acceptance of these rules and of a world with greater equality among civilizations will not be easy for the West or for those civilizations which may aim to supplement or supplant the West in its dominant role. In such a world, for instance, core states may well view it as their prerogative to possess nuclear weapons and to deny such

weapons to other members of their civilization. Looking back on his efforts to develop a "full nuclear capability" for Pakistan, Zulfikar Ali Bhutto [the nation's president from 1971–1977] justified those efforts: "We know that Israel and South Africa have full nuclear capability. The Christian, Jewish and Hindu civilizations have this capability. Only the Islamic civilization was without it, but that position was about to change." The competition for leadership within civilizations lacking a single core state may also stimulate competition for nuclear weapons. Even though it has highly cooperative relations with Pakistan, Iran clearly feels that it needs nuclear weapons as much as Pakistan does. On the other hand, Brazil and Argentina gave up their programs aimed in this direction, and South Africa destroyed its nuclear weapons, although it might well wish to reacquire them if Nigeria began to develop such a capability. While nuclear proliferation obviously involves risks, . . . a world in which one or two core states in each of the major civilizations had nuclear weapons and no other states did could be a reasonably stable world.

Most of the principal international institutions

date from shortly after World War II and are shaped according to Western interests, values, and practices. As Western power declines relative to that of other civilizations, pressures will develop to reshape these institutions to accommodate the interests of those civilizations. The most obvious, most important, and probably most controversial issue concerns permanent membership in the U.N. Security Council. That membership has consisted of the victorious major powers of World War II and bears a decreasing relationship to the reality of power in the world. Over the longer haul either changes are made in its membership or other less formal procedures are likely to develop to deal with security issues. . . . In a multicivilizational world ideally each major civilization should have at least one permanent seat on the Security Council. At present only three do. The United States has endorsed Japanese and German membership but it is clear that they will become permanent members only if other countries do also. Brazil has suggested five new permanent members, albeit without veto power, Germany, Japan, India, Nigeria, and itself. That, however, would leave the world's 1 billion Muslims unrepresented, except in so far as Nigeria might undertake that responsibility. From a civilizational viewpoint, clearly Japan and India should be permanent members, and Africa, Latin America, and the Muslim world should have permanent seats, which could be occupied on a rotating basis by the leading states of those civilizations, selections being made by the Organization of the Islamic Conference, the Organization of African Unity, and the Organization of American States (the United States abstaining). It would also be appropriate to consolidate the British and French seats into a single European Union seat, the rotating occupant of which would be selected by the Union. Seven civilizations would thus each have one permanent seat and the West would have two, an allocation broadly representative of the distribution of people, wealth, and power in the world.

Some Americans have promoted multiculturalism at home; some have promoted universalism abroad; and some have done both. Multiculturalism at home threatens the United States and the West; universalism abroad threatens the West and

the world. Both deny the uniqueness of Western culture. The global monoculturalists want to make the world like America. The domestic multiculturalists want to make America like the world. A multicultural America is impossible because a non-Western America is not American. A multicultural world is unavoidable because global empire is impossible. The preservation of the United States and the West requires the renewal of Western identity. The security of the world requires acceptance of global multiculturality.

Does the vacuousness of Western universalism and the reality of global cultural diversity lead inevitably and irrevocably to moral and cultural relativism? If universalism legitimates imperialism, does relativism legitimate repression? Once again, the answer to these questions is yes and no. Cultures are relative; morality is absolute. Cultures . . . are "thick"; they prescribe institutions and behavior patterns to guide humans in the paths which are right in a particular society. Above, beyond, and growing out of this maximalist morality, however, is a "thin" minimalist morality that embodies "reiterated features of particular thick or maximal moralities." Minimal moral concepts of truth and justice are found in all thick moralities and cannot be divorced from them. There are also minimal moral "negative injunctions, most likely, rules against murder, deceit, torture, oppression, and tyranny." What people have in common is "more the sense of a common enemy [or evil] than the commitment to a common culture." Human society is "universal because it is human, particular because it is a society." At times we march with others; mostly we march alone. Yet a "thin" minimal morality does derive from the common human condition, and "universal dispositions" are found in all cultures. Instead of promoting the supposedly universal features of one civilization, the requisites for cultural coexistence demand a search for what is common to most civilizations. In a multicivilizational world, the constructive course is to renounce universalism, accept diversity, and seek commonalities. . . .

This effort would contribute not only to limiting the clash of civilizations but also to strengthening Civilization in the singular (hereafter capitalized for clarity). The singular Civilization presumably refers to a complex mix of higher levels of morality, religion, learning, art, philosophy, technology, material well-being, and probably other things. These obviously do not necessarily vary together. Yet scholars easily identify highpoints and lowpoints in the level of Civilization in the histories of civilizations. The question then is: How can one chart the ups and downs of humanity's development of Civilization? Is there a general, secular trend, transcending individual civilizations, toward higher levels of Civilization? If there is such a trend, is it a product of the processes of modernization that increase the control of humans over their environment and hence generate higher and higher levels of technological sophistication and material well-being? In the contemporary era, is a higher level of modernity thus a prerequisite to a higher level of Civilization? Or does the level of Civilization primarily vary within the history of individual civilizations?

This issue is another manifestation of the debate over the linear or cyclical nature of history. Conceivably modernization and human moral development produced by greater education, awareness, and understanding of human society and its natural environment produce sustained movement toward higher and higher levels of Civilization. Alternatively, levels of Civilization may simply reflect phases in the evolution of civilizations. When civilizations first emerge, their people are usually vigorous, dynamic, brutal, mobile, and expansionist. They are relatively un-Civilized. As the civilization evolves it becomes more settled and develops the techniques and skills that make it more Civilized. As the competition among its constituent elements tapers off and a universal state emerges, the civilization reaches its highest level of Civilization, its "golden age," with a flowering of morality, art, literature, philosophy, technology, and martial, economic, and political competence. As it goes into decay as a civilization, its level of Civilization also declines until it disappears under the onslaught of a different surging civilization with a lower level of Civilization.

Modernization has generally enhanced the material level of Civilization throughout the world. But has it also enhanced the moral and cultural dimensions of Civilization? In some respects this appears to be the case. Slavery, torture, vicious abuse of individuals, have become less and less acceptable in the contemporary world. Is this, however, simply the result of the impact of Western civilization on other cultures and hence will a moral reversion occur as Western power declines? Much evidence exists in the 1990s for the relevance of the "sheer chaos" paradigm of world affairs: a global breakdown of law and order, failed states and increasing anarchy in many parts of the world, a global crime wave, transnational mafias and drug cartels, increasing drug addiction in many societies, a general weakening of the family, a decline in trust and social solidarity in many countries, ethnic, religious, and civilizational violence and rule by the gun prevalent in much of the world. In city after city—Moscow, Rio de Janeiro, Bangkok, Shanghai, London, Rome, Warsaw, Tokyo, Johannesburg, Delhi, Karachi, Cairo, Bogota, Washington—crime seems to be soaring and basic elements of Civilization fading away. People speak of a global crisis in governance. The rise of transnational corporations producing economic goods is increasingly matched by the rise of transnational criminal mafias, drug cartels, and terrorist gangs violently assaulting Civilization. Law and order is the first prerequisite of Civilization and in much of the world—Africa, Latin America, the former Soviet Union, South Asia, the Middle East—it appears to be evaporating, while also under serious assault in China, Japan, and the West. On a worldwide basis Civilization seems in many respects to be yielding to barbarism, generating the image of an unprecedented phenomenon, a global Dark Ages, possibly descending on humanity.

In the 1950s [Canadian politician] Lester Pearson warned that humans were moving into "an age when different civilizations will have to learn to live side by side in peaceful interchange, learning from each other, studying each other's history and ideals and art and culture, mutually enriching each others' lives. The alternative, in this overcrowded little world, is misunderstanding, tension, clash, and catastrophe." The futures of both peace and Civilization depend upon understanding and cooperation among the political, spiritual, and intellectual leaders of the world's major civilizations. In the clash of civilizations, Europe and America will hang together or hang separately. In the greater clash, the global "*real clash*," between Civilization and barbarism, the world's great civilizations, with their rich accomplishments in religion, art, literature, philosophy, science, technology, morality, and compassion, will also hang together or hang separately. In the emerging era, clashes of civilizations are the greatest threat to world peace, and an international order based on civilizations is the surest safeguard against world war.

After reading this selection, consider these questions:
1. According to Huntington, what will the world of the twenty-first century look like?
2. What must the West, and particularly the United States, learn about itself within this world?
3. What do all civilizations share in common, according to Huntington?

# SELECTION 2:

# The Non-Western World

$O$*ne of the most prominent voices to have emerged from the postcolonial world was that of Frantz Fanon (1925–1961). Born in the French colony of Martinique, Fanon trained as a psychiatrist in both Martinique and France. In opposition to those in the colonial and decolonizing world who spoke of nonviolent resistance to the imperial powers, Fanon called for armed resistance. In making this argument, Fanon was concerned not just with immediate political results but also with long-term psychological effects. In addition to the obvious problems of colonialism, he pointed to the traumatic psychic impact foreign rule had on colonized populations. Violence, Fanon claimed, was individually and collectively therapeutic. In the 1950s Fanon joined with the Algerian resistance movement to French rule. He died of cancer in 1961. The following selection is taken from Fanon's best-known work,* The Wretched of the Earth *(1961).*

The violence of the colonial regime and the counter-violence of the native balance each other and respond to each other in an extraordinary reciprocal homogeneity. This reign of violence will be the more terrible in proportion to the size of the implantation from the mother country. The development of violence among the colonised people will be proportionate to the violence exercised by the threatened colonial regime. In the first phase of this insurrectional period, the home governments are the slaves of the settlers, and these settlers seek to intimidate the natives and their home governments at one and the same time. They use the same methods against both of them. . . . For the settlers, the alternative is not between *Algérie algérienne* [Algerian Algeria] and *Algérie française* [French Algeria] but between an independent Algeria and a colonial Algeria, and anything else is mere talk or attempts at treason. The settler's logic is implacable and one is only staggered by the counter-logic visible in the behaviour of the native insofar as one has not clearly understood beforehand the mechanisms of the settler's ideas. From the moment that the native has chosen the methods of counter-violence, police reprisals automatically call forth reprisals on the side of the nationalists. However, the results are not equivalent, for machine-gunning from aeroplanes and bombardments from the fleet go far beyond in horror and magnitude any answer the natives can make. This recurring terror demystifies once and for all the most estranged members of the colonised race. They find out on the spot that all the piles of speeches on the equality of human beings do not hide the commonplace fact that the seven Frenchmen killed or wounded at the Col de Sakamody kindles the indignation of all civilised consciences, whereas the sack of the douars [a temporary village of Algerian shepherds] of Guergour and of the dechras of Djerah and the massacre of whole populations—which had merely called forth the Sakamody ambush as a reprisal—all this is of not the slightest importance. Terror, counter-terror, violence, counter-violence: that is what observers bitterly record when they describe the circle of hate, which is so tenacious and so evident in Algeria. . . .

Today, national independence and the growth of national feeling in under-developed regions take on totally new aspects. In these regions, with the exception of certain spectacular advances, the different countries show the same absence of infrastructure. The mass of the people struggle against the same poverty, flounder about making the same gestures and with their shrunken bellies outline what has been called the geography of hunger. It is an under-developed world, a world inhuman in its poverty; but also it is a world without doctors, without engineers and without administrators. Confronting this world, the European nations sprawl, ostentatiously opulent. This European opulence is literally scandalous, for it has been founded on slavery, it has been nourished with the blood of slaves and it comes directly from the soil and from the subsoil of that under-developed world. The well-being and the progress of Europe have been built up with the sweat and the dead bodies of Negroes, Arabs, Indians and the yellow races. We have decided not to overlook this any longer. When a colonialist country, embarrassed by the claims for independence made by a colony, proclaims to the nationalist leaders: "If you wish for independence, take it, and go back to the middle ages," the newly-independent people tend to acquiesce and to accept the challenge; in fact you may see colonialism withdrawing its capital and its technicians and setting up around the young State the apparatus of economic pressure. The apotheosis of independence is transformed into the curse of independence, and the colonial power through its immense resources of coercion condemns the young nation to regression. In plain words, the colonial power says: "Since you want independence, take it and starve." The nationalist leaders have no other choice but to turn to their people and ask from them a gigantic effort. A regime of austerity is imposed on these starving men; a disproportionate amount of work is required from their atrophied muscles. An autarkic regime is set up and each state, with the miserable resources it has in hand, tries to find an answer to the nation's great hunger and poverty. We see the mobilisation of a people which toils to exhaustion in front of a suspicious and bloated Europe. . . .

But it so happens that for the colonised people this violence, because it constitutes their only work, invests their characters with positive and creative qualities. The practice of violence binds them together as a whole, since each individual forms a violent link in the great chain, a part of the great organism of violence which has surged upwards in reaction to the settler's violence in the beginning. The groups recognise each other and the future nation is already indivisible. The armed struggle mobilises the people; that is to say, it throws them in one way and in one direction.

The mobilisation of the masses, when it arises out of the war of liberation, introduces into each man's consciousness the ideas of a common cause, of a national destiny and of a collective history. In the same way the second phase, that of the building-up of the nation, is helped on by the existence of this cement which has been mixed with blood and anger. Thus we come to a fuller appreciation of the originality of the words used in these under-developed countries. During the colonial period the people are called upon to fight against oppression; after national liberation, they are called upon to fight against poverty, illiteracy and under-development. The struggle, they say, goes on. The people realise that life is an unending contest.

We have said that the native's violence unifies the people. By its very structure, colonialism is separatist and regionalist. Colonialism does not simply state the existence of tribes; it also reinforces it and separates them. The colonial system encourages chieftaincies and keeps alive the old Marabout con-fraternities. Violence is in action all-inclusive and national. It follows that it is closely involved in the liquidation of regionalism and of tribalism. Thus the national parties show no pity at all towards the caids and the customary chiefs. Their destruction is the preliminary to the unification of the people.

At the level of individuals, violence is a cleansing force. It frees the native from his inferiority complex and from his despair and inaction; it makes him fearless and restores his self-respect. Even if the armed struggle has been symbolic and the nation is demobilised through a rapid movement of decolonisation, the people have the time to see that the liberation has been the business of each and all and that the leader has no special merit. . . .

The imperialist states would make a great mistake and commit an unspeakable injustice if they contented themselves with withdrawing from our soil the military cohorts, and the administrative and managerial services whose function it was to discover the wealth of the country, to extract it and to send it off to the mother countries. We are not blinded by the moral reparation of national independence; nor are we fed by it. The wealth of the imperial countries is our wealth too. On the universal plane this affirmation, you may be sure, should on no account be taken to signify that we feel ourselves affected by the creations of Western arts or techniques. For in a very concrete way Europe has stuffed herself inordinately with the gold and raw materials of the colonial countries: Latin America, China and Africa. From all these continents, under whose eyes Europe today raises up her tower of opulence, there has flowed out for centuries towards that same Europe diamonds and oil, silk and cotton, wood and exotic products. Europe is literally the creation of the Third World. The wealth which smothers her is that which was stolen from the under-developed peoples. The ports of Holland, the docks of Bordeaux and Liverpool were specialised in the Negro slave-trade, and owe their renown to millions of deported slaves. So when we hear the head of a European state declare with his hand on his heart that he must come to the help of the poor under-developed peoples, we do not tremble with gratitude. Quite the contrary; we say to ourselves: "It's a just reparation which will be paid to us."

After reading this selection, consider these questions:

1. According to Fanon, why is violence inevitable between native peoples and colonizers?
2. How is violence beneficial for colonial peoples?
3. What does Europe owe its former colonies?

# SELECTION 3:

# Orientalism

*Debates over colonialism and postcolonialism in the West and not just in the West have been animated in large measure by the appearance of Edward Said's* Orientalism *in 1978. A Palestinian by birth and American by training, Said points to the ways in which the West has constructed a notion of the Middle East that speaks more of European conditions and needs than of an understanding of the Middle East as a region with its own cultures and religions. The following selection is taken from portions of Said's introduction and his concluding remarks.*

I have begun with the assumption that the Orient is not an inert fact of nature. It is not merely *there,* just as the Occident itself is not just *there* either. We must take seriously [the] great observation that men make their own history, that what they can know is what they have made, and extend it to geography: as both geographical and cultural entities—to say nothing of historical entities—such locales, regions, geographical sectors as "Orient" and "Occident" are man-made. Therefore as much as the West itself, the Orient is an idea that has a history and a tradition of thought, imagery, and vocabulary that have given it reality and presence in and for the West. The two geographical entities thus support and to an extent reflect each other.

Having said that, one must go on to state a number of reasonable qualifications. In the first place, it would be wrong to conclude that the Orient was *essentially* an idea, or a creation with no corresponding reality. When [English politician and author Benjamin] Disraeli said in his novel *Tancred* that the East was a career, he meant that to be interested in the East was something bright young Westerners would find to be an all-consuming passion; he should not be interpreted

as saying that the East was *only* a career for Westerners. There were—and are—cultures and nations whose location is in the East, and their lives, histories, and customs have a brute reality obviously greater than anything that could be said about them in the West. About that fact this study of Orientalism has very little to contribute, except to acknowledge it tacitly. But the phenomenon of Orientalism as I study it here deals principally, not with a correspondence between Orientalism and Orient, but with the internal consistency of Orientalism and its ideas about the Orient (the East as career) despite or beyond any correspondence, or lack thereof, with a "real" Orient. My point is that Disraeli's statement about the East refers mainly to that created consistency, that regular constellation of ideas as the pre-eminent thing about the Orient, and not to its mere being. . . .

A second qualification is that ideas, cultures, and histories cannot seriously be understood or studied without their force, or more precisely their configurations of power, also being studied. To believe that the Orient was created—or, as I call it, "Orientalized"—and to believe that such things happen simply as a necessity of the imagination, is to be disingenuous. The relationship between Occident and Orient is a relationship of power, of domination, of varying degrees of a complex hegemony, and is quite accurately indicated in the title of K.M. Panikkar's classic *Asia and Western Dominance.* The Orient was Orientalized not only because it was discovered to be "Oriental" in all those ways considered commonplace by an average nineteenth-century European, but also because it *could be*—that is, submitted to being—*made* Oriental. There is very little consent to be found, for example, in the fact that [French novelist Gustav] Flaubert's encounter with an Egyptian courtesan produced a widely influential model of the Oriental woman; she never spoke of herself, she never represented her emotions, presence, or history. *He* spoke for and represented her. He was foreign, comparatively wealthy, male, and these were historical facts of domination that allowed him not only to possess Kuchuk Hanem physically but to speak for her and tell his readers in what way she was "typically Oriental." My argument is that Flaubert's situation of strength in relation to Kuchuk Hanem was not an isolated instance. It fairly stands for the pattern of relative strength between East and West, and the discourse about the Orient that it enabled.

This brings us to a third qualification. One ought never to assume that the structure of Orientalism is nothing more than a structure of lies or of myths which, were the truth about them to be told, would simply blow away. I myself believe that Orientalism is more particularly valuable as a sign of European-Atlantic power over the Orient than it is as a veridic discourse about the Orient (which is what, in its academic or scholarly form, it claims to be). Nevertheless, what we must respect and try to grasp is the sheer knitted-together strength of Orientalist discourse, its very close ties to the enabling socio-economic and political institutions, and its redoubtable durability. After all, any system of ideas that can remain unchanged as teachable wisdom (in academies, books, congresses, universities, foreign-service institutes) from the period of [French philosopher and historian] Ernest Renan in the late 1840s until the present in the United States must be something more formidable than a mere collection of lies. Orientalism, therefore, is not an airy European fantasy about the Orient, but a created body of theory and practice in which, for many generations, there has been a considerable material investment. Continued investment made Oriental-ism, as a system of knowledge about the Orient, an accepted grid for filtering through the Orient into Western consciousness, just as that same investment multiplied—indeed, made truly productive—the statements proliferating out from Orientalism into the general culture.

[Italian socialist Antonio] Gramsci has made the useful analytic distinction between civil and political society in which the former is made up of voluntary (or at least rational and noncoercive) affiliations like schools, families, and unions, the latter of state institutions (the army, the police, the central bureaucracy) whose role in the polity is direct domination. Culture, of course, is to be found operating within civil society, where the influence of ideas, of institutions, and of other persons works not through domination but by what Gramsci calls consent. In any society not totalitarian, then, certain cultural forms predominate over others, just as certain ideas are more influential than others; the form of this cultural leadership is what Gramsci has identified as *hegemony,* an indispensable concept for any understanding of cultural life in the industrial West. It is hegemony, or rather the result of cultural hegemony at work, that gives Orientalism the durability and the strength I have been speaking about so far. Orientalism is never far from . . . the idea of Europe, a collective notion identifying "us" Europeans as against all "those" non-Europeans, and indeed it can be argued that the major component in European culture is precisely what made that culture hegemonic both in and outside Europe: the idea of European identity as a superior one in comparison with all the non-European peoples and cultures. There is in addition the hegemony of European ideas about the Orient, themselves reiterating European superiority over Oriental backwardness, usually overriding the possibility that a more independent, or more skeptical, thinker might have had different views on the matter.

In a quite constant way, Orientalism depends for its strategy on this flexible *positional* superiority, which puts the Westerner in a whole series of possible relationships with the Orient without ever losing him the relative upper hand. And why should it have been otherwise, especially during the period of extraordinary European ascendancy from the late Renaissance to the present? The scientist, the scholar, the missionary, the trader, or the soldier was in, or thought about, the Orient because he *could be there,* or could think about it, with very little resistance on the Orient's part. Under the general heading of knowledge of the Orient, and within the umbrella of Western hegemony over the Orient during the period from the end of the eighteenth century, there emerged a complex Orient suitable for study in the academy, for display in the museum, for reconstruction in the colonial office, for theoretical illustration in anthropological, biological, linguistic, racial, and historical theses about mankind and the universe, for instances of economic and sociological theories of development, revolution, cultural personality, national or religious character. Additionally, the imaginative examination of things Oriental was based more or less exclusively upon a sovereign Western consciousness out of whose unchallenged centrality an Oriental world emerged, first according to general ideas about who or what was an Oriental, then according to a detailed logic governed not simply by empirical reality but by a battery of desires, repressions, investments, and projections. If we can point to great Orientalist works of genuine scholarship like Silvestre de Sacy's *Chrestomathie arabe* or Edward William Lane's *Account of the Manners and Customs of the Modern Egyptians*, we need also to note that Renan's . . . racial ideas came out of the same impulse, as did a great many Victorian pornographic novels.

And yet, one must repeatedly ask oneself whether what matters in Orientalism is the general group of ideas overriding the mass of material—about which who could deny that they were shot through with doctrines of European superiority, various kinds of racism, imperialism, and the like, dogmatic views of "the Oriental" as a kind of ideal and unchanging abstraction?—or the much more varied work produced by almost uncountable individual writers, whom one would take up as individual instances of authors dealing with the Orient. In a sense the two alternatives, general and particular, are really two perspectives on the same material: in both instances one would have to deal with pioneers in the field. . . . And why

would it not be possible to employ both perspectives together, or one after the other? Isn't there an obvious danger of distortion (of precisely the kind that academic Orientalism has always been prone to) if either too general or too specific a level of description is maintained systematically? . . .

Since the demise of the Soviet Union there has been a rush by some scholars and journalists in the United States to find in an Orientalized Islam a new empire of evil. Consequently, both the electronic and print media have been awash with demeaning stereotypes that lump together Islam and terrorism, or Arabs and violence, or the Orient and tyranny. And there has also been a return in various parts of the Middle and Far East to nativist religion and primitive nationalism, one particularly disgraceful aspect of which is the continuing Iranian *fatwa* against [British novelist] Salman Rushdie. But this isn't the whole picture, and what I want to do in the remaining part of this essay is to talk about new trends in scholarship, criticism, and interpretation that, although they accept the basic premises of my book, go well beyond it in ways, I think, that enrich our sense of the complexity of historical experience.

None of those trends has emerged out of the blue, of course; nor have they gained the status of fully established knowledges and practices. The worldly context remains both perplexingly stirred-up and ideologically fraught, volatile, tense, changeable, and even murderous. Even though the Soviet Union has been dismembered and the Eastern European countries have attained political independence, patterns of power and dominance remain unsettlingly in evidence. The global south—once referred to romantically and even emotionally as the Third World—is enmeshed in a debt trap, broken into dozens of fractured or incoherent entities, beset with problems of poverty, disease, and underdevelopment. . . . Gone are the non-Aligned movement and the charismatic leaders who undertook decolonization and independence. An alarming pattern of ethnic conflict and local wars, not confined to the global south, as the tragic case of the Bosnians attests, has sprung up all over again. And in places like Central America, the Middle East, and Asia, the United States still remains the dominant power, with an anxious and still un-unified Europe straggling behind.

Explanations for the current world scene and attempts to comprehend it culturally and politically have emerged in some strikingly dramatic ways. I have already mentioned fundamentalism. The secular equivalents are a return to nationalism and theories that stress the radical distinction—a falsely all-inclusive one, I believe—between different cultures and civilizations. Recently, for example, Professor Samuel Huntington of Harvard University advanced the far from convincing proposition that Cold War bipolarism has been superseded by what he called the clash of civilizations, a thesis based on the premise that Western, Confucian, and Islamic civilizations, among several others, were rather like watertight compartments whose adherents were at bottom mainly interested in fending off all the others.

This is preposterous, since one of the great advances in modern cultural theory is the realization, almost universally acknowledged, that cultures are hybrid and heterogenous and . . . that cultures and civilizations are so interrelated and interdependent as to beggar any unitary or simply delineated description of their individuality. How can one today speak of "Western civilization" except as in large measure an ideological fiction, implying a sort of detached superiority for a handful of values and ideas, none of which has much meaning outside the history of conquest, immigration, travel, and the mingling of peoples that gave the Western nations their present mixed identities? This is especially true of the United States, which today cannot seriously be described except as an enormous palimpsest of different races and cultures sharing a problematic history of conquests, exterminations, and of course major cultural and political achievements. And this was one of the implied messages of *Orientalism,* that any attempt to force cultures and peoples into separate and distinct breeds or essences exposes not only the misrepresentations and falsifications that ensue, but also the way in which understanding is complicit with the power to produce such things as the "Orient" or the "West."

After reading this selection, consider these questions:

1. What does Said mean when he writes that "orientalism is an idea"?
2. How does he introduce the notion of power?
3. How does Said counter Samuel P. Huntington's argument from the previous selection?

# SELECTION 4:

# A Reply to Said

*Since the publication of works like Edward Said's in the late 1970s, a new field of study has arisen with its own definitions, problems, and debates. It has come to be called "postcolonial studies." Amidst these debates, Arif Dirlik has recently emerged as one of the leading voices. Dirlik is critical of Said's notion of Orientalism, especially as it has been extended to all other non-Western cultures. In the following selection from his work* The Postcolonial Aura: Third World Criticism in the Age of Global Capitalism *(1997), Dirlik speaks directly to this notion of Orientalism as a product of a Eurocentric worldview.*

Orientalism emerged historically in accompaniment to Eurocentrism. The consequence of Eurocentrism historically was to erase the part that non-Europe had played in European development in the course of centuries of interaction, and, on the contrary, to distance other histories from the European. The emergence of Eurocentrism also coincided historically with the establishment of EuroAmerican domination and colonialization of the world. Eurocentrism served the cause of colonialism by representing the world outside of Europe as "empty," at least culturally speaking, or backward, defined in terms of "lack," and hence in need of European intervention. Europe had everything to give to the world; what it received in return were images of its own past—and the rightful material returns from its civilizing activity.

The "Orientalization" of Asian societies not only erased the part they had played in "the making of Europe," but also the spatial and temporal complexities of these societies. The question of representation raised in Said's *Orientalism* is not the correctness or erroneousness of Orientalist representation, but the metonymic reductionism that led to the portrayal of these societies in terms of some cultural trait or other, that homogenized differences within individual societies, and froze them in history. Where the representation was extended to Asia as a whole, metonymic reductionism took the form of projecting upon Asia as a whole the characteristics of the particular society of the individual Orientalist's acquaintance.

However individual Orientalists may have responded to Asia, moreover, Orientalism as *discourse* implied also a power relationship: Europeans, placed at the pinnacle of progress, were in a better position than the natives themselves to know what Asians were about, since they had the advantage of a more prodigious (and panoptical) historical hindsight. I noted above that Orientalists did not just speak about Asia, they also spoke for Asia. While this points to perturbations within Orientalism, it also raises the question of power: power to speak for the Other. The Oriental may speak about the past, of which s/he is an embodiment, but not about the present, in which s/he is not a genuine participant; especially the critical Oriental, who appears as a degeneration of the ideal type to the extent that s/he has learned to speak in the language of the present. Advocates of a "China-centered history". . . have suggested that contemporary Chinese, who have been touched by "Western" ideas and methods (especially Marxism, it seems), have lost touch with their own past, and are at a disadvantage, therefore, in providing a truly China-centered history.

Where Orientalism as articulated by Said is wanting, I think, is in ignoring the "Oriental's" participation in the unfolding of the discourse on the Orient, which raises some questions both about the location of the discourse and, therefore, its implications for power. I have suggested above that Orientalism, regardless of its ties to Eurocentrism both in origin and in its history, in some basic ways required the participation of "Orientals" for its legitimation. And in its practice, Orientalism from the beginning took shape as an exchange of images and representations, corresponding to the circulation of intellectuals and others, first the circulation of Europeans in Asia, but increasingly with a counter-circulation of Asians in Europe and the United States.

Rather than view Orientalism as an autochtonous product of a European modernity, therefore, it makes some sense to view it as a product of those "contact zones" in which Europeans encountered non-Europeans, where a European modernity produced and was also challenged by alternative modernities as the Others in their turn entered the discourse on modernity. I borrow the term "contact zone" from [American scholar] Mary Louis Pratt, who has described it as "the space of colonial encounters, the space in which peoples geographically and historically separated come into contact with each other and establish ongoing relations, usually involving conditions of coercion, radical inequality, and intractable conflict." But the contact zone is not merely a zone of domination, it is also a zone of exchange, even if it is unequal exchange, which Pratt de-

From *The Postcolonial Aura: Third World Criticism in the Age of Global Capitalism*, by Arif Dirlik. Copyright © 1997 by Westview Press. Reprinted by permission of Westview Press, a member of Perseus Books, LLC.

scribes as "transculturation," whereby "subordinated or marginal groups select and invent from materials transmitted to them by a dominant or metropolitan culture. While subjugated peoples cannot readily control what emanates from the dominant culture, they do determine to various extents what they absorb into their own, and what they use it for." We may note also that, in the contact zone, in the process of the very effort to communicate with the dominated, the dominant or the metropolitan culture goes through a language change, if to a lesser extent than the dominated.

The idea (and the reality) of the contact zone enable the explanation of some of the contradictions in Orientalism that I have described above. The contact zone is a zone of domination, because it does not abolish the structures of power of which it is an expression, and to which it serves as a zone of mediation. But the contact zone also implies a distance, a distance from the society of the Self, as well as of the Other. The Orientalist, I suggested above, is "Orientalized" himself or herself in the very process of entering the "Orient" intellectually and sentimentally. Same with the "Oriental," whose very contact with the Orientalist culminates in a distancing from native society, where s/he becomes an object of suspicion, and who in the long run is better able to communicate with the Orientalist than with the society of the Self. . . . In some ways, it is this distancing from the complexities of everyday life in either society that facilitates the metonymic cultural representations that I have described above as a basic feature of Orientalism—whether by the Orientalist, or by the self-Orientalizing "Oriental." Is it very surprising that nationalism in China, which was as much a source of cultural reification as Orientalism, was the production of intellectuals who were themselves products of contact zones, be they Chinese in China, Chinese intellectuals studying abroad, or Chinese overseas?

If locating Orientalism in the contact zone modifies our understanding of the processes whereby Orientalist representations are produced, the same location also reveals different relationships between Orientalism and power. [University of Indiana professor] Chen Xiaomei's reminder that Ori-entalism (or Occidentalism) may have different meanings in different contexts is a valuable one; so long as we relocate the context of which she speaks not in "China," but in the contact zone of "Westernized" Chinese intellectuals. As Chen argues, Occidentalism (the mirror image of Orientalism) serves as a source of critique of an oppressive state ideology. But there is arguably another aspect to such self-Orientalization. However closely Orientalism may be tied in with EuroAmerican power historically, its contemporary manifestations are difficult to explain in terms of a past relationship between Orientalism and EuroAmerican power. The Confucian revival of the [1980s], I would like to suggest, is an expression not of powerlessness, but of a newfound sense of power, that has accompanied the economic success of East Asian societies, who now reassert themselves against an earlier EuroAmerican domination. In this sense, the Confucian revival (and other cultural nationalisms) may be viewed as an articulation of native culture (and an indigenous subjectivity) against EuroAmerican cultural hegemony.

The challenge to Eurocentrism in the Confucian revival, within the context of a Global Capitalism, has had reverberations within a EuroAmerican context as well, raising questions about another fundamental premise of Orientalism: the idea of an Occident with a unified culture. Interestingly, even as capitalism has emerged victorious over existing forms of socialism, and global unity under a globalized capitalism seems a real possibility for the first time in nearly a century, new fissures have appeared that are expressed in the affirmation of cultural differences not just in Asia or what used to be the Second and Third Worlds, but within the First World itself. The notion of different "cultures of capitalism," to which I referred above, has been extended by some to differences among EuroAmerican societies themselves, as in a recent work that identifies "seven cultures of capitalism," all but one (Japan) located in Europe and North America. The contradiction may be a contradiction of proliferating "contact zones" under a globalized capitalism, which has been accompanied not by the abolition of but by a simultaneous proliferation of national and ethnic reification of cultures. The idea of a "West" is called into question in a Europe or North America striving for economic and political unification, just as claims to a Confucian zone run aground on claims to national uniqueness in East and Southeast Asia.

The part that self-orientalization may play in the struggle against internal and external hegemony, and its claims to alternative modernities, however, must not be exaggerated. In the long run, self-Orientalization serves to perpetuate, and even to consolidate, existing forms of power. Partha Chatterjee has observed that "nationalist thought accepts the same essentialist conception based on a distinction between 'the East' and 'the West,' the same typology created by a transcendent studying subject, and hence the same 'objectifying' procedures of knowledge constructed in the post-Enlightenment age of Western science." Self-essentialization may serve the cause of mobilization against "Western" domination; but in the very process also consolidates "Western" ideological hegemony by internalizing the historical assumptions of Orientalism. At the same time, it contributes to internal hegemony, by suppressing differences within the nation.

Examples of the latter abound in contemporary cultural nationalisms. Most obvious is the use of "culture" to reject calls for "democracy" and "human rights," which is common to a diverse group from Lee Kuan Yew to Mahathir Mohamad to the Government of the People's Republic of China. While there is no denying that "democracy" and "human rights" as they are conceived are EuroAmerican in origin, and are often misused by the latter in the pursuit of power, their denial on the grounds of "cultural imperialism" also justifies oppression at home—and makes little sense when the regimes involved incorporate so much else that is also EuroAmerican in origin.

This "official Occidentalism," as Chen Xiaomei calls it, however, is only part of the problem. "Anti-official Occidentalism" may be just as complicit in oppression in its resort to self-Orientalization as a protest against the oppression of the state. The essentialization and homogenization of the national terrain serves in that case as much as in the case of the state to disguise differences within the nation, including class,

gender and ethnic differences. I have suggested above that elites in Asian societies have been complicit all along in the production of Orientalism. This may be more the case than ever in the past, as the idea of the "nation" has become problematic, and the nation difficult to define as a cultural entity, as globalization and diasporic motions of people complicate cultures and challenge state-defined national cultures with localized cultures. Culturalist essentialism, regardless of its origins in the state or with intellectuals, serves to contain and to control the disruptive consequences of globalization. This helps explain the simultaneous appearance of cultural nationalism with calls for economic globalization. . . .

While as an advocate of the revival of Confucianism someone such as Tu Weiming is quite different in his evaluation of China's past, in terms of power relationships his position is revealing of a similar elitism that nourishes off his privileged status as a Westernized Chinese intellectual. In speaking of Cultural China, Tu has suggested that the creation of a Cultural China must proceed from the "periphery" to the "center," from Chinese overseas to Chinese in China (or, in terms of the metaphor used here, from the "contact zone" to China proper). In terms of Chinese societies, the center-periphery distinction suggests that "Cultural China" is to be created by the transformation of the centers of power by intellectuals from the margins with little or no power; as this is the configuration of power that the center-periphery model usually suggests. Viewed from a global perspective, however, the power relationship appears quite differently, because in that perspective, the periphery coincides with the centers of global power while the "center" of Chinese society appears as the location of the periphery. "Diasporic Chinese," to the extent that they are successful in a global economy or culture, then, become the agents of changing China. But their very location suggests that they are no longer "Chinese" in any simple identifiable sense, but the products of the "contact zone," in which the West or the East, or the Occident or the Orient, are no longer identifiable with any measure of clarity. The assertion of "Chineseness" against this uncertainty seeks to contain the very dispersal of a so-called "Chinese culture" into numerous local cultures which more than ever makes it impossible to define a Chinese national culture. This strategy of containment is the other side of the coin to the pursuit of a "Chinese" identity in a global culture. If in the former case it may serve to counter a EuroAmerican hegemony, in the latter case it is itself an expression of establishing a cultural hegemony that denies the diversity of what it means to be Chinese. In this latter case, ironically, it is empowered by the very EuroAmerican hegemony that it seeks to displace.

[Indian scholar] Aijaz Ahmad in a recent study has criticized Said for ignoring class relations in the emergence of Orientalism. Orientalism is not just a matter of continents or nations representing one another; it also entails class (or, for that matter, gender and ethnic) representations; not only in terms of who is engaged in representation, but how a society is represented. It was the upper-class upper-caste Brahmins who provided British Orientalists with the texts of Hinduism, as well as their assumptions about Hindu spirituality. Jesuits in China, who were initially drawn to Buddhism as a means of entry into China, decided that Confucianism served better than Buddhism in the representation of China because their friends in officialdom pointed them toward the lifestyles of the elite. In our day, Confucianism may be subjected to different evaluations, which also suggest different relations of power within Chinese societies, and between Chinese societies and the outside world. Recent experience also indicates that it is insufficient to conceive of Orientalism simply in terms of Eurocentrism or nationalism. It is its position in the capitalist structuring of the world that ultimately accounts for the changing relationships between Orientalist discourse (Eurocentric or self-Orientalizing) and power. Just as it was the apparent Chinese incapability to make the transition to capitalism that once condemned Confucianism to a defunct past, it is Chinese success in the world of capitalism that now enables its admission to the center of a global modernity as an alternative to EuroAmerican capitalisms—acknowledged as such even by the ideologues of the latter. Intellectuals who themselves have become part of a global elite (not to speak of the managers of cap-

ital) play a crucial part in the transformation.

Ironically, the self-assertiveness of "Orientals" under these circumstances would seem to represent not an alternative to, as they claim, but a consolidation of Eurocentric hegemony; or, more accurately, the hegemony of capital globally. As I noted above, Orientalism was a product of capitalist modernization (and colonialism) in Europe; and the very notion of modernization incorporated Orientalist assumptions as an integral premise. Where Orientalism earlier represented the past of modernity, it is now rendered into one of its versions—but still without history. The cultural nationalisms of recent years, while they make claims to the uniqueness of essentialized national cultures, all share one thing in common: that the unique national culture is a force of modernization, more precisely, capitalist modernization. Rather than question capitalism with Confucian or other Chinese values, for example, the tendency has been to render it into a value-system conducive to capitalist development. While this has dislodged the claim that only Europeans had the value-system appropriate to capitalism, and has asserted the possibility of multiple paths, the multiple paths are all contained within a teleology of capitalism as the end of history.

Said has suggested that the solution to overcoming Orientalism may lie in the cultivation of a "decentered consciousness" that resists totalization and systematization, something, I take it, along the lines of "multiculturalism." If my analysis based on the "contact zone" has any validity, this may not be sufficient, because Orientalism itself may be a product of a consciousness already decentered, if not completely. There is no self-evident reason why a decentered consciousness should not find relief in culturalist fundamentalism, or the reification of ethnicity and culture; the history of Orientalism provides evidence of this strong possibility. Multiculturalism, ironically, may enhance tendencies to Orientalism in its insistence on the cultural definition of ethnicity, which reifies cultural origins at the expense of the historicity of both ethnicity and culture.

It seems to me to be more important to question the assumptions of capitalist modernity (not merely Eurocentrism) of which Orientalism is an integral expression. To the extent that they have assimilated the teleology of capitalism, recent challenges to Eurocentrism (such as with the Confucian revival) have promoted rather than dislodged Orientalism. What is necessary is to repudiate historical teleology in all its manifestations. This would entail the historicization of capitalist modernity itself, and the identification of alternative modernities, not in terms of reified cultures, but in terms of alternative historical trajectories that have been suppressed by the hegemony of capitalist modernity. It also requires questioning not just of continental distinctions (Orient/Occident), but of nations as units of analysis, since the latter also thrive on cultural homogenization and reification. It is necessary, I think, to restore full historicity to our understanding of the past—and the present—historicity not in the sense that Said uses "historicism" (that presupposes organically holistic cultures) but historicity that is informed by the complexity of everyday life, which accounts not only for what unites but, more importantly, for diversity in space and time, which is as undesirable to national power as it is to Eurocentrism. A thoroughgoing historicism subjects culture to the structures of everyday life, rather than erase those structures by recourse to a homogenizing culturalism. This, of course, requires also that we conceive of alternative modernities that take as their point of departure not a reified past legacy, but a present of concrete everyday cultural practices where . . . it is no longer possible to tell what is identifiably Chinese or identifiably Western.

After reading this selection, consider these questions:

1. What are Dirlik's criticisms of Orientalism?
2. How does Dirlik describe the formation of Orientalism?
3. What does he mean by the term *zone of contact*?

# SELECTION 5:

# A Defense of the West

*The debates generated by postcolonialism have raised questions about the definition of the West. There has not yet emerged a clear set of issues and terms of the debate, but several scholars and thinkers have begun to question the nature of the West. The West can no longer just be understood as a number of imperialistic powers nor simply equated with modern scientific knowledge and technological "progress." In the 1970s the progressive-minded French sociologist and political scientist Jacques Ellul (1912–1985) attempted to rethink the identity of the West. By pointing to the contribution of the West through its long historical evolution, Ellul suggests the civilization's significance to world history. The following selection is taken from Ellul's* The Betrayal of the West *(1978).*

From *Betrayal of the West*, by Jacques Ellul, translated by Matthew O'Connell. Copyright © 1978, Matthew O'Connell. Reprinted by permission of The Continuum Publishing Company.

I am not criticizing or rejecting other civilizations and societies; I have deep admiration for the institutions of the Bantu and other peoples (the

Chinese among them) and for the inventions and poetry and architecture of the Arabs. I do not claim at all that the West is superior. In fact, I think it absurd to lay claim to superiority of any kind in these matters. What criterion would you apply? What scale of values would you use? I would add that the greatest fault of the West since the seventeenth century has been precisely its belief in its own unqualified superiority in all areas.

The thing, then, that I am protesting against is the silly attitude of western intellectuals in hating their own world and then illogically exalting all other civilizations. Ask yourself this question: If the Chinese have done away with binding the feet of women, and if the Moroccans, Turks, and Algerians have begun to liberate their women, whence did the impulse to these moves come from? From the West, and nowhere else! Who invented the "rights of man"? The same holds for the elimination of exploitation. Where did the move to socialism originate? In Europe, and in Europe alone. The Chinese, like the Algerians, are inspired by western thinking as they move toward socialism. [Karl] Marx was not Chinese, nor was [French revolutionist] Robespierre an Arab. How easily the intellectuals forget this! The whole of the modern world, for better or for worse, is following a western model; no one imposed it on others, they have adopted it themselves, and enthusiastically.

I shall not wax lyrical about the greatness and benefactions of the West. Above all, I shall not offer a defense of the material goods Europe brought to the colonies. We've heard that kind of defense too often: "We built roads, hospitals, schools, and dams; we dug the oil wells. . . ." And the reason I shall say nothing of this invasion by the technological society is that I think it to be the West's greatest crime. . . . The worst thing of all is that we exported our rationalist approach to things, our "science," our conception of the state, our bureaucracy, our nationalist ideology. It is this, far more surely than anything else, that has destroyed the other cultures of the world and shunted the history of the entire world onto a single track.

But is that all we can say of the West? No, the essential, central, undeniable fact is that the West was the first civilization in history to focus attention on the individual and on freedom. Nothing can rob us of the praise due us for that. We have been guilty of denials and betrayals (of these we shall be saying something more), we have committed crimes, but we have also caused the whole of mankind to take a gigantic step forward and to leave its childhood behind.

This is a point we must be quite clear on. If the world is everywhere rising up and accusing the West, if movements of liberation are everywhere under way, what accounts for this? Its sole source is the proclamation of freedom that the West has broadcast to the world. The West, and the West alone, is responsible for the movement that has led to the desire for freedom and to the accusations now turned back upon the West.

Today men point the finger of outrage at slavery and torture. Where did that kind of indignation originate? What civilization or culture cried out that slavery was unacceptable and torture scandalous? Not Islam, or Buddhism, or Confucius, or Zen, or the religions and moral codes of Africa and India! The West alone has defended the inalienable rights of the human person, the dignity of the individual, the man who is alone with everyone against him. But the West did not practice what it preached! The extent of the West's fidelity is indeed debatable: the whole European world has certainly not lived up to its own ideal all the time, but to say that it has never lived up to it would be completely false.

In any case, that is not the point. The point is that the West originated values and goals that spread throughout the world (partly through conquest) and inspired man to demand his freedom, to take his stand in the face of society and affirm his value as an individual. I shall not be presumptuous enough to try to "define" the freedom of the individual. . . .

The West turned the whole human project into a conscious, deliberate business. It set the goal and called it freedom, or, at a later date, individual freedom. It gave direction to all the forces that were working in obscure ways, and brought to light the value that gave history its meaning. Thereby, man became man.

The West attempted to apply in a conscious,

methodical way the implications of freedom. The Jews were the first to make freedom the key to history and to the whole created order. From the very beginning their God was the God who liberates; his great deeds flowed from a will to give freedom to his people and thereby to all mankind. This God himself, moreover, was understood to be sovereignly free (freedom here was often confused with arbitrariness or with omnipotence). This was something radically new, a discovery with explosive possibilities. The God who was utterly free had nothing in common with the gods of eastern and western religions; he was different precisely because of his autonomy.

The next step in the same movement saw the Greeks affirming both intellectual and political liberty. They consciously formulated the rules for a genuinely free kind of thinking, the conditions for human freedom, and the forms a free society could take. Other peoples were already living in cities, but none of them had fought so zealously for the freedom of the city in relation to other cities, and for the freedom of the citizen within the city.

The Romans took the third step by inventing civil and institutional liberty and making political freedom the key to their entire politics. Even the conquests of the Romans were truly an unhypocritical expression of their intention of freeing peoples who were subject to dictatorships and tyrannies the Romans judged degrading. It is in the light of that basic thrust that we must continue to read Roman history. Economic motives undoubtedly also played a role, but a secondary one; to make economic causes the sole norm for interpreting history is in the proper sense superficial and inadequate. You can not write history on the basis of your suspicions! If you do, you only project your own fantasies.

I am well aware, of course, that in each concrete case there was darkness as well as light, that liberty led to wars and conquests, that it rested on a base of slavery. I am not concerned here, however, with the excellence or defects of the concrete forms freedom took; I am simply trying to say (as others have before me) that at the beginning of western history we find the awareness, the explanation, the proclamation of freedom as

the meaning and goal of history.

No one has ever set his sights as intensely on freedom as did the Jews and Greeks and Romans, the peoples who represented the entire West and furthered its progress. In so doing, they gave expression to what the whole of mankind was confusedly seeking. In the process we can see a progressive approach to the ever more concrete: from the Jews to the Greeks, and from the Greeks to the Romans there is no growth in consciousness, but there is the ongoing search for more concrete answers to the question of how freedom can be brought from the realm of ideas and incarnated in institutions, behavior, thinking, and so on.

Today the whole world has become the heir of the West, and we Westerners now have a twofold heritage: we are heirs to the evil the West has done to the rest of the world, but at the same time we are heirs to our forefathers' consciousness of freedom and to the goals of freedom they set for themselves. Other peoples, too, are heirs to the evil that has been inflicted on them, but now they have also inherited the consciousness of and desire for freedom. Everything they do today and everything they seek is an expression of what the western world has taught them. . . .

Similarly, and as part of the same process, the West brought about the division of societies and the world into rich and poor. Please note, however: I am not saying that there had not been rich and poor earlier and in other parts of the world. The point is, rather, that everything used to be so organized that wealth and poverty were stable states, determined (for example) by the traditional, accepted hierarchy, and that this arrangement was regarded as due to destiny or an unchangeable divine will. The West did two things: it destroyed the hierarchic structures and it did away with the idea of destiny. It thus showed the poor that their state was not something inevitable. This is something Marx is often credited with having done, but only because people are ignorant. It was Christianity that did away with the idea of destiny and fate. . . .

Once Christianity had destroyed the idea of destiny or fate, the poor realized that they were poor, and they realized that their condition was not inevitable. Then the social organisms that had made it possible to gloss over this fact were challenged and undermined from within.

Against all this background we can see why the whole idea of revolution is a western idea. Before the development of western thought, and apart from it, no revolution ever took place. Without the individual and freedom and the contradictory extremes to which freedom leads, a society cannot engender a revolution. Nowhere in the world—and I speak as one with a knowledge of history—has there ever been a revolution, not even in China, until the western message penetrated that part of the world. Present-day revolutions, whether in China or among the American Indians, are the direct, immediate, unmistakable fruit of the western genius. The entire world has been pupil to the West that it now rejects. . . .

I wish only to remind the reader that the West has given the world a certain number of values, movements, and orientations that no one else has provided. No one else has done quite what the West has done. I wish also to remind the reader that the whole world is living, and living almost exclusively, by these values, ideas, and stimuli. There is nothing original about the "new" thing that is coming into existence in China or Latin America or Africa: it is all the fruit and direct consequence of what the West has given the world.

In the [1950s] it was fashionable to say that "the third world is now entering upon the stage of history." The point was not, of course, to deny that Africa or Japan had a history. What the cliché was saying, and rightly saying, was that these peoples were now participating in the creative freedom of history and the dialectic of the historical process. Another way of putting it is that the West had now set the whole world in motion. It had released a tidal wave that would perhaps eventually drown it. There had been great changes in the past and vast migrations of peoples; there had been planless quests for power and the building of gigantic empires that collapsed overnight. The West represented something entirely new because it set the world in movement in every area and at every level; it represented, that is, a coherent approach to reality. Everything—ideas, armies, the state, philosophy, rational methods, and social organi-

zation—conspired in the global change the West had initiated.

It is not for me to judge whether all this was a good thing or bad. I simply observe that the entire initiative came from the West, that everything began there. I simply observe that the peoples of the world had abided in relative ignorance and a hieratic repose until the encounter with the West set them on their journey.

Please, then, don't deafen us with talk about the greatness of Chinese or Japanese civilization. These civilizations existed indeed, but in a larval or embryonic state; they were approximations, essays. They always related to only one sector of the human or social totality and tended to be static and immobile. Because the West was motivated by the ideal of freedom and had discovered the individual, it alone launched society in its entirety on its present course.

Again, don't misunderstand me. I am not saying that European science was superior to Chinese science, nor European armies to Japanese armies; I am not saying that the Christian religion was superior to Buddhism or Confucianism; I am not saying that the French or English political system was superior to that of the Han dynasty. I am saying only that the West discovered what no one else had discovered; freedom and the individual, and that this discovery later set everything else in motion. Even the most solidly established religions could not help changing under the influence. . . .

It was not economic power or sudden technological advances that made the West what it is. These played a role, no doubt, but a negligible one in comparison with the great change—the discovery of freedom and the individual—that represents the goal and desire implicit in the history of all civilizations. That is why, in speaking of the West, I unhesitatingly single out freedom from the whole range of values. After all, we find justice, equality, and peace everywhere. Every civilization that has attained a certain level has claimed to be a civilization of justice or peace. But which of them has ever spoken of the individual? Which of them has been reflectively conscious of freedom as a value?

The decisive role of the West's discovery of freedom and the individual is beyond question, but the discovery has brought with it . . . tragic consequences. First, the very works of the West now pass judgment on it. For, having proclaimed freedom and the individual, the West played false in dealing with other peoples. It subjected, conquered, and exploited them, even while it went on talking about freedom. It made the other peoples conscious of their enslavement by intensifying that enslavement and calling it freedom. It destroyed the social structures of tribes and clans, turned men into isolated atoms, and shaped them into a worldwide proletariat, and all the time kept on talking of the great dignity of the individual: his autonomy, his power to decide for himself, his capacity for choice, his complex and many-sided reality. . . .

Reason makes it possible for the individual to master impulse, to choose the ways in which he will exercise his freedom, to calculate the chances for success and the manner in which a particular action will impinge upon the group, to understand human relations, and to communicate. Communication is the highest expression of freedom, but it has little meaning unless there is a content which, in the last analysis, is supplied by reason. . . .

Here precisely we have the magnificent discovery made by the West: that the individual's whole life can be, and even is, the subtle, infinitely delicate interplay of reason and freedom.

This interplay achieved its highest form in both the Renaissance and classical literature since the Enlightenment. No other culture made this discovery. We of the West have the most rounded and self-conscious type of man. For, the development of reason necessarily implied reason's critique of its own being and action as well as a critique of both liberty and reason, through a return of reason upon itself and a continuous reflection which gave rise to new possibilities for the use of freedom as controlled by new developments of reason. . . .

Let me return to my main argument. It was the West that established the splendid interplay of freedom, reason, self-control, and coherent behavior. It thus produced a type of human being that is unique in history: true western man. (I repeat: the type belongs neither to nature nor to the animal world; it is a deliberate construct achieved through effort.) I am bound to say that I regard this type as superior to anything I have seen or known elsewhere. A value judgment, a personal and subjective preference? Of course. But I am not ready on that account to turn my back on the construction and on the victory and affirmation it represents. Why? Because the issue is freedom itself, and because I see no other satisfactory model that can replace what the West has produced.

After reading this selection, consider these questions:
1. Does Ellul believe the West is "better" than other civilizations?
2. What, according to Ellul, has the West given to the world?
3. How does Ellul sketch a history of Western civilization?

# INDEX

absolutism, 49
  Bossuet's definition of, 54–55
  witch-hunting as manifestation of, 59–61
*Account of the Manners and Customs of the Modern
  Egyptians* (Lane), 285
Ackerley, J.R., 219
Age of Restoration, 98
Ahmad, Aijaz, 290
Alembert, Jean La Rond d', 20, 69, 71
Algeria
  liberation movement in, 280–82
*Allgemeiner Deutscher Frauenverein,* 26
"Alliance of Throne and Altar," 175
American Revolution
  and legitimacy of government, 22
Anderson, Adam, 47
Anderson, Michael, 144
*And Yet Another Philosophy of History* (Herder), 108–10
anti-Semitism
  of Nazis, 232, 233
    implementation of, 237–42
  racial character of, 203
Appleby, Joyce, 264
Archimedes, 43
Arendt, Hannah, 210
aristocracy
  Austrian, 207
  Ortega y Gasset on, 34
Aristotelian physics, 42–44
Aristotle, 36, 39
Ashton, T.S., 125
Astell, Mary, 24, 25, 27
Aston, Francis, 47
*Autobiographical Study, An* (Freud), 172–74

Bacon, Francis, 40, 64, 264, 265
Badoglio, Marshall, 256
Bailly, Jean-Sylvain, 83
Bakunin, Mikhail, 27
Barentin, François de, 84
Barth, Karl, 190
Beauvoir, Simone de, 27
Beecher, Catherine, 24, 25
Benes, Edvard, 256
Benoist, Charles, 141
Bentham, Jeremy, 101

Berlin Conference (1884–1885), 200
Bernstein, Eduard, 250
*Betrayal of the West, The* (Ellul), 291–95
*Beyond Good and Evil* (Nietzsche), 168
Bhutto, Zulfikar Ali, 277
*Bible, The*
  on royal authority, 55
  women's scholarship on, 23
Biddiss, Michael D., 199
Bismarck, Otto von, 100, 153, 155, 197, 229
*Black Dwarf* (newspaper), 149
Blomberg, Werner von, 228
Bodin, Jean, 52
Boer War, 198
Boeters, Gerhard, 235
Bolshevik Revolution, 225
  reasons for success of, 252–54
  roots of, 243–44
*Bolsheviks Come to Power, The* (Rabinowitch), 251
Bonaparte, Napoléon, 80, 95, 98
Bossuet, Jacques-Bénigne, 54
bourgeoisie, 134
  Austrian, 206–207
  and nationalism, 204
Bouvier, Jeanne, 142
Boxer, Marilyn, 144
Boxer Rebellion (1900), 201
Bracher, Karl Dietrich, 225
Briggs, Henry, 47
Brontë, Charlotte, 146
Brooke, Rupert, 218
Brüning, Heinrich, 227
Buffon, Georges-Louis Leclerc de, 158
Bühler, Joseph, 242
bureaucracy
  origins of, 57–59
Burke, Edmund, 27, 104, 107, 108
Burleigh, Michael, 233
Byrnes, James, 255

*Cahiers de Doléance,* 86
Calvin, John, 192
Camus, Albert, 27
capitalism
  and the new imperialism, 211
Catholicism

Austrian, 208
Central Place System, 127
Chadwick, Edwin, 125
Chamberlain, Houston Stewart, 203
Charles I (king of England), 51, 61, 62
Chatterjee, Partha, 289
Cheidze, Nikolai Semenovich, 247
Chen Xiaomei, 288
Chesterton, Gilbert, 210
child labor, 136–39, 144
    conditions of, 117, 119–20, 124
China
    cultural nationalism in, 288–90
*Chrestomathie arabe* (Sacy), 285
Christianity, 293
    Feuerbach on essence of, 179–81
    forms of, in post-Napoleonic Europe, 175
    philosophes' critique of, 66
    and the Scientific Revolution, 36
Churchill, Winston, 255, 256
Cicero, 11
civilizations
    definition of, 10–11
    effects of modernization on, 279
    first centers of, 11
    non-Western, as approximations, 294
    Western
        defense of, 291–95
        morals of, Nietzsche's attack on, 168–73
        vs. non-Western, clash of, 277–80
Cixous, Hélène, 272
*Clash of Civilizations, The* (Huntington), 277–80
class consciousness, 135
    of working class, 149–51
Cobbett, William, 126
*Code Napoléon,* 28
    women's status under, 25
Colbert, Jean-Baptiste, 49–50
Cold War, 245
    origins of, 254–58
colonialism, 200–201, 210–14
    end of, problems arising from, 276–77
    violence of, and resistance movements, 280–82
*Communist Manifesto, The* (Marx and Engels), 136
Comte, August, 156, 160
Condorcet, Marquis de, 20
Confucianism, 290, 291
    Chinese revival of, 288
Congress of Vienna, 98
conservatism
    origins of, 104–107
Cooper, Anna, 27
Copernicus, Nicolaus, 36, 64
Council of Trent, 59, 186
Counter Reformation, 48, 59
    acculturation of rural areas during, 60–61

*Course of Positive Philosophy* (Comte), 160–61
Covington, Elizabeth, 264
*Creation of the Feminist Consciousness, The* (Lerner), 23
culture
    definition of, 11
    Herder's idea of, 108
Czechoslovakia, 246
    Soviet control of, 256

Darwin, Charles, 157, 162, 233–34
Declaration of the Rights of Man and Citizen, 89–91
Declaration of the Rights of Woman and Female Citizen
    (Gouges), 91–94
*Democracy in America* (Tocqueville), 95
Demuth, Helene, 152
Derrida, Jacques, 264, 265, 268, 269
Descartes, René, 40, 67
    on right reasoning, 67–68
    and Scientific Revolution, 29–30
*Descent of Man, The* (Darwin), 162, 234
dialectical theology, 190
Diderot, Denis, 65, 66, 156
    on purpose of *The Encyclopedia,* 71–74
Dirlik, Arif, 286
*Discipline and Punish* (Foucault), 266, 267, 268
discourse
    Orientalism as, 287
    and power, Foucault on, 266–68
*Discourse on Method* (Descartes), 67–68
*Discourse on the Moral Effects of the Arts and Sciences*
    (Rousseau), 77–79
divinity
    female representation of, 23
    questions on nature of, 12
dreams
    Freud on symbolism of, 173–74
Drexler, Anton, 222
Dryden, John, 126
Dürsterberg, Theodor, 227
"Duties of Man" (Mazzini), 111–12

Edict of Nantes, 48
education, universal
    Condorcet on, 21
    and Counter Reformation, 60
    Ortega y Gasset on, 33
    for women, 24, 26
Elizabeth I, 51
Ellul, Jacques, 291
*Émile* (Rousseau), 77
empiricism, 65
Enabling Act, 221, 226, 229
*Encyclopedia, The,* 66, 69
    Diderot on purpose of, 71–74
Engels, Friedrich, 136, 145, 250
England

and colonial imperialism, 200–202
emergence of, as major power, 50–51
franchise in, 200
industrialization in, 115, 127, 129
  impact of, on workers, 125–26
Parliament-monarchy struggle in, 61–62
pre–World War I, 197–98
Victorian, single women's status in, 146–47
*English Bill of Rights,* 62–63
English civil war (1642–1649), 62
Enlightenment, 22
  Herder's satire of, 108
  motto of, 69
  original principles of, 64
  postmodernist critique of, 264–65
*Enlightenment: An Interpretation, The* (Gay), 68
Entente Cordiale, 198
environment
  Scientific Revolution and humanity's view of, 30–31
*Epistle to the Romans* (Saint Paul), 190
*Essence of Christianity, The* (Feuerbach), 179–81
Estates General, 51, 80, 81
ethnic nationalism, 202–203
eugenics, 234–35
Europe
  colonial view of, 281, 282
  after Congress of Vienna, 98
  Eastern, post–World War II division of, 255–57
  in era of mass society, 195–98
  Industrial Revolution in, 115–17
  post-Napoleonic, forms of Christianity in, 175
  post–World War I troubles in, 220–21
  Revolutions of 1848 in, 99–100, 153
  rise of parliamentary institutions in, 199
  urbanization in, 126–29
evolution, theory of, 158–59

faith
  Barth on, 192
Fanon, Frantz, 280
Feder, Gottfried, 222
Fell, Margaret, 27
feminism, postmodern, 272–75
Feuerbach, Ludwig, 179, 182
Final Solution, 237–42
First Estate, 81
Flamsteed, John, 47
Flaubert, Gustav, 284
Foucault, Michel, 264
  on relation between discourse and power, 266–68
Fourier, Charles, 136
France
  franchise in, 200
  peasant uprisings in, 82
  rise of bureaucracy in, 58
  of the Second Republic, 196–97

women and industrialization in, 141–44
women's roles in revolutionary movements of, 25
Francis Joseph (emperor), 206
French Revolution, 18–19, 80, 95
  events leading to, 83–85
  and legitimacy of government, 22
  origins of, 81–82
  stages of, 98
French Wars of Religion (1564–1598), 48, 49, 60, 62
Freud, Sigmund, 157, 158, 206, 267
  on psychoanalysis, 172–74
Frick, Wilhelm, 228
functionalism, 159
Fussell, Paul, 214

Galilei, Galileo, 28, 35, 64
  scientific method of, 40–41
Galton, Francis, 234
Gay, Peter, 68
Gellibrand, Henry, 47
*German Dictatorship, The* (Bracher), 225
German Workers' Party
  program of, 222–24
Germany
  and colonial imperialism, 200–202
  franchise in, 200
  industrialization in, 116, 128
  nationalism in, 204
    and feminist consciousness, 25–26
  under National Socialism, 221–22, 224–30
    Hitler on goals of, 230–32
    racial ideologies of, 235–37
  nineteenth-century, life of worker in, 130–33
  pre–World War I, 197–98
    naval policy of, 213
  socialist movement in, 153
  Weimar Republic of, 220
Gladstone, William, 213
glasnost, 245
Goebbels, Joseph, 229
Goethe, Johann von, 158
Goldman, Emma, 27
Gorbachev, Mikhail, 245, 246
  on perestroika, 258–62
Göring, Hermann, 228, 238
Gouges, Olympe de, 91
government
  legitimacy of, 22
  Leo XIII on role of, 187
  Ortega y Gasset on, 33
  power of, effects of religious wars on, 48
  and utility principle, 101–102
Gramsci, Antonio, 284
Grant, Reginald, 216, 218
gravitation, law of, 44
Great Depression, 220

*Great War and Modern Memory, The* (Fussell), 214–19
Grey, Sir Edward, 217
Guchkov, Alexandr Ivanovich, 248
Gunter, Edmund, 47

Haeckel, Ernst, 234
Haggard, Rider, 216
Haig, Douglas, 218
Halley, Edmond, 47
*Hammer of Witchcraft,* 61
Harriman, Averell, 255
Head, George, 129
Hegel, Georg Wilhelm Friedrich, 179, 182, 270
Heidegger, Martin, 269
Hemingway, Ernest, 215
Henry IV (king of France), 48
Henry VIII (king of England), 51
Henty, George Alfred, 216
Herder, Johann, 11, 108
Heydrich, Reinhard, 237
Himmler, Heinrich, 237
Hindenberg, Paul von, 221, 227, 228
*History of Sexuality, The* (Foucault), 266
Hitler, Adolf, 221, 224, 235
    seizure of power by, 226–29
Hobsbawm, E.J., 202
Hofmann, Otto, 240, 241
Hohenberg, Paul M., 126
Holbach, baron d', 70
Hölderlin, Friedrich, 270
Holy Roman Empire, 50
Hooke, Robert, 47
Howarth, Patrick, 218
Hoyt, David, 264
Hugenberg, Alfred, 227
*humanitas,* 11
human rights, 292
Hume, David, 65, 101
Hungary, 246
Huntington, Samuel, 277
    criticism of, 286

ideology
    Foucault on, 267
imperialism, 200
    colonial, 210–14
    factors behind, 201
individualism, 29
industrialization
    impact of, on workers, 125–26
    of Soviet Union, 245
Industrial Revolution, 115–17
    in England, 115–16
    social impacts of, 134–35
*Inquiry into the Nature and Causes of the Wealth of Nations, An* (Smith), 74–76, 135

International Society, 153–54
*Interpretation of Dreams, The* (Freud), 173
*Introduction to the Principles of Morals and Legislation, An* (Bentham), 101–102
Isherwood, Christopher, 217
Isherwood, Kathleen, 217
Italy
    fascism in, 225, 229

James, Henry, 216
James I, 51, 61
James II, 105–106
Jullien, Stéphanie, 146

Kamenev, Lev, 247
Kant, Immanuel, 65, 69
*Kapital, Das* (Marx), 151–55
Kapp Putsch, 226
Kay, James Phillips, 121
Kennan, George, 256
Kepler, Johannes, 37, 44, 64
Kerensky, Alexander, 244, 253
Kierkegaard, Søren, 182, 192
Kleist-Schmenzin, Ewald von, 228
*Knowledge and Postmodernism in Historical Perspective* (Appleby et al.), 264
Koyré, Alexandre, 40
*Kraft durch Freude,* 222
Krille, Otto, 130
Kristallnacht, 237
Krupp, Friedrich, 128

labor
    Adam Smith on division of, 74–76
    effects of industrialization on, 150–51
    Leo XIII on, 187–89
    nineteenth-century factory, conditions of, 117–20, 121–24
        in Germany, 130–33
    *see also* child labor; trade unions
laissez-faire economics, 135
Lamarck, Jean, 158
Lane, Edward William, 285
Lapouge, Vacher de, 203
Larkin, Philip, 215
Lassalle, Ferdinand, 153
Latham, Michael, 264
"Laugh of the Medusa, The" (Cixous), 272–75
Lee Kuan Yew, 289
Lees, Lynn Hollen, 126
Lefebvre, Georges, 82
Lenin, Vladimir, 244, 252, 259
    on Bolshevik program, 249–51
    and October Revolution, 247–49
Leo XIII, 186
Lerner, Gerda, 23

liberalism
    Austrian, 205–206
    and nationalism, tensions between, 99
    nineteenth-century, principles of, 102–104
    and socialism, shared features of, 156
Liebknecht, Karl, 248
literature
    of pre–World War I era, 216–17
Lithuania, 246
living conditions
    of nineteenth-century workers, 122–24
Locke, John, 65, 101
*Lord Northcliffe's War Book* (Northcliffe), 218
Louis XII, 48–49, 52
Louis XIII, 51, 57
Louis XIV, 48–49, 51, 54, 57
Louis XV, 51
Louis XVI, 81, 83, 84–85
    administrative reforms of, 95–97
Lowe, David, 217
Lublin Committee, 255
Lueger, Karl, 206, 207–208, 209
Luther, Martin, 190, 192
Luther, Martin (German undersecretary of state), 240
Lvov, Georgii Evgen'evich, 248
Lyle, Charles, 157–58

Machiavelli, Niccolò, 112
MacMahon, Marshal, 154
*Madness and Civilization* (Foucault), 267
Maier, Charles S., 254
Makin, Bathsua, 25
*Making of Urban Europe, The* (Hohenberg and Lees), 126
Malthus, Thomas, 125
Maria Theresa, 59
Married Women's Property Bill, 25
Martin, Emma, 27
Marx, Karl, 27, 136, 179, 250
    on socialism, 151–55
Marxism
    Gorbachev on, 260–61
    Lenin on, 249–50
mass democracy, age of, 195
materialism
    of Feuerbach, 179
    Herder on, 112
mathematization of nature, 41
Mayer, Jacob, 128
Mazzini, Giuseppe, 110, 202
McCulloch, J.R., 125
"MCMXIV" (Larkin), 215
*Mein Kampf* (Hitler), 233
Melanchthon, Philipp, 192
Mensheviks, 253
Merton, Robert K., 46
Metternich, Clemens von, 98

Meyer, Alfred, 242
Michelet, Jules, 147
Mill, John Stuart, 102, 125, 160
Mirabeau, Honoré-Gabriel Riqueti, comte de, 85, 171
Mohamad, Mahathir, 289
Montesquieu, baron et de LaBrède, 20
moon
    Galileo's observations on, 37–39
*Moral and Physical Condition of the Working Classes Employed in the Cotton Manufacture in Manchester* (Kay), 121–24
Morris, William, 216
mortality rate
    in Europe, decline in, 195
Muchembled, Robert, 59
Muller, Max, 203
multiculturalism, 290
Mussolini, Benito, 221, 225

Napier, John, 47
Napoléon III (Louis Napoléon), 100, 196
nationalism, 99, 156, 286
    in China, 288
    cultural, 289
    of 1880–1914, 202–205
    in Germany, 204
        and feminist consciousness, 25–26
    imperialist tendency of, 213–14
    and links with racism, 203
    and World War I, 198
National Socialist German Workers' Party, 222, 226
    *see also* Nazism
National Society for Women's Suffrage, 25
*Nations and Nationalism Since 1780* (Hobsbawm), 202–205
Native Americans
    environmental view of, 31
natural selection, 163–64
nature
    mathematization of, 41
    Newton's universal laws of, 44
Nazism, 221–22
    Hitler on goals of, 230–32
    racial ideologies of, 235–37
Necker, Jacques, 83, 84, 85
Network System, 127–28
*Neue Freie Presse,* 206
Neumann, Erich, 242
Nevill, W.P., 219
Newbolt, Sir Henry, 218
Newton, Isaac, 35, 36, 41, 47, 64
    on scientific method, 44–46
Nicholas II, 243
    abdication of, 244
Nietzsche, Friedrich, 157, 159–60, 265, 266, 269
    on Western morals, 168–71

*Nouvelle Héloïse, La* (Rousseau), 77
Nuremberg Laws, 237, 240

Occidentalism, 288
October Revolution, 246, 253–54
    *see also* Bolshevik Revolution
*Old Regime and the French Revolution, The* (Tocqueville),
    95–97
*On Liberty* (Mill), 102
*On the Genealogy of Morals* (Nietzsche), 168–73
*Orientalism* (Said), 283–86
    critique of, 287–91
*Origin of Species, The* (Darwin), 158, 162–64, 233
*Origins of the Cold War and Contemporary Europe, The*
    (Maier), 254
*Origins of Totalitarianism* (Arendt), 210
Orsini, Felice, 155
Ortega y Gasset, José, 32
Otto, Louise, 25, 26
"Our Program" (Lenin), 249
Owen, Wilfred, 218

Papen, Franz von, 227, 228
Paris Commune (1870–1871), 154
    women's roles in, 25
Paul, Saint, 56
Pearson, Lester, 279
Peel, Robert, 137
Péguy, Charles-Pierre, 210
Perdiguier, Agricole, 140
perestroika, 245, 246
    Gorbachev on, 258–62
Petkov, Nikola, 256
philosophes, 65–66, 68–70
*Philosophy of Manufactures, The* (Ure), 117–20
Pius IX, 186
Plekhanov, Georgy, 250
Poland, 246
    post–World War II, 255
politics
    application of scientific method to, 19
Pope, Alexander, 65
population
    urban, of Europe, 195
positivism, 156–57
    Comte on, 161
*Postcolonial Aura: Third World Criticism in the Age of
    Global Capitalism* (Dirlik), 286–91
postcolonial studies, 286
postmodern feminism, 272–75
postmodernism
    as critique of the Enlightenment, 264–65
    problem with definition of, 263
Pratt, Mary Louis, 287
*Pravda* (newspaper), 247–48
"Present Age, The" (Kierkegaard), 182

*Principia Mathematica* (Newton), 44, 47
"Progress: Its Law and Causes" (Spencer), 165–68
Protestantism
    liberal, origins of, 176–78
    Neo-Reformation, 190–92
Protestant Reformation, 48
    Kierkegaard on, 182
    women in, 24
Prudhomme, René-François-Armand, 136
psychoanalysis
    Freud on, 172–74

Quataert, Jean, 144
"Question Concerning Technology, The" (Heidegger),
    269–71

Rabinowitch, Alexander, 251
*Racial State: Germany, 1933–1945, The* (Burleigh and
    Wippermann), 233
racism
    and nationalism, 203
*Reflections on the Revolution in France* (Burke), 104–107
Reformation. *See* Protestant Reformation
Reign of Terror, 80, 96
religion
    Feuerbach on, 179–81
*Religion: Speeches to Its Cultured Despisers*
    (Schleiermacher), 176–78
religious wars, 48
    *see also* French Wars of Religion
Renaissance, 18, 295
Renan, Ernest, 284
*Rerum Novarum* (Leo XIII), 186
*Revolt of the Masses* (Ortega y Gasset), 32–34
Revolutions of 1848, 99, 153
    consequences of, 100
Rhodes, Cecil, 212
Richelieu, Cardinal, 52
Rickman, John, 125
Roosevelt, Franklin D., 255
Rorty, Richard, 265
Rosenberg, Hans, 57
Rousseau, Jean-Jacques, 69, 77, 89
Rowntree, Seebohm, 141
rural life
    Christian acculturation of, 60–61
Rushdie, Salmon, 285
Russia
    Bolshevik Revolution in, 225
    franchise in, 200
    *see also* Soviet Union

Sacy, Silvestre, 285
Said, Edward, 283
Saint-Simon, Claude-Henri de Rouvroy comte de, 135
Sartre, Jean-Paul, 27

Schleicher, Kurt von, 227
Schleiermacher, Friedrich, 176, 190
Schönborn, Franz Cardinal, 209
Schönerer, Georg von, 207, 208, 209
Schopenhauer, Arthur, 168
Schorske, Carl E., 205
*Science and the Modern World* (Whitehead), 29
scientific method, 19
    Galileo's use of, 40–41
    Newton on, 44–46
    and technological innovation, 46–47
Scientific Revolution, 19, 20
    consequences of, 35
    Descartes' contribution to, 29–30
    effects of, on morals, Rousseau on, 77–79
    origins of, 35–36
Scott, Joan W., 140, 145
Second Estate, 81
Seeckt, Hans von, 226
*Shirley* (Brontë), 146
Sieyès, Emmanuel-Joseph, 83, 86
Sitwell, Osbert, 217
*Six Books of the Commonwealth* (Bodin), 52
"Sketch for the Historical Progress of the Human Mind"
    (Condorcet), 20
slavery, 292
Smith, Adam, 65, 74, 77, 135
Smith, Bonnie, 146
Sneider, Allison, 264
*Social Contract, The* (Rousseau), 77
Social Darwinism, 159, 165–68, 233–34
socialism, 135–36, 156
    Christian, 186–89
    Marx on, 151–55
        goals of, 152, 153
    under perestroika, 259, 260, 261
socialist internationalism, 204–205
social mobility
    during age of mass society, 199–202
*Société du Suffrage des Femmes,* 25
society
    application of scientific method to, 19
Society of Vincent de Paul, 146
*S.O.S. Stand To* (Grant), 216
South Africa, 212
Southey, Robert, 125
sovereignty
    concept of, 51–53
    Declaration of the Rights of Man and Citizen on
        authority of, 90
Soviet Union
    breakup of, 246
    establishment of, 243
    role of, in Cold War, 255–58
    during World War II, 244–45
Spain, 50

Spencer, Herbert, 165, 234
Stalin, Joseph, 221, 245, 248, 254–55
"Starry Messenger, The" (Galileo), 37–39
Stimson, Henry, 256
Stückart, Wilhelm, 241
suffrage
    expansion of, in Europe, 200
    Ortega y Gasset on, 33
    women's struggle for, 25
Sweden, 50
*Syllabus of Errors* (Pius IX), 186

Tacitus, 11
Taylor, A.J.P., 215
Teheran Conference, 255
Terraine, John, 217
textile manufacture, 115
    female labor force in, 145
    labor conditions in, 117–20, 121–24
    and urban industrialization, in England, 126–27, 129
theology of the word, 190
*Theory of Moral Sentiments, The* (Smith), 135
Theresienstadt, 240
Third Estate, 81, 83
    Sieyès on, 86–88
Thirty Years' War (1618–1648), 53, 62
*Thus Spoke Zarathustra* (Nietzsche), 160
Tilly, Louise A., 140, 145
Tocqueville, Alexis de, 95
trade unions, 152
    growth of, in Europe, 200
    Leo XIII on, 189
transportation
    advances in, 195
    and growth of urban industry, 129
Treaty of Versailles, 220
Triple Entente, 198
Trotsky, Leon, 246, 253
    on October Revolution, 247–49
Truman, Harry, 255
Tseretelli, Iraklii Georgevich, 248
Tu Weiming, 289
"tyranny of the majority," 104

Ulyanov, Vladimir Ilich. *See* Lenin, Vladimir
unions. *See* trade unions
United Nations Security Council
    membership in, 278
United States
    eugenics in, 234
    role of, in Cold War, 255
urbanization
    in Europe, 126–29
        during era of mass society, 195
Ure, Andrew, 117
utilitarianism, 101, 102

Vatican I, 186
Vienna
    mass politics in, 205–209
Vincent de Paul, 60
"Vitaï Lampada" (Newbolt), 218
Vlacq, Adrian, 47
*Volksgemeinschaft,* 221
Voltaire, 11, 20, 69, 70
voting rights. *See* suffrage

Wagner, Richard, 168
Wallace, Henry, 256
Wannsee Conference, 237–42
Watt, James, 115
Waugh, Alec, 217
Weimar Republic, 220
West, the
    Nietzsche on morals of, 168–71
"What is the Third Estate?" (Sieyès), 86–88
Wheeler, Anna, 27
Whitehead, Alfred North, 29
Wilhelm II, 229
Wippermann, Wolfgang, 233

witch-hunting, 59–61
Wollstonecraft, Mary, 24, 27
women
    and development of feminist consciousness, 23–28
    Gouges on rights of, 91–94
    and industrial labor, 139–44
    opportunities for, during Industrial Revolution, 144–48
    status of, in Nazi Germany, 236
    *see also* feminism, postmodern
*Women, Work, and Family* (Tilly and Scott), 140
*Word of God and the Word of Man, The* (Barth), 190–92
World War I
    causes of, 197–98
    disillusionment following, 201–202
    psychological consequences of, 215–19
    role of, in Bolshevik Revolution, 243, 252
    significance of, 197
World War II
    roots of Cold War in, 255
*Wretched of the Earth, The* (Fanon), 280

Yalta Conference, 255
Young Plan, 227